Laws and Legislation

snova
New York

Laws and Legislation

Conundrums of Paternalism in International Criminal Justice
Farhad Malekian
2024. ISBN: 979-8-89113-284-9 (Hardcover)
2024. ISBN: 979-8-89113-743-1 (eBook)

Concreting Righteousness in International Criminal Justice
Farhad Malekian
2024. ISBN: 979-8-89113-297-9 (Hardcover)
202-. ISBN: 979-8-89113-677-9 (eBook)

Islamic Sources and International Law
Nehaluddin Ahmad, LLD, Gary I. Lilienthal, PhD
2023. ISBN: 979-8-89113-173-6 (Hardcover)
2023. ISBN: 979-8-89113-264-1 (eBook)

Maritime Law Perspectives Old and New, Volume I
Proshanto K. Mukherjee
2023. ISBN: 979-8-88697-765-3 (Hardcover)
2023. ISBN: 979-8-88697-924-4 (eBook)

Maritime Law Perspectives Old and New, Volume II
Proshanto K. Mukherjee, Jingjing Xu, Maximo Q. Mejia Jr.
2023. ISBN: 979-8-88697-778-3 (Hardcover)
2023. ISBN: 979-8-88697-938-1 (eBook)

More information about this series can be found at
https://novapublishers.com/product-category/series/laws-and-legislation-series/

Katie A. Hilbert
Editor

Policies to Reverse the Damage Caused by the War on Drugs

snova
New York

NOTICE TO THE READER

The Publisher has taken reasonable care in the preparation of this book but makes no expressed or implied warranty of any kind and assumes no responsibility for any errors or omissions. No liability is assumed for incidental or consequential damages in connection with or arising out of information contained in this book. The Publisher shall not be liable for any special, consequential, or exemplary damages resulting, in whole or in part, from the readers' use of, or reliance upon, this material. Any parts of this book based on government reports are so indicated and copyright is claimed for those parts to the extent applicable to compilations of such works.

Independent verification should be sought for any data, advice or recommendations contained in this book. In addition, no responsibility is assumed by the Publisher for any injury and/or damage to persons or property arising from any methods, products, instructions, ideas or otherwise contained in this publication.

This publication is designed to provide accurate and authoritative information with regards to the subject matter covered herein. It is sold with the clear understanding that the Publisher is not engaged in rendering legal or any other professional services. If legal or any other expert assistance is required, the services of a competent person should be sought. FROM A DECLARATION OF PARTICIPANTS JOINTLY ADOPTED BY A COMMITTEE OF THE AMERICAN BAR ASSOCIATION AND A COMMITTEE OF PUBLISHERS.

Library of Congress Cataloging-in-Publication Data

ISBN: 979-8-89113-829-2 (Hardcover)
ISBN: 979-8-89113-857-5 (eBook)

Published by Nova Science Publishers, Inc. † New York

Contents

Preface

The war on drugs marked the start of a dramatic rise in the U.S. prison population. This policy became an engine for mass incarceration, as it resulted in an increase of Federal funding for drug control agencies, proposed measures such as mandatory and excessive sentencing laws and, yes, the now well-known and destructive no-knock warrants. The totality of these punitive measures does not increase public safety; rather, it produces permanent harm and disrupts the entire equilibrium of justice. This book examines how to repair the damage wrought by these overly excessive penalties.

Chapter 1

Undoing the Damage of the War on Drugs: A Renewed Call for Sentencing Reform*

Committee on the Judiciary

Thursday, June 17, 2021
House of Representatives
Subcommittee on Crime, Terrorism,
and Homeland Security
Committee on the Judiciary
Washington, DC

The Subcommittee met, pursuant to call, at 10:07 a.m., in Room 2141, Rayburn House Office Building, Hon. Sheila Jackson Lee [chair of the subcommittee] presiding.

Present: Representatives Jackson Lee, McBath, Dean, Scanlon, Bush, Lieu, Escobar, Cohen, Jordan, Biggs, Chabot, Tiffany, Massie, Spartz, Fitzgerald, and Owens.

Staff Present: Cierra Fontenot, Chief Clerk; John Williams, Parliamentarian; Merrick Nelson, Digital Director; Monalisa Dugue, Deputy Chief Counsel; Veronica Eligan, Professional Staff Member/ Legislative Aide; Tieffa Harper, Detailee; Jason Cervenak, Minority Chief Counsel for Crime; Ken David, Minority Counsel; Andrea Woodard, Minority Professional Staff Member; Kiley Bidelman, Clerk; and Carter Robertson, U.S. Secret Service Detailee.

* This is an edited, reformatted and augmented version of Hearing before the Subcommittee on Crime, Terrorism, and Homeland Security, of the Committee on the Judiciary, House of Representatives, One Hundred Seventeenth Congress, First Session, Serial No. 117–29, dated June 17, 2021.

In: Policies to Reverse the Damage Caused by the War on Drugs
Editors: Katie A. Hilbert
ISBN: 979-8-89113-829-2

Ms. JACKSON LEE. Good morning. The Committee will come to order. Without objection, the chair is authorized to declare recesses of the Subcommittee at any time.

Let me, first, thank all of you for your indulgence. This morning we had the enrollment signing of the Juneteenth holiday that was declared yesterday, and I am certainly ecstatic, but I also want to acknowledge my respect for this hearing and my role as Chair.

My tardiness was not for any other reason, for the historic enrollment signing of the Juneteenth independent national holiday day, so thank you all, as witnesses and my Committee Members, for your indulgence. Thank you so very much.

We welcome everyone to this morning's hearing on undoing the damage of the war on drugs, a renewed call for sentencing reform. Long overdue.

Before we begin, I'd like to remind Members that we have established an email address and distribution list dedicated to circulating exhibits, motions, or other written materials that Members may want to offer as part of our hearing today. If you would like to submit materials, please send them to the email address that has been previously distributed to your offices, and we will circulate the materials to Members and staff as quickly as we can.

For those in the room, current guidance from the Office of Attending Physician is that individuals who are fully vaccinated for COVID–19 do not need to wear a mask or maintain social distancing. Fully vaccinated individuals may, of course, choose to continue wearing masks based on their specific risk considerations. If you're not fully vaccinated, the Office of Attending Physician requires you to continue wearing a mask and maintaining 6 feet of social distancing.

I would also like Members to mute your microphones when you are not speaking. This will help prevent feedback and other technical issues. You may unmute yourself any time you seek recognition. I will now recognize myself for an opening statement.

Today marks the 50th anniversary of the war on drugs, and the 1970s marked the start of a dramatic rise in U.S. prison population. Mass incarceration grew, developed, imploded, and continued. This has only increased and is unmatched globally with over 2 million people currently incarcerated, even though the U.S. only accounts for less than 5 percent of the world's population.

On June 17th, 1971, President Nixon declared his new policy— war on drugs—in response to a rising tide of the use and/or trafficking of drugs. This policy became an engine for mass incarceration, as it resulted in an increase of Federal funding for drug control agencies, proposed measures such as mandatory and excessive sentencing laws and, yes, the now well-known and destructive no-knock warrants.

The totality of these punitive measures does not increase public safety; rather, it produces permanent harm and disrupts the entire equilibrium of justice. We examine sentencing reform through a punitive lens, rather than rehabilitation.

Consequently, a significant wave of destruction has amassed billions of dollars in human costs through our communities of color, while destroying families.

I remember just a few years ago, under a former chairman of this committee, as the siege of opioids were facing us. We did a different approach. We did approach of rehabilitation, treatment. What a difference. I offered an amendment that this new approach would cover crack cocaine as well.

New thinking needs to be the call of the day. When looking back at the true reason for the war on drugs, several top aides within Nixon's immediate orbit have revealed that by getting the public to associate the hippies with marijuana, Blacks with heroin, and then criminalizing both heavily, they could disrupt the communities; they would arrest their leaders, raid their homes, break up their meetings, and vilify them night after night on the evening news. They did so while knowing that the false narrative would work, and it did.

As ACLU says, the drug war has achieved only the harmful purposes President Nixon intended—disrupting, vilifying, and oppressing communities of color.

I agree with the leadership conference, that Congress must be bold to effectively repair the damage wrought by these overly excessive penalties.

Do you know who else was caught up in all this? Juveniles, under 25, under 20. Their lives off track, because of the use of drugs, or the co-opting of those who were engaged in drug use and/or drug trafficking—juveniles, children, who got sentencing 25 years, 30 years, in that time.

The impact of the war on drugs is still being felt today as evidenced in the alarming number of individuals incarcerated under these laws even 50 years later. According to the Federal Bureau of Prisons' own data, nearly half of all inmates are incarcerated on drug offenses.

Every month, approximately 1,600 people are sentenced for drug offenses in Federal court, most of which receive harsh sentences. In the '80s–'90s, we passed several legislations which continue to move away from rehabilitation and focus instead on excessive punishment when dealing with drugs.

Several bills continue to emphasize the prison focus. For example, the Anti-Drug Abuse Act of 1986 implemented the initial 100– 1 disparity and created mandatory minimum penalties for drug offenses, including life imprisonment.

In the '90s we passed the three strikes penalty that mandated life sentence for anyone convicted of a certain prior drug or violent felonies, and incentivized States to adopt similar policies.

In 1995, the U.S. Sentencing Commission called upon Congress to revisit these Draconian mandatory minimum sentencing laws, because of the racial disparities in cocaine versus crack cocaine sentencing.

Congress, however, overrode the recommendation made. We must use and undo the damage caused by the war on drugs. *Terry* v. *U.S.*, June 2017, the most recent drug case before the Supreme Court, the court held that crack offenders who did not trigger a mandatory minimum are not eligible for a sentence reduction under the First Step Act of 2018.

Justice Sotomayor concurs with Justice Thomas and essentially said that Congress has the necessary tools at its disposal to remedy the issue in Terry. I agree, and this is why I am working on legislation with the Senate, and we intend to introduce legislation in short order to address this issue in Terry.

We're also delighted that other Members, such as Mr. Jeffries, are working on legislation that is important to this discussion, and many other Members on this Subcommittee. In making its finding, Justice Thomas pointed to instances in which Congress has responded with proposed legislation with disproportionate ratios in how drugs of equal effect are treated differently.

The court explained and I quote, "Senator Sessions and Hatch introduced legislation in 2001 to lower the 100–1 ratio to 20–1." Representative Lee led a similar effort in the House that would have created a 1–1 ratio in H.R. 4545.

As the Supreme Court has acknowledged, I've been fighting to change these disparities for over a decade, and I will continue to do so as we seek to end mandatory minimum sentencing, beginning with the drug mandatory minimums, and I reserve the balance of my time.

It is my pleasure now to recognize the Ranking Member's opening statement, and that is the gentleman from Arizona, Mr. Biggs, for his opening statement.

Mr. BIGGS. I thank the Chair and appreciate all the witnesses being here today, both in person and remotely as well.

I look forward to a robust conversation surrounding sentencing reform, and I believe it's the job of Congress to examine the efficacy of our laws from time to time, see if updates are needed.

In fact, we should be looking, in my opinion, at our entire Federal Criminal Code to see what changes need to be made.

Shockingly, no one really knows how many Federal crimes are in statute, but some estimates put the figure above 4,000. Keep in mind that at its inception, the United States Code included only 30 crimes.

It has been nearly 40 years since retired Justice Department Official Ronald Gainer managed the last comprehensive attempt to count the number of Federal crimes and concluded, quote, "You will have died and resurrected three times," close quote, and will still not have an answer to how many Federal crimes are on the books in the United States.

I would suggest that many of those are duplicative and irrelevant. Not even the Congressional Research Service or the American Bar Association are able to calculate the number of Federal crimes.

According to one analysis, legislators introduced 154 bills in the 115th Congress alone that sought to add more criminal penalties to the United States Code.

Congress is not even the most egregious culprit in this over-criminalization. The sheer number of regulatory crimes in this country is mind-boggling. I have stated there are more than 4,000 Federal crimes in the U.S. Code, but there are also, astonishingly, more than 300,000 Federal crimes throughout various Federal regulations. That is absurd.

Many of these crimes are already crimes at the State level, and that's exactly where they should be prosecuted. Last, I checked, murder is a crime in every State, for instance.

The saturation of criminal conduct prevents law enforcement from focusing only on the severe and dangerous Federal crimes. Andrew McCarthy, a former Federal prosecutor said that time and money, quote, "spent investigating conduct that is not inherently criminal are time and money lost to the thwarting of much more serious crime," close quote.

Over-criminalization, coupled with the left's desire to defund the police, has real world consequences. In New York City, NYPD data showed murders jumped by nearly 14 percent through March 28th of this year, the latest figures the Department has made public, while shootings were up nearly 50 percent. The jump in crime came on the heels of New York City defunding its police department by $1 billion.

In L.A., homicides have increased nearly 36 percent from 67 to 91 through March 30th of this year. The increased homicide rate occurred after Los Angeles defunded its police department by $150 million.

Detroit, Michigan, suffered 327 homicides in 2020, as opposed to 275 in 2019, and aggravated assaults rose to 12,003 in 2020 from 9,467 in 2019. Detroit began defunding its police force in 2014 due to a city-wide bankruptcy. Since 2014, the Detroit Police Department has been cut by 20 percent.

As leaders, we should not be encouraging States and localities to defund their police. In fact, we should condemn it when we see it. That is why I was dismayed to see that the majority invited at least one witness who advocates for defunding our police.

In sum, we know that over-criminalization has led to a backlog in our courts and an overflow of inmates in our prisons. It's duplicative, it's unnecessary, and quite frankly, in my opinion, it's unconstitutional.

No one really knows how many Federal crimes are in statute, and that is a crime, in and of itself, rhetorically speaking.

Then, I will say also, generally crime in the United States had been trending downward over the last 30 years—violent crime and property crime. Last year, the United States tallied more than 20,000 murders, the highest since 1995.

No doubt, the impact of COVID was there, but it was 4,000 more than in 2019. Sixty-three of the 66 largest police jurisdictions saw increases in at least one category of violent crime in 2020.

I'm looking forward to a robust discussion that I'm sure we will have today. I appreciate the Chair for convening this very important Committee hearing, and I look forward to hearing from all the witnesses today. Thank you. I yield back.

Ms. JACKSON LEE. The gentleman yields back. We'll now move to introducing our witnesses. Thank you very much, Mr. Biggs, for your statement.

Ms. Rachel Barkow, that is on virtual, is the Vice Dean and Charles Seligson Professor of Law and Faculty Director of the Center on the Administration of Criminal Justice at NYU School of Law. She's recognized as one of the country's leading experts on criminal law and policy.

In June of 2013, the Senate confirmed Ms. Barkow as a Member of the Sentencing Commission, which she served until January 2019. She's been a Member of the Manhattan District Attorney's Office Conviction Integrity Policy Advisory Panel since 2010.

Mr. William Underwood is Senior Fellow at the Sentencing Project. Mr. Underwood served 33 of a 60-year sentence and life sentence in Federal prison after being sentenced in 1990 under then newly enacted sentencing guidelines of 1987, and the Anti-Drug Abuse Act of 1988.

His mentoring of countless young men in custody attracted the attention of a Federal circuit judge who wrote to thank him for making a difference in the lives of people around him.

On January 15th, 2021, the Federal judge granted his motion for compassionate release on an exemplary disciplinary record and found that he had transformed himself into a model prisoner and an American father. Today, Mr. Underwood works on criminal justice reform.

Ms. Kyana Givens is an Assistant Federal Public Defender for the Eastern District of North Carolina. In addition to her Federal criminal defense practice, Ms. Givens teaches and trains attorneys across the country on trial advocacy, emerging digital technology, and unconscious bias.

Ms. Givens was the Albert M. Sax fellow at Harvard Law School, where she worked closely with clinical professors, teaching and training in trial advocacy. Ms. Givens is a faculty member at the National Criminal Defense College and serves on the faculty for the Trial Skills Academy for Federal defenders.

Ms. Kassandra Frederique is the Executive Director of the Drug Policy Alliance. She has built and led campaigns on the overdose crisis and marijuana legalization. Ms. Frederique has been instrumental in grounding the national drug policy conversation around reparative justice and restitution for communities harmed by the war on drugs.

Among other victories, Ms. Frederique was the architect of the campaign that cut the number of New York City marijuana arrests by more than 99 percent.

Ms. Marta Nelson is Director of Government Strategy, Advocacy, and Partnership Department at the Vera Institute of Justice. She joined Vera in 2019, to research and write on sentencing reform, particularly sentencing involving people convicted of violent offenses.

Prior to joining Vera, Ms. Nelson served from 2014 to 2019 as Executive Director of Reentry and Special Counselor for criminal justice initiatives in New York, where she helped deliver comprehensive bail reform in 2019.

Ms. Jillian Snider is the Director of Criminal Justice and Civil Liberties at the R Street Institute. She is also a lecturer at John Jay College of Criminal Justice, and a retired officer from the New York City Police Department.

Ms. Snider also teaches as an Adjunct Lecturer at John Jay College of Criminal Justice in the Department of Law, police science, and criminal justice.

Mr. John Malcolm is the Vice President for the Institute for Constitutional Government, director at the Meese Center for Legal and Judicial Studies, and

Ed Gilbertson and Sherry Lindberg Gilbertson, Senior Legal Fellow, Institute for Constitutional Government at The Heritage Foundation.

He brings a wealth of legal expertise in both the public and private sectors. Mr. Malcolm is past Chair of the criminal law practice group of the Federalist Society and serves on the Board of Directors of Legal Services.

We welcome all our distinguished witnesses and thank them for participating in today's hearing. I'll begin by swearing in the witnesses. I will ask that our witnesses in person please rise and raise your right hand. I ask that those that are remote witnesses, please turn on their audio, make sure that I can see your face and your raised right hand while I administer the oath.

Do you swear or affirm, under penalty of perjury, that the testimony you're about to give is true and correct to the best of your knowledge, information, and belief so help you God? I need to hear you orally.

I do.

Ms. JACKSON LEE. Thank you. Let the record show the witnesses answered in the affirmative. You may be seated. Thank you.

Please note that each of your written statements will be entered into the record in its entirety. Accordingly, I ask that you summarize your testimony in 5 minutes. To help you stay within that time, there is a timing light on your table.

When the light switches from green to yellow, you have 1 minute to conclude your testimony. When the light turns red, it signals your 5 minutes have expired.

For our witnesses appearing virtually, there's a timer on your screen to help you keep track of time.

Ms. Barkow, you may begin, and you are virtual. Thank you very much and welcome again.

Statement of Rachel E. Barkow

Ms. BARKOW. Thank you, Chair Jackson Lee, Chair Nadler, Ranking Member Jordan, Ranking Member Biggs, and distinguished Members of the Subcommittee. Thank you so much for inviting me to testify on the important topic of sentencing reform.

The United States leads the world in incarceration and its harsh sentencing policies have separated families, destroyed communities, and produced gross racial disparities.

The biggest tragedy of all is that these policies haven't made us any safer. It's just the opposite. Our severe and punitive practices have increased the risk of crime.

Now, the conventional wisdom for decades has been the more severe the punishment, the greater the crime-fighting benefits. While that view might be common, it's actually mistaken.

In fact, we have a great deal of evidence showing that excessively punitive practices cause more crimes than they prevent. So, consider long sentences. When we give out disproportionate sentences, they undermine public confidence in criminal laws, and that, in turn, leads to reduced compliance with laws. People stop reporting crimes and cooperating with law enforcement, and that makes it harder to detect and solve crimes.

Long sentences also undermine public safety, because they make it that much harder for people to adjust when they're released from prison. Ninty-five percent of all people who are incarcerated return to free society, and we should want their reentry to be successful. The longer they stay in prison, the harder that is.

It's no wonder researchers find evidence that long sentences increase the risk of crime when people get out, even when you control for their underlying crime and criminal record.

For example, a study from Texas found that after a certain point, each additional year of incarceration caused an increased risk of recidivism between 4 and 7 percent.

Now, some might say, even if these sentences aren't deterring, at least they're incapacitating people from committing crimes outside the prison walls. Here too, reality is much more complicated than the gut instinct.

For starters, most people age out of most criminal behaviors, even without any governmental intervention. Besides aging out of crime, people stop committing crimes for other reasons. They address underlying substance abuse problems; they get mental health treatment or employment.

So, keeping people behind bars for decades doesn't bring incapacitation benefits after a certain point for so many people, because there's nothing to incapacitate.

In addition, because most people eventually rejoin society, we need to weigh whatever incapacitation benefit we're getting against that increased risk of recidivism from longer terms of incarceration.

All too often, the risks outweigh the benefits precisely because the person would have stopped committing crimes in any case, and time away from society has made it so much harder for them, when they're released, to stay on a law-abiding path.

So, a comprehensive analysis of this issue, looking at all the studies, has concluded incarceration certainly reduces crime outside prison as long as it lasts, but it appears to cause more crime later.

So, unfortunately, the flawed premise that we need to be as harsh as possible underlies so many of our laws and practices. We're spending a fortune on punitive practices that don't work to make us safer, and they tend to make things worse.

So, whether your concern is fiscal conservatism, racial justice, public safety, or a fundamental respect for human dignity, all roads point to the same solutions. We need to roll back the harsh policies of the past four decades.

Now, I'm just going to briefly offer a checklist of what those reforms should look like. It's not meant to be exhaustive, but it does give you a guidepost.

It means eliminating mandatory minimums, which have failed in all their policy objectives.

It means allowing the Sentencing Commission to make decisions based on evidence instead of congressional directives that aren't based on any evidence or data.

It means making retroactive relief available for anyone who is punished under a law that has since been changed to reduced sentences, something we've seen works, because the Sentencing Commission has that authority and has retroactively reduced sentences to great effect.

There should be second-look mechanisms for individuals, either through parole or allowing a judge to make adjustments because circumstances and people change.

We need to eliminate the harsh collateral consequences that are attached to convictions that make it harder for people to reenter, and we need to limit the use of pretrial detention.

Again, not an exhaustive list, but it gives you an idea. There aren't many areas left in public life that offer this kind of win-win, but criminal law is one of them.

It's why it's been the rare space of bipartisanship, even in these polarizing times, and it's my hope that it will continue to be a place where we can all come together to make us all better off.

Thank you for allowing me to testify and share my thoughts, and I'd be happy to answer any questions you may have.

[The statement of Ms. Barkow follows:]

Statement of Rachel E. Barkow, Vice Dean and Seligson Professor of Law, Faculty Director, Center on the Administration of Criminal Law, New York University School of Law, before the House Committee on the Judiciary, Subcommittee on Crime, Terrorism, and Homeland Security, Undoing the Damage of the War on Drugs: A Renewed Call for Sentencing Reform, June 17, 2021

Chairwoman Jackson Lee, Chairman Nadler, Ranking Member Jordan, Ranking Member Biggs, and Distinguished Members of the Subcommittee: Thank you for inviting me to testify on the topic of sentencing reform.

The United States leads the world in incarceration, and its harsh sentencing policies have separated families, destroyed communities, and produced gross racial disparities. The biggest tragedy of all is that these policies have not made us any safer. Just the opposite, too many severe sentences and punitive practices make crime more likely, not less.

In my remarks today, I would like to start by explaining what the evidence tells us about harsh punishments and crime. The conventional wisdom for decades has been that the more severe the punishment, the greater the crime fighting benefits. While that view might be common, it is mistaken. In fact, we have countless examples of excessively punitive practices that have been shown to cause more crimes than they prevent. This is true of excessively long sentences, of pretrial detention, and of collateral consequences attached to convictions. Yet that flawed premise – that we need to be as harsh as possible in response to criminal activity – underlies so many of our laws and practices, and it accounts for the rise of mass incarceration in the United States. We are spending a fortune on punitive practices that do not work to make us safer and, in fact, tend to make things worse.

Whether your concern is fiscal conservatism, racial justice, public safety, or fundamental respect for human dignity, all roads point to the same solutions. We need to roll back the harsh policies of the past four decades, make retroactive relief available for those punished under those laws, and adopt policies that we know work to reduce crime.

I will conclude by highlighting several specific policies that need reform. It is not an exhaustive list, but it will point out some of the major areas where we can promote public safety, save money, reduce racial disparities, and stop destroying families and communities. There are not many areas left in public life that offer this kind of win-win, but criminal law is one of them. That is why this has been the rare space of bipartisanship even in the polarizing times we live in, and it is my hope it will continue to be a place where we can come together to make us all better off.

The Costs of Excessive Punishment

For decades, Members of Congress and politicians around the country have hewed to the view that longer sentences promote public safety. They seem to believe that is true either because these harsh sentences and collateral consequences will deter the behavior from occurring in the first place, or because a long sentence incapacitates someone and therefore prevents that person from committing crimes while they are locked up. Both premises are flawed.

Let's start with the assumption that long sentences deter crime. It is one of the more settled aspects of criminology that the best way to deter crime is by increasing the odds of detection, not by changing the length of the sentence.[1] So if you have limited resources, you are better off spending them on mechanisms that improve detection and not increasing sanctions. Far too often, however, policymakers, including Congress, have ignored this evidence. For decades, the dominant approach in Congress and in the states has been to ratchet up punishments while clearance rates for violent crimes are abysmally low. Nationwide, the police solve less than half of all crimes involving physical violence, and in some communities the numbers are even lower. The clearance rate for homicides is less than 30% in some communities, and rates are lowest when the victim of the crime is Black.[2] If people think they have a 70% chance of committing a crime without getting caught, sentence length will do little to deter.

The problem with long sentences is not just that resources spent on sentencing could be better spent on detecting crime. Long sentences themselves can be harmful to public safety because they undermine public confidence in criminal laws. People see disproportionate sentences and lose

---

1 COUNCIL OF ECONOMIC ADVISERS, ECONOMIC PERSPECTIVES ON INCARCERATION AND THE JUSTICE SYSTEM 37-38 (2016); Steven Durlauf & Daniel Nagin, *Imprisonment and Crime: Can Both Be Reduced?*, 10 CRIMINOLOGY & PUB. POL'Y 13 (2011); Paul J. Larkin, Jr. *Swift, Certain, and Fair Punishment—24/7 Sobriety and HOPE: Creative Approaches to Alcohol- and Illicit Drug-Using Offenders*, 105 J. CRIM. L. & CRIMINOLOGY 39 (2016).

2 RACHEL E. BARKOW, PRISONERS OF POLITICS: BREAKING THE CYCLE OF MASS INCARCERATION 161 (2019).

faith that government is operating fairly and equitably. That, in turn, leads to reduced compliance with the laws themselves.[3] People stop reporting crimes and cooperating with law enforcement, which makes it harder to detect and solve crimes.[4] "If the legal system imposes more, or less, punishment on some crimes than citizens believe is deserved, the system seems unfair; it loses its credibility and, eventually, its effectiveness."[5]

Long sentences also undermine public safety because they make it that much harder for people to adjust when they are released from prison. Ninety-five percent of the people who are incarcerated return to free society.[6] We should want their reentry to be successful. But the longer they stay in prison, the harder that is.[7] "People who have served long periods of time in prison have a difficult time adjusting to an environment that is not highly controlled because their social skills and ability to make independent decisions atrophy when they are incarcerated."[8] And the greater number of people we incarcerate, which is a product of longer sentences, the more stretched prison resources become to provide rehabilitative programming and help to those who need it. For instance, a recent study of federal prisons found that the demand exceeded the capacity for many programs found to lower recidivism and assist with reentry.[9]

It is no wonder, then, that researchers find evidence that longer sentences can increase the risk of crime when people get out, even controlling for their underlying crime. For example, a study from Texas found that, after a certain point, each additional year of incarceration caused an *increase* in the risk of recidivism from 4-7%.[10]

Some might say that, even if these long sentences do not deter, at least they are incapacitating people from committing crimes outside the prison walls. But here, too, reality is much more complicated than this gut instinct. For starters, most people age of most criminal behaviors even without any

---

[3] Tom R. Tyler, *Procedural Justice, Legitimacy, and the Effective Rule of Law*, 30 CRIME & JUST. 321 (2003).

[4] Tom R. Tyler, *Popular Legitimacy and the Exercise of Legal Authority: Motivating Compliance, Cooperation and Engagement*, 20 PSYCHOL. PUB. POL'Y & L. 78 (2014).

[5] STUART P. GREEN, THIRTEEN WAYS TO STEAL A BICYCLE 53 (2012).

[6] TIMOTHY HUGHES & DORIS JAMES WILSON, BUREAU OF JUSTICE STATISTICS, REENTRY TRENDS IN THE UNITED STATES, http://www.bjs.gov/content/reentry/reentry.cfm.

[7] CHARLES COLSON TASK FORCE ON FEDERAL CORRECTIONS, TRANSFORMING PRISONS, RESTORING LIVES ix, 15 (2016).

[8] BARKOW, *supra* note 2, at 44.

[9] COLSON TASK FORCE, *supra* note 7, at 17.

[10] BARKOW, *supra* note 2, at 44.

government intervention.[11] In addition to aging out of crime, people stop committing crimes for other reasons, like addressing an underlying substance abuse problem or getting mental health treatment.[12] Keeping people behind bars for decades is thus not bringing any incapacitation benefit after a certain point because there is no criminal risk to incapacitate.

In addition, because most people eventually rejoin society, we need to weigh whatever incapacitation benefit we get against the increased risk of recidivism from longer terms of incarceration. And all too often, the risk outweighs the benefits precisely because the person would have stopped committing crimes but incarceration itself and time away from society has made it much harder for them to pursue a law-abiding path. A comprehensive analysis of this issue has concluded that, while "incarceration certainly reduces crime outside prison as long as it lasts, [it] appears to cause more crime later."[13]

The analysis thus far has considered the tradeoffs only from the perspective of the person serving the sentence. But long sentences have downsides that go beyond their effects on the offender. Long sentences cause enormous hardships to families, from the physical separation of parents and children, to lost wages that are often the difference between subsistence and ruin. It thus should come as no surprise that the children of incarcerated parents have an increased risk of a host of behavioral problems that, in turn, increase the risk that the children themselves will end up committing crimes.[14]

When researchers have studied all these costs and benefits of long sentences, they have concluded the costs are too great to justify this approach.[15] Moreover, this analysis underestimates the costs of long sentences because it does not quantify the many things communities and families lose when people are incarcerated for excessive amounts of time.

The stories of people who are granted relief and released early provide a glimpse of the lost talent and productivity we are keeping behind bars. Gerald Tarboro received a 15-year sentence for drug charges. Thanks to the First Step Act, he was released four years earlier. Since his release in March 2019, he has been working as a welder, pursuing a graduate degree in Public Policy, and advocating for the rights of other people still incarcerated.

---

[11] *Id.* at 44-45.

[12] *Id.* at 80-81.

[13] DAVID ROODMAN, THE IMPACTS OF INCARCERATION ON CRIME 98 (2017), http://files.openphilanthropy.org/files/Focus_Areas/Criminal_Justice_Reform/The_impacts_of_incarceratio n_on_crime_10.pdf.

[14] BARKOW, *supra* note 2, at 47-48.

[15] *Id.* at 49.

Or consider Rudy Martinez. He was given a life sentence as a first-time, non-violent drug offender. He was released after serving more than two-and-a-half decades in prison thanks to a commutation from President Obama. Since his release, he has been employed as a truck driver, attending community college to obtain an associate's degree in social work, and advocating for others.[16] He is a positive presence in the life of his children and his granddaughter.

There are countless stories just like Mr. Tarboro's and Mr. Martinez's.[17] People released through commutations, compassionate release, or retroactive sentencing adjustments are thriving despite the long odds against them, and all their contributions would have been lost had they been forced to serve the entirety of their original sentences. They are living proof of the costs of excessively long sentences.

But the costs of long sentences are all too often completely ignored. You can scour the Congressional Record from the 1980s and 1990s and not find any discussion of the downsides to long sentences. Instead, the assumption is the longer, the better. But in so many cases, these long sentences are leading to more crimes than they are preventing.

The best evidence demonstrating this point is looking to see what happens in places that have started to take a different course. We have seen jurisdiction after jurisdiction reduce sentences and reduce crime.[18] "[S]tates that lowered their incarceration rates have seen a greater drop in their crime rates than states where imprisonment rates have increased."[19]

This is not just a state phenomenon. We see the same positive results when federal sentences have been reduced. The United States Sentencing Commission has studied the effect of retroactive sentencing reductions on recidivism and found that shortening sentences does not increase recidivism. On multiple occasions, the Commission has compared the recidivism rates of those who receive sentencing reductions with similarly situated people who do not get the reductions solely because they served their full sentences before the changes were made. These are ideal comparison groups because the only difference between them is the sentence length. And the Commission has

---

16 Rudy Martinez, *Who Is My Brother's Keeper?*, 16 U. ST. THOMAS L.J. 353, 357 (2020).

17 FAMM has an excellent collection of such stories, available at https://famm.org/stories/.

18 PEW CHARITABLE TRUSTS, MOST STATES CUT IMPRISONMENT AND CRIME, http://www.pewtrusts.org/en/multimedia/data-visualizations/2014/imprisonment-and-crime; BARKOW, *supra* note 2, at 43.

19 BARKOW, *supra* note 2, at 43.

found, time and time again, that lowering sentences does not increase recidivism.[20]

Unfortunately, reductions at the federal level have been relatively rare, and retroactive adjustments in statutes have been even rarer. Instead, most often Congress has increased sentences on the assumption doing so is the right course for public safety. Its failure to consider the tradeoffs of an excessively punitive approach and the resulting damage it does to public safety is not limited to long sentences. We see the same counterproductive hit to public safety when we overuse pretrial detention,[21] fail to grant compassionate release or take other actions to correct excessive sentences[22] and impose harsh collateral consequences when someone is convicted.[23] In all these areas, we see that a "tough" approach actually backfires and makes crime more likely.

Congress may not have understood these tradeoffs at the peak of the drug war and tough-on-crime politics in the 1980s and 1990s, but we know better now. It is long past time to change the laws to take advantage of what we know about public safety.

It is particularly urgent given that these same policies not only fail to make us safer, but have so many other troubling outcomes. We incarcerate more people per capita than any other country on earth, and the negative

---

[20] U.S. SENTENCING COMM'N, RECIDIVISM AMONG OFFENDERS RECEIVING RETROACTIVE SENTENCE REDUCTIONS: THE 2007 CRACK COCAINE AMENDMENT 3 (2014) (2007 Amendment Report), https://www.ussc.gov/sites/default/files/pdf/research-and-publications/research-projects-and-surveys/miscellaneous/20140527_Recidivism_2007_Crack_Cocaine_Amendment.pdf; U.S. SENTENCING COMM'N, RECIDIVISM AMONG OFFENDERS RECEIVING RETROACTIVE SENTENCE REDUCTIONS: THE 2011 FAIR SENTENCING ACT GUIDELINE AMENDMENT 1 (2018) (FSA Amendment Report), https://www.ussc.gov/sites/default/files/pdf/research-and-publications/research-publications/2018/20180328_Recidivism_FSA-Retroactivity.pdf; U.S. SENTENCING COMM'N, RETROACTIVITY & RECIDIVISM: THE DRUGS MINUS TWO AMENDMENT 6 (2020) (Drugs Minus Two Report), https://www.ussc.gov/sites/default/files/pdf/research-and-publications/research-publications/2020/20200708_Recidivism-Drugs-Minus-Two.pdf.

[21] CHRISTOPHER T. LOWENKAMP, MARIE VANNOSTRAND & ALEXANDER HOLSINGER, THE HIDDEN COSTS OF PRETRIAL DETENTION, LAURA AND JOHN ARNOLD FOUNDATION (Nov. 2013), https://craftmediabucket.s3.amazonaws.com/uploads/PDFs/LJAF_Report_hidden-costs_FNL.pdf; Paul Heaton, Sandra Mayson & Megan Stevenson, *The Downstream Consequences of Misdemeanor Pretrial Detention*, 69 STAN. L. REV. 711 (2017).

[22] BARKOW, *supra* note 2, 84-86.

[23] *Id.* at 88-97.

consequences do not fall evenly on everyone in society. They disproportionately affect poor people and people of color.[24]

And we are not just punishing an individual with these sentences and draconian policies. We are punishing their innocent loved ones as well. Ironically, the law recognizes that third party effects have to be central to a punishment decision when the target is a corporation.[25] Yet when it comes to individuals, all too often the collateral damage to others is completely ignored.

Examples of Federal Laws and Policies That Undermine Public Safety

There are numerous examples of federal laws that stem from the flawed premise that they needed to be as harsh as possible, and these laws have turned out to be counterproductive to safety and fundamentally flawed in practice.

The biggest shift in federal punishment policy took place in the 1980s when Congress passed Comprehensive Crime Control Act of 1984 (CCCA).[26] Members of Congress on both sides of the aisle were dissatisfied with the federal approach to punishment that existed up to that point.[27] Under the pre-CCCA model, judges had wide discretion to set sentences, and the ultimate release date for a given person was determined by parole officials. Legislators lost faith in this model mainly because it rested on the idea of rehabilitation, with the parole board deciding when someone had rehabilitated and could therefore be released. A Senate report summed up the prevailing view of the time that "almost everyone involved in the criminal justice system now doubts that rehabilitation can be induced reliably in a prison setting, and it is now quite certain that no one can really detect whether or when a prisoner is rehabilitated."[28] Many legislators (particularly those on the left) also wanted to address what they saw as unwarranted disparities associated with the wide

---

[24] LEAH SAKALA, BREAKING DOWN MASS INCARCERATION IN THE 2010 CENSUS: STATE-BY-STATE INCARCERATION RATES BY RACE/ETHNICITY (May 28, 2014), https://www.prisonpolicy.org/reports/rates.html.

[25] Rachel E. Barkow, *Using the Corporate Prosecution and Sentencing Model for Individuals: The Case for a Unified Federal Approach*, 83 LAW & CONTEMP. PROBS. 159, 175 (2020).

[26] Pub. L. No. 98-473, tit. II, 98 Stat. 1976 (1984) (codified as amended in scattered sections of 18 and 28 U.S.C.).

[27] Rachel E. Barkow, *Categorical Mistakes: The Flawed Framework of the Armed Career Criminal Act and Mandatory Minimum Sentencing*, 133 HARV. L. REV. 200, 209-210 (2019).

[28] S. REP. NO. 98-225, at 38 (1983).

discretion the indeterminate model gave judges and parole officials.[29] And still other legislators (particularly those on the right) thought the prior regime was flawed because the sentences were too lenient and not doing enough to prevent crime.[30]

The CCCA aimed to address these concerns and ushered in "the most significant series of changes in the federal criminal justice system ever enacted at one time."[31] A centerpiece of the CCCA was creating harsher punishments for federal offenses, including creating mandatory minimum sentences, increasing maximum sentences, raising fines, and expanding asset forfeiture.[32]

Another part of the CCCA fundamentally changed federal pretrial practice. The Bail Reform Act of 1984[33] dramatically expanded the availability of pretrial detention.[34] Congress allowed courts to consider a defendant's risk of danger to the community, but "danger" was not limited to a concern with violence. This was the peak of the war on drugs, so Congress created a rebuttable presumption that a defendant is dangerous (and therefore should be detained) if he is charged with a drug violation that carries a maximum penalty of at least ten years.[35] Congress aimed to "increase dramatically the number of people detained pretrial."[36]

The Sentencing Reform Act[37] was another key component of the CCCA, and it created the United States Sentencing Commission and instructed that body to promulgate mandatory sentencing guidelines to limit the discretion of judges.[38] But instead of letting that expert body study sentencing and research to create the guidelines, Congress acted on its own before the Commission even had a chance to pass a single guideline. Congress passed harsh mandatory

---

[29] *See* Barbara S. Barrett, *Sentencing Guidelines: Recommendations for Sentencing Reform*, 57 MO. L. REV. 1077, 1079 (1992); Edward M. Kennedy, *Toward a New System of Criminal Sentencing: Law with Order*, 16 AM. CRIM. L. REV. 353, 356–57 (1979).

[30] *See* Barrett, *supra* note 27, at 1079; Donald W. Dowd, *What Frankel Hath Wrought*, 40 VILL. L. REV. 301, 303–04 (1995).

[31] Joseph E. diGenova & Constance L. Belfiore, *An Overview of the Comprehensive Crime Control Act of 1984 — The Prosecutor's Perspective*, 22 AM. CRIM. L. REV. 707, 707 (1985).

[32] Comprehensive Crime Control Act of 1984, Pub. L. No. 98-473, tit. II, §§ 211–216, 98 Stat. 1976, 1987–2017 (1984) (codified as amended in scattered sections of 18 U.S.C.); S. REP. NO. 98-225, at 3, 66, 105; Barkow, supra note 25, at 210.

[33] Pub. L. No. 98-473, tit. II, ch. I, §§ 202–209, 98 Stat. 1976, 1976–87 (1984) (codified as amended in scattered sections of 18 U.S.C.).

[34] 18 U.S.C. § 3142 (2012); diGenova & Belfiore, *supra* note 29, at 708–12.

[35] *See* 18 U.S.C. § 3142(e).

[36] Barkow, *supra* note 25, at 211.

[37] Pub. L. No. 98-473, tit. II, ch. II, 98 Stat. 1987 (1984) (codified as amended in scattered sections of 18 and 28 U.S.C.).

[38] 28 U.S.C. §§ 991–998 (2012).

minimums for individuals with certain prior felony convictions who were charged federally with possessing a firearm pursuant to the Armed Career Criminal Act (ACCA),[39] which was also part of the CCAA. It instituted even more sweeping mandatory minimum sentences in the Anti-Drug Abuse Act of 1986,[40] which was also the law that created what came to be known as the 100-to-1 ratio between powder and crack cocaine, requiring 100 times the quantity of powder cocaine than crack cocaine to trigger the same mandatory minimum penalties.[41] And Congress continued to pass its own sentencing laws and sweeping collateral consequences for those convicted of federal crimes without consulting the Commission even after the Guidelines were promulgated.[42] Congress even ordered the Commission to take specific actions to increase sentences no matter what the Commission's own research might have said.[43]

It was bad enough that Congress failed to consult the expert agency it created to address sentencing. But Congress did no independent research, either. For decades, it has passed ever harsher laws with no evidence that they would further public safety or that they would make the most of limited resources.

Congress's approach to crack cocaine is emblematic of the process it followed across the board. When it set the penalties for crack, it responded to sensational media accounts and hysterical anecdotes characterizing crack as a uniquely addictive drug that prompted violent behavior.[44] One member of Congress candidly admitted that they set crack penalties without "really hav[ing] an evidentiary basis."[45] If Members of Congress had taken the time to consult the Sentencing Commission or study the issue on its own, it would have discovered that crack and powder are pharmacologically indistinguishable and that crack is no more addictive. They would have also learned that individuals on crack are no more prone to violence than

---

[39] Pub. L. No. 98-473, tit. II, ch. XVIII, 98 Stat. 2185 (1984) (codified as amended at 18 U.S.C. § 924(e) (2012)).

[40] Pub. L. No. 99-570, 100 Stat. 3207 (1986) (codified as amended primarily in scattered sections of 18 and 21 U.S.C.); *see id.* §§ 1401–1402, 100 Stat. at 3207-30 to -40.

[41] Pub. L. No. 99-570, § 1002, 100 Stat. 3207, 3207-2 to -4 (1986) (codified as amended at 21 U.S.C. § 841 (2012)).

[42] Barkow, *supra* note 25, at 213-214.

[43] *Id.* at 214.

[44] *Id.* at 215.

[45] NAOMI MURAKAWA, THE FIRST CIVIL RIGHT: HOW LIBERALS BUILT PRISON AMERICA 125 (2014) (quoting 156 CONG. REC. H6202 (daily ed. July 28, 2010) (statement of Rep. Daniel E. Lungren)).

individuals on powder cocaine.[46] They would have further learned that treating crack and powder so dramatically differently would create enormous racial disparities in sentencing, punishing Black people far more harshly than White people because of different arrest rates for the two forms of the drug based on race.[47]

We see the same basic pattern – a failure to consider evidence, a lack of consultation with subject matter experts, no evaluation of what would be best to promote public safety – in Congress's passage of the ACCA. The legislative history indicates that Congress wanted to target the relatively small number of people who commit a disproportionate share of the most violent crimes. The actual legislation it enacted, however, fails to achieve that objective. Prior drug felonies trigger the harsh mandatory minimum even if they involved no violence at all. Almost 99% of drug offenses involve no physical injury to anyone. And people with drug-only convictions pose little risk of future violence – with only 1.6% of them being rearrested for a violent felony.[48] That is why the Sentencing Commission has concluded that "drug trafficking only offenders generally do not warrant similar (or at times greater) penalties than those career offenders who have committed a violent offense" and has urged Congress to amend the law "to more effectively differentiate between career offenders with different types of criminal records."[49] Prior burglary offenses also trigger ACCA, and they, too, lack an association with violence. Congress included this offense because prosecutors requested it and claimed, without evidence, that burglary is a dangerous offense linked to violence.[50] The data show otherwise. More than 97% of burglaries involve no physical injury.[51] Congress just never looked at any data.

The entire framework of mandatory minimum sentences suffers from the same shortcomings. When Congress set the mandatory minimums for drug sentences in the Anti-Drug Abuse Act of 1986, it made assumptions that those minimums would reach high-level dealers and leaders of drug-trafficking operations.[52] Congress did not take the time to learn how conspiracy law

---

[46] Barkow, *supra* note 25, at 215-216.

[47] *Id.* at 216.

[48] *Id.* at 230.

[49] U.S. SENTENCING COMM'N, REPORT TO THE CONGRESS: CAREER OFFENDER SENTENCING ENHANCEMENTS 8, 27 (2016).

[50] Armed Career Criminal Legislation: Hearing on H.R. 4639 and H.R. 4768 Before the Subcomm. on Crime of the H. Comm. on the Judiciary, 99th Cong. 26 (1986) (testimony of James Knapp, Deputy Assistant Att'y Gen., Criminal Division, U.S. Department of Justice).

[51] Barkow, *supra* note 25, at 231-232.

[52] Id. at 216-217.

works, so it did not understand that low-level participants in trafficking operations would also get hit would those mandatory minimum penalties. The result was sadly predictable. A bipartisan task force evaluating criminal law concluded that "that the mandatory minimum framework . . . is fundamentally broken" because "judges find their hands tied by an extraordinarily punitive one-size-fits-all structure."[53] And that size is set for the most culpable leaders of trafficking operations, even though the punishments are overwhelmingly applied to low-level participants, many of whom sell to support a drug habit. The Sentencing Commission has issued multiple reports laying out the problems with mandatory minimum sentences, but Congress has continued to ignore its expert advice. It is hardly surprising that numerous commutations granted by recent presidents have come in cases involving mandatory minimum sentences.[54]

It is no wonder that mandatory minimum sentences have failed to achieve their policy objectives. They have not reduced crime, they have increased rather than reduced racial disparities, and they have "lumped together people of vastly different levels of culpability, thus resulting in excessive and disproporionate sentences for tens of thousands."[55]

The federal legal landscape is overrun with laws like these. They set severe mandatory minimums, direct the Commission to establish harsh guidelines, and they give prosecutors leverage to impose huge penalties on anyone who wants to exercise their right to a jury trial. They play a huge role in filling federal prisons and contributing to mass incarceration. They lead to gross racial disparities.[56] They cost a fortune. What they do not do is make us any safer.

---

[53] COLSON TASK FORCE, *supra* note 7, at 21.

[54] Rachel E. Barkow, *Clemency and Presidential Administration of Criminal Law*, 90 N.Y.U. L. REV. 802, 837 n.208 (2015).

[55] Rachel E. Barkow, *The Evolving Role of the United States Sentencing Commission*, 33 FED. SENT. REP. 3, 5 (2020).

[56] The Sentencing Commission has concluded that mandatory minimums and mandatory sentencing guidelines had a greater adverse impact on Black people who commit offenses than did the sentencing regime that existed before the 1984 legislation. U.S. SENTENCING COMM'N, FIFTEEN YEARS OF GUIDELINES SENTENCING: AN ASSESSMENT OF HOW WELL THE FEDERAL CRIMINAL JUSTICE SYSTEM IS ACHIEVING THE GOALS OF SENTENCING REFORM 135 (2004).

Suggested Reforms

There is a better path forward, one that Congress itself recognized at one point.

When it sought to reform federal sentencing in the mid-1980s, it conceded that "[s]entences that are disproportionate to the seriousness of the offense create a disrespect for the law."[57] It also approvingly cited the Minnesota approach to sentencing guidelines as the one it wanted to follow.[58] Tragically, somewhere along the way, Congress veered off this course and took a punitive path that ignored expert advice and data. But it is not too late to fix the federal framework.

Eliminate Mandatory Minimums

The first key step is to make policy grounded in evidence and data instead of flawed intuitions like the harsher, the better. That means Congress needs to repeal mandatory minimums or effectively do the same thing by creating a safety valve that is available to anyone and allows judges not to impose the mandatory minimum if the punishment would be disproportionate to the facts of the case. Mandatory minimums have been a complete policy failure, and they should not be part of any functioning sentencing scheme. The Commission has amply documented these problems, and it is long past time for Congress to take note of the evidence and repeal them.

Congress has already begun to recognize the need for this change. The First Step Act reduced many drug mandatory minimums.[59] But that was, as the law's title indicates, but a first step, and it is time for Congress to finish what it started by repealing all mandatory minimums. They rest on the flawed premise that they work to reduce crime and disparities when in fact they do not achieve any of their objectives.

Fix the Sentencing Commission Framework

The next critical step is to fix flaws with the Sentencing Commission and Guidelines. Congress should start by passing a new directive to the Sentencing Commission to reconsider all of its prior Guideline sentences without being bound by any previous congressional directives. Those prior directives were not grounded in evidence or analysis, but instead were based on political impulses to call for increases based on the fatally flawed assumption that

---

[57] S. REP. NO. 98-225, at 46 (1983).
[58] *Id.* at 46.
[59] Barkow, *supra* note 53, at 8 (describing the reductions).

increasing sentence length was good for public safety.[60] I have explained the flaw with that assumption, and it is important to allow the Commission to balance all relevant interests in setting guidelines without a thumb on the scale in favor of an increase when it might not be warranted. A new directive relieving the Commission from any prior directives will allow it to fix guidelines that are problematic, which are most easily identified by the fact that large numbers of judges are not complying with them. That is a key sign that the guideline is not proportional in most cases and needs to be right-sized.

Congress should reform other aspects of the Commission's operation. While successful state commissions like Minnesota must make sure its punishments fit within existing prison capacity – a restraint that helps make state sentencing more rational and prioritizes limited resources so they are used most effectively and to avoid overcrowding and overspending – the federal commission does not currently have such a constraint.[61] But it should. It should also have to engage in a cost-benefit analysis before passing a new guidelines, something that is standard for other administrative agencies and an approach that helps keep important tradeoffs in view and makes it more likely that the government is operating efficiently.

Congress should also balance the composition of the Commission. Since its inception, it is an agency that has been dominated by former prosecutors, a byproduct of the fact that the only specified requirement for commissioners is to have a certain number of judges, who themselves largely come from the ranks of former prosecutors.

Unfortunately, that means a majority of the Commission at any one time has tended to have a view that longer sentences are better for public safety. A more balanced Commission would include commissioners who are criminologists, defense lawyers, and formerly incarcerated people – perspectives sorely lacking on the Commission now. The original idea for a sentencing commission came from Judge Marvin Frankel, but Congress ignored Frankel's suggestion that the body should be made up of "criminologists, sociologists, and former or present prisoners."[62] Requiring the president to nominate individuals with those backgrounds will help improve the Commission's decisions and bring relevant expertise on what works to reduce crime and what life inside prisons is like – perspectives that will help the Commission set sentence lengths with a full range of information.

---

[60] Barkow, *supra* note 53, at 5.
[61] Rachel E. Barkow, *Administering Crime*, 52 UCLA L. REV. 715, 760 (2005).
[62] MARVIN E. FRANKEL, CRIMINAL SENTENCES: LAW WITHOUT ORDER 120 (1973).

Retroactivity

Whenever Congress modifies a law so that sentences are lower, that change must be retroactively available to all individuals currently serving sentences under the old regime. Congress recognized the importance of retroactivity when it gave the Sentencing Commission the authority to determine when its changes to the Sentencing Guidelines should be retroactive. The Commission's use of this authority shows how effective it has been. When it reduced crack sentences in 2007, it made those reductions retroactively available and then studied what happened to those who served their full sentences and those who received the retroactive reductions (which averaged 26 months).[63] Those who received reductions in 2007 had, five years later, recidivated at a rate of 43.6% compared to 47.8% for those who served their full sentence.[64] (With recidivism measuring arrest rates.) When it conducted a study of the 2011 reductions, it also found no stastitically significant difference in the two groups three years later.[65]

The Commission lowered sentences for all drug offenses, not just crack cocaine, in 2013, and made those changes retroactive. More than 30,000 people received an average reduction of 37 months.[66] When those receiving a reduction were compared three years later with a similarly situated group who had served their full sentences before retroactivity took effect, the Commission found the group that received a reduced sentence recidivated at a rate of 27.9% compared to 30.5% for the group that served their full sentence.[67] This data shows that retroactive adjustments do not compromise public safety.

Congress itself recognized the need for retroactive sentencing adjustments in the First Step Act when it allowed individuals sentenced before the Fair Sentencing Act to seek adjustments based on the FSA's changes to crack sentences.[68] Almost 2400 people have received a sentencing reduction thanks to the First Step Act's retroactivity provision, and roughly 91% of them are Black.[69]

Congress should similarly provide for retroactive eligibility whenever it makes statutory changes that result in lower sentences. No one should serve a

63 2007 Amendment Report, note 19, at tbl. 8.
64 2007 Amendment Report, *supra* note 19, at 3.
65 FSA Amendment Report, *supra* note 19, at 1.
66 Drugs Minus Two Report, *supra* note 19, at 1.
67 Drugs Minus Two Report, *supra* note 19, at 6.
68 Pub. L. No. 115-391 § 404, 132 Sta. 5194 (2018).
69 U.S. SENTENCING COMM'N, FIRST STEP ACT OF 2018 RESENTENCING PROVISIONS RETROACTIVITY DATA REPORT tbl.4 (2020).

sentence today that has been recognized as harsher than it needs to be. No society can justify keeping people locked up under laws they now recognize were flawed and too harsh.

Second Look Mechanisms

Even if the laws themselves do not change, people and circumstances do. Consequently, there need to be second-look mechanisms in place in addition to retroactive legislative adjustments to account for changes in individual circumstances over time. The federal sentencing regime is notable among all jurisdictions in the United States for its lack of viable second look mechanisms. No one sentenced after November 1, 1987, is eligible for parole in the federal system. Individuals must either turn to clemency or compassionate release, neither of which has been up to the task of dealing with all the meritorious cases. Clemency is fundamentally flawed because the Department of Justice is in charge of screening petitions. Given that DOJ brought the cases in the first place, it is hardly surprising that they do not look favorably on requests to overturn its decisions.[70] Compassionate release has failed to pick up the slack. Until the First Step Act passed, the Bureau of Prisons had to file a petition with a court for anyone to be considered for compassionate release, and the BOP's failure to do so was subject to two critical inspector general reports.[71] That awful track record led Congress in the First Step Act to allow people to file directly with courts for compassionate release.

That has been a welcome reform. But even with that change, some courts have been generous with their grants, while others have been less so.[72] Part of the variation is due to the fact that there is uncertainty about the grounds on which a sentence can be reconsidered as a matter of compassionate release.[73]

---

[70] Rachel E. Barkow & Mark Osler, *Designed to Fail: The President's Deference to the Department of Justice in Advancing Criminal Justice Reform*, 59 WM. & MARY L. REV. 387 (2017).

[71] OFFICE OF THE INSPECTOR GEN., U.S. DEP'T OF JUSTICE, THE IMPACT OF AN AGING INMATE POPULATION ON THE FEDERAL BUREAU OF PRISONS 2 (2016), https://perma.cc/9T6H-5GGN; OFFICE OF THE INSPECTOR GEN., U.S. DEP'T OF JUSTICE, THE FEDERAL BUREAU OF PRISONS' COMPASSIONATE RELEASE PROGRAM 1 (2013), https://perma.cc/KQX2-R5GC.

[72] U.S. SENT. COMM'N, COMPASSIONATE RELEASE DATA REPORT, tbl. 1 (2021), https://www.ussc.gov/sites/default/files/pdf/research-and-publications/federal-sentencing-statistics/compassionate-release/20210609-Compassionate-Release.pdf?utm_medium =email&utm_source=govdelivery.

[73] There is a split between the 11th Circuit, which takes the more limited view, and decisions from the Fourth, Fifth, Sixth, Seventh, Ninth, and Tenth Circuits that take the broader view.

Congress must expand the available second look options. Specifically, it should make clear that any sentence can be reconsidered after a certain period of time, either by reestablishing parole or making clear that the compassionate release second look under the First Step Act is not limited to situations of ill health or extraordinary family circumstances but includes taking a second look for any compelling reason, which can include the fact the sentence is excessive. People and circumstances change over time – particularly over the long periods of incarceration that are so often handed down in the federal system. Having a second look allows a decision maker to account for the ways in which people change, particularly as they age out of criminal behaviors. It also provides a mechanism for reflecting changes in attitudes to particular kinds of crime. For example, marijuana is now legal in many states and federal prosecutors have been largely let those state schemes stand without federal interference. Yet individuals continue to serve decades in federal prison for selling marijuana. Parole eligibility or the opportunity to appear before a judge for resentencing after a certain length of time can help account for inevitable changes in circumstances.

Relief from Collateral Consequences

Although not officially part of a defendant's sentence, collateral consequences of convictions effectively amount to additional punishment of defendants – and in ways that compromise public safety. Federal law renders individuals convicted of drug offenses ineligible for public housing, welfare assistance, and food stamps, all of which are often critical transitional tools for individuals trying to reenter society after terms of incarceration. Federal law also mandates the reduction of state highway funds if states do not suspend drivers' licenses for people with drug offenses, which ends up hampering people's ability to get to jobs, again in opposition to public safety goals.[74] Congress paid little attention to public safety effects when these laws were passed. For example, it passed the restrictions on welfare and food stamps after two minutes of discussion, and inexplicably carves out drug offenses for ineligibility.[75] These laws have nothing to do with public safety and everything to do with the hysteria that surrounded the start of the drug war. Repealing these collateral consequences would improve public safety by allowing more people to successfully transition to law-abiding lives after serving their sentences.

---

[74] BARKOW, *supra* note 2, at 93.
[75] *Id.*

Pretrial Detention Reform

Detention before trial is not technically part of a defendant's sentence because individuals are presumed innocent before they are convicted. But although it is not considered punishment in a legal sense, pretrial detention affects sentencing and public safety. Individuals detained pretrial are more likely to plead guilty than similarly situated defendants who are not detained. That is, even controlling for offense and criminal record, the detention itself leads to more convictions.[76] Pretrial detention also leads to longer sentences, regardless of a defendant's risk, crime, or criminal history.[77] And just as long sentences can lead to more criminal offending upon release than shorter ones, all else being equal, pretrial detention can have the same consequences. It is so disruptive on individuals' lives – leading to job loss, eviction, loss of custody of children – that it is no wonder that individuals detained pretrial have a greater risk of offending than individuals who were not detained, even when controlling for the offense type and risk level. Pretrial detention itself leads to a 20% increase in misdemeanors and a 30% increase in felonies.[78]

Because of their inextricable connection, sentencing reform must include pretrial detention reform. The federal scheme is fundamentally flawed because it assumes individuals should be detained if they are a risk to engage in drug trafficking, and it creates a presumption that the risk exists if an individual is merely charged with drug trafficking offenses that carry a maximum sentence of at least ten years.[79] That covers most drug defendants in the federal system and leads to far too much pretrial detention. Congress should reform its pretrial detention practices, just as many states are doing, and base its determinations on evidence, not unsubstantiated assumptions based on the hysteria that surrounded the drug war. States like New Jersey that have reformed their pretrial detention practices have seen their jail populations decline substantially without an increase in crime. It is time for the federal government to lead in this effort as well.

This is not meant to be an exhaustive list. Congress should fix all the areas in which it was guided by the flawed premise that the most punitive approach is the most effective approach. Data, evidence, and experience show that not to be the case, and thousands of lives have been destroyed as a result.

---

[76] Heaton et al., *supra* note 19, at 717.
[77] LOWENKAMP ET AL., *supra* note 19, at 4.
[78] Heaton et al., *supra* note 19, at 718.
[79] 18 U.S.C. § 3142(e).

Conclusion

Thank you for allowing me to testify and share my thoughts on sentencing reform.

I would be happy to answer any questions that you might have.

* * *

Ms. JACKSON LEE. The gentlelady's time has expired. Thank you very much. I yield now to Mr. Underwood for 5 minutes.

Statement of William R. Underwood

Mr. UNDERWOOD. I first want to thank Chair Jackson Lee, Chair Nadler, Ranking Member Biggs, and Members of this Committee for holding this hearing today, and for sharing this space to hear stories about the impact that the war on drugs has had on people like me and families like mine.

My name is William Underwood, and I am a Senior Fellow at the Sentencing Project's campaign to end life imprisonment.

One hundred and fifty years ago today, President Nixon declared the war on drugs. I was a 17-year-old father at the time. It was fast money to be made, and I was not going to allow my son to grow up in a world of hunger and pain that I had.

Just like any other war, this one has eviscerated entire generations and communities like the one where I grew up in, in Harlem. While it's called the war on drugs, it's disparate impact over the decades has made clear that this is actually a war on the poor, a war on inner city youth, and a war on Black people and other communities of color.

I witnessed that reality every day of my 33 years of incarceration after being sentenced to life without the possibility of parole, and a concurrent 20-year sentence for leading a violent drug operation during the 1970s and the early '80s in New York City.

From the beginning of my incarceration, I was surrounded by other men of color, serving life-long and other extreme sentences, including for drug offenses handed down under a mandatory minimum sentencing structure that never accounts for an individual's growth, rehabilitation, and transformation while incarcerated.

This experience wasn't unique to the prisons in which I served. In fact, 1 in every 7 people in U.S. prisons are serving a life sentence, or virtual life sentence, of at least 50 years.

Nearly 4,000 of those people are serving life sentences for a drug-related offense, 38 percent of whom are in the Federal prison system in which I served, men like Tony Lewis, Sr., Wayne Pray, Todd Vassell, Thomas Jackson, Steven Petersen, Darryl Riley, Spencer Bolis (ph), and Steven Brown.

I was extremely lucky that I was granted compassionate release in January at 67 years old. Judge Sidney H. Stein found my sentence reflected the seriousness of my criminal behavior when I was convicted 33 years ago, but its extremeness did not account for the person I am today.

Judge Stein's order stated, in light of Underwood's exemplary record over the last three decades, his consequential mentorship of young men and contribution to a culture of responsibility in Federal prison, and his commendable efforts in raising and supporting his children and grandchildren from behind bars, the court finds that Underwood's good deeds exceed the bounds of what we consider rehabilitation, and amount to extraordinary and compelling reasons meriting a sentence reduction.

I was not the exception in prison. Many others like me remain and will take their last breaths there. Like me, those are men that have also spent decades having to get to know their children through 15-minute phone calls. Like me, they have had to see grandchildren grow up through nothing but photographs.

I'm very fortunate to have four successful children who have always fought for me, supported me, and helped me maintain a piece of the music publishing rights that I owned before my incarceration.

It comes as no surprise that the lack of preparation provided in prisons leaves so many young people returning to their communities to end up on the streets or back in prison.

There's got to be a better way. Regardless of their intended purpose, mandatory minimums go against the Rule of law by perpetuating disproportionate prison sentences and aggravating racial disparities in the criminal justice system.

A wealth of research shows that prosecutors bring charges carrying a mandatory minimum sentence against Black defendants at higher rates than White defendants. Research also illustrates that people age out of criminal conduct as they get older.

Life sentences do nothing to promote public safety and only perpetuate cycles of poverty and trauma. Extreme sentences ignore people's capacity for change as human beings.

We are capable of painful, yet transformative self-reflection, maturity, and growth, and to deny a person this opportunity is to deny them their humanity.

There is no reason to wait decades until a person's sentence to begin evaluating their growth and readiness to rejoin their families and communities.

By granting a second look after 10 years and releasing those who have proven they have worked for it, deserve it, and are ready for it, we can reunite families and free up resources in the justice system to prepare those inside for a successful release.

So, I come before you a reformed man, an atoned man, with the hope that you will hear my words, hear the honesty and commitment in my voice, and be moved to understand why each and every one of us, when given the chance, can be better than the worse thing we have ever done.

We all deserve a second chance. Thank you.

[The statement of Mr. Underwood follows:]

Testimony of William R. Underwood, Senior Fellow, the Sentencing Project, on Undoing the Damage of the War on Drugs: A Renewed Call for Sentencing Reform, before the U.S. House of Representatives' Committee on the Judiciary, Subcommittee on Crime, Terrorism and Homeland Security, June 17, 2021

I first want to thank Chairwoman Jackson Lee and the members of this committee for holding this hearing today, and for sharing this space to hear stories about the impact that the war on drugs has had on people like me and families like mine. My name is William Underwood and I am a Senior Fellow with The Sentencing Project's Campaign to End Life Imprisonment.

Fifty years ago today, President Nixon declared the war on drugs. I was a 17-year-old father at the time; there was fast money to be made, and I was not going to allow my son to grow up in the world of hunger and pain that I had.

Just like any other war, this one has eviscerated entire generations in communities like the one where I grew up in Harlem. While it's called the war on drugs, its disparate impact over the decades has made clear that this is actually a war on the poor, a war on inner city youth, and a war on Black people and other communities of color.

If this were actually a war on drugs, it would not be true that while white Americans engage in drug offenses at similar rates to Black and Brown Americans, over half of the 250,000 people imprisoned nationwide for a drug offense are African American or Latinx.[80]

I witnessed that reality every day of my 33 years of incarceration, after being sentenced to life without the possibility of parole and a concurrent 20-year sentence for leading a violent drug operation during the 1970s and early 80s in New York City.

From the beginning of my incarceration, I was surrounded by other men of color serving lifelong and other extreme sentences, including for drug offenses — handed down under a mandatory minimum sentencing structure that never accounts for an individual's growth, rehabilitation and transformation while incarcerated.

This experience wasn't unique to the prisons in which I served time. In fact, one in every seven people in U.S. prisons are serving a life sentence or virtual life sentence of at least 50 years. Nearly 4,000 of those people are serving life sentences for a drug-related offense, 38 percent of whom are in the federal prison system in which I served.[81] Men like Wayne Pray, Todd Vassell, Thomas Jackson, Steven Petersen, Darryl Riley, and Steven Brown.

I was lucky that I was granted compassionate release in January at 67 years old. Judge Sidney H. Stein found my sentence reflected the seriousness of my criminal behavior when I was convicted 33 years ago, but its extremeness did not account for the person I am today. Judge Stein's release order cited letters from the men I mentored while in prison, including this excerpt:

> I watched him mentor other young men in prison and it was a well-known fact and still is that when you speak to Mr. Underwood and are around him, "no nonsense is allowed!" This brings about a culture of responsibility of all the men that he comes into contact with and I can attest that not only other prisoners respect each other, but respect the staff there as well. In turn the staff respects the prisoners.[82]

---

[80] Carson, A. (2020). *Prisoners in 2019*. Bureau of Justice Statistics.

[81] Nellis, A. (2021). *No End in Sight: America's Enduring Reliance on Life Imprisonment*. The Sentencing Project.

[82] *United States v. Underwood,* 88-Cr-822 (SHS) (S.D.N.Y. Jan. 15, 2021).

I was not the exception in prison. Many others like me remain and will take their last breaths there.

Like me, those men have also spent decades having to get to know their children through 15-minute phone calls. Like me, they have had to see their grandchildren grow up through nothing but photographs. And after each rare in-person visit, they have had to return to the same prison cell while their families return to the quickly changing and developing world outside.

Since so much of the justice system's resources go toward warehousing people serving life sentences, there is a completely inadequate amount of resources being spent on preparing people to return to this quickly changing world. It's no mystery as to why those fortunate enough to get out of prison and re-enter their communities struggle to handle a computer, find work and housing, secure health insurance, claim Social Security, or open a bank account.

I'm lucky to have four successful children who have always fought for me, supported me, and helped me maintain a piece of the music publishing rights that I owned before my incarceration. While it has been a struggle, my support team, my children, have given me the tools I need to survive in the 21st Century. But it comes as no surprise that the lack of preparation provided in prisons leads so many young people returning to their communities to end up on the streets or back in prison.

There's got to be a better way.

For one, our criminal legal system must move away from mandatory minimums.

Regardless of their intended purpose, mandatory minimums go against the rule of law by perpetuating disproportionate prison sentences and exacerbating racial disparities in the criminal justice system. A wealth of research shows that prosecutors bring charges carrying a mandatory minimum sentence against Black defendants at higher rates than white defendants.

Second, there is absolutely no need for lifelong sentences.

As criminological research illustrates, people age out of criminal conduct as they get older, and lengthy prison terms keep people behind bars well after they are no longer likely to commit another crime. Life sentences do nothing to promote public safety, and only perpetuate cycles of poverty and trauma.

Extreme sentences also ignore people's capacity for change. During my incarceration, I thought daily about the moments I was missing out on with my children and grandchildren, and dreamed about the man I could be for them if I could just find a way out. My desire to be that man inspired me to spend every day of my time in prison educating and working on myself, and educating and mentoring others.

As human beings, we are capable of painful yet transformative self-reflection, maturity, and growth, and to deny a person this opportunity is to deny them their humanity.

Finally, ten years is long enough to be able to reevaluate someone's growth and rehabilitation, and to begin to consider their release.

There's no reason to wait decades into a person's sentence to begin evaluating their growth and readiness to rejoin their families and communities. By granting a second look after ten years, and releasing those who have proven they have worked for it, deserve it, and are ready for it, we can reunite families and free up resources in the justice system to prepare those inside for successful release.

So, I come before you a reformed man, an atoned man, with the hope that you will hear my words, hear the honesty and commitment in my voice, and be moved to understand why each and every one of us, when given the chance, can be better than the worst thing that we have ever done. That we all deserve a Second Chance; a Second Chance which is the promise of America.

* * *

Ms. JACKSON LEE. Mr. Underwood, I'm going to take the liberty of saying, thank you so very much for your powerful testimony.

Mr. UNDERWOOD. Thank you.

Ms. JACKSON LEE. We thank you for being here today, and I hope that we will all learn from, among others, your testimony, which is extremely important.

Ms. Frederique, you're recognized now for 5 minutes.

Statement of Kassandra Frederique

Ms. FREDERIQUE. Chair Jackson Lee, Ranking Member Biggs, and Members of the Committee, thank you for the opportunity to submit this statement upon the committee.

I am the Executive Director of the Drug Policy Alliance, the Nation's leading organization advancing drug policies that are grounded in science, compassion, health, and human rights.

Today is not just the anniversary of a policy agenda around drugs. Today is also the anniversary of the calcification of this country's commitment to using punishment, surveillance, and imprisonment of people who disagree with those in power.

Today, I sit here testifying that our country's principles of freedom, autonomy, liberty, and joy are for all and not for some. A day after Congress has made Juneteenth a Federal holiday, I'm sitting here today to say that not all of us are free, and that there is much work to do by this body to make freedom realized.

For more than 50 years, the United States has adopted and expanded punitive policies toward the possession, use, and distribution of drugs, enacting increasingly harsh sentencing laws that lead to mass incarceration and mass criminalization, while ignoring the destructive impacts of those laws.

The sentencing laws at the heart of that deeply flawed strategy have led to mass incarceration, fractured families and communities, interrupted educational and vocational progress, lost opportunities to contribute to society, and killed American Dreams.

The human and fiscal impacts of this destructive policy are staggering. Every month, approximately 1,600 people, on average, are sentenced for drug offenses in Federal court, and over 1,000 people are sent back to prison for violations of supervised release or parole related to drugs.

Drug convictions still account for the incarceration of almost half a million people. One in five people currently incarcerated in the U.S. are locked up for a drug offense, while over 750,000 people, or 25 percent of all people under community supervision, are on probation or parole for drug law violation.

Although rates of drug use and sales are similar across racial lines, Black and Latinx people are far more likely to be criminalized than White people. Every year, the Federal Government spends $35 billion on law enforcement, Federal courts, forensic scientists, community supervision, and drug testing. What if we had invested that much money in education, health, and employment opportunities for our communities?

Yet, the drug war has achieved no meaningful reduction in drug supply or prices. Instead, it has exacerbated the dangers of illicit markets. Long prison sentences have done nothing to stem the rate of drug overdoses, but instead, have prevented the implementation of robust, harm-reduction systems and driven people who need and want help further from the public health resources.

In fact, overdoses have reached an all-time high. Nearly 850,000 people have died from a drug overdose since 1999. More than 70,000 died in 2019, and almost 90 K in 2020.

For Breonna Taylor, Carlos Ingram-Lopez, Andrea Circle Bear, and for my dear friend Alexis' son Jeff, and for my aunt and uncle's son, Stanley Frederique, who we buried last week, Congress must take bold steps to refocus the Federal strategy, pivoting from the central premise that drug use is something that should be punished.

Instead, the Federal approach should be health-focused, evidence-based, and respectful of self-determination. Congress should move quickly to reduce sentences of incarceration for all drug offenses, particularly those related to possession and the distribution of personal use quantities of controlled substances.

Additionally, it should fully repeal mandatory minimum sentences, and vastly broaden the safety valve provisions.

Enact substantial reforms to supervised release to limit drug-related technical violations and reincarceration.

Revisit harsh drug enhancements, like the distribution resulting in death statute that allows for excessive and arbitrary sentences, while discouraging others close to a person experiencing overdose from seeking medical help.

Ensure that drug possession is no longer the cause of mandatory detention and deportation of noncitizens, or otherwise lead to immigration consequences tearing apart families.

Reject efforts to further criminalize fentanyl and its analogues, and, instead, embrace a public health approach to drug use.

Madam Chair, this must be a turning point. For 50 years, the drug war has filled our prisons and derailed individual lives and disrupted families and communities. The fiscal and human costs are incalculable.

We must start enacting evidence-based policies rather than those based on arbitrary punishments and have no demonstrated benefit in keeping people safe.

Thank you for the opportunity to submit testimony. I look forward to working with you all to create a world where we no longer waste money, destroy lives, decimate communities, but, rather, support people in getting services, support, and treatment they need to thrive.

[The statement of Ms. Frederique follows:]

Written Testimony of Kassandra Frederique, Executive Director, Drug Policy Alliance, June 15, 2021, U.S. House of Representatives, Judiciary Subcommittee on Crime, Terrorism, and Homeland Security, Hearing on "Undoing the Damage of the War on Drugs: A Renewed Call for Sentencing Reform"

Chairwoman Jackson Lee and Members of the Subcommittee, thank you for the opportunity to submit this statement for the Subcommittee's hearing on "Undoing the Damage of the War on Drugs: A Renewed Call for Sentencing Reform." I am the executive director of the Drug Policy Alliance, the nation's leading organization advancing drug policies that are grounded in science, compassion, health and human rights.

At Least Fifty Years of Failed Policy

For more than 50 years the United States has adopted and expanded punitive policies toward the possession, use and distribution of drugs - enacting increasingly harsh sentencing laws that led to mass incarceration and mass criminalization while ignoring the destructive impacts of those laws. The sentencing laws at the heart of that deeply flawed strategy have led to mass incarceration, fractured families and communities, interrupted educational and vocational progress, blocked opportunities to contribute to society, and killed American dreams. The human and fiscal impacts of this destructive policy are staggering:

- Every month approximately 1,600 people[83] on average are sentenced for drug offenses in federal courts and over a thousand people[84] are sent back to prison for violations of supervised release or parole related to drugs.

---

[83] U.S. Department of Justice, Office of Justice Programs, Bureau of Justice Statistics. *Federal Justice Statistics, 2017-2018*, https://bjs.ojp.gov/content/pub/pdf/fjs1718.pdf. (Accessed June 14, 2021).

[84] Sheil et al., *Federal Supervised Release Revocation for Drug Use: The Rest of the Story*, December 2018, https://www.uscourts.gov/sites/default/files/83_1_3_0.pdf. (Accessed June 14, 2021).

- Every day federal agents make more than 60 arrests[85] for drug offenses, mostly of those who are themselves experiencing substance use disorder or desperate economic circumstances.
- Drug convictions still account for the incarceration of almost half a million people[86] – one in five people currently incarcerated in the U.S. are locked up for a drug offense – while over 750,000 people[87] - or 25 percent of all people under community supervision - are on probation or parole for a drug law violation."
- Misguided drug laws and draconian sentencing have produced profoundly unequal outcomes for communities of color. Although rates of drug use and sales are similar across racial and ethnic lines, black and Latinx people are far more likely to be criminalized than white people.[88]
- A drug conviction can prevent a person from accessing housing, employment, public benefits, educational opportunities, and has cascading effects that impact families and communities for generations.
- Every year, the federal government spends over $35 billion[89] on law enforcement, federal courts, forensic scientists, community supervision, and drug testing.

And yet the Drug War has achieved no meaningful reduction in the drug supply or prices. Instead it has exacerbated the dangers of illicit markets and created unnecessarily risky and harmful conditions for people who use drugs. Long prison sentences have done nothing to stem the rate of drug overdoses, but instead have prevented the implementation of robust harm reduction systems and driven people who need and want help further away from public health resources. In fact, overdoses have reached an all time high. Nearly

---

[85] U.S. Department of Justice, Office of Justice Programs, Bureau of Justice Statistics. *Federal Justice Statistics, 2017-2018*, https://bjs.ojp.gov/content/pub/pdf/fjs1718.pdf. (Accessed June 14, 2021).

[86] Prison Policy Initiative, *Mass Incarceration: The Whole Pie 2020,* March 24, 2020, https://www.prisonpolicy.org/reports/pie2020.html (Accessed June 14, 2021).

[87] Prison Policy Initiative, *Mass Incarceration: The Whole Pie 2020,* March 24, 2020, https://www.prisonpolicy.org/reports/pie2020.html (Accessed June 14, 2021).

[88] Drug Policy Alliance, *The Drug War, Mass Incarceration and Race,* January 25, 2018, https://drugpolicy.org/resource/drug-war-mass-incarceration-and-race-englishspanish.

[89] Executive Office of the President of the United States, *National Drug Control Strategy FY 2021 Budget and Performance Summary,* June 2020, (Accessed June 14, 2021) https://trumpwhitehouse.archives.gov/wp-content/uploads/2020/06/2020-NDCS-FY-2021-Budget-and-Performance-Summary.pdf (Accessed June 14, 2021).

850,000 people have died from a drug overdose since 1999; more than 70,000 died in 2019 alone.[90]

This year must mark a significant turning point. As the United States marks the 50th anniversary of the Drug War, Congress must recognize the harms of this approach and move the country in a new direction.

Congress must take bold steps to refocus the federal strategy, pivoting away from the central premise that controlling unauthorized drug possession and use is something that should be punished. Instead, the federal approach should be health focused, evidence-based, and respectful of self-determination.

A Policy Solution: Decriminalization

Drug decriminalization is an important step toward achieving a rational drug policy that prioritizes health over punishment. Decriminalization is a sensible step forward that would reap vast human and fiscal benefits, while protecting families and communities.[91] While drug decriminalization cannot fully repair our broken and oppressive criminal legal system or the harms of an unregulated drug market, shifting from prohibition to drug decriminalization helps reduce dangerous and unnecessary police interactions, reduce the number of people caught up in the criminal justice system, better assist those in need, and save tax dollars.

The concept is neither new nor radical. Other nations, including Portugal, have successfully decriminalized possession of drugs for personal use and achieved meaningful improvements in treating problematic drug use and reducing the harms of policing drugs. Support for eliminating criminal penalties for drug possession is growing across the U.S. and around the world.

At the state level, Oregon decriminalized the possession of drugs for personal use last November, and in 2021 bills have been introduced in several other states, including New York, Maine, Massachusetts, Maryland, Vermont, Rhode Island, and elsewhere to enact similar reforms.

At the federal level, we are excited that Representatives Bonnie Watson Coleman and Cori Bush announced their intention to introduce

---

[90] Centers for Disease Control and Prevention, https://www.cdc.gov/drug overdose/data/statedeaths.html (Accessed June15, 2021).

[91] Drug Policy Alliance, *It's Time for the U.S. to Decriminalize Drug Use and Possession*, July 2017, https://drugpolicy.org/resource/its-time-us-decriminalize-drug-use-and-possession (Accessed June 14, 2021).

groundbreaking legislation, the *Drug Policy Reform Act*, in this body very soon. The Drug Policy Reform Act will decriminalize low-level possession of controlled substances, shift the regulatory responsibility for classifying drugs away from law enforcement to the Department of Health and Human Services, begin repairing past harms, and make other changes to shift toward a system that prioritizes health and harm reduction.

Support Pending Reform Proposals

We commend members of the House who have introduced the following legislation to reduce sentences for drug offenses:

- The *EQUAL Act, introduced by Rep. Jeffries,* to once and for all end the federal disparity between crack cocaine offenses and make this policy retroactive. Passing this law is even more important now in light of the recent Supreme Court case that upholds the First Step Act's limitations when it comes to crack cocaine offenses.[92]
- The *Prohibiting Punishment of Acquitted Conduct Act,* introduced by Rep. Steven Cohen, to end the unjust practice of judges increasing sentences based on conduct for which a defendant has been acquitted by a jury.
- The *COVID-19 Safer Detention Act,* by Chair Jerrold Nadler (D-NY) and Representatives Sheila Jackson Lee (D-TX) and Ted Deutch (D-FL), to expand compassionate release from federal prisons and allow some of the most vulnerable individuals in custody an opportunity to reunite with loved ones.
- Of course the *MORE Act,* led by Chairman Jerrold Nadler, Subcommittee Chairwoman Sheila Jackson Lee, and Reps. Earl Blumenauer, Barbara Lee, Hakeem Jeffries and Nydia Velázquez, to declassify marijuana as a controlled substance under federal law, expunge marijuana convictions, and reduce marijuana sentences.

In addition to the legislative proposals above, Congress should do more to immediately reform federal drug sentencing. Congress should reduce sentences of incarceration for all drug offenses, particularly those related to

[92] *See Terry v. United States*, slip opinion issued June 14, 2021.

possession and distribution of personal use quantities of controlled substances. Additionally, it should:

- Fully repeal mandatory minimum sentences and vastly broaden the safety valve provisions. Mandatory minimum sentences take discretion away from judges and require the imposition of often absurdly harsh sentences, regardless of the circumstances of the individual – regardless of whether they were suffering from substance use disorder and sometimes even when they did not fully know the contents of a substance. In 2020 nearly two thirds[93] of those sentenced in drug cases were convicted of an offense carrying a mandatory minimum penalty.
- Enact substantial reforms to supervised release to limit unnecessary drug-related conditions of release and prevent further incarceration for drug related technical violations.
- Revisit harsh drug enhancements like the "distribution resulting in death" statute[94] that allows for excessive and arbitrary sentences, while undermining the safety of people who use drugs by discouraging others close to a person experiencing overdose from seeking medical help.
- Ensure that that drug possession is no longer the cause of mandatory detention and deportation of non-citizens, or otherwise leads to immigration consequences, tearing apart families.
- Reject efforts to further criminalize fentanyl and its analogues and instead embrace a public health response to drug use.[95]

Madame Chair, this must be the turning point. For 50 years the Drug War has filled our prisons and derailed individual lives and disrupted families and communities. We must start enacting evidence-based policies rather than those based on arbitrary punishments that have no demonstrated benefit in keeping people safer.

Although we appreciate the Committee holding this hearing to discuss sentencing reform, it is important to recognize the vast array of reforms that are necessary to dismantle the excesses of the Drug War.

---

[93] United States Sentencing Commission, *Annual Report 2020,* https://www.ussc.gov/about/annual-report-2020 (Accessed June 14, 2021).

[94] See 21 U.S.C. § 841(b)(1)(C).

[95] See for example, https://drugpolicy.org/sites/default/files/classwide-scheduling-fentanyl-analogues-oppositionletter-congress.pdf (Accessed June 14, 2021).

- We need to pass comprehensive police reform that should contain meaningful changes in how search warrants are executed and limits on the militarization of our police forces. We must also end the practice of civil asset forfeiture based on suspected drug activity.
- We must dramatically reduce the funding for drug enforcement agencies, particularly the DEA, which are incentivized only to make increasing numbers of arrests, which leads to more arrests of the least culpable and most vulnerable, such as low level sellers who themselves suffer from substance use disorder.
- We need Congress to pass legislation that stops revocation of parole and supervised release for drug technical violations.
- We must pass legislation to clarify the "drug-involved premises" law to prevent the criminalization of harm reduction providers seeking to prevent overdoses.
- We must pass the MEAL Act to lift restrictions on the receipt of Supplemental Nutrition Assistance Program (SNAP) and Temporary Assistance for Needy Families (TANF) benefits for people with prior felony drug convictions in order to ensure people are able to feed and support their families.
- And fundamentally, we need Congress to start crafting a true replacement for the Controlled Substances Act - and to develop in a manner that is led by the people most impacted by the Drug War.

Thank you for the opportunity to submit testimony. We look forward to working with you to develop and enact meaningful reforms centered on removing criminal penalties for drug possession and facilitating access to voluntary harm reduction, treatment, recovery, and other social services.

* * *

Ms. JACKSON LEE. Thank you for your testimony, and now we yield to Ms. Nelson for her testimony.

Members, at the inclusion of Ms. Nelson's testimony, we will recess for votes. We thank the witnesses for their indulgence. We will continue after votes on the floor of the House.

Ms. Nelson, you are recognized.

Statement of Marta Nelson

Ms. NELSON. Good morning. Thank you, Chair Jackson Lee, Ranking Member Biggs, and Members of the Subcommittee. I'm Marta Nelson, Director of Government Strategy at the Vera Institute of Justice, a 60-year-old organization that provides data, evidence, and solutions to fight mass incarceration, and to transform the criminal, legal, and immigration systems until they are fair for all.

I have worked for over 25 years on efforts to stem the effects of our country's addiction to punishment, and I am delighted to offer remarks on behalf of Vera on this long overdue topic of sentencing reform.

This hearing notes the 50th anniversary of the war on drugs, but the early '70s also marked the start of mass incarceration and extreme sentences.

We have as many people, over 200,000 to be exact, serving life sentences today, as we had total in prison in 1970. Black and Latinx people bear the brunt of this policy. They comprise 32 percent of our country's population yet, make up 56 percent of the prison population.

It doesn't have to be like this. If we incarcerated our citizens at the same rate as the rest of the world, we would have one-sixth of the people we do in prison, about 360,000 instead of over 2 million. It's not that people in other countries do not engage in violent or harmful behavior and are not convicted of crime. They do, and they are. The difference is in how our systems respond.

In stark contrast to the United States, criminal legal system in Europe, the default, even after a felony conviction, is a community-based sanction.

To change where we are, we need to take bold steps. We suggest seven legislative changes that, taken together, could reduce the Federal prison population by 80 percent, according to preliminary Vera modeling.

They are: Removing sentencing enhancements based on prior conviction records; creating a maximum incarcerative sentence of 20 years for the most serious crimes; significantly expanding opportunities to earn good time off of sentences; abolishing mandatory minimums; allowing people convicted of all crimes the opportunity for community-based sentences; creating second-look, resentencing options; and requiring racial impact statements before criminalizing any new behavior and enhancing punishments to already criminalized behavior.

These reforms share three attributes:

First, they promote actual safety, not performative safety. One influential meta-analysis of studies on deterrence concludes it is clear that lengthy prison sentences cannot be justified on a deterrence-based crime-prevention basis.

Instead, community-based programming, even for people who have been charged with violent crimes, has been shown to reduce future unlawful conduct. Indeed, many of the rehabilitative innovations of the last 30 years were pioneered in the community.

There may be a need to incapacitate those few people who truly cannot walk safely amongst us, but that is a small minority of the people behind bars now.

Second, these repairs repair harm. By a margin of 3–1, survivors of crime prefer holding people accountable through more proactive measures like mental health treatment, drug treatment, restorative justice, or community service, rather than prison sentences.

This is because prison sentences are not proactive. They are reactive. At bottom, they don't require the person to do anything other than to be removed from society.

Sentencing could instead create a community-based process for the person to acknowledge and address the harm they have caused.

Third, these reforms address racial justice. Our current excessive sentences grow from the harsh-on-crime policies of the '70s to the '90s, following the gains of the civil rights era amidst a racialized panic over crime and drugs.

Recognizing this origin, jurisdictions must assume racial biases will continue to impact every part of the criminal legal system, and should sentence with a light touch, privileging liberty as much as possible.

Finally, urging these reforms now, when homicide rates across the country have increased, regardless of criminal legal policies and when gun violence has also increased may seem challenging to those who think this is the time to be tough on crime. That would be a serious mistake.

Again, increasing jail and prison sentences is a poor crime-deterrent strategy.

In addition to approving crime clearance rates, which research shows it can deter crime, jurisdictions should invest heavily in proven solutions to gun violence, such as violence interruption, hospital-based interventions, and focused deterrence.

The best crime-prevention solution of all is to invest in the services, resources, and support that help communities flourish and thrive, especially after the devastation of the pandemic. Thank you.

[The statement of Ms. Nelson follows:]

Written Testimony to the House Committee on the Judiciary: "Undoing the Damage of the War on Drugs: A Renewed Call for Sentencing Reform," June 17, 2021

Marta Nelson, Director of Government Strategy Vera Institute of Justice
On behalf of the Vera Institute of Justice, I am honored to submit written testimony and offer remarks at this important hearing on sentencing reform. We commend Chair Nadler and Subcommittee Chair Jackson Lee for opening up this long overdue conversation.

The Vera Institute is a 60 year-old organization that delivers data, evidence, and solutions to fight mass incarceration and transform the criminal legal and immigration systems until they are fair for all. I have worked for over 25 years—as a lawyer for prisoners' rights, the director of several reentry programs, and as special counsel for criminal justice initiatives to the current governor of New York—on efforts to stem the effects of our country's addiction to punishment.

Sentencing's Role in the Rise of Mass Incarceration

This hearing notes the 50th anniversary of the "War on Drugs," a war whose damage since the 1970s has decimated communities and families and done little to deliver either public safety or health.[96] But 1970 marks another important data point as well. It is the start as we know it of mass incarceration, excessive punishment, and extreme sentences. In 1970, the U.S. incarcerated at the same rate as most other countries.[97] However, with the advent of "tough on crime" rhetoric, "truth in sentencing" laws, and sentencing enhancements, from the 1970s through the 1990s, our nation did more than wage a war on drugs—we indulged our thirst for perpetual punishment, particularly on Black people who were routinely considered beyond rehabilitation and in need of

---

[96] D. Baum, *Smoke and Mirrors: The War on Drugs and The Politics of Failure* (Waltham, MA: Little, Brown and Co; 1996); On how the War on Drugs has affected education, housing, employment, child welfare, immigration, and public benefits systems 50 years later, see Drug Policy Alliance, "Uprooting the Drug War," https://uprootingthedrugwar.org/resources/.

[97] National Research Council, *The Growth of Incarceration in the United States: Exploring Causes and Consequences* (Washington, DC: The National Academies Press, 2014), Chapter 4.

control.[98] This is not hyperbole. The public record of sentencing enhancements in this period is littered with racialized references to the "superpredator," "inner city," and "drug user." In the media's coverage of crime and public safety, Blackness became synonymous with criminality, drug use, and violence.[99] The result? Today we have a jail and prison system that incarcerates over 2 million people,[100] we lead the world in incarceration, and we have as many people—over 200,000, to be exact—serving life sentences as we had total in prison in 1970.[101] The impact of this punitive approach did not land equally across our citizenry.

Black and Latinx people comprise about 32 percent of our country's population yet make up 56 percent of the prison population.[102]

Once someone has been convicted of a crime, the U.S. criminal legal system acts as if a switch were flipped. Notions about the importance of

---

[98] On the history of mass incarceration and evolution of U.S. sentencing policies from the 1940s-present, see National Research Council, *The Growth of Incarceration in the United States: Exploring Causes and Consequences* (Washington, DC: The National Academies Press, 2014), Chapters 2-4. On Black people being viewed as "incurable" and unable to be rehabilitated, see Anthony Grasso, "Broken Beyond Repair: Rehabilitative Penology and American Political Development," *Political Research Quarterly*, vol. 70 issue 2 (2017).

[99] John DiLulio, "The Coming of the Super Predators," https://www.washingtonexaminer.com/weekly-standard/the-coming-of-the-super-predators. See also Edward Huntington Williams, "NEGRO COCAINE "FIENDS" ARE A NEW SOUTHERN MENACE; Murder and Insanity Increasing Among Lower Class Blacks Because They Have Taken to "Sniffing" Since Deprived of Whisky by Prohibition," https://www.nytimes.com/1914/02/08/archives/negro-cocaine-fiends-are-a-new-southern-menace-murder-and-insanity.html; Peter Kerr, "NEW VIOLENCE SEEN IN USERS OF COCAINE," https://www.nytimes.com/1987/03/07/nyregion/new-violence-seen-in-users-of-cocaine.html; and Carl Hart, "How the Myth of the 'Negro Cocaine Fiend' Helped Shape American Drug Policy," https://www.thenation.com/article/archive/how-myth-negro-cocaine-fiend-helped-shape-american-drug-policy/.

[100] Jacob Kang-Brown, Chase Montagnet, and Jasmine Heiss, "People in Jail and Prison in 2020, Table 1 lists the pre-pandemic prison and jail population. https://www.vera.org/downloads/publications/people-in-jail-and-prison-in-2020.pdf.

[101] The Sentencing Project, "People Serving Life Exceeds Entire Prison Population of 1970," February 2020, https://www.sentencingproject.org/publications/people-serving-life-exceeds-entire-prison-population-1970/.

[102] The Bureau of Justice Statistics reported that in 2019, 452,800 Black people were sentenced to prison across the United States (or 32.8% of all those sentenced to prison). There were 320,700 Hispanic or LatinX people sentenced to prison that same year (or 23.2% of all those sentenced to prison). For more, see Bureau of Justice Statistics, "Prisoners in 2019," October 2020, Table 3: https://www.bjs.gov/content/pub/pdf/p19.pdf#:~:text=At%20year-end%202019%2C%20an%20estimated%201%2C430%2C800%20prisoners%20were,prisoners%20in%202018%20an d%2011%25%20from%20the%20peak. According to 2019 population estimates from the US Census Bureau, Black people comprise 13.4% of the US population and Hispanic or LatinX individuals make up 18.5% of the population. For more, see United States Census Bureau, "Quick Facts," https://www.census.gov/quickfacts/fact/table/US/RHI725219.

liberty, proportionality, restraint, and human capacity to change go out the window, and no punishment is too harsh. After all, "You do the crime, you do the time, right?"

That approach has led to the dubious distinction of the U.S. having the highest average rate of incarceration in the world compared to other countries.[103] If we incarcerated at the same rate as the rest of the world, we would have one-sixth of the people we do in jail and prison—about 360,000, instead of the pre-pandemic census of 2.2 million.[104] We got to this place because we reflexively sentence nearly everyone convicted of a felony to incarceration. In the state courts, over 70 percent of people convicted of felonies are sentenced to time in jail or prison, while in the federal system, 89 percent of felonies result in an incarcerative sentence.[105] By contrast, Finland and Germany send 3 percent and 5 percent of people convicted of a felony to jail or prison, respectively, and, across Europe, felony convictions result in incarceration on average only 20 percent of the time.[106] It is not that people in other countries do not engage in violent or harmful behavior or are not convicted of crimes—they do and they are. The difference is how the system responds. In stark contrast to the U.S. criminal legal system, in Europe the default, even after a felony conviction, is a community-based sanction.

---

103 Institute for Crime & Justice Policy Research, "World Prison Brief," https://www.prisonstudies.org/world-prison- brief-data.

104 Vera researchers took a sample of incarceration data from 17 other countries to compare to the United States on or around 2019 (those countries data was available from the World Prison Brief, and they are Argentina, Australia, Brazil, Canada, England and Wales, France, Germany, India, Italy, Japan, Mexico, Nigeria, Portugal, Russia, South Africa, South Korea, and Spain). The U.S. incarceration rate is 6.6 times higher than that of other nations in the sample, at 685 per 100,000 compared to 104 per 100,000. To be in line with the international estimate, United States incarceration would need to be reduced 85 percent. Applying this 85 percent reduction to the number of people incarcerated on a given day before the pandemic, 2.240 million, there would have been only 341,900 people incarcerated in the United States.

105 On state figures, see Brian Reaves, Bureau of Justice Statistics, "Felony Defendants in Large Urban Counties, 2009 – Statistical Tables" (December 2013), Table 24 https://bjs.ojp.gov/content/pub/pdf/fdluc09.pdf. On federal figures, see United States Sentencing Commission, "2019 Sourcebook," Figure 6, https://www.ussc.gov/sites/default/files/pdf/research-and-publications/annual-reports-and-source books/2019/Figure06.pdf.

106 Aebi, Akdeniz, Barclay, Campistol, Caneppele, Gruszcynska, Harrendorf, Heiskanen, Hysi , Jehle et al., *European Sourcebook of Crime and Criminal Justice Statistics*, 5th ed. (Helsinki: HEUNI Publications Series 80), Second Printing, 2017, Table 3.2.3.1, 196.

Traditional Justifications for Harsh Punishment Are Not Supported by Evidence

To begin to restrain our use of incarceration, we have to reexamine the foundational rationales for sentencing against the evidence and our assumptions about what sentencing should accomplish. Since the inception of the U.S. criminal legal system, two of the primary justifications for sentencing have been deterrence and retribution.[107] Deterrence theory assumes that harsh sentences meted out to people convicted of a crime keeps society safe overall by influencing others to think twice before engaging in unlawful behavior.[108] This justification was part of the rationale in the 1980s and 1990s behind expanding mandatory minimums and predicate sentencing—both designed to lengthen incarcerative sentences.[109] Retribution, or "just deserts," is premised on the notion that punishment supposedly restores the moral balance that is disrupted by a criminal act, and delivers some semblance of satisfaction and resolution to the victim harmed by that crime.[110]

Until recently, the validity of those theories remained unquestioned and deterrence and retribution were time and again trotted out as justification for the laws, policies, and practices that delivered mass incarceration.

Politics aside, what does the evidence prove when it comes to harsh punishment and long incarcerative sentences? First, severe sentences do not deter crime. This may seem counterintuitive, but study after study shows that people do not change their unlawful behavior based on the future possibility of facing a harsh sentence.[111] First, people typically do not know the legal sentence or punishment for a particular crime—even as legislatures pass sentencing laws, the public's awareness of them is slim.[112] Second, most people decide to desist from crime not because they fear a specific sanction

---

[107] The political philosophers Immanuel Kant and Jeremy Bentham, writing in the late 1700s, promoted two rival goals of "modern" sentencing: to punish crime, retribution, and to prevent crime, deterrence, along with incapacitation and rehabilitation. For more, see Rauscher & Frederick, "Kant's Social and Political Philosophy," The Stanford Encyclopedia of Philosophy (Spring 2017 Edition), Edward N. Zalta (ed.); Jeremy Bentham, *An Introduction to the Principles of Morals and Legislation* (1789), Chapter XIV.

[108] Nora Deimleitner, Douglas Berman, Marc Miller, and Ronald Wright, *Sentencing Law and Policy* (New York: Wolters Kluwer, 4th Edition, 2018), 2.

[109] National Research Council, *The Growth of Incarceration in the United States: Exploring Causes and Consequences* (Washington, DC: The National Academies Press, 2014), Chapter 4.

[110] On the purposes of federal sentencing, see 18 U.S.C. § 3553 (a)(2).

[111] Daniel Nagin, *Deterrence in the Twenty-First Century: A Review of the Evidence* (Carnegie Mellon University, 2013), 7-8, https://doi.org/10.1184/R1/6471200.v1.

[112] Ibid., 7-8.

but because of non-legal considerations, such as a moral worldview that a particular behavior is prohibited, breaks the social code, or their own fear of social censure.[113] One influential meta-analysis of studies on deterrence concludes, "[I]t is clear that lengthy prison sentences cannot be justified on a deterrence-based, crime-prevention basis."[114] If there is any deterrence effect to be had in the state's response to crime, the research shows the certainty and swiftness of being caught influences behavior far more than the sanction that follows.[115]

As for retribution? Pushing for long sentences as "justice" for a victim presupposes a zero sum game—that someone's pain as a survivor of a crime cannot be honored unless the responsible party is severely punished by losing their freedom.[116] Crime survivors, however, by a margin of three to one, do not default to incarceration as the preferred response.[117] Polling shows they prefer holding people accountable through measures like rehabilitative programming, mental health treatment, drug treatment, community supervision, or community service.[118] Again, this may seem counterintuitive, but it lies in the fact that incarcerative sentences are reactive, not proactive, and the use of jail or prison serves little value beyond excommunication. The majority of survivors of crime in the U.S. are people who are intimately familiar with the criminal legal system—they themselves have been defendants in it, or have seen its impact on family, friends, and neighbors—and they know how violent and damaging incarceration can be and how little rehabilitation occurs behind bars.[119]

---

[113] Ibid., 8.

[114] Ibid., 5.

[115] Ibid., 4.

[116] For an example of this zero-sum thinking, see John Eligon, "It's a Slap in the Face: Victims are Angered as Jails Free Inmates," https://www.nytimes.com/2020/04/24/us/coronavirus-jail-inmates-released.html.

[117] Alliance for Safety and Justice, "Nationwide Survey of Crime Survivors," 2016, 5, https://allianceforsafetyandjustice.org/wp-content/uploads/documents/Crime%20Survivors%20Speak%20Report.pdf. This nationwide survey of over 800 crime survivors has been repeated after 2016 on state populations in Florida, Texas, Illinois, Michigan, and California with similar results.

[118] Ibid.

[119] Allison Hastings and Kaitlin Kall, "Opening the Door to Healing: Reaching and Serving Crime Victims Who Have a History of Incarceration," February 2020, https://www.vera.org/downloads/publications/opening-the-door-to- healing.pdf.

Three Foundational Principles to Approach Sentencing Decisions

At Vera, we have extensively studied the literature, research, and evidence about sentencing reform, and are piloting new approaches in some of our initiatives, such as our work with reform-minded prosecutors to offer alternatives to incarceration even in serious felony cases.[120] In our view, to be successful in ending mass incarceration and delivering public safety, any effort at sentencing reform must offer a new set of guiding principles and a new framework for fashioning a fair, accountable, and just sentence after conviction. At its core, a sentence must promote racial justice, create real safety, and indeed repair the harm caused by the unlawful behavior.

We recommend that legislatures answer the following three questions to galvanize sentencing reform efforts:

1. How can this sentence advance racial justice?

While the 1970s formally marked the beginning of mass incarceration as we know it in this country, the criminal legal system has targeted and subjugated Black people for generations before—from slave patrols that controlled every aspect of enslaved people's lives, to the exception in the Thirteenth Amendment that abolished slavery except as punishment for a crime, and the Reconstruction-era Black Codes that criminalized Black people's freedom, mobility, and political and economic power.[121] The racialized panic of the "law and order" era of the 1970s, and even today, is a continuation of the criminalization of Blackness and a direct legacy of slavery.

When undertaking reform, jurisdictions cannot look away from that history and must assume racial biases will continue to impact every part of the criminal legal system, including sentencing, and that court system actors will act in ways, conscious or not, that punish Black people more harshly than others. Given that fraught legacy and the racial implications of the sentencing decision, a conviction alone cannot be the bright line behind which freedom disappears.[122] In other words, in order to redress racial disparities, the vast

[120] See Vera Institute of Justice, "Reshaping Prosecution Project," Reshaping Prosecution | Vera Institute.

[121] Elizabeth Hinton, LeShae Henderson, and Cindy Reed, "An Unjust Burden: The Disparate Treatment of Black Americans in the Criminal Justice System," Vera Institute of Justice 2018, https://www.vera.org/downloads/publications/for-the-record-unjust-burden-racial-disparities.pdf.

[122] Sherry F. Colb, *Freedom from Incarceration: Why is the Right Different from All Other Rights* (69 NYU L. Rev. 781, 799, 1994) (arguing that courts should enforce the fundamental right

majority of convictions, including for felonies, should not carry an incarcerative sentence or one that unduly takes away a person's freedom.

How Can This Sentence Produce Actual Safety?

The most important priority for many victims and survivors of crime is that the party who committed the harm never engages in that behavior again, either towards the harmed party or anyone else.[123] Community-based programs that focus on rehabilitation and addressing the harmful behavior, even for people who have been charged with violent crimes, have been shown to reduce future unlawful conduct.[124] Indeed, many of the most important rehabilitative programming innovations of the last 30 years, including cognitive behavioral programming, were pioneered in the community.[125]

A 2019 meta-analysis of 35 U.S. community-based restorative justice programs found that participants were 41.5 percent less likely to be rearrested than people who were prosecuted and sentenced through the traditional criminal legal process.[126] Another meta-analysis from 2013 of 10 programs in Australia, the United Kingdom, and the U.S. found that using face-to-face restorative justice conferencing as an alternative to regular court processing resulted in less reoffending among program participants compared to people who went through the traditional criminal legal process.[127] Perhaps surprisingly, these positive outcomes from community-based restorative programs were especially pronounced for people who committed serious and repeat offenses.[128]

---

of liberty by subjecting incarcerative sentencing laws to strict scrutiny and require a compelling state purpose and narrow tailoring).

[123] Danielle Sered, *Until We Reckon: Violence, Mass Incarceration and a Road to Repair* (New York, The New Press 2019), 30.

[124] Michael Tonry, "Community Punishments," *Reforming Criminal Justice: A Report from the Academy of Justice,* (Vol. 4, 2017), 189, *https://law.asu.edu/sites/default/files/pdf/academy_for_justice/10_Criminal_Justice_Reform_Vol_4_Community-Punishments.pdf.*

[125] Francis Cullen, Cheryl Lero Johnson, and Daniel Mears, "Reinventing Community Corrections," *Crime and Justice* 46 (University of Chicago Press, 2016), 29.

[126] Kyle Ernest, "Is Restorative Justice Effective in the U.S.?," (PhD. Diss., Arizona State University, August 2019), 101.

[127] Heather Strang, Lawrence W Sherman, Evan Mayo-Wilson, Daniel Woods, and Barak Ariel, "Restorative Justice Conferencing (RJC) Using Face-to-Face Meetings of Offenders and Victims: Effects on Offender Recidivism and Victim Satisfaction. A Systematic Review" (48 Campbell Systematic Review, 2013), https://restorativejustice.org.uk/sites/default/files/resources/files/Campbell%20RJ%20review.pdf.

[128] Ibid.

How Does This Sentence Repair Harm?

Giving people who commit crimes the opportunity to acknowledge and repair the harm they caused can bring healing to victims and rehabilitate the person who harmed them in a way that serving a jail or prison sentence cannot. The state's fallback option for addressing a violent crime—prosecuting and punishing a person with lengthy incarceration—does not specifically address a survivor's trauma. Again, polling of crime victims and survivors reflect the dissatisfaction they feel with the traditional criminal legal process—three in four victims surveyed said that they received no help from the criminal legal system, and only eight percent of violent crime survivors received assistance from a victims services organization.[129] Even in the domestic violence context, where resources have been invested in recent years to support survivors of intimate partner violence, a 2019 survey found that only 26 percent received help.[130] By contrast, a study of crime survivors who experienced a reparative experience, such as face-to-face conferencing with the person who harmed them as part of a restorative justice process, reported feeling more satisfied at the end of the process than people who participated in traditional court processing and sentencing.[131]

When repair is an operative principle in sentencing, the question for each proven offense would not be how many months or years of incarceration are needed to right the moral wrong, but what processes and actions—such as listening, apologies, restitution, and service—are needed to help repair the harm to the specific victim, if there is one, and to help the person who committed harm grow and change so that they are less likely to harm others in

---

[129] Alliance for Safety and Justice, Crime Survivors Speak: The First-Ever National Survey on Victims' Views on Safety and Justice, 11, https://allianceforsafetyandjustice.org/wp-content/uploads/2019/04/Crime-Survivors-Speak- Report-1.pdf.

[130] United States Department of Justice Bureau of Justice Statistics, "Criminal Victimization 2019," September 2020, 9, https://bjs.ojp.gov/content/pub/pdf/cv19.pdf.

[131] Findings from a 2019 meta-analysis of 35 restorative justice programs in the United States from the 1970s to 2018 find that victims in restorative justice processes are 86.7% more likely to be satisfied with their experience than those going through the regular criminal justice. For more, see Kyle Ernest, "Is Restorative Justice Effective in the U.S.?," (PhD. Diss., Arizona State University, August 2019), 101. See also, Strang et al., "Restorative Justice Conferencing (RJC) Using Face-to-Face Meetings of Offenders and Victims: Effects on Offender Recidivism and Victim Satisfaction. A Systematic Review," 38, 40 (70% of restorative justice conferencing participants reported themselves satisfied, in comparison to 42% of the regular court participants. The conferencing process aids repair by providing what 58% of survivors consider to be a sincere apology, compared to 10% of survivors going through court processing and sentencing as usual. That leaves them feeling much more healed – to the point where they wouldn't contemplate seeking vengeance if it were available to them (9% of reparative process participants versus 45% of regular court participants)).

the future.[132] In contrast to an incarcerative sentence, essentially a "time out" from society, a reparative criminal sentence requires the person convicted to engage in work to address the harm caused to others. This reinvention is hard work—requiring more action and effort from the person sentenced than is required by simple punishment or retribution. It also has better outcomes.[133]

Putting These Principles into Practice through Seven Legislative Reforms

How does the criminal legal system operationalize racial justice, public safety, and repair? Below are seven discrete areas of legislation that will significantly reduce racial disparities by promoting more freedom over confinement, advance safety by moving people out of prison who do not "need" to be there for safety, and build community-based sanctions, which are in the long term better investments for public safety by keeping people together with their families and communities as they engage in repair. These seven legislative recommendations represent a paradigm shift, most certainly, but are already in the political discourse:

1. *Remove prior conviction enhancements*. The federal sentencing guidelines increase a person's sentence by their prior criminal history, and nearly every state has some version of a prior record sentencing enhancement on the books, such as mandatory sentences for second- or third-time felony convictions, "habitual offender" sentences. or California's infamous "three strikes" law.[134] The justification to remove prior conviction enhancements is that they are based heavily on deterrence theory, which, as discussed above, is ineffective and does not enhance public safety. Beyond the inefficacy of prior conviction enhancement laws, they drive racial disparities by compounding the impact of discriminatory arrest and conviction practices that have disproportionately impacted Black people who are

---

[132] Restorative justice is one way of centering the survivor's harm and requiring the responsible party to address it. That frame can be written into statute, for example, see Montana Rev. Code Ann. §46-18-101(3)(i) ("Sentencing practices should promote and support practices, policies and programs that focus on restorative justice principles").

[133] Danielle Sered, "Accounting for Violence: How to Increase Safety and Break Our Failed Reliance on Mass Incarceration," 2017, 18. See also Francis Cullen, "Correctional Rehabilitation" in *Reforming Criminal Justice: A Report from the Academy of Justice,* (Vol. 4, 2017), 239-240, https://law.asu.edu/sites/default/files/pdf/academy_for_justice/12_Criminal_Justice_Reform_Vol_4_Correctional-Rehabilitation.pdf.

[134] Douglas Berman, *Sentencing Law and Policy: Cases, Statutes and Guidelines* (2018), 288.

more likely to be arrested, prosecuted, and sentenced than their white counterparts for the same behavior.[135] We propose that sentences at the time of conviction are fashioned only based on the instant behavior and charges, not on past actions for which a person has already faced sanction and punishment.

2. *Cap maximum sentences at 20 years.* The Sentencing Project, which has focused on the U.S.'s outsized and racially discriminatory sentencing system for more than three decades, in 2019 launched a campaign to have a backstop to the sentencing system—a term of years beyond which no sentence can go.[136] They propose a maximum of 20 years of incarceration for the most serious of crimes, including convictions that carry life sentences or life without parole, such as murder.[137] Within 20 years, these incarcerative sentences will have served whatever safety, retributive, or separation purpose they offer, and, in the rare instance that a person continues to pose a safety threat after serving that sentence, an expert review board can review the release decision and order civil commitment if such a threat is confirmed.[138] We agree with their proposal and promote it as well.
3. *Earn good time of one day off a sentence per day of reparative behavior.* The vast majority of states and, to a lesser extent, the federal government, have long recognized the power of giving incarcerated people the ability to earn time off their sentences for positive behavior while incarcerated.[139] Known as "good time," the scheme offers people some agency, however limited, in determining when they will go home by rewarding efforts to follow institutional rules and participate in required programming with less time behind bars.[140] We

---

[135] U.S. Sentencing Commission, "Simplification Draft Paper," Chapter Four (1995) (summarizing the arguments for and against prior record enhancements).

[136] Marc Mauer and Ashley Nellis, *The Meaning of Life: The Case for Abolishing Life Sentences* (The New Press, 2018); See also The Sentencing Project, "The Campaign to End Life Imprisonment," https://endlifeimprisonment.org/.

[137] Ibid., 145.

[138] Ibid., 150.

[139] Total number from the NCSL chart. For a general discussion of the purpose and applicability of good time credits, see Nora Demleitner, "Good Conduct Time: How Much and For Whom? The Unprincipled Approach of the Model Penal Code," 2009 (critiquing the Model Penal Code: Sentencing's limiting good time credits to 15% of a sentence because more needs to be done to combat the extreme length of American sentences).

[140] 32 states allow for the ability to earn time off a sentence for rule-following and good discipline, usually called "good time." For more, see National Conference of State Legislators, "Good Time and Earned Time Policies for State Prison Inmates," January 2016 (link unavailable online).

support a good time proposal of a day for a day so that, if a person maintains a positive disciplinary and programming record, they can earn as much as half the time off their incarcerative sentence.

4. *Abolish mandatory minimums.* Several states and the federal government require a judge to order a set, minimum period of incarceration if a person is convicted of certain crimes, including many drug crimes and other nonviolent offenses, in addition to more typically violent crimes.[141] Mandatory minimums limit judicial discretion to consider a person's individual circumstances and promote repair. We support eliminating them entirely so that prosecutors and judges must approach each case individually, consider a community-based sanction, and, if jail or prison is appropriate, wrestle with the length of incarceration to be imposed.[142]
5. *Allow community-based sanctions on any conviction, regardless of severity.* Alternative to incarceration programs—known as ATIs—are community-based sanctions that a person may participate in instead of a jail or prison sentence. These programs have repeatedly been shown to be as effective, if not more, than incarceration in promoting behavior change and reducing future offending behavior.[143] However, mandatory minimum laws and prosecutorial and judicial aversion to offering ATIs limit the potential of these programs, and many ATIs themselves bar people from participating if it is their second offense or if they are facing charges involving violence.[144] We support legislation that requires the courts to consider alternatives to incarceration as a sanction for all convictions, regardless of severity, based on the individual circumstances of that case.

---

[141] The Anti-Drug Act of 1986, 2 Pub. L. No. 99-570, 100 Stat. 3207 (codified in several sections of 26 U.S.C. 2012); The Armed Career Criminal Act (ACCA), 18 U.S.C. 924(e).

[142] Groups such as FAMM and its coalition have been advocating for this for years. Sentencing Reform | FAMM. This year Attorney General Merrick Garland joined this recommendation during his confirmation hearing. Sarah Lynch, Doina Chiaru "Key quotes from U.S. attorney general nominee Garland on criminal justice policies | Reuters" February 22, 2021.

[143] Don Stemen "The Prison Paradox: More Incarceration Will Not Make Us Safer" Vera Institute of Justice 2017. for-the-record-prison-paradox_02.pdf (vera.org).

[144] Alexi Jones, "Reforms without Results: Why States should stop excluding violent offenses from criminal justice reforms," The Prison Policy Initiative, April 2020, Chart 1, https://www.prisonpolicy.org/reports/violence.html#:~:text=Community-based%20 programs%20run%20by%20nonprofit%20organizations%20are%20newer,also%20typica lly%20exclude% 20people%20convicted%20of%20violent%20offenses.

6. *Institute "second look" resentencing at 10 years.* "Second look" laws would allow courts to reexamine a sentence after a person has served a significant period of time in prison—to determine if the sentence still serves the interests of justice and promotes public safety.[145] Our recommendation is that a "second look" be required for all cases at the 10-year mark in a prison sentence.
7. *Incorporate racial impact assessments.* Legislatures often conduct fiscal impact assessments or consider other public policy implications when making new law. When engaging in sentencing law reform, they should be required to conduct racial impact assessments (or racial impact statements) to evaluate the cost in racial disparities of the proposed criminal justice legislation, just as fiscal impact assessments measure their cost in dollars.[146] We support requiring these statements to publicize and acknowledge that most legislation that creates new crimes, or makes sentences harsher, likely will exacerbate racial disparities. Legislatures should be forced to see this data and determine whether to change course in light of it.[147]

Vera is conducting an analysis, still in progress, that estimates the impact of these seven legislative reforms on the U.S. Bureau of Prisons population in 2016 if the federal government had implemented them ten years earlier, in 2006. Our initial findings suggest that the federal prison population would have been 80 percent less as a result. We intend to publish these results in a report to be released later this year.

---

[145] An example is the District of Columbia's Incarceration Reduction Amendment Act, in which a person who committed the offense of which they were committed before they were 25 years old may petition the court for resentencing after 15 years. The court must find that "the defendant is not a danger to the safety of any person or the community and that the interests of justice warrant a sentence modification." See D.C. Rev. Code. §24-403.03 (revised December 2020 to include individuals who committed crimes up to age 25, https://lims.dccouncil.us/downloads/LIMS/41814/Signed_Act/B23-0127-Signed_Act.pdf).

[146] See generally Catherine London, "Racial Impact Statements: A Proactive Approach to Addressing Racial Disparities in Prison Populations," 2011: https://scholarship.law.umn.edu/cgi/viewcontent.cgi?article=1164&context=lawineq.

[147] Ibid. 211-212 ("IF lawmakers had confronted the potential racial impact of these sentencing policies before enacting the ADAA, they might have considered alternatives that would have prevented the subsequent surge in African American incarceration rates); See also Marc Mauer, "Racial Impact Statements: Changing Policies to Address Disparities," 2009, 1: https://jjie.org/wp-content/uploads/2018/09/ABA-Racial-Impact-Statements.pdf https://scholarship.law.umn.edu/cgi/viewcontent.cgi?article=1164&context=lawineq.

Sentencing Reform Will Support, Not Undermine, Public Safety

We recognize that legislatures across the country are in a difficult moment to move criminal justice reform that will result in fewer people behind bars. Urging these reforms now, when homicide rates across the country last year increased on average by 30 percent over the previous year, and when gun violence has also increased, may seem challenging to lawmakers who may reflexively think that this is time to be "tough on crime."[148]

This is an opportunity to learn from recent history and make investments in long-term public safety, not short-term responses driven by politics and fearmongering that will perpetuate the status quo. As noted above, increasing jail and prison sentences is a poor crime deterrence strategy. Instead, it is the swiftness and certainty of responding to crime that has a greater a deterrent effect on behavior. In a moment when clearance rates of solving serious crimes, especially homicides and gun assaults, are at a serious low in many cities, the best immediate response is to reassign police officers to investigate these cases within the first 48 hours.[149] In addition to improving crime clearance rates, jurisdictions should also invest heavily in proven solutions to gun violence, such as violence interruption, hospital based interventions, and focused deterrence.[150] On average, the U.S. spends $352 per capita on policing.[151] Jurisdictions that have invested heavily in gun violence prevention—like Massachusetts and New York—have spent on average only $1-$2 per capita on these efforts and seen gun homicide declines of 16 to 30 percent.[152] And the best crime prevention solution of all? To invest in the services, resources, and supports that help communities to flourish and thrive, especially after the devastation of the pandemic.

---

148 Richard Rosenfeld and Ernesto Lopez, "Pandemic, Social Unrest and Crime in U.S. Cities: March 2021 Update," Council on Criminal Justice, https://counciloncj.z2systems.com/np/viewDocument?orgId=counciloncj&id=40288796796495d701798bc365f4026a.

149 For example, homicide clearance rates as of 2018 (latest Uniform Crime Report data) were 45% for Houston, 45% for Philadelphia and 52% for Detroit. Vera Institute of Justice "Arrest Trends: Clearance Rates" Brooklyn, NY Clearance Rates | Arrest Trends (vera.org).

150 Law Center to Prevent Gun Violence and the PICO National Network, "Healing Communities in Crisis: Lifesaving Solutions to the Urban Gun Violence Epidemic," 2016, https://giffords.org/wp-content/uploads/2016/04/Healing- Communities-in-Crisis-4-3.pdf.

151 Per capital investment in Police, State and Local Government Expenditures on Police Protection in the U.S., 2000- 2017 | Bureau of Justice Statistics (ojp.gov).

152 Giffords Law Center, Community Justice Reform Coalition, Pico National Network "Investing in Intervention: The Critical Role of State-Level Support in Breaking the Cycle of Gun Violence" Investing-in-Intervention- 02.14.18.pdf (giffords.org).

* * *

Ms. JACKSON LEE. Thank you for your testimony. Your time has expired.

Again, Members, we are now in recess until the completion of the vote on the floor.

Witnesses, thank you very much for both your testimony and those that we will hear when we return, and thank you for your indulgence. The hearing is now in recess.

[Recess.]

Ms. JACKSON LEE. We are resuming the hearing on "Undoing the Damage of the War on Drugs: A Renewed Call for Sentencing Reform," before the Subcommittee on Crime, Terrorism, and Homeland Security of the Committee on the Judiciary. I am please now to yield 5 minutes to Ms. Snider.

Statement of Jillian E. Snider

Ms. SNIDER. Good morning, Chair Jackson Lee, Ranking Member Biggs, and Members of the Committee. Thank you for the invitation to testify today. My name is Jillian Snider, and I'm the director of criminal justice and civil liberties policy at the R Street Institute, which is a nonprofit, nonpartisan public policy research organization.

Our mission is to engage in policy research and outreach to promote free markets and limited, effective government in many areas, including criminal justice reform. That is why today's hearing is of special interest to us.

In addition to my current role, I'm also a lecturer at John Jay College of Criminal Justice and a retired New York City police officer.

Today, I'm here to speak to you about the critical nature of bipartisan support for the EQUAL Act.

Although the aggressive law enforcement approach to the crack epidemic of the 1980s was initially designed to decrease the spread of drug-related disease and death and to combat organized crime, we now know that it instead led to an overreliance on arrests, incarcerations, and sentencing disparities, all of which have had a disproportionate impact on Black and Latinx men in urban communities.

Indeed, for far too long now the United States has relied on a system of overcriminalization that overuses and at times outright misuses criminal law to address societal problems that are more effectively handled through civil channels or by other interventions.

Recent data shows our Nation's incarcerated population boasts approximately 2.3 million individuals, 430,000 of which were imprisoned for drugs offenses. In fact, an overwhelming 92 percent of individuals in Federal prison have a drug offense as their most serious criminal charge.

This is largely because lawmakers of the past assumed that the use or sale of drugs had a causal effect on violence, and, by this logic, stricter penalties on drug-related offenses would deter future criminal activity.

However, subsequent data indicates that this is not the case. On the contrary, increased incarceration has had only a small impact on crime rates, and most of the benefits relate only to property crimes.

Moreover, although drug abuse may cause income-generating crimes like burglary and larceny, it is not directly causal of violent crime. In fact, a recent cross-sectional analysis of more than 7,000 prisoners indicates that binge consumption of alcohol is more closely correlated to violent crime than the use of cocaine.

Currently, approximately 35 percent of Federal drug offenders are considered Category 1 by the U.S. Sentencing Commission, which means they have no previous terms of imprisonment or extremely minimal criminal records.

Additionally, of individuals with linked U.S. Sentencing Commission records, less than 5 percent have a violent crime as their most serious offense and less than 25 percent of federally sentenced drug offenders possessed an illegal firearm as part of their arresting offense.

Recognizing our past mistakes, several States have reclassified and downgraded drug offenses and increased the quantity thresholds necessary to raise offenses to the felony level. In many States, there is no difference in statutory penalties between powder cocaine and crack cocaine. In New York, for example, the are treated the same, recognized in the State penal law as "controlled substances."

Over the course of my policing career, I have seen how these positive changes at the State level are too often nullified when the Federal Government asserts jurisdiction over what is clearly a State matter.

A decisive 67 percent of Americans who self-identify as Republicans, Democrats, and Independents believe that government should focus more on providing treatment for illegal drug users than prosecuting them.

What's more, national law enforcement organizations, such as the Law Enforcement Action Partnership, also recognize that while drugs are potentially addictive and cause self-harm, drug abuse is a public health problem that requires a more nuanced approach.

The United States relies on the principles of justice and equality for all, but the past 50 years have clearly demonstrated that, in the case of narcotics enforcement, the law has been not equally or justly applied.

Rather, the war on drugs arrested and sentenced tens of thousands of individuals, ultimately for an often victimless, though socially intolerable behavior, and its effects were profound: The disruption of families, the loss of housing and potential employment, the inexcusable disparity based all too often on race, ethnicity, or financial status, rather than public safety concerns.

Luckily, the EQUAL Act represents a golden and popular opportunity to reform sentencing to reduce these disparities and to focus on a more humane, rehabilitative approach instead of a largely failed punitive one.

That is why support for the EQUAL Act cannot by mired in partisan politics—lives are at stake. Instead, bipartisan support must continue as you strive to achieve a meaningful solution to this ongoing crisis.

Thank you to the Subcommittee for holding this hearing. If I could be of any assistance to Members of the committee, please feel free to contact me or my colleagues at the R Street Institute.

Thank you.

[The statement of Ms. Snider follows:]

Submitted Statement for the Record of Jillian E. Snider, Policy Director, Criminal Justice and Civil Liberties, R Street Institute, before the Subcommittee on Crime, Terrorism, and Homeland Security, Committee on the Judiciary, United States House of Representatives, Hearing on Undoing the Damage of the War on Drugs: A Renewed Call for Sentencing Reform, June 17, 2021

Chairwoman Jackson Lee, Ranking Member Biggs, and Members of the Committee:

Thank you for the invitation to testify today. My name is Jillian E. Snider, and I am the director of criminal justice and civil liberties policy at the R Street Institute, which is a nonprofit, nonpartisan, public policy research organization. Our mission is to engage in policy research and outreach to promote free markets and limited, effective government in many areas, including criminal justice reform, and that is why today's hearing is of special interest to us.

In addition to my current role, I am also a Lecturer at John Jay College of Criminal Justice and a retired police officer from the New York City Police Department. I am here to speak to you today about the critical nature of bipartisan support for the EQUAL Act. Current drug prohibition has resulted in an overreliance on enforcement, arrests and incarceration—which has had a disproportionate impact on Black and Brown men in urban communities.[153]

The crack epidemic of the 1980s triggered an aggressive enforcement approach, initially established to decrease the spread of drug-related diseases and deaths, and to combat organized crime. Cocaine, and its derivative crack cocaine, is dangerous, has a high potential for abuse, and may lead to severe psychological or physical dependence.[154] The chemical composition of powder cocaine and crack cocaine are nearly identical, and both produce similar results when ingested. The only true variation between the two is the method of consumption: powder cocaine is typically snorted, injected, or swallowed, while crack cocaine is smoked.

The 1986 Anti-Drug Abuse Act created a disparity between the amount of crack cocaine and the amount of powder cocaine that triggers a federal mandatory minimum sentence. This meant that 5 grams of crack mandated a five-year sentence, while 500 grams of powder cocaine was the threshold for the same sentence. The 2010 Fair Sentencing Act was a positive step in reducing this disparity, but the time has come to do away with the disparity altogether, because, as we know, there are no significant differences between the two forms.

Our criminal justice system is not a one-size-fits-all solution. For far too long now, the United States has relied on a system of overcriminalization, in which we overuse—and at times misuse—criminal law to address societal problems that could be more effectively handled through civil channels or other institutions. This is evident by our nation's present incarcerated population, which boasts approximately 2.3 million individuals.[155]

Law enforcement strategies and sentencing policies of the War on Drugs era is one of the biggest contributors to this level of mass incarceration, with the number of Americans imprisoned for drug offenses reaching more than

---

153 Betsy Pearl, "Ending the War on Drugs: By the Numbers," Center for American Progress, June, 27, 2018. https://www.americanprogress.org/issues/criminal-justice/reports/2018/06/27/452819/ending-war-drugs- numbers.

154 "Drug Scheduling," United States Drug Enforcement Administration, last accessed June 15, 2021. https://www.dea.gov/drug-information/drug-scheduling.

155 Wendy Sawyer and Peter Wagner, "Mass Incarceration: The Whole Pie 2020," Prison Policy Initiative, March 24, 2020. https://www.prisonpolicy.org/reports/pie2020.html.

430,000 in 2019.[156] An overwhelming 92 percent of individuals in federal prison have a drug offense as their most serious criminal charge.[157]

Law-makers assumed that the use or sale of drugs had a causal effect on both theft and violence, inspiring stricter penalties on drug-related offenses to deter future criminal activity. Research and evidence-based findings indicate this is not the case. Increased incarceration has demonstrated only a small impact on crime rates, and the majority of crime reduction benefits are only related to property crimes.[158] Drug abuse, specifically the use of cocaine or heroin, while consistent with patterns of income-generating crime like burglary and larceny, are not significantly correlated with violent crime.[159] A recent cross-sectional analysis of more than 7,000 prisoners indicates that binge consumption of alcohol is more closely correlated to violent crime than the use of cocaine.[160]

Approximately 35 percent of federal drug offenders fall within the U.S. Sentencing Commission Category I for criminal history, meaning these individuals have no previous terms of imprisonment or extremely minimal criminal records. Additionally, of individuals with linked U.S. Sentencing Commission records, less than 5 percent have a violent crime as their most serious offense.[161] Less than 25 percent of federally sentenced drug offenders possessed an illegal firearm in the instant matter.[162]

---

156 "Criminal Justice Facts," The Sentencing Project, 2020. https://www.sentencingproject.org/criminal-justice-facts.

157 Bureau of Justice Statistics, " Drug Offenders in Federal Prison: Estimates of Characteristics Based on Linked Data," U.S. Dept. of Justice, October 2015. https://bjs.ojp.gov/content/pub/pdf/dofp12.pdf.

158 Don Stemen, "The Prison Paradox: More Incarceration Will Not Make Us Safer," Vera Institute of Justice, July 2017. https://www.vera.org/downloads/publications/for-the-record-prison-paradox_02.pdf.

159 Denise C. Gottfredson, et al., "Substance Use, Drug Treatment, and Crime: An Examination of Intra-Individual Variation in a Drug Court Population," *Journal of Drug Issues* 38:2 (April 2008). https://journals.sagepub.com/doi/10.1177/002204260803800211.

160 Anders Hakansson and Virginia Jesionowska, "Associations Between Substance Use and Type of Crime in Prisoners with Substance Use Problems – A Focus on Violence and Fatal Violence," *Substance Abuse and Rehabilitation* 9 (January 2018). https://www.ncbi.nlm.nih.gov/pmc/articles/PMC5774467/pdf/sar-9-001.pdf.

161 Bureau of Justice Statistics. https://bjs.ojp.gov/content/pub/pdf/dofp12.pdf.

162 Ibid.

In recent years, many states have modified their drug sentencing laws by reclassifying and downgrading drug offenses and by increasing the quantity thresholds necessary to raise the offense to felony-level.[163] In many states, there is no difference in statutory penalties between powder cocaine and crack cocaine. In New York, for example, the two are treated the same, recognized in the state penal law as "controlled substances."[164]

While it is a collective belief that drug abuse in the United States is a serious problem, a national survey found that 67 percent of Americans—including self-identified Republicans, Democrats and Independents—believe the government should focus more on providing treatment for those who use illegal drugs as opposed to harsher prosecution.[165] National law enforcement organizations, such as the Law Enforcement Action Partnership, recognize that drugs are both dangerous and potentially addictive, but believe drug abuse is a public health problem and should not be solely a law enforcement matter.[166]

The United States relies on the principles of justice and equality for all. The differential enforcement of narcotics over the past fifty years has clearly demonstrated that the law has not been equally applied. The "War on Drugs" resulted in the arrest and sentencing of tens of thousands of individuals, resulting in the disruption of families, the loss of housing and potential employment, and ultimately the loss of many years for an often victimless, socially intolerable behavior. Strict enforcement and punitive punishment have not been a successful deterrent, and may be counterproductive: they limit opportunity, resulting in a repetitive cycle of abuse and incarceration. What we need is reform that calls for equal sentencing, less disciplinary penalties, and a more rehabilitative and humane approach. That is why support for the EQUAL Act cannot be mired in partisan politics: lives are at stake. Instead, the EQUAL Act must continue to be bipartisan as you strive to solve part of this ongoing crisis.

---

163 Don Stemen, "Beyond the War: The Evolving Nature of the U.S. Approach to Drugs," *Harvard Law & Policy Review* 11:2 (June 2017). https://ecommons.luc.edu/cgi/viewcontent.cgi?article=1026&context=criminaljustice_facpubs.

164 "The Laws of New York: Part 3 Specific Offenses," The New York State Senate, last accessed Jun 15, 2021. https://www.nysenate.gov/legislation/laws/PEN/220.00.

165 "America's New Drug Policy Landscape," Pew Research Center, April 2014. https://www.pewresearch.org/politics/2014/04/02/americas-new-drug-policy-landscape.

166 "Drug Policy: War on Drugs," Law Enforcement Action Partnership, October 2018. https://lawenforcementactionpartnership.org/our-issues/drug-policy.

Thank you to the Subcommittee on Crime, Terrorism, and Homeland Security for holding this hearing. If I can be of any assistance to members of the Committee, please feel free to contact me or my colleagues at the R Street Institute.

Jillian E. Snider
Director, Criminal Justice and Civil Liberties Policy R Street Institute
(917) 417-5680
jsnider@rstreet.org

* * *

Ms. JACKSON LEE. We thank you very much for your testimony. Now, we'll yield for 5 minutes to Ms. Givens for her testimony.

Statement of Kyana Givens

Ms. GIVENS. Good morning, again. Thank you, Committee Chair Jackson Lee, Committee Chair Nadler, and Ranking Member Biggs.

I am a Federal public defender from the Eastern District of North Carolina. I've been proud to serve as a public defender for 16 years in three jurisdictions, both the West Coast and the East Coast.

I agree with so many of the recommendations already shared by our esteemed panel member witnesses—most importantly, abolishing the mandatory minimum.

As I sit here today, I can't help but think about who is on my caseload, and I want the Committee to remember who our policies affect.

As I sit here today, 48 percent of the people on my caseload are eligible for mandatory minimums. Many of these young people are between the ages of 18–26 years old.

That is entirely too young during developing adolescence to throw these young people into our prison system for time periods that equal 5–15 years. We are erasing entire phases of life for a whole generation.

I'm asking the Committee to remember that the laws that you pass impact real lives. Some of those lives that I see on my caseload include a whole bunch of young people who landed at the prison system by falling through the education system. Let us not forget also, a whole bunch of our prisoners are people who grew up in the foster care system.

I have represented a young couple who was expecting preemies and I could not get the young man out. He missed the birth of his children. The one family he ever knew, he was removed from for a mandatory minimum period.

I'm asking the Committee to really consider some specific areas of the mandatory minimum and the impact it has. That is the recidivist statute of 851, the drug recidivist statute, and the 924(c), which is a combination of drugs plus a gun or drugs plus a violent crime.

These are some of the most popular convictions that we see in our Nation and they also come with mandatory minimums. Simply making an impact on this area could seriously reduce and have a positive impact on reducing mass incarceration.

I submitted in my testimony a young woman who represents something we often see, which is young people in a car with a gun and drugs ending up with a 924(c) and a mandatory minimum of 5 years. This was a young student-athlete who was not the driver, she was a passenger, and she is serving a sentence today for at least 70 months.

I also want to touch on something that Ranking Member Biggs alluded to, which is the overfederalization of local crime. It results in task forces like Project Safe Neighborhoods that actually does not accomplish the goals that it intended. We have got to take a close look at the overfederalizing of local crime and bring it back to the place that it belongs.

The impact of these task forces usually means oversurveilling and overpolicing communities of color; that is, Black and Brown individuals. We hide behind pretty names like Project Safe Neighborhoods when this does not make our neighborhoods safer.

Long sentences do not ensure public safety. We have got to sentence like we believe it, we have got to sentence like supported by data.

Last by not least, I'm going ask the Committee to really think about our youth, this 18–26-year-old group. We need to reclaim them. We need to recover them and remove them from the Federal prison system. They should not be subject to mandatory minimums under 851 or 924.

Last, we should recenter drug misuse as the public crisis it is. Drug addiction and mental illness are a public health crisis, and the criminal justice system is so closely linked we have got to address it is as a public health crisis.

I look forward to working with you, accepting your questions, and ask the Committee to take action. The war on drugs was a failure and we need to leave it where it was. Thank you.

[The statement of Ms. Givens follows:]

Testimony of Kyana Givens, Assistant Federal Public Defender, Federal Public Defender for the Eastern District of North Carolina, before the Judiciary Committee of the House of Representatives, Subcommittee on Crime, Terrorism, and Homeland Security, Hearing on Undoing the Damage of the War on Drugs: A Renewed Call for Sentencing Reform

Chairman Nadler, Subcommittee Chair Jackson-Lee, and members of the Subcommittee, thank you for inviting me to participate in this important hearing. My name is Kyana Givens and I am an Assistant Federal Public Defender in Raleigh, North Carolina. At any given time, Federal Public and Community Defenders and other appointed counsel under the Criminal Justice Act represent 80 to 90 percent of all individuals in the federal criminal system because they cannot afford counsel.

Introduction

Today I will focus my remarks on two drivers of mass incarceration: mandatory minimum sentences and the federalization of local crime. But first, I want to speak a little bit about where my perspective comes from.

I have spent 16 years as a public defender on the front lines of the so-called "War on Drugs." From this vantage point, I have watched the implementation of law enforcement policies purportedly adopted in the name of ending drug misuse, reducing supply, and making streets safer. I have watched as harsh mandatory minimums and the unjust discriminatory 100-to-1 (now 18-to-1) crack cocaine penalties sent my clients—many young men of color—to crowd our prisons. I have seen the broken families and communities left behind. And I've witnessed through my clients that these policies are a failure.

Tens of millions of Americans continue to struggle with addiction and its consequences.[167] Near-daily headlines reporting large scale seizures of a variety of drugs prove that our nation's choice to address drug dependence

[167] Substance Abuse and Mental Health Serv. Admin., *Key Substance Use and Mental Health Indicators in the United States: Results from the 2019 National Survey on Drug Use and Health* 2 (2020), https://bit.ly/2RvoZQp (In 2019, approximately 20.4 million people aged 12 or older had a substance use disorder related to their use of alcohol or illicit drugs in the past year).

through sweeping and severe law enforcement efforts, rather than public health responses, has failed to alleviate the demand for illicit drugs or decrease overdose deaths.[168]

Meanwhile, these laws and enforcement policies have destroyed communities, broken families, and branded millions of people as felons. Perversely, these extreme levels of incarceration *undermine* public safety. There is overwhelming research that long prison sentences do not deter future crime.[169] Lengthy prison terms weaken family structure, limit economic opportunity, and discourage rehabilitation.

Evidence gathered by the Sentencing Commission and the Colson Task Force has shown that many of these oversize sentences can be reduced with no increase in recidivism.[170]

I have been encouraged by the last decade's bipartisan movement toward reform. In 2010, Congress enacted the Fair Sentencing Act to reduce the unjust disparity between crack and cocaine from 100-to-1 to 18-to-1.[171] President Obama granted clemency to almost 2,000 individuals serving lengthy sentences for drug offenses, and during his administration the Department of Justice (Department) curtailed its use of mandatory minimums.[172] Two-and-a-

---

[168] *See, e.g.,* U.S. Customs and Border Protection, *CBP Air and Marine Operations and Partners Seize Combined 4 Tons of Cocaine in Eastern Pacific* (Apr. 7, 2021), https://bit.ly/327YXo6; News Release, *Law Enforcement Seizures of Methamphetamine, Marijuana Rose During Pandemic,* Nat'l Inst. on Drug Abuse (Mar. 2, 2021), https://bit.ly/3wOCLxq; U.S. Customs and Border Control, *Border Patrol Agents Seize Over 800 Pounds of Marijuana* (Apr. 6, 2021), https://bit.ly/3dabduG; Stella Chan & Amanda Jackson, *DEA Announces Biggest Domestic Seizure of Meth in Agency History*, CNN (Oct. 14, 2020), https://cnn.it/3uFeSGO.

[169] U.S. Dep't of Just., Off. of Just. Programs, Nat'l Inst. of Just., *Five Things About Deterrence* 1 (2016); *see also* Nat'l Res. Council, *The Growth of Incarceration in the United States: Exploring Causes and Consequences* 134–40, 337 (Jeremy Travis *et al.* eds., 2014); Daniel S. Nagin, *Deterrence in the Twenty-First Century*, 42 Crime & Justice 199, 202 (2013); Donald P. Green & Daniel Winik, *Using Random Judge Assignments to Estimate the Effects of Incarceration and Probation on Recidivism among Drug Offenders*, 48 Criminology 357 (2010); Francis T. Cullen *et al.*, *Prisons Do Not Reduce Recidivism: The High Cost of Ignoring Science*, 91 Prison J. 48S (2011).

[170] The Commission found no statistically significant difference in the rates of recidivism after five years of prisoners released early under the retroactive amendment to the crack guidelines and prisoners who served their full sentences; in fact, the recidivism rate for those who served their full sentences was slightly higher. U.S. Sent'g Comm'n, *Recidivism Among Offenders Receiving Retroactive Sentence Reductions: The 2007 Crack Cocaine Amendment* at 1, 3 (May 2014), https://bit.ly/3pPHD2t; *see also* Transforming Prisons, Restoring Lives: Final Recommendations of the Colson Task Force on Federal Corrections at 21 (Jan. 2016), https://urbn.is/3cJNj8Q.

[171] Fair Sentencing Act of 2010, Pub. L. No. 111-220, 124 Stat 2372 (Aug. 3, 2010).

[172] Sari Horwitz, *Obama Grants Final 330 Commutations to Nonviolent Drug Offenders*, Wash. Post (Jan. 19, 2017) (granting a total of 1,715 clemencies) https://wapo.st/3cFZHq9; United

half years ago, Congress passed the First Step Act of 2018 with overwhelming bipartisan support, reducing sentences for certain drug offenses, curtailing "stacking" of § 924 charges, and making the Fair Sentencing Act of 2010 retroactive.[173] To date, more than 3,770 individuals serving unduly long sentences imposed under the discriminatory 100-to-1 crack-cocaine ratio have seen reductions in their sentences.[174] But other critical aspects of the First Step Act were *not* made retroactive, leaving far too many behind.[175]

Just this week, the Supreme Court ruled unanimously in *Terry v. United States,* 593 U.S., Slip Op. (May 4, 2021), that the First Step Act does not entitle individuals convicted of extremely low-level crack offenses to reduced sentences. The petitioner, Tarahrick Terry, pled guilty to possession with the intent to distribute about four grams of crack or, as Justice Sotomayor wrote, "less than the weight of four paper clips."[176] Justice Sotomayor explained that "[h]is Guidelines range would normally have been about three to four years. But Terry was sentenced as a career offender because of two prior drug convictions committed when he was a teenager and for which he spent a total of only 120 days in jail."[177] The bipartisan lead sponsors of the First Step Act, Senators Durbin, Grassley, Booker and Lee, urged the Supreme Court to hold that the First Step Act "makes retroactive relief broadly available to all individuals sentenced for crack-cocaine offenses before the Fair Sentencing Act."[178] But the Supreme Court held that the language of the First Step act would not "bear that meaning."[179]

The First Step Act of 2018 was just that—a step. But it was not transformational. Since the First Step Act, Congress has not acted to eliminate or reduce pervasive one-size-fits-all mandatory minimums. Without serious reform, prosecutors remain armed with the cudgel of outsize mandatory minimums that they deploy disproportionately against communities of color. Decades of data show that Black, Indigenous, Hispanic, and other people of

---

States Dep't of Just. *In Milestone for Sentencing Reform, Attorney General Holder Announces Record Reduction in Mandatory Minimums Against Nonviolent Drug Offenders* (Feb. 17, 2015), https://bit.ly/2U9hCiV.

173 First Step Act of 2018, Pub. L. No. 115-391, 132 Stat 5194 (Dec. 21, 2018).

174 Federal Bureau of Prisons, *First Step Act*, https://bit.ly/3vqD13J (Jan. 24, 2020).

175 *See* FAMM, *Bill Summary: First Step Implementation Act, S.1014* (summarizing sentencing provisions of the First Step Act that were not made retroactive), https://bit.ly/3wsv5jY.

176 *Terry*, 593 U.S. at 5 (Sotomayor, J. concurring).

177 *Id.*

178 *Id.* at 8.

179 *Id.*

color are over-represented in mandatory minimum sentences.[180] Fortunately, as Justice Sotomayor reminded us this week in *Terry*, "Congress has numerous tools to right this injustice."[181]

It is impossible to address all the factors that fuel mass incarceration in the United States today. Instead, I will focus on two issues I encounter on a near-daily basis in the courtrooms of Raleigh, North Carolina: (1) the excessive and disparate application of mandatory minimums prison sentences, particularly those for drug offenses,[182] and (2) the shift in focus of federal prosecutors from crimes with obvious interstate connections to crimes that were once thought of as purely local.[183]

---

[180] Marit Rehavi and Sonja B. Starr, *Racial Disparity in Federal Criminal Sentences*, 122 J. of Pol. Econ. 6 at 1350–1351 (Dec. 2014) (hereinafter Rehavi, *Racial Disparity*); U.S. Sent'g Comm'n, *Quick Facts, Mandatory Minimum Penalties*, https://bit.ly/2Tu5LLZ.

[181] *Terry*, 593 U.S. at 8.

[182] Rehavi, *Racial Disparity*, 122 J. of Pol. Econ. 6 at 1323 (Dec. 2014) (finding "black men have 1.75 times the odds of facing such charges, which is equivalent to a 5-percentage point (or 65 percent) increase in the probability for the average defendant. The initial mandatory minimum charging decision alone is capable of explaining more than half of the black-white sentence disparities not otherwise explained by precharge characteristics"). We have known for decades that not only are mandatory minimums themselves a "significant driver of this population increase," *Reevaluating the Effectiveness of Mandatory Minimum Sentences*, Hearing Before the Comm. on the Judiciary at 5, 113th Cong. (Sept. 2013) (Statement of Judge Patti B. Saris, Chair, United States Sentencing Commission), (hereinafter Saris, *Reevaluating Mandatory Minimums*) (reporting a 178.1 percent increase in the number of federal prisoners convicted of an offense carrying a mandatory minimum from 1995 to 2010), https://bit.ly/3pVQ2Bf, but the drug guidelines are linked to the two mandatory minimum levels specified in 21 U.S.C. § 841, and spread across seventeen levels between, above, and below those levels. "Given that drug trafficking constitutes the largest offense group sentenced in federal courts," the increase in prison terms due to the mandatory minimums and their incorporation into the guidelines "has been the single sentencing policy change having the greatest impact on prison populations." U.S. Sent'g Comm'n, *Fifteen Years of Guideline Sentencing* at 76 (2004), https://bit.ly/2TxvGlF (hereinafter U.S.S.C, *Fifteen Years of Guideline Sentencing*); *see also id.* at 48, 54.

[183] *See* David Patton, *Criminal Justice Reform and Guns: The Irresistible Movement Meets the Immovable Object*, 69 Emory L.J. 1011, 1012–1021 (2020) (hereinafter, Patton, *Criminal Justice Reform and Guns*); Bonita R. Gardner, *Separate and Unequal: Federal Tough-on-Guns Program Targets Minority Communities for Selective Enforcement*, 12 Mich. J. Race & L. 305, 317 (2007) (hereinafter Gardner, *Separate and Unequal*); Sara Sun Beale, *The Unintended Consequences of Enhancing Gun Penalties: Shooting Down the Commerce Clause and Arming Federal Prosecutors*, 51 Duke L. J. 1641, 1660–68 (2002); Daniel Richman, *"Project Exile" and the Allocation of Federal Law Enforcement Authority*, 43 Ariz. L. Rev. 369. 374–75, 279 (2001).

Mandatory Minimums Fuel Mass Incarceration and Racial Disparities

The most significant driver of the five-fold increase in the federal prison population has been mandatory minimums, particularly those for drug offenses.[184] In 1971, President Nixon declared drug abuse as "America's public enemy number one."[185] "In order to fight and defeat this enemy," he said, "it is necessary to wage a new, all-out offensive."[186] Fifteen years later, Ronald Reagan warned that "illegal drugs were every bit as much a threat to the United States as enemy planes and missiles." We must "do all we can to defeat the drug menace threatening our country."[187] Congress heeded this command, enacting sweeping and severe penalties like the Comprehensive Crime Control Act of 1984 and the Anti-Drug Abuse Act of 1986.[188] A decade later, on the eve of his reelection, Bill Clinton reported "we passed 'three strikes and you're out' and the death penalty for drug kingpins and cop killers," touting the accomplishments of the Violent Crime Control and Law Enforcement Act of 1994.[189] The laws from this era imposed harsh mandatory minimums for a variety of offenses, including drug offenses, and introduced the now-discredited 100-to-1 ratio between crack and powder cocaine.[190] The racial impact built into the design of these laws soon became clear; imposing severe sentences based on a person's criminal record disproportionately targets people of color, who are more likely to have a record in the first place because of unequal contact with police and unequal charging practices.[191]

---

[184] *See* Fed. Bureau of Prisons, *Statistics* (40,330 in 1985, 219,298 in 2013), https://bit.ly/35kjcRm (The federal prison population quintupled from 1986 when Congress enacted the current mandatory minimums for drug offenses to its highest point in 2013.).

[185] Richard Nixon, *Remarks About an Intensified Program for Drug Abuse Prevention and Control* (Jun. 17, 1971), https://bit.ly/3wutoTi.

[186] *Id.*

[187] *Remarks on Signing the Just Say No to Drugs Week Proclamation*, Ronald Reagan Presidential Libr. & Museum (May 20, 1986), https://bit.ly/3gyPOf3.

[188] *See* Comprehensive Crime Control Act of 1984, Pub. L. No. 98-473, tit. II, 98 Stat.1976 (Oct. 12, 1984); Anti-Drug Abuse Act of 1986, Pub. L. No. 99-570, 100 Stat. 3207 (Oct. 27, 1986).

[189] The President's Radio Address, 32 Weekly Comp. Pres. Doc. 2282 (Nov. 2, 1996), https://bit.ly/3xk816X; Violent Crime Control and Law Enforcement Act of 1994, Pub. L. No. 103-322, 108 Stat. 1796 (Jan. 25, 1994).

[190] See Rachel E. Barkow, *Categorical Mistakes: The Flawed Framework of the Armed Career Criminal Act and Mandatory Minimum Sentencing*, 133 Harv. L. Rev. 200, 212 (2019); *see also* Ranya Shannon, *3 Ways the 1994 Crime Bill Continues to Hurt Communities of Color*, Ctr. for Am. Progress (May 10, 2019), https://ampr.gs/3cIriHv.

[191] Ranya Shannon, *3 Ways the 1994 Crime Bill Continues to Hurt Communities of Color*, Center for American Progress (May 10, 2019), https://ampr.gs/3cIriHv.

The harms from "War on Drugs" enforcement priorities were exacerbated by the misguided belief—which emerged forcefully during the 1990s—that some of our children are incurable "super-predators" deserving of long prison sentences.[192] We now know from neurodevelopmental research that, in general, adolescents lack the capacity to effectively contemplate the risks and consequences of their actions.[193] Neurologists, psychiatrists, and the U.S. Sentencing Guidelines all recognize that youthful offenders' brain development continues after age 18 and up to age 26.[194] Yet the stain from the "superpredator" myth has left an indelible mark on our country: current data from the Bureau of Prisons ("BOP") shows that over 8,000 young people under the age of 26 are federally incarcerated, and many over that age are serving sentences enhanced by prior convictions for crimes committed in adolescence.

One of the most pernicious vestiges of the "tough on crime" rhetoric that fueled the War on Drugs is the outsize power wielded by federal prosecutors. The federal criminal system places enormous power into the hands of the Department and its prosecutors: they control who is charged, what they're charged with, and often, the severity of a potential sentence.[195] Mandatory minimum statutes equip prosecutors with unchecked power that is inconsistent with due process, the separation of powers, and fundamental fairness. They also distort the traditional role of the judge by improperly transferring sentencing authority from neutral judges to prosecutors, and restricting judges from applying the breadth of individualized sentencing discretion otherwise mandated by Congress in 18 U.S.C § 3553(a). The decision to charge mandatory minimums, or not, is entirely in the hands of prosecutors. And that

---

192 *See* The Campaign for the Fair Sentencing of Youth, *The Superpredator: The Child Study Movement to Today* (May 2021), https://bit.ly/2RYN2aY.

193 *Miller v. Alabama*, 567 U.S. 460, 492 (2012) (Sotomayor, J. concurring) (Yet "the ability to consider the full consequences of a course of action and to adjust one's conduct accordingly is precisely what we know juveniles lack capacity to do effectively.").

194 *Roper v. Simmons*, 543 U.S. 551, 569 (2005) (citing Steinberg & Scott, *Less Guilty by Reason of Adolescence: Developmental Immaturity, Diminished Responsibility, and the Juvenile Death Penalty*, 58 Am. Psychologist 1009, 1014 (2003)); *Graham v. Florida*, 560 U.S. 48, 68 (2010) (Noting "developments in psychology and brain science continue to show fundamental differences between juvenile and adult minds. For example, parts of the brain involved in behavior control continue to mature through late adolescence."); U.S.S.G. § 5H1.1. (age, including youth may be relevant in determining whether a departure is warranted).

195 Although the court decides the ultimate sentences, prosecutors can control the options available to the judge through choices about the initial charges levied, whether a plea is offered (and its terms), relief from the mandatory minimum under 18 U.S.C. § 3553(e), and sentencing recommendations.

power is routinely abused. Emily Bazelon has explained that "[t]he unfettered power of prosecutors is the missing piece for explaining how the number of people incarcerated in the United States has *quintupled* since the 1980s …"[196]

Mandatory minimum sentences also are a major contributor to wrongful convictions because they incentivize unreliable cooperator testimony.[197] Often the only way a person facing a mandatory minimum can try to escape it is to cooperate. "This reality introduces an extraordinary incentive to lie. Empirical evidence shows that lying cooperators account for an astounding 15 percent to 45 percent of wrongful convictions."[198] Further, prosecutors generally decide if and how to reward cooperation. There are only two ways individuals can receive a sentence below the mandatory minimum: safety valve and substantial assistance.[199] To get either from of relief, individuals must satisfy—in the prosecutor's view—several difficult criteria. As a result, relief under the provisions is granted unevenly, and in a racially disparate manner.[200]

To this day, mandatory minimums fuel mass incarceration and will do so until Congress takes decisive action. Contrary to congressional intent, prosecutors routinely seek lengthy mandatory minimum sentences against minimally-involved individuals. Too often, that is because prosecutors depend on the threat of extreme sentences to deter individuals from exercising their right to trial. Meanwhile, enforcement efforts continue to target Black and

---

[196] Emily Bazelon, Charged: The New Movement to Transform American Prosecution and End Mass Incarceration xxv (2019).

[197] Reliance on cooperators can also "focus" racial disparities. *See*, e.g., Alexandra Natapoff, *Snitching: The Institutional and Communal Consequences*, 73 U. Cin. L. Rev. 645, 673 (2004). Cooperators typically can cooperate only against people they know. *Id.* To the degree that they live racially segregated lives, then law enforcement reliance on them "becomes a kind of focusing mechanism guaranteeing that law enforcement will expend resources in" their "community whether or not the situation there independently warrants it." *Id.*

[198] *Controlled Substances: Federal Polices and Enforcement*, Hearing Before the Subcomm. on Crime, Terrorism, and Homeland Security of the H. Comm. on the Judiciary at 17, 117th Cong. (Mar. 2021) (Statement of Alison Siegler, Erica Zunkel, and Judith P. Miller) (hereinafter Siegler, *University of Chicago Statement*"), https://bit.ly/3iHq2s0 (gathering sources).

[199] Cong. Res. Serv., *Federal Mandatory Minimum Sentences: The Safety Valve and Substantial Assistance Exceptions* 3 (2019), https://bit.ly/2RX0uMm.

[200] It is up to the government whether to offer 18 U.S.C. §3553(e) mandatory minimum relief or §5K1.1 sentencing reductions for cooperation. In the last five years, white individuals sentenced under primary guideline §2D1.1 received §5K1.1 departures almost twice as often as Black or Hispanic individuals. See USSC, FY 2016 – 2020 Individual Datafiles ((In Fiscal Years 2016 through 2020, 32.5 percent of white individuals sentenced under primary guideline §2D1.1 received §5K1.1 reductions, while only 18.6 percent of Black individuals and 17.7 percent of Hispanic individuals received §5K1.1 reductions).

Brown individuals with mandatory minimum offenses, fueling stark racial disparities in the federal system.

A. Sentences intended for kingpins and serious traffickers are routinely and mostly applied to minimally-involved individuals and street-level dealers, an enforcement approach that exacerbates racial disparities and does not deter crime.

When Congress enacted mandatory minimums for drug transactions in 1986 and extended them to conspiracies in 1988, it was taking aim at high-level operators in drug trafficking organizations. It intended that the ten-year mandatory minimum would apply to "kingpins—the masterminds who are really running these operations," that the five-year mandatory minimum would apply to "middle-level dealers," and thought that an individual's role in the offense would correspond to the quantity of drugs involved in the offense.[201] Congress also expected that this structure would encourage the Department to direct its "most intense focus" on "major traffickers" and "serious traffickers" in order "to focus scarce law enforcement resources."[202]

Congress was mistaken that an individual's role in the offense would correspond to the quantity involved in the offense.[203] A decade ago, the U.S. Sentencing Commission determined that the "quantity of drugs involved in an offense is not closely related to an individual's function in the offense."[204] But for most of its history, the Department has charged mandatory minimums indiscriminately, subjecting minimally involved individuals to mandatory

---

[201] Senator Robert Byrd, then the Senate Minority Leader, summarized the intent behind the legislation:

> For the kingpins—the masterminds who are really running these operations—and they can be identified by the amount of drugs with which they are involved—we require a jail term upon conviction. If it is their first conviction, the minimum term is 10 years. Our proposal would also provide mandatory minimum penalties for the middle-level dealers as well. Those criminals would also have to serve time in jail. The minimum sentences would be slightly less than those for the kingpins, but they nevertheless would have to go to jail—a minimum of 5 years for the first offense.

132 Cong. Rec. 27,193–94 (Sept. 30, 1986).

[202] H.R. Rep. No. 99-845, pt. 1, at 11–12 (1986).

[203] *United States v. Dossie*, 851 F. Supp.2d 478, 480–81 (E.D.N.Y. 2012) (providing a thorough explanation of the history and mistaken rationale of mandatory minimum sentences in drug cases).

[204] U.S. Sent'g Comm'n, 2011 Report to the Congress: Mandatory Minimum Penalties in the Federal Criminal Justice System at 168, https://bit.ly/3iNd8sa (hereinafter USSC, *2011 Report*).

minimums intended for kingpins and serious traffickers.[205] Indeed, the category of individuals "most often subject to mandatory minimum penalties at the time of sentencing" in 2010 were "street level dealers, who were many steps down from high-level suppliers and leaders of drug organizations."[206]

From 2013 through 2016, the Department, for the first time, discouraged prosecutors from using mandatory minimums against minimally involved individuals charged with drug offenses. Under this "Smart on Crime" policy, the percentage of individuals facing federal drug charges who were convicted of an offense carrying a mandatory minimum dropped to 44.5 percent by 2016,[207] a significant decrease from 2010, when approximately two-thirds of individuals facing drug charges were convicted of such an offense.[208] But still, the vast majority of these cases did not involve violence, or leadership roles: 98.7 percent did not use, threaten or direct the use of violence, 88 percent played no aggravated role, and 77.5 percent had no weapon involvement.[209] In 2017, the Inspector General found that progress had been made, but that "some districts did not develop or update their policies as directed, while others developed policies that are in whole or in part inconsistent with *Smart on Crime*."[210]

Any progress that was made was reversed by former Attorney General Sessions' May 2017 directive to charge and pursue those offenses carrying the most substantial sentences. I was glad to see the rescission of the Sessions' Directive by the Department on January 29, 2021,[211] but am troubled that

---

205 "Mandatory minimum penalties currently apply in large numbers to every function in a drug organization, from couriers and mules who transport drugs often at the lowest levels of a drug organization all the way up to high-level suppliers and importers who bring large quantities of drugs into the United States. For instance, in the cases the Commission reviewed, 23 percent of individuals charged with drug offenses were couriers, and nearly half of these were charged with offenses carrying mandatory minimum sentences." Saris, *Reevaluating Mandatory Minimums Sentences* at 5.

206 *Id.*

207 *See* Letter from Neil Fulton, David Patton, and Jon Sands, Co-Chairs, Federal Pubic & Community Defenders Legis. Comm., to the Hons. Mitch McConnell & Chuck Schumer, *Re: The First Step Act* (H.R. 5682); *Sentencing Reform* (Aug. 13, 2018), https://bit.ly/3grpKDX (hereinafter "Fulton Letter").

208 U.S. Sent'g Comm'n, Mandatory Minimum Penalties for Drug Offenses in the Federal Criminal Justice System (October 2017), https://bit.ly/3xeR4e6.

209 Fulton Letter at 14.

210 U.S. Dep't of Just., Off. of the Inspector Gen., Review of the Department's Implementation of Prosecution and Sentencing Reform Principles under the *Smart on Crime* Initiative at 9 (June 2017), https://bit.ly/35jZogO.

211 Mem. from Monty Wilkinson, Act'g Att'y Gen., U.S. Dep't of Just., to All Federal Prosecutors on Interim Guidance on Prosecutorial Discretion, Charging, and Sentencing (Jan. 29, 2021), https://bit.ly/3gB1aiG (rescinding the Sessions directive and reinstating guidance May 19, 2010 charging guidance from former Attorney General Holder, which

Attorney General Garland has not issued new charging policies that even reinstate, let alone expand, on the "Smart on Crime" policy. The 2017 OIG report found that the delays in promulgating and disseminating that policy limited its impact. Any delays by Attorney Garland in promulgating and disseminating new policies may cripple effort to ameliorate and reverse Trump-era polices, and to redress mass incarceration.

B. Prosecutors misuse severe mandatory enhancements to coerce guilty pleas and punish defendants for exercising their right to trial.

For most in the federal system, "the right to a trial is a choice in name only."[212] "Individuals who choose to exercise their Sixth Amendment right to trial face exponentially higher sentences if they invoke the right to trial and lose."[213] The potential consequences of going to trial are so extreme that in the federal criminal legal system, trials are "on the verge of extinction."[214] In 2019, about 97.9 percent of federal criminal convictions came from guilty pleas.[215]

Prosecutors wield disproportionate and often unilateral power in charging offenses carrying mandatory minimum sentences. In nonviolent drug distribution offenses, for example, the simple act of including the weight of the drugs in the charging document can have drastic consequences by invoking the mandatory minimum penalty.[216]

Even after filing the initial charge, prosecutors retain a variety of mechanisms to influence sentencing outcomes and force pleas.[217] Certain federal statutes require mandatory, non-discretionary sentencing enhancements—but they apply only if the prosecution has charged an individual for the conduct triggering the enhancement. Two of the most common enhancements are penalties under 18 U.S.C. § 924(c), and recidivist

---

directs prosecutors to conduct an individualized assessment of relevant facts in making charging and sentencing decisions).

[212] Nat'l Ass'n of Crim. Def. Lawyers, *The Trial Penalty: The Sixth Amendment Right to Trial on the Verge of Extinction and How to Save It* at 6 (2018), https://bit.ly/3zo7ZwJ ("Trial Penalty Report").

[213] *Id.* at 5.

[214] *Id.* at 1.

[215] U.S. District Cts., *Criminal Defendants Disposed of, by Type of Disposition and Offense, During the 12-Month Period Entering Dec. 31, 2019* (Dec. 2019), https://bit.ly/2TsmJKv.

[216] Mem. from Eric H. Holder, Jr., Attorney Gen., U.S. Dep't of Just., to All Federal Prosecutors on Department Policy on Charging Mandatory Minimum Sentences and Recidivist Enhancements in Certain Drug Cases (Aug. 12, 2013), https://bit.ly/3guWPxD.

[217] *Trial Penalty Report* at 25–30.

enhancements charged under 18 U.S.C. § 851. In the First Step Act of 2018, Congress voted on an overwhelmingly bipartisan basis to reform certain aspects of these statutes, but it did not make those changes retroactive. And even after those reforms, the penalties triggered by § 924(c) and § 851 remain harsh and coercive.

Section 924(c) Penalties

The penalties attached to § 924(c) are among the most commonly imposed mandatory-minimum sentences in the United States.[218] According to the U.S. Sentencing Commission, convictions for § 924(c) offenses "significantly contribute" to the federal prison population, constituting 14.3 percent of that population.[219] I am all too familiar with the harm wrought by these harsh penalties: the Eastern District of North Carolina has the second highest number of cases involving § 924(c) convictions in the country.[220]

Section 924(c) requires a mandatory consecutive sentence of 5, 7 or 10 years if an individual possessed, carried, brandished or discharged a firearm during or in furtherance of a drug trafficking crime or a crime of violence.[221] In addition, for every "second or subsequent" firearms offense, individuals face a 25-year enhancement.[222] Prior to the First Step Act, the Supreme Court interpreted § 924(c) such that it did not require a previous final conviction and could include multiple counts in the same indictment.[223] As a result, courts were sometimes required to impose overly harsh, decades-long sentences for charges brought in a single indictment. This practice, called "stacking," resulted in a sentence of at least 30 years for two counts, 55 years for three counts, and up to hundreds of years, even when the person charged has no prior record, and even when they did not use a gun, or even touch a gun. In the First Step Act of 2018, Congress ended this abusive practice. But many individuals who were punished for exercising their trial right with enhanced 924(c) sentences are still serving prison terms that would not be imposed today.

---

218 U.S. Sentencing Commission, *Mandatory Minimum Penalties for Firearm Offenses in the Federal Criminal Justice System* 16 (March 2018), https://bit.ly/3wqZQFM.

219 U.S. Sent'g Comm'n, *Quick Facts: Federal Offenders in Prison- March 2021*, https://bit.ly/3wkMhrw.

220 U.S. Sent'g Comm'n, *Quick Facts: 18 U.S.C. § 924(c) Firearms Offenses* https://bit.ly/2SARInD.

221 18 U.S.C. 924(c)(1)(A)(i)–(iii).

222 *Id.* at 924(c)(1)(C)(i).

223 *See Deal v. United States*, 508 U.S. 129 (1993).

Consider the case of Robert Bernhardt, or "Bob" to those who know him. Mr. Bernhardt is a 65-year-old U.S. Army Vietnam veteran serving a mandatory life sentence for weapons-for-drugs transactions in the District of Colorado. Mr. Bernhardt was a law-abiding citizen until he began to abuse methamphetamine at the age of 38 and engaged in crime to support his addiction. Although the prosecutor offered a plea deal of 12 years, Mr. Bernhardt exercised his right to a jury trial. Upon conviction, he faced mandatory life because of the "stacking" of his two 924(c) convictions. Were he sentenced today, he would face a 35-year sentence, not life. A federal district judge in Colorado concluded that Mr. Bernhardt "could not be sentenced today as he was in 1998."[224] During his 25 years in prison, Mr. Bernhardt has maintained a spotless disciplinary record without a single infraction. BOP staff have described him as a "model inmate." And Mr. Bernhardt's original prosecutor believes that "his life sentence is now far greater than necessary to achieve the ends of justice in this case," and Mr. Bernhardt "has done enough time." Despite this, Mr. Bernhardt's life sentence remains in place.[225]

Although the First Step Act curtailed the worst abuses of § 924(c), prosecutors still misuse the statute to ratchet up sentences for individuals charged with non-violent drug offenses and transfer discretion away from the sentencing judge. The case of my client, "Margo Smith,"[226] illustrates this point. Ms. Smith, a 24-year old college student athlete, juggled low-wage jobs and schoolwork as she tried to complete her education after her school arbitrarily reduced her scholarship. But she could not make ends meet and turned to selling drugs to bridge the financial gap. In 2019, police stopped and searched a car her friend was driving and found less than an ounce of marijuana and methamphetamine. When police searched Ms. Smith, they

---

[224] *United States v. Bernhardt*, No. 96-CR-203-WJM, 2020 WL 2084875, at *2 (D. Colo. Apr. 30, 2020).

[225] Since the passage of the First Step Act of 2018, Mr. Bernhardt has sought a reduction in his sentence two times. In early 2019, Mr. Bernhardt filed pro se motion arguing his stacked 924(c)s were invalid under the First Step Act. The district court recognized that Mr. Bernhardt "could not be sentenced today as he was in 1998," but concluded that the changes to the 924(c) provisions did not apply retroactively and denied relief. United States v. Bernhardt, No. 96-CR-203-WJM, 2020 WL 2084875, at *2 (D. Colo. Apr. 30, 2020). In June 2020, Mr. Bernhard tried again, filing a motion for compassionate release. Again, the Court acknowledged that Mr. Bernhardt couldn't be sentenced to mandatory life today for his crimes, described him as "an exemplary inmate" who found "ways to serve children and the underprivileged," but denied him relief because it wanted him to serve "half of the sentence" Mr. Bernhardt could have received if he were sentenced today. United States v. Bernhardt, No. 96-CR-203-WJM, 2020 WL 4041458, at *3 (D. Colo. July 17, 2020).

[226] I have changed my client's name to protect her privacy.

recovered a gun. Although non-mandatory minimum charges were available, prosecutors charged her with a violation of 18 U.S.C. § 924(c), triggering a five-year mandatory sentence and stripping away the judge's discretion to tailor a sentence that would reflect her youth and minimal history.

Section 851 Enhancements

The opportunity for prosecutors to file § 851 enhancements lends itself to similar abuses. Prior to the enactment of the First Step Act of 2018, if an individual charged with a drug offense had one or more prior convictions of a "felony drug offense," the prosecutor had the option to file a § 851 enhancement.[227] The prosecutor's filing would double the otherwise applicable mandatory minimum (from 5 to 10 years, or from 10 to 20 years), or increase it to mandatory life. In practice, the definition of "felony drug offense" allowed prosecutors to seek enhanced mandatory minimums based on relatively minor prior convictions, regardless of how long ago, including simple possession of drugs, misdemeanors in some states, offenses for which the defendant served no jail time, diversionary dispositions where the defendant was not convicted under state law.

Congress expected, based on the Department's express representation, that prosecutors would file enhancements under 21 U.S.C. § 851 only for "hardened," "professional criminals."[228] Instead, prosecutors improperly use § 851 enhancements to coerce individuals to plead guilty and to punish those who exercise their right to trial. A judge and former federal prosecutor explained:

> The single most important factor that influences the government's decision whether to file or threaten to file a prior felony information (or to withdraw or promise to withdraw one that has previously been filed) is illegitimate. ... To coerce guilty pleas, and sometimes to coerce cooperation as well, prosecutors routinely threaten ultra-harsh, enhanced

---

[227] U.S. Sent'g Comm'n, *Application and Impact of 21 U.S.C. § 851: Enhanced Penalties for Federal Drug Trafficking Offenders*, https://bit.ly/3cFXOtO (hereinafter USSC, *§ 851 Report*).

[228] See *Kupa v. United States*, 976 F. Supp. 2d 417, 419, 424–27 (E.D.N.Y. 2013); Drug Abuse Control Amendments 1970, Part 1: Hearing on H.R. 11701 and H.R. 13743 Before the Subcomm. on Pub. Health and Welfare of the H. Comm. on Interstate and Foreign Commerce, 91st Cong. (1970), H.R.Rep. No. 91–45, at 81 (Statement of John N. Mitchell, Att'y Gen. of the United States); id. (Statement of John Ingersoll, Comm'r of Bureau of Narcotics and Dangerous Drugs); Narcotics Legislation: Hearing on S. Res. 48, S. 1895, S. 2590, and S. 2637 Before the Subcomm. to Investigate Juvenile Delinquency of the S. Comm. on the Judiciary, 91st Cong., S. Doc. No. 521–3, at 681 (1969).

> mandatory sentences that *no one* – not even the prosecutors themselves – thinks are appropriate. And to demonstrate to defendants generally that those threats are sincere, prosecutors insist on the imposition of the unjust punishments when the threatened defendants refuse to plead guilty.[229]

One example is *United States v. Midyett*, 07-CR-874 (E.D.N.Y. June 17, 2010). Tyquan Midyett was charged with selling small quantities of crack cocaine at the age of 26 after a short lifetime of substance abuse which began at the age of 14 when he was in foster care. He was charged when the 100:1 crack/powder cocaine disparity was still in effect. His guideline range called for approximately 7 to9 years imprisonment (it would have been 4 to 4 ½ years had the law treated crack the same as cocaine), but the government charged him with the 10-year mandatory minimum intended for kingpins despite its own assertion that he played only a minor role. Mr. Midyett declined to plead guilty, at which point the government filed a prior "felony drug offense" information pursuant to § 851. Mr. Midyett went to trial, lost, and was sentenced to the mandatory minimum of 20 years, a sentence twice what the government offered before he went to trial, and five times the guideline sentence for a comparable amount of cocaine.[230]

In the First Step Act of 2018, Congress somewhat blunted the coercive power of § 851 enhancements by reducing the life mandatory minimum to 25 years and the 20-year mandatory minimum to 15 years, and by limiting the applicability of the enhancement to individuals with prior "serious drug offenses," i.e., those with at least a ten-year statutory maximum for which the defendant served more than 12 months and was released within 15 years of the commencement of the instant offense.[231] But it did not make those changes to the law retroactive, and to this day, thousands of individuals subjected to the unjust law remain locked in prison.

C. Mandatory Minimums Exacerbate Stark Racial Disparities in the Federal Legal System

The Discredited Crack-Cocaine Ratio

As part of the 1986 drug laws passed during the escalating drug panic, the Anti-Drug Abuse Act of 1986 established mandatory minimum sentences for

---

229 *Kupa*, 976 F. Supp.2d at 432–34 (E.D.N.Y. 2013).
230 Tyquan Midyett's story is relayed in *Kupa*, 976 F. Supp. 2d at 436-37.
231 First Step Act of 2018, Pub. L. No. 115-391, 132 Stat 5194 (Dec. 21, 2018).

possession of specific amounts of cocaine but established a 100-to-1 ratio between distribution of powder and crack cocaine.

Crack, it was claimed, was more harmful, more dangerous, than powder cocaine. These claims lacked a scientific basis—the two have similar effects.[232] The difference between crack and powder cocaine is that crack contains water and baking soda, and crack use is correlated to low income.[233] A media frenzy, incorporating racial stereotyping associating crack use with Black communities, fed hysterical narratives about inner city crime that spurred an expansive enforcement approach.[234] In Terry, Justice Sotomayor explains that "Black people bore the brunt of this disparity. Around 80 to 90 percent of those convicted of crack offenses between 1992 and 2006 were Black, while Black people made up only around 30 percent of powder cocaine offenders in those same years."[235]

Congress has twice acted to correct the unfairness and racial disparities caused by the crack-cocaine disparity: first, by reducing the ratio to 18-to-1 in the Fair Sentencing Act of 2010, and then by making that change retroactive in the First Step Act of 2018. The demographics of those who have received relief from that change show how Black communities were targeted for crack-cocaine enforcement. Since the First Step Act of 2018's passage, courts have granted 3,705 motions for a sentence reduction; 91.8 percent of which were for Black individuals.[236] The average reduction in sentence has been six years.[237]

But work remains to be done. Despite overwhelming evidence that distinguishing between crack and cocaine drives flawed policy, crack cocaine is still penalized more harshly than powder cocaine, and prosecutors continue to target Black individuals for enforcement. In fiscal year 2019, over 80 percent of those prosecuted for crack offenses were Black, even though Black

---

[232] D.K. Hatsukami & M.W. Fischman, *Crack Cocaine and Cocaine Hydrochloride. Are the Differences Myth or Reality?*, *J. Am. Med. Assoc.* (Nov. 1996), https://bit.ly/3cZhWY7.

[233] Joseph J. Palamar, *et al.*, *Powder Cocaine and Crack Use in the United States: An Examination of Risk for Arrest and Socioeconomic Disparities in Use*, *J. Drug Alcohol Depend.* (Apr. 2015), https://bit.ly/3gw5NdW.

[234] Drug Pol'y Alliance, *A Brief History of the Drug War* (last visited June 14, 2021), https://to.pbs.org/3iH6js8.

[235] *Terry*, 593 U.S. at 3.

[236] U.S. Sent'g Comm'n, *First Step Act of 2018 Resentencing Provisions Retroactivity Data Report* at tbl. 4 (May 2021), https://bit.ly/2SzsqGj.

[237] *Id.* at tbl. 6.

individuals make up about 13 percent of the total United States population.[238] Yet studies have shown that upwards of 66 percent crack users are white.[239]

Disparate Charging Decisions

There is overwhelming evidence, stretching back to 1993, that prosecutors disparately charge mandatory minimum offenses and enhancements against Black and Brown individuals.[240] These disparities are overwhelming in the Eastern District of North Carolina. From 2016-2020, 57.5 percent of individuals subjected to a federal mandatory minimum in my district were Black, and 18.4 percent of individuals were Hispanic.[241] But in North Carolina, Black individuals make up only 22.2 percent and Hispanic individuals only 9.8 percent of the total population.[242]

Repeated analyses have also shown racial disparity in the decision whether to charge the severe enhancements under 21 U.S.C. § 851 and 18 U.S.C. § 924(c) among those eligible for such enhancements. Eligible Black individuals are charged with § 851 enhancements at a higher rate than eligible White individuals.[243] A 2018 analysis by the U.S. Sentencing Commission showed that Black individuals were 42 percent of those eligible for a § 924(c) enhancement, but 51 percent of those against whom the government sought an 851 enhancement, and 57 percent of those convicted under it.[244] Importantly, although Congress has reduced some penalties associated with § 851 enhancements, they still trigger severe mandatory minimums. And even after the First Step Act's § 851 reforms, prosecutors still disproportionately target

---

[238] U.S. Sent'g Comm'n, *Quick Facts: Crack Cocaine Trafficking Offenses* (FY 2019), https://bit.ly/3wkMhrw; U.S. Census Bureau, *United States Quick Facts*, (last accessed Jun. 14, 2021), https://www.census.gov/quickfacts/fact/table/US/PST045219 (U.S. population estimates as of July 2019).

[239] Joseph J. Palamar, *et al.*, *Powder Cocaine and Crack Use in the United States: An Examination of Risk for Arrest and Socioeconomic Disparities in Use*, J. Drug Alcohol Depend. (Apr. 2015), https://bit.ly/3gw5NdW (67.4% in this study); Deborah Vagins & Jesselyn McCurdy, *Twenty Years of the Unjust Federal Crack Cocaine Law*, The Am. Civil Liberties Union; Washington, DC: 2006. (Oct. 2006), https://bit.ly/3gv98Ks.

[240] U.S. Gov't Accounting Office, GAO/T-GGD-93-40, *Mandatory Minimum Sentences: Are They Being Imposed and Who is Receiving Them?* at 4 (1993), https://bit.ly/3xrMmdj.

[241] *See* USSC, *FY 2016 – FY 2020 Individual Datafiles*.

[242] United States Census, *Quick Facts: North Carolina*, https://bit.ly/2SAbdg4 (last accessed on June 15, 2021).

[243] *See* USSC, *2011 Report* at 257 (30 percent of eligible African American offenders received § 851 enhancements, while 25 percent of eligible white offenders received the enhancement); U.S.S.C, *Fifteen Years of Guideline Sentencing* at 90 (2004) (African Americans were 48 percent of offenders eligible for a § 924(c) enhancement, but 64 percent of those who received it).

[244] USSC, *§ 851 Report* at 7.

black individuals with these enhancements. In the year after the First Step Act was enacted, 53.8 percent of the § 851 of enhancements prosecutors chose to file were against Black individuals.[245]

Similar racial disparities exist when it comes to § 924(c) enhancements. An analysis by the Sentencing Commission showed that Black defendants were 48 percent of those eligible for a § 924(c) enhancement, but 64 percent of those who received it.[246] There are also significant disparities for individuals convicted of multiple counts under § 924(c): Black individuals accounted for more than two-thirds of individuals convicted of multiple counts under § 924(c) but comprised just over half of individuals convicted of § 924(c) overall.[247]

These statistics show that Congress's failure to make the First Step Act's changes to § 851 and § 924 retroactive fall hardest on people of color. Correcting this imbalance is not only a matter of fundamental fairness, it is a matter of racial equity.

Federal Initiatives to Crack Down on "Local" Crime Drive Mass Incarceration and Systematically Target Minority Communities

Another key driver of mass incarceration in America has been federal prosecutor's shift of "focus from crimes with obvious interstate connections to crimes once thought of as purely local."[248] For three decades, federal initiatives touted by prosecutors as the panacea to violent crime have targeted minority communities, with questionable benefit to public safety.[249] Under these initiatives, people who are arrested by state and local police for certain offenses are prosecuted in federal court for the express purpose of imposing more severe prison sentences.[250] The people prosecuted are overwhelmingly people of color."[251]

---

[245] U.S. Sentencing Commission, *First Step Act of 2018 Resentencing Provisions Retroactivity Data Report* at 16 (May 2021), https://bit.ly/2SzsqGj.

[246] U.S.S.C, *Fifteen Years of Guideline Sentencing* at 90 (2004), https://bit.ly/2TxvGlF.

[247] U.S. Sentencing Commission, *Mandatory Minimum Penalties for Firearm Offenses in the Federal Criminal Justice System* at 24 (May 2021), https://bit.ly/2SzsqGj.

[248] Patton, *Criminal Justice Reform and Guns* at 1011.

[249] *Id.*

[250] *Id.*; *see also Legitimacy and Federal Criminal Enforcement Power*, 123 Yale L.J. 2236, 2246 (2014) ("On the whole, federal prosecution results in a more certain conviction and a likely higher sentence than a defendant would receive were he prosecuted in a local county courthouse").

[251] Patton, *Criminal Justice Reform and Guns* at 1012.

The Trump Department doubled down on "tough-on-crime" polices that disproportionately targeted Black and Brown communities. Former Attorney Generals Sessions and Barr established a series of task forces and enforcement initiatives that prioritized federal prosecution of drug, gun and immigration offenses—all categories in which non-white individuals are consistently over-represented.[252]

Policymakers must resist pressure to perpetuate and expand these failed strategies as a "rise in crime rates threatens to push cities back toward old patterns, imperiling the many overdue experiments in public safety finally taking place."[253] But there are troubling signs that the Department will not heed the lessons of the past.

On May 26, 2021, Deputy Attorney General Lisa Monaco announced the Department's "Comprehensive Strategy for Reducing Violent Crime," which centers on expanding a nationwide program called "Project Safe Neighborhoods."[254] Project Safe Neighborhoods, launched by President Bush, was an effort to increase firearm prosecutions nationwide. The federal government hired hundreds of new prosecutors and law enforcement agents to bring federal prosecutions for gun crimes—largely simple possession—that would have otherwise proceeded in state courts.[255] Under the program, which has been in place since 2001, federal prosecutions for "felon-in-possession" have proliferated.[256] Since 1968, it has been a federal crime for anyone previously convicted of a felony to possess a gun—with no requirement that the person used the gun in a crime or traveled across state lines.[257] The

---

[252] *See, e.g.*, Mem. From Jeff Sessions, Att'y Gen., U.S. Dep't of Just., to all Federal Prosecutors on *Commitment to Targeting Violent Crime* (March 8, 2017), https://bit.ly/2StYoUJ; Press Release, Dep't of Just., Attorney Jeff Sessions Announces the Formation of Operation Synthetic Opioid Surge(S.O.S) (Jul. 12, 2018) ("Each participating United States Attorney's Office (USAO) will choose a specific county and prosecute every readily provable case involving the distribution of fentanyl, fentanyl analogues, and other synthetic opioids, regardless of drug quantity."), https://bit.ly/3gBdm33; Press Release, Dep't of Just., Attorney General William P. Barr Announces Launch of Operation Legend (Jul. 8, 2020), https://bit.ly/3iJkzkd.

[253] *See* Editorial Board, *Violent Crime is Spiking. We Must Still Reimagine Public Safety*, Wash. Post (Jun. 5, 2021), https://wapo.st/3xpwRSP.

[254] Mem. from Lisa Monaco, Deputy Att'y Gen., U.S. Dep't of Just., to Department of Justice Employees on *Comprehensive Strategy for Reducing Violent Crime* (May 26, 2021), https://bit.ly/3guWPxD (describing Project Safe Neighborhoods as the "leading initiative that brings together federal, state, local, and tribal law enforcement officials, prosecutors, and a broad array of community stakeholders to identify the most pressing violent crime problems in an area and to develop comprehensive solutions to address them").

[255] Gardner, *Separate and Unequal* at 311.

[256] Patton, *Criminal Justice Reform and Guns* at 1013–1022.

[257] Gun Control Act of 1968, Pub. L. No. 90-618, § 102, 82 Stat. 1213, 1221 (1968).

overwhelming majority of Project Safe Neighborhoods gun prosecutions focus on felon-in-possession charges, despite the existence of "twenty major federal gun crimes—including gun trafficking, corrupt gun dealers, stolen guns, selling to minors, obliterating serial numbers, and lying on the background check form."[258] From 2016-2020, 78.5 percent of federal firearm convictions nationally were for being a felon in possession of a firearm.[259]

"[Project Safe Neighborhoods]specifically targets communities of color for punishment above and beyond what would already be significant punishment in state court."[260] More than half of all Black individuals in the United States live in just 30 cities, all of which were targeted as part of Project Safe Neighborhoods.[261] In the Eastern District of Michigan, "almost ninety percent of those prosecuted under Project Safe Neighborhoods [were] African American."[262] Likewise, in the Southern District of New York, "testimony show[ed] that more than eighty percent of defendants prosecuted under the project were African American."[263] And in the Southern District of Ohio, "more than ninety percent" of individuals prosecuted under the program were Black.[264] These are the disparities from cities that collect and disclose their task force priorities and data, or were required to produce discovery about them in civil rights litigation. But there are many local police departments and sheriffs' offices that do not collect and/or disclose special enforcement data. Without transparency, special enforcement projects are not accountable to this body or the public. Task forces supported with federal funds should be required to keep and disclose data. These consistent disparities in cities spread across the country show that policies which divert gun crimes to federal court disproportionately subject Black individuals to federal prosecution and sentencing. This is true in the Eastern District of North Carolina, where the government prosecutes Black people in 81.4. percent of felon-in-possession cases.[265]

The racial disparities in federal firearm prosecutions are inextricably linked to the War on Drugs. The disparate enforcement of drug laws against

---

[258] Gardner, *Separate and Unequal* at 313.

[259] *See* U.S. Sent'g Comm'n, *FY 2016 – FY 2020 Individual Datafiles.*

[260] Patton, *Criminal Justice Reform and Guns* at 1203.

[261] Emma Shreefter, *Federal Felon-in-Possession Gun Laws: Criminalizing a Status, Disparately Affecting Black Defendants, and Continuing the Nation's Centuries-Old Methods to Disarm Black Communities*, 21 CUNY L. Rev. 143,163 (2018); Gardner, *Separate and Unequal* at 316.

[262] Gardner, *Separate and Unequal* at 313–317.

[263] *Id.*

[264] *Id.*

[265] *See* U.S. Sent'g Comm'n, *FY 2016 – FY 2020 Individual Datafiles.*

Black and Brown individuals has shaped a criminal justice system in which people of color are overrepresented: A 2021 Sentencing Project report found that Black men are six times more likely than white men to be incarcerated at some point during their lifetimes.[266] And there is little to show in improvements to public safety for this devastating approach: "[E]mpirical research on the relationship between federal gun possession prosecutions and crime rates strongly suggests that the prosecutions have little or no impact."[267]

The Department's newest iteration of Project Safe Neighborhoods shows some awareness of these issues, and Senior Justice Department officials have emphasized that Project Safe Neighborhoods will include non-prosecutorial strategies, and "measure progress based on how many crimes were averted, rather than on the number of arrests and prosecutions."[268] But past experience gives good reason to fear that the prosecutorial component of Project Safe Neighborhoods will dominate, further entrenching stark racial disparities and continuing to drive mass incarceration. In original form, the Project Safe Neighborhoods toolkit included both prosecutorial and non-prosecutorial tools, but the latter were "much less frequently and sporadically implemented."[269]

Policy Recommendations

President Biden has pledged to move away from the failed War on Drugs by ending the use of mandatory minimums[270] and to eradicate racial inequities in the criminal justice system.[271] These principles should guide the Subcommittee's deliberations about how to respond to the daunting challenge of overincarceration. It is time for the government to adjust its policies to prioritize evidence-based strategies to stop people from entering prison, shorten the length of sentences, and better support individuals who reenter the community from prison. It goes without saying that we cannot incarcerate our

---

[266] The Sentencing Project, *Trends in U.S. Corrections* at 5 (updated May 2021) https://bit.ly/3vyC6i5.

[267] Patton, *Criminal Justice Reform and Guns* at 1020–21.

[268] Blake Diaz, *'Culture of Transparency,' Police Overhauls Can Reduce Violent Crime: DOJ* (May 27, 2021), https://bit.ly/3vmfGQN.

[269] Patton, *Criminal Justice Reform and Guns* at 1019.

[270] Joe Biden, *The Biden Plan for Strengthening America's Commitment to Justice*, https://bit.ly/32l6Abb (last visited April 12, 2021).

[271] Proclamation 10171, *A Proclamation on Second Chance Month, 2021*, 86 Fed. Reg. 64, 17689–90 (March 31, 2021), https://bit.ly/328V8ze.

way out of a mass incarceration crisis. Professors Alison Siegler, Erica Zunkel, and Judith P. Miller of the Federal Criminal Justice Clinic, have proposed a comprehensive set of policy reforms that could correct many of these problems; I recommend them and incorporate them here.[272]

End Mandatory Minimums

The most important step that Congress and the Administration could take to remediate America's harmful and ineffective sentencing would be to enact legislation to end mandatory minimums, especially in drug cases, and apply those changes retroactively. There is widespread, bipartisan agreement that mandatory minimum drug laws are "inhumane, racially discriminatory, waste taxpayer money, and deprive judges of sentencing discretion."[273] Further, any reform legislation must be retroactive: legal reforms that are not unfairly leave far too many behind bars.

Short of repealing all mandatory minimums, there are several existing legislative proposals to address mandatory minimums and make sentencing fairer:

- The First Step Implementation Act would allow courts to apply the sentencing reform provisions of the First Step Act of 2018 to reduce sentences that were imposed prior to the enactment of the FSA, modestly expand the safety valve, and make technical corrections to the First Step Act[274];
- The EQUAL Act (Eliminating a Quantifiably Unjust Application of the Law) would eliminate the crack-powder 18-1 crack ratio.[275]
- Pass legislation to expand safety valve provisions to allow judges to sentence below the mandatory minimum. The Justice Safety Valve Act of 2019 gives courts broad discretion to impose a sentence below a mandatory minimum if the court finds that it is necessary to do so in order to impose a sentence that is not greater than necessary to comply with the statutory purposes of sentencing enumerated in 18 U.S.C. 3553(a). It requires courts to give the parties reasonable notice

---

[272] Siegler, *University of Chicago Statement*.
[273] *Id.* at 17.
[274] First Step Implementation Act of 2021, S. 1014, 117th Cong. (2021).
[275] EQUAL Act, S. 79., 117th Cong. (2021); Reps. Jeffries, Scott, Armstrong, and Bacon Introduce Bipartisan Bill to Eliminate Sentencing Disparity Between Crack and Powder Cocaine (Mar. 9, 2021), https://bit.ly/3xnewWQ.

of its intent to do so and provide a written statement of reasons for imposing a sentence below the mandatory minimum.[276]

- The Mandatory Minimum Reform Act of 2020 would eliminate mandatory minimum sentences for drug offenses.[277]
- The Second Look Act would allow any individual who has served at least 10 years in federal prison to petition a court to take a "second look" at their sentence before a judge and determine whether they are eligible for a sentence reduction or release. The legislation would create a rebuttable presumption of release for petitioners who are 50 years of age or older.[278]
- The Smarter Sentencing Act would reduce the mandatory minimums for certain drug offenses in the Controlled Substances Act (21 U.S.C. § 841(b)(1) and the Controlled Substances Import and Export Act (21 U.S.C. § 960(b)) from 5, 10, and 20 years to 2, 5, and 10 years.[279]
- The MORE Act (Marijuana Opportunity Reinvestment and Expungement Act) would begin to repair the racially-disparate effects of past marijuana policy and begin to curb the destructive effects of longstanding federal policy.[280]
- Congress should also allow the classwide scheduling of fentanyl analogues to expire in October 2021.[281] Classwide scheduling returns us to the failed and unjust strategies of the drug war by expanding mandatory minimums and prosecutorial discretion to target communities of color.[282]

---

276 Justice Safety Valve Act of 2019, S. 399, 116th Cong. (2019).

277 Mandatory Minimum Reform Act of 2020, 116th Cong. (2019).

278 Second Look Act of 2019, S. 2146, 116th Cong. (2019); Booker, Bass to Introduce Groundbreaking Bill to Give "Second Look" to Those Behind Bars (Jul. 15, 2019). https://bit.ly/3wrElVA.

279 Smarter Sentencing Act, S. 1013, 117th Cong. (2021); Press Release, Durbin, Lee Introduce Smarter Sentencing Act (Mar. 26, 2021), https://bit.ly/3pV24e4.

280 Marijuana Opportunity Reinvestment and Expungement (MORE) Act, H.R. 3884, 116th Cong. (2019–2020); *see also* Siegler, *University of Chicago Statement* at 46–50.

281 *Extending Temporary Emergency Scheduling of Fentanyl Analogues Act*, Pub. L. 117-12 (2021).

282 *Hearing on "An Epidemic within a Pandemic: Understanding Substance Use and Misuse in America*: Hearing Before the Subcomm. on Health of the H. Comm. on Energy and Commerce, 117th Cong. 4 n.18 (Apr. 14, 2021) (Testimony of Patricia L. Richman, National Sentencing Resource Counsel for the Federal Public & Community Defenders), https://bit.ly/3iGCOa4.

In addition to proposals already included in proposed laws, Congress should consider other interventions to ameliorate the severity of the federal legal system:

- Congress should eliminate or reduce recidivist enhancements, by repealing 21 U.S.C. § 851 and amending 21 U.S.C. § 841 and § 960 accordingly;
- Follow the U.S. Sentencing Commission's recommendation to remove individuals with prior drug convictions from the Career Offender directive in 21 U.S.C. § 994(h).[283]
- Congress must act to clarify that the First Step Act of 2018 entitles individuals who commit the least serious crack-cocaine offenses to a reduced sentence.
- Marijuana convictions should not trigger recidivist mandatory minimum enhancements in cases prosecuted in federal jurisdictions where marijuana is legal.
- Marijuana possession in connection with a 924(c) should not be eligible for the five-year mandatory minimum for individuals below the age 26 and first-time federal offenders.

There are also several steps that Congress could take to blunt the coerciveness of the Trial Penalty:

- Under current law, an individual may be sentenced for conduct that a jury has acquitted him or her of at trial. This is deeply unfair, weakens the finality and citizen oversight that a jury trial provides, and disincentivizes defendants from going to trial. The bipartisan Prohibiting Punishment of Acquitted Conduct Act, introduced during the 116th Congress, would eliminate consideration of acquitted conduct by federal courts during sentencing;[284]
- Enact open-file discovery to ensure fair trails, by ensuring that individuals are given full access to all relevant evidence, including any exculpatory information, and grand jury transcripts prior to entry of a guilty plea and trial.

---

283 U.S. Sent'g Comm'n, *Report to Congress: Career Offender Sentencing Enhancements* 27 (2016), https://bit.ly/35kQxvg; *see also* Siegler, *University of Chicago Statement* at 34-35.

284 Prohibiting Punishment of Acquitted Conduct Act of 2021, S. 601, 117th Cong. (2021).

Curtail the Federalization of Local Crime

Congress can also intercede to reduce the footprint of the federal legal system and decrease federal prosecutions for local crime:

- Programs like Project Safe Neighborhoods are driven by federal grant dollars that focus on enforcement-oriented goals and outcomes. Congress should overhaul the Department of Justice's grantmaking strategy to focus on goals of ending mass incarceration, promoting comprehensive public health and safety, and ensuring accountability in policing. Department grant recipients should be required to keep enforcement data like locations, age of arrestees, race, ethnicity and Use of Force criteria.
- This subcommittee should also conduct oversight hearings to examine the Department of Justice's charging and enforcement policies for simple gun and drug possession offenses in majority Black and Brown communities.

Adopt a Public Health Approach to Drug Misuse and Mental Health

It is time for the government to adjust its drug policy to prioritize evidence-based strategies to effectively fight this critical public health issue. Congress should encourage robust partnerships with doctors, psychiatrists, psychologists and public health experts. Further, the government must prioritize delivering quality mental health and substance abuse treatment to incarcerated and reentering individuals by adequately funding substance abuse rehabilitation and reentry centers.

Several legislative proposals under consideration in the 117th Congress hold the potential to move drug policy in our country in the right direction, including:

- The Medicaid Reentry Act of 2021[285] provides a bridge for individuals reentering the community by providing health care 30 days prior to release and on reentry. Ninety-five percent of the more than 2 million adults who are incarcerated in the United States will be released and the transition back into the community is a critical period for those with mental illness and substance use disorder.[286] One study

---

[285] H.R. 955 (2021).

[286] *See* Lakeesha Woods et al., *The Role of Prevention in Promoting Continuity of Health Care in Prisoner Reentry Initiatives*, 103 Am. J. Pub. 830–8 (2013), https://bit.ly/3mGuA1N.

found that risk of a fatal drug overdose is 129 times as high as it is for the general population during the two weeks after release.[287]

- The Mainstreaming Addiction Treatment Act of 2021[288] eliminates the redundant "X-waiver" to prescribe buprenorphine for substance use disorder treatment. Buprenorphine is one of the three medications approved by the FDA to treat opioid use disorder and reduces mortality by up to fifty percent.[289]
- The Support, Treatment, and Overdose Prevention of Fentanyl Act of 2021[290] proposes a comprehensive health- and evidence-based response to fentanyl and its analogues. Rather than turn to policing and incarceration, the STOP Fentanyl Act adopts an evidence-based response to the opioid crisis.

Ensure Parity in Sentencing Policy

Finally, Congress must also make structural changes to the criminal justice system to diversify the voices who shape federal sentencing policy. For example, the composition of the U.S. Sentencing Commission shows the pervasive tilt towards law enforcement in sentencing policy. The U.S. Sentencing Commission is tasked, inter alia, with "advis[ing] and assist[ing] Congress and the executive branch in the development of effective and efficient crime policy."[291] The seven voting members on the Commission are appointed by the President and confirmed by the Senate to serve six-year terms. The Attorney General and the Parole Commission serve as nonvoting, ex officio members of the Commission. But the Commission has no such role for the federal public defenders—who represent most of the individuals in the federal criminal legal system. Congress should improve the quality of, and public confidence in, the U.S. Sentencing Commission's work by adding a Federal Defender ex officio representative to balance existing representatives from the executive branch. The Judicial Conference has long endorsed the need for this reform.

---

[287] *See* Ingrid A. Binswanger, et al., *Release from Prison—A High Risk of Death for Former Inmates*, 356 New Eng. J. Med. 157–65 (Jan. 11, 2007), https://bit.ly/3uDbMTE.

[288] H.R. 1384 (2021).

[289] Nat'l Acads. of Sci., Eng'g, and Med, *Medications for Opioid Use Disorder Save Lives* (2019), https://bit.ly/3uJfWto.

[290] H.R. 2366 (2021).

[291] 18 U.S.C. § 994.

Conclusion

It is a myth that longer sentences improve public safety. The wide net of "tough on crime" policies disproportionally impact people of color, our youth, and vulnerable individuals with addiction and mental illness. In the words of Chairman Nadler, "[m]andatory minimum penalties are unwise, unjust, and unfair. The status quo is unacceptable, and we need to take a hard look at reforming these penalties."[292] Congress is equipped to tackle these problems and to chart a new path. I urge this Subcommittee to treat these issues with the urgent attention they need and thank the Subcommittee and appreciate the invitation to share my perspective on this important issue.

* * *

Ms. JACKSON LEE. Thank you for your testimony. Mr. Malcolm, you're now recognized for 5 minutes.

Statement of John Malcolm

Mr. MALCOLM. Chair Jackson Lee, Vice-Chair Bush, Ranking Member Biggs, and distinguished Members of Congress, I am the Vice President of the Institute for Constitutional Government and the Director of the Meese Center for Legal and Judicial Studies at The Heritage Foundation.

Although I have spent much of my career as a Federal prosecutor, I recognize that our criminal justice system is far from perfect and that when it comes to sentences in drug cases, the pendulum can swing too far.

Based on recent changes in State laws, it also seems clear that a lot of people believe that we should recalibrate how we tackle the drug problem that continues to plague our country. Sentencing reform is part of that ongoing discussion.

Let me offer a few thoughts on some of the proposals that you are considering.

---

[292] Press Release, House Committee on the Judiciary, Chairman Nadler Statement for Subcommittee Hearing on "Controlled Substances: Federal Policies and Enforcement," (Mar. 11, 2021), https://bit.ly/3gvUSRw.

Regarding the First Step Implementation Act, I endorse any effort to ensure that the First Step Act is fully implemented. While there are many parts of this bill that I support, there are some that give me pause.

So, the First Step Act modestly reduced mandatory minimum penalties for certain repeat drug offenders, but only on a prospective basis. In addition to making these changes retroactive, the First Step Implementation Act would expand eligibility to those who commit a serious violent felony.

I question whether this expansion makes sense at a time when we have experienced a dramatic spike in violent crime, although I recognize that eligibility for sentencing reconsideration does not mean that an offender will automatically—or even very often—get his sentence reduced.

The Act would also enable a judge to take a second look at the sentence imposed on a juvenile offender who has served a minimum of 20 years.

I have similar concerns with respect to juvenile offenders who commit unspeakably violent crimes. I recognize that such offenders would not be eligible for relief until they had spent over half their lives behind bars.

The Act would also expand the current safety valve to allow a judge to impose a sentence below a mandatory minimum if the judge determines that a defendant's criminal record substantially overrepresents the seriousness of the defendant's criminal history or the likelihood that the defendant will commit other crimes.

While I believe that the safety valve was too stringent prior to the passage of the First Step Act, I'm a bit uncomfortable with expanding the safety valve to recidivists who have more than four criminal history points based on such inherently subjective factors or criteria.

The EQUAL Act would eliminate altogether the current 18–1 disparity between crack cocaine and powder cocaine offenders when it comes to imposing mandatory minimum penalties, and it would make this change retroactive.

There is some evidence that suggests that crack is more addictive than powder cocaine based on the different ways that the two drugs are ingested and the fact that crack is much cheaper. The vast majority of States, though, do not treat crack cocaine any differently from powder cocaine.

Additionally, regardless of the intent behind these laws, it is clear that the greatest impact, both in terms of extremely long sentences handed down to offenders and the devastation that drugs have wrought, has been felt in communities of color.

While I don't have a settled view on whether it makes sense to completely eliminate the differential, the current 18–1 disparity certainly does strike me as excessive.

Both the First Step Implementation Act and the EQUAL Act have provisions that would apply retroactively. While I respect the legitimate concerns expressed by many about applying changes in sentencing laws retroactively, I believe that if society has made a judgment that certain sentences are unduly harsh, then it must believe that those sentences were too harsh and unjust when they were originally imposed.

In my opinion, enabling a judge to reconsider a sentence is a smaller price to pay than allowing offenders to languish in prison for longer than society now deems is just.

In conclusion, let me say that the work you're doing will have a dramatic impact on both the victims and perpetrators of crime and their families. It will also shape how people view our criminal justice system in terms of its effectiveness and its fairness.

Over the years, I have dealt with many people who approach these issues from different ideological perspectives. Some believe the system should be changed because of systemic racism or mass incarceration. Others believe we do not place enough emphasis on rehabilitation and redemption.

While I don't always agree with them, I acknowledge that people who espouse these views believe them passionately and sincerely. In speaking to these thought leaders, I have often been struck at how often people agree about what ought to be done even if they disagree about why those measures are warranted.

Sadly, too often nothing gets done, either because people get caught up on the "why" rather than focusing on the "what" or because they insist on an all-or-nothing approach with respect to the proposals they support.

As you deliberate, I would urge you to focus on your areas of agreement and not let the perfect be the enemy of the good.

I thank you for inviting me here to testify today, and I would be happy to answer any questions you might have.

[The statement of Mr. Malcolm follows:]

Legislative Testimony, "Undoing the Damage of the War on Drugs: A Renewed Call for Sentencing Reform," Testimony before the Committee on the Judiciary, Subcommittee on Crime, Terrorism, and Homeland Security, U.S. House of Representatives, June 17, 2021

John G. Malcolm
Vice President, Institute for Constitutional Government
Director and Ed Gilbertson and Sherry Lindberg Gilbertson Senior Legal Fellow, Edwin Meese III Center for Legal and Judicial Studies
The Heritage Foundation

Chairwoman Lee, Vice Chair Bush, Ranking Member Biggs, and distinguished Members of Congress:

Thank you for the opportunity to appear before you today to discuss some of the various criminal justice reform proposals that you are currently considering. My name is John Malcolm. I am the Vice President of the Institute for Constitutional Government and the Director and Ed Gilbertson and Sherry Lindberg Gilbertson Senior Legal Fellow in the Edwin Meese III Center for Legal and Judicial Studies at The Heritage Foundation.[293] I have also spent a good deal of my career involved in the criminal justice system—as an Assistant United States Attorney, an Associate Independent Counsel, a Deputy Assistant Attorney General in the Criminal Division at the U.S. Justice Department, and a criminal defense attorney.

A lot of my scholarship has focused on various aspects of our criminal justice system.[294] In 2013, I had the privilege of testifying before the House

[293] The title and affilia tion are for identification purposes. Members of The Heritage Foundationstaff testify as individuals discussing their own independent research. The views expressed here are my own and donot reflect an institutional positionfor The Heritage Foundation or its board of trustees. The Heritage Foundation is a public policy, research, and educationalorganizationrecognized as exemptunder section 501(c)(3) of the Internal Revenue Code. It is priva tely supported andreceives no funds from anygovernment atany level, nor does it perform any government or other contract work. The Heritage Foundation is the most broadly supportedthinktank in the United States. During 2017, it hadhundreds of thousands of individuals, foundation, and corporate supporters representing every sta te in the U.S. Its 2017 incomecame from thefollowing sources: Individuals 71%, Foundations 9%, Corporations 4%, Program revenue andother income 16%. The topfive corporate givers provided The Heritage Foundationwith 3.0% of its 2017 income. The Heritage Foundation's books a re auditedannually by the national accounting firm of RSM US, LLP.

[294] John G. Malcolm, *Do We Have a Mass Incarceration Problem? Compared to What?*, CATO UNBOUND, July 16, 2020, available at https://www.cato-unbound.org/2020/07/16/john-

malcolm/do-we-have-mass-incarceration- problem-compared-what; John G. Ma lcolm and Cully Stimson, *Reform of Policing: What Makes Sense—and What Doesn't*, DAILY SIGNAL, June 11, 2020, available at https://www.dailysignal.com/2020/06/11/reform-of-policing- wha t-makes-sense-and-what-doesnt/; John G. Ma lcolm and Brett Tolman, *A Bill to Give Former Inmates a Second Chance*, DAILY SIGNAL, Aug. 26, 2019, availa ble athttps://www.dailysignal.com/2019/08/26/a-bill-to-give-former- inma tes-a-second-chance/; John G. Malcolm and Brett Tolman, *Why It's Not "Soft On Crime" to Support Criminal Justice Reform*, DAILY SIGNAL, Aug. 20, 2018, available at https://www.dailysignal.com/2018/08/20/why-its-not- soft-on-crime-to-support-criminal-justice-reform/; John G. Ma lcolm, *Criminal Justice Reform a Big Part of Orrin Hatch's Legacy*, DAILY SIGNAL, June 25, 2018, available athttps://www.dailysignal.com/ 2018/06/25/criminal-justice-reform-a-big-part-of-orrin-hatchs-legacy/; John G. Ma lcolm and John-Michael Seibler, *House-Passed Prison Reforms Would Help Strengthen Families and Communities*, DAILY SIGNAL, May 23, 2018, available at https://www.dailysignal.com/2018/05/23/house-passed-prison-reforms-would-help-strengthen-families-and- communities/; John G. Ma lcolm, *The Problem with the Proliferation of Collateral Consequences*, FEDERALIST SOC'Y REV., Jan. 29, 2018, available at https://fedsoc.org/commentary/publications/the-problem-with-the-proliferation-of-colla teral-consequences; John G. Ma lcolm, *Morally Innocent, Legally Guilty: The Case for Mens Rea Reform*, FEDERALIST SOC'Y REV., Sept. 7, 2017, available at https://fedsoc.org/commentary/publications/morally-innocent-legally-guilty-the-case-for-mens-rea-reform; John G. Ma lcolm and Hon. Michael Mukasey, *Criminal Lawand the Administrative State: How the Proliferation of Regulatory Offenses Undermines the Moral Authorityof Our Criminal Laws*, *in* LIBERTY'S NEMESIS: THE UNCHECKED EXPANSION OF THE STATE 283 (Dean Reuter & John Yoo eds., Encounter Books 2016); John G. Ma lcolm, *Criminal Justice Reform at the Crossroads*, 20 TEX. REV. LAW & POL. 249 (2016), availa ble at https://static1. squarespace.com/static/57cd857d3e00bed93bb34aea/t/57cd9d09725e25df3efd2203/1473 092875109/F INAL-FORMAT-Malcolm_Website-1.pdf; John G. Ma lcolm and Hon. Michael Mukasey, *The Importance of Meaningful Mens Rea Reform*, HERITAGE FOUND., Feb. 17, 2016, availa ble athttps://www.heritage.org/crime-and- justice/ commentary/the-importance-meaningful-mens-rea-reform; John G. Malcolm, *The Pressing Need for Mens Rea Reform*, HERITAGE FOUND., Sept. 1, 2015, available at https://www.heritage.org/crime-and-justice/report/the- pressing-need-mens-rea-reform; John G. Ma lcolm and Paul Larkin, *Obama Is Right That We Need to Reform the Criminal Justice System*, DAILY SIGNAL, Jan. 20, 2015, available at https://www. dailysignal.com/2015/01/20/obama-got-right-wrong-state-union/#headline4; John G. Ma lcolm, *Criminal Law and the Administrative State: The Problems with Criminal Regulations*, HERITAGE FOUND., Aug. 6, 2014, available at https://www.heritage.org/crime-and-justice/report/criminal-law-and-the-administrative-state-the- problem-criminal-regulations; John G. Malcolm, *The Case for the Smarter Sentencing Act*, HERITAGE FOUND., July 28, 2014, availa ble athttps://www.heritage. org/crime-and-justice/commentary/the-case-the-smarter-sentencing-act; John G. Malcolm, *Over-Criminalization Undermines Respect for Legal System*, HERITAGE FOUND., Dec. 11, 2013, availa ble athttps://www.heritage.org/crime-and-justice/commentary/over-criminalization-undermines-respect-legal- system.

Judiciary Committee's Over-Criminalization Task Force,[295] and I was an outspoken supporter of the First Step Act[296] and other criminal justice reform proposals. Although I spent much of my career as a federal prosecutor and am a scholar at a prominent conservative think tank, I recognize that our criminal justice system is far from perfect and that, when it comes to creating new crimes or increasing sentences for new and old crimes, sometimes the pendulum can swing too far.

I am aware that you are currently considering a number of criminal justice reform proposals including the Eliminating a Quantifiably Unjust Application of the Law (EQUAL) Act,[297] the Reforming Alternatives to Incarceration and Sentencing to Establish a Better Path for Youth (RAISE) Act,[298] the Community-Based Sentencing Alternatives for Caretakers Act,[299] the First Step Implementation Act,[300] and the Prohibiting Punishment of Acquitted Conduct Act,[301] among others. Even though I have concerns about some of these proposals, I applaud you for debating these issues. All of you care about public safety, although I recognize that there may be disagreements among you about whether some of these proposals will enhance or hurt public safety in the long run.

These are particularly difficult issues in relation to the "war on drugs," a phrase first used by President Richard Nixon in 1971 at a press conference where he identified drug abuse as "public enemy number one in the United States." There is no question that this effort has entailed a high social and economic cost.

A complicating factor in any discussion about drug offenses is that while many consider drug dealing to be a nonviolent offense, there are others, myself included, who are uncomfortable with this label "since drug dealing is often

---

[295] *Defining the Problem and Scopeof Over-Criminalization and Over-Federalization—Testimony before the Committeeon the Judiciary Over-criminalization Task Force, U.S. House of Representatives on June 14, 2013*, HERITAGE FOUND., available at https://www.heritage.org/testimony/defining-the-problem-and-scope-over-criminalization-and-over-federalization.

[296] First Step Act of 2018, Pub. L. No. 115-391, 132 Stat. 5194, untitled (congress.gov).

[297] EQUAL Act, H.R. 1693, 117th Cong. (2021), BILLS-117hr1693ih.pdf (congress.gov). A companion bill, S. 79, has been introduced in the Senate.

[298] RAISE Act of 2021, H.R. 128, 117th Cong. (2021), BILLS-117hr128ih.pdf (congress.gov).

[299] Community-Based Sentencing Alternatives for Caretakers Act of 2021, H.R. 2277, 117th Cong. (2021), BILLS- 117hr2277ih.pdf (congress.gov).

[300] First Step Implementation Act of 2021, S. 1014, 117th Cong. (2021), BILLS-117s1014is.pdf (congress.gov).

[301] Prohibiting Punishment of Acquitted Conduct Act of 2021, H.R. 1621 & S. 601 (a s amended bythe Senate Judicia ry Committee), 117th Cong. (2021), BILLS-117s601is.pdf (congress.gov).

carried out by gangs, and almost invariably involves the actual or threatened use of violence and the inherent risk of overdose."[302] It seems clear, though, based on recent efforts in many states to decriminalize or legalize the possession of certain drugs that are still prohibited under federal law, that many members of the public believe that we need to recalibrate how we tackle the drug problems that continue to plague our country, as evidenced, for example, by the current opioid epidemic.[303] Many states have instituted drug courts[304] and other specialized courts. Sentencing reform at both the state and federal levels is, of course, part of that ongoing discussion.

The following are my thoughts on a couple of the proposals that you are considering.

The First Step Implementation Act

The First Step Act of 2018 modestly reduced the mandatory minimum penalties for certain repeat drug offenders[305] and eliminated the ability of prosecutors to "stack" mandatory minimum sentences under 18 U.S.C. § 924(c) for using a firearm during a crime of violence or drug crime.[306] The

---

[302] John G. Ma lcolm and Jason Snead, *As Justice Department Ramps Up Fight Against Violent and Drug Crime, Property Owners Put at Risk*, DAILY SIGNAL, July 21,2017, available at https://www.heritage.org/crime-and- justice/commentary/justice-department-ramps-fight-against-violent-and-drug-crime-property.

[303] According to the Na tional Institute on Drug Abuse (internal footnotes omitted): "In 2019, nearly 50,000 people in the United Sta tes died from opioid-involved overdoses. Themisuse of andaddiction to opioids—including prescription pain relievers, heroin, andsynthetic opioids such as fentanyl—is a serious national crisis that affects public hea lth as well as socialandeconomic welfare. The Centers for Disea se Controland Preventionestimates that the total 'economic burden' of prescription opioid misuse alone in the United States is $78.5 billion a year, including the costs of healthcare, lost productivity, addiction treatment, andcriminal justice involvement." *Opioid Overdose Crisis*, NAT'L INST. ON DRUG ABUSE, https://www.drugabuse.gov/drug-topics/opioids/opioid-overdose-crisis (la st visited June 14, 2021).

[304] *See, e.g.*, *What Are Drug Courts?*, NAT'L. DRUG CT. RES. CTR., availa ble athttps://ndcrc.org/what-are-drug- courts/ (la st visited June 14, 2021).

[305] For example, the mandatory minimum penalty for a second drug offense was reduced from 20 years to 15 years, and the mandatory minimum penalty for a third drug offense was reduced from life imprisonment to 25 years.

[306] The Act clarified that an offender cannot receive the 25-year mandatory sentence for a repeat 924(c) offense unless he had previously been convicted and served a sentence for such an offense.

First Step Act made these changes applicable only to offenses committed after December 21, 2018, the effective date of the statute.[307]

Section 101 of the First Step Implementation Act would enable offenders who committed their crimes prior to that date to petition a court for a reduction in sentence based on the new sentencing structure brought about by the First Step Act. It would also expand eligibility from those who committed a "felony drug offense" to those who committed a "serious drug felony or serious violent felony."

Section 102 of the First Step Implementation Act would expand the current "safety valve"[308] to allow a court to impose a sentence below a mandatory minimum if the judge "specifies in writing the specific reasons why reliable information indicates that excluding the defendant pursuant to [the limitations set forth in the current safety valve] substantially overrepresents the seriousness of the defendant's criminal history or the likelihood that the defendant will commit other crimes."

Section 201 provides potential relief to juvenile offenders—defined as those who "committed and completed" their crimes before turning 18 years of age—who were "convicted as an adult" by providing a "second look" after the offender has served a minimum of 20 years in prison, thereby enabling a judge to reduce that offender's sentence but only if the judge concludes that "the defendant is not a danger to the safety of the community and that the interests of justice warrant a sentence modification." The defendant would not be permitted to file more than three applications for relief, with a minimum of five years having elapsed between applications.

In order to give certain juvenile offenders the opportunity to start with a clean slate upon reaching adulthood, Section 202 would facilitate the sealing or expungement of juvenile delinquency adjudications and juvenile criminal records for certain eligible, nonviolent offenders.[309] It would also "prevent the unauthorized use or disclosure of [such records] and any potential employment, financial, psychological, or other harm that would result from

---

[307] This is in sta rk contrast to another provision of the First Step Act, Section 404, which enabled certain crack cocaineoffenders sentenced prior to the effective dateof the Fa ir Sentencing Act of 2010 to petition for a reduction in sentence based onthe changes in the la wthat were brought about bythat Act.

[308] *See* 18 U.S.C. § 3553(f) (listing the current list of criteria that must be met for a person to qualify for the safety valve).

[309] Many states have already enacted laws providing for the sealing or expungement of certain criminal convictions, including for juvenile offenders. See *50-State Comparison: Expungement, Sealing & Other Record Relief* RESTORATION OF RTS. PROJECT, ava ilable at https://ccresourcecenter.org/state-restoration-profiles/50-state- comparison judicial-expungement-sealing-a nd-set-aside/ (last visited June 14, 2021).

such unauthorized use or disclosure," subjecting those who intentionally violate this provision to potential criminal penalties.[310] The section includes some sensible exceptions related to investigations conducted by, or potential employment with, certain federal agencies involved in law enforcement, national security, the military, and other designated "high-risk, public trust position[s]" within federal agencies. The section also includes an exception whenever a juvenile offender whose records have been sealed or expunged testifies "in a criminal or other proceeding if such disclosure is required by the Constitution of the United States, the constitution of a State, or a Federal or State statute or rule."

Section 203 would require the Attorney General to establish and enforce procedures to ensure the accuracy of criminal records that are sought for employment-related purposes. This is important because such records, which are often inaccurate or incomplete,[311] are routinely sought by would-be employers who are conducting background checks and can have a devastating effect on an individual's employment prospects. Accordingly, this section provides a process for people to challenge or correct records regarding their criminal history (or lack thereof).

I wholeheartedly endorse and applaud any effort to ensure that all parts of the First Step Act are fully and effectively implemented, and there are several provisions in this bill that I support. That having been said, there are parts of this bill that give me some pause. For example, regarding Section 101, I question whether expanding eligibility for sentencing reconsideration to those who have been convicted of a "serious violent felony" makes sense during a time in which we have experienced a dramatic spike in violent crime in this country,[312] although I do recognize that eligibility for sentencing

[310] I note that there a re other currently existing federal sta tutes thatwould most likely apply to such conduct, including 18 U.S.C. § 402 (contempts constituting crimes). If Congress wishes to ensure thatuses anddisclosures of the type envisioned in this section are treatedsolely as misdemeanors, it might wa nt to consider addinglanguage that would preclude a federal prosecutor from charging such uses anddisclosures as felonies. Additionally, while I acknowledge that thesection provides a mens rea standard that is reasonably strong, I would encourage Congress to consider utilizing the more robust "willfulness" standard here.

[311] *See* Nicole Weissman and Marina Duane, *Five problems with Criminal Background Checks*, URB. INST., March 13, 2017, available at https://www.urban.org/urban-wire/five-problems-criminal-background-checks; *Faulty FBI Background Checks for Employment: Correcting FBI Records Is Key to Criminal Justice Reform*, NAT'L EMP. LAW PROJECT, December 2015, available at https://s27147.pcdn.co/wp-content/uploads/NELP-Policy-Brief-Faulty-FBI- Background-Checks-for-Employment.pdf.

[312] *See, e.g.*, Emma Tucker and Peter Nickeas, *The US Saw Significant Crime Rise Across Major Cities in 2020. And It's Not Letting Up*, CNN, April 3, 2021, available at

reconsideration does not mean that such an offender will automatically, or even very often, get his sentence reduced.

I have similar concerns about Section 201 with respect to juvenile offenders who commit unspeakably violent crimes, but I recognize that such offenders would not be eligible for relief under this provision until they had spent over half of their lives behind bars[313] and can only assume and hope that if this bill is enacted in its present form, judges will take seriously the directive that such offenders should not be released early unless the judge determines that the defendant no longer poses "a danger to the safety of the community…."

Regarding Section 102, while I expressed the view that the safety valve was too stringent prior to passage of the First Step Act,[314] I am discomfited by the thought of expanding the safety valve to offenders who have more than four criminal history points—and have therefore made clear that they are recidivists—based on such subjective criteria as a judge's belief that this

---

https://www.cnn.com/2021/04/03/us/us-crime-rate-rise- 2020/index.html; Neil MacFarquhar, *With Homicides Rising, Cities Brace for a Violent Summer*, N.Y. TIMES, June 1, 2021, available at https://www.nytimes.com/2021/06/01/us/shootings-in-us.html; Leonard A. Sipes, Jr., *Violent and Property Crime Rates in the U.S.*, CRIME IN AMERICA, April 2021, available at https://www.crimeinamerica.net/crime-rates-united-states/; Rafael A. Mangual, *Cities Got Deadlier in 2020: What's Behind the Spike in Homicides?*, THE HILL, April 5, 2021, available at https://thehill.com/opinion/criminal-justice/546445-cities-got-deadlier-in-2020-whats-behind-the-spike-in-homicides.

[313] I am also a ware of a significant body of research concluding that adolescent brain development is such that juveniles are likely to act more impulsively and be less risk averse than adults. *See*, *e.g*., Dustin Albert, Jason Chein & Laurence Steinberg, *The Teenage Brain: Peer Influences on Adolescent Decision Making*, 22 CURRENT DIRECTIONS IN PSYCH. SCI. 114, 114–15 (2013) (describing heightened susceptibility to peer influence and resulting increased risky behavior in adolescents); Leah H. Somerville, *The Teenage Brain: Sensitivity to Social Evaluation*, 22 CURRENT DIRECTIONS IN PSYCH. SCI. 121, 125 (2013) (noting the disproportionate effect of peer reaction on juvenile decision-making compared to adults); Beatriz Luna et al., *The Teenage Brain: Cognitive Control and Motivation*, 22 CURRENT DIRECTIONS IN PSYCH. SCI. 94, 98–99 (2013) (noting that even when adolescents are capable of exercising control akin to adults, they show less consistency and less integration of brain processes in decision-making); Nico U. F. Dosenbach, Steven E. Peterson & Bradley L. Schlaggar, *The Teenage Brain: Functional Connectivity*, 22 CURRENT DIRECTIONS IN PSYCH. SCI. 101, 104 (2013); Laurence Steinberg & Elizabeth Cauffman, *Maturity of Judgment in Adolescence: Psychosocial Factors in Adolescent Decision Making*, 20 LAW & HUM. BEHAV. 249, 253–54 (1996); JOHN H. FLAVELL, PATRICIA H. MILLER & SCOTT A. MILLER, COGNITIVE DEVELOPMENT (3d ed. 1993) (discussing the advances in deductive reasoning that occur as children mature into adulthood including the ability to think hypothetically, abstractly, and multi-directionally as well as the development of metacognition).

[314] John G. Ma lcolm, *The Case for the Smarter Sentencing Act*, HERITAGE FOUND., July 28, 2014, available at https://www.heritage.org/crime-and-justice/commentary/the-case-the-smarter-sentencing-act.

record "substantially overrepresents the seriousness of the defendant's criminal history or the likelihood that the defendant will commit other crimes." I do recognize, though, that the judge must specify the reasons why he or she has reached this conclusion based on "reliable information" (another somewhat nebulous and subjective term) and take comfort in the fact that defendants who commit "a serious drug felony or a serious violent felony" as those terms are defined under federal law[315] would be ineligible unless, of course, the defendant provides "substantial assistance" to the government.[316]

The EQUAL Act

In 1986, Congress passed the Anti-Drug Abuse Act, which established many mandatory minimum penalties for drug offenses, including amending 21 U.S.C. § 841 to provide a 100-to-1 ratio in the quantities of powder cocaine and crack cocaine that would trigger a mandatory minimum penalty. For example, the law established a five-year mandatory minimum term of imprisonment for offenses involving 500 grams of powder cocaine or five grams of crack cocaine, and a 10-year mandatory minimum penalty for offenses involving five kilograms of powder cocaine or 50 grams of crack cocaine. In 2010, through the Fair Sentencing Act, Congress lowered the disparity to 18-to-1—an arbitrary number to be sure—so that the amount of crack cocaine was raised to 28 grams to trigger a five-year mandatory minimum penalty and 280 grams to trigger a 10-year mandatory minimum penalty while the amounts for powder cocaine remained unchanged. While the Fair Sentencing Act implemented this change on a prospective basis only, Section 404 of the First Step Act of 2018 made those changes retroactive, enabling many offenders who had been sentenced under the old 100-to-1 regime to petition a court for a reduction in sentence. While courts retain the discretion to grant or deny such relief, many offenders have in fact had their sentences reduced as a result of this change in the law.[317] The EQUAL Act would eliminate the disparity altogether and apply this change retroactively.

---

315 *See* 21 U.S.C. §§ 802(57), (58).

316 *See* 18 U.S.C. § 3553(e), §5K1.1 (Substantial Assistance to Authorities).

317 *See* U.S. SENT'G COMM'N, THE FIRST STEP ACT OF 2018: ONE YEAR OF IMPLEMENTATION, August 2020 ("Since authorized by the First Step Act, 2,387 offenders received a reduction in sentence as a result of retroactive application of the Fair Sentencing Act of 2010."), available at https://www.ussc.gov/sites/default/files/pdf/research-and-publications/research-publications/2020/20200831_First-Step-Report.pdf.

From a pharmacological perspective, there is really no difference between powder and crack cocaine.

> Cocaine is a hydrochloride salt in its powdered form, while crack cocaine is derived from powdered cocaine by combining it with water and another substance, usually baking soda (sodium bicarbonate). After cocaine and baking soda are combined, the mixture is boiled, and a solid forms. Once it's cooled and broken into smaller pieces, these pieces are sold as crack.[318]

According to pharmacologists, the major differences are how the drug is administered and its effects on the user. Although it can be injected, powder cocaine is usually snorted, while crack cocaine can only be smoked. When cocaine is injected or smoked, the drug takes effect more quickly, resulting in a more intense high of shorter duration.[319] For this reason, as well as the fact that crack cocaine is much cheaper than powder cocaine, many believe that crack cocaine users are more likely to become addicted than powder cocaine users are. Moreover, while some believe that crack users are more prone to violent reactions than powder cocaine users are, others dispute this.[320]

Additionally, regardless of the intent behind these laws, as has been pointed out many times, it is clear that the largest impact, both in terms of the devastation that drugs have wrought and in terms of the imposition of extremely long sentences on offenders, has been felt most keenly in communities of color.[321] I further note that the vast majority of states do not

---

318 *What Is Crack? Differences Between Crack and Cocaine?,* AM. ADDICTION CTRS., availa ble at https://americanaddictioncenters.org/cocaine-treatment/differences-with-crack (la st visited June 14, 2021).

319 *Id.* ("The intensity andduration of the high la rgely rela te to howthe drug is taken, per the Na tional Institute on Drug Abuse. Generally, when cocaine is injectedor smoked, thedrugtakes effect more quickly, resulting in a more intense but shorter high. When cocaine is snorted, it takes longer to feel its effects but theresulting high la sts longer. According to a clinica lpharmacist, cocaine and crackproduce very different effects in the body, la rgely related to howthey a re usually administered. When cocaine is snorted, its effects occur in about 1–5 minutes; theypeakwithin 20–30 minutes; and theydissipate within 1–2 hours. The effects of cracktake hold in under a minute, peak in 3–5 minutes, and la st 30–60 minutes. If cocaine is injected, however, theeffects begin, peak, and for about as longas crack. While injection is not the mostcommonmethod of cocaine consumption, it is used by some people.").

320 *See, e.g.*, Michael G. Vaughn, Qiang Fu, Brian E. Perron, Amy S. B. Bohnert, Matthew O. Howard, *Is Crack Cocaine Use Associated with Greater Violence than Powdered Cocaine Use? Results from a National Sample*, AM. J. OF DRUG AND ALCOHOL ABUSE, 36: 181–186 (2010).

321 *See, e.g.*, USSC, *Quick Facts: Crack Cocaine Trafficking Offenses*, The United States Sentencing Commission (June 2020), available at https://www.ussc.gov/sites/default/

treat crack cocaine any differently from powder cocaine in terms of sentencing[322] and that this bill has attracted bipartisan support[323] as well as support from major prosecutorial and law enforcement organizations.[324] While I do not have a settled view on whether it makes sense to completely eliminate the differential when it comes to sentencing, the current disparity between how crack cocaine offenders are treated compared to powder cocaine offenders does strike me as being excessive.

Retroactivity

Let me say a few words about retroactivity. Both the First Step Implementation Act and the EQUAL Act have retroactivity provisions that might enable offenders who committed their offenses prior to passage of these Acts to take advantage of some of the changes that these laws, if enacted, would bring about, leaving it to the court's discretion whether to grant or deny a petition for relief.

There are many who object to the retroactive application of changes in sentencing laws. In addition to those who did not support the change in the first place, others object because it runs counter to the general principle of

files/pdf/research-and-publications/quick-facts/Crack_Cocaine_FY19.pdf (reporting that in FY2019, 80.9 percent of defendants convicted of federal cra ck cocaine distribution charges were black).

322 FAMM, CRACK COCAINE DISPARITY IN THE STATES, available at https://famm.org/wp-content/uploads/Crack- Dispa rity-in-the-States.pdf (last visited June 14, 2021).

323 In addition to the fact that the EQUAL Act was introduced by a bipartisan group of Congressmen—Reps. Hakeem Jeffries (D-NY), Bobby Scott (D-VA), Kelly Armstrong (R-ND), and Don Bacon (R-NE)—and has a bipartisan list of co-sponsors, *see* https://www.govtrack.us/congress/bills/117/hr1693/details, Arkansas Governor Asa Hutchison, a Republican and former director of the Drug Enforcement Administration under President George W. Bush, recently voiced his support for the bill. Gov. Asa Hutchison, *It's Time to Fix an Old Wrong and End the Disparity Between Crack and Cocaine Offenses*, FOX NEWS, June 8, 2021, available at https://www.foxnews.com/opinion/end-crack- cocaine-offenses-gov-asa-hutchinson.

324 *See, e.g.,* Letter of support from the Major Cities Chiefs Association to Sen. Booker and Rep. Jeffries (April 26, 2021), available at https://majorcitieschiefs.com/wp-content/uploads/2021/05/2021.04.26-S.-79_H.R.-1693-EQUAL-Act-Endorsement.pdf; Press Release, National District Attorneys Association, Na tion's Largest Prosecutor Organiza tion Endorses Endingthe Disparity in Sentencing Between Crackand Powder Cocaine (Feb. 24, 2021), availa ble athttps://ndaa.org/wp-content/uploads/NDAA-Press-Release-on-EQUAL-Act.pdf.

desiring finality in criminal cases,[325] which can be particularly unsettling to victims and their families. Some have mentioned the need to conserve judicial resources and the burden that would be placed on judges who would be tasked with reconsidering sentences that were imposed long ago at the expense of attending to other matters.[326] Others have noted that the original sentence that was imposed may have been the result of a plea bargain in which other, more serious charges were dismissed; enabling an offender to petition a court for a reduction in sentence could upset the "benefit of the bargain," at least from the prosecutor's perspective. One might also object that retroactivity is a one-way ratchet, in that an offender can petition a court for resentencing when a penalty is reduced by subsequent legislation, but a prosecutor cannot petition a court to resentence a defendant when a penalty is increased by subsequent legislation.[327]

While I recognize the legitimacy of all of these arguments, I come down on the side that if society has made a judgment, as reflected through legislation passed by its elected representatives, that certain punishments are simply too harsh and therefore unjust, then the current sentiment presumably is that they were too harsh and unjust when they were originally imposed, at least theoretically. Enabling a judge to reconsider a sentence, taking into account all factors including the nature of the crime that was committed, the views of

---

[325] *See* Mackey v. United States, 401 U.S. 667, 691 (1971) (Harlan, J., concurring in judgment in part and dissenting in part) ("No one, not criminal defendants, not the judicial system, not society asa whole is benefitted by a judgment providing a man shall tentatively go to jail today, but tomorrow and every day thereafter his continued incarceration shall be subject to fresh litigation on issues alreadyresolved."); Sanders v. United States, 373 U.S. 1, 24–25 (1963) (Harlan, J., dissenting) ("Both the individual criminal defendant and society have an interest in insuring that there will at some point be the certainty that comes with an end to litigation, and that attention will ultima tely be focused not on whether a conviction was free from error but rather on whether the prisoner can be restored to a useful place in the community."); Paul M. Bator, *Finality in Criminal Law and Federal Habeas Corpus for State Prisoners*, 76 HARV. L. Rev. 441, 452 (1963) (stating that a lack of finality can undermine the functions of criminal law).

[326] *See, e.g.*, Solem v. Stumes, 465 U.S. 638, 654 (1984) (Powell, J., concurring in judgment) (cited by the Teague plurality in support of claim that retroactivity overburdens judicial resources); Mackey v. United States, 401 U.S. 667, 691 (1971) (Harlan, J., concurring in part and dissenting in part) (arguing that finality conserves judicial resources).

[327] U.S. CONST. art. I, § 9, cl. 3 provides: "No... ex post facto Law shall be passed." The phrase "ex post facto," Latin for "after the fact," refers to laws that apply retroactively. Ever since Calder v. Bull, 3 U.S. 386 (1798), in which Justice Samuel Chase stated that the Ex Post Facto Clause applies to any law that renders criminal an action that was legal when it was taken, aggravates the severity of a crime, increases the resulting punishment, or alters the applicable rules of evidence after the crime was committed, courts have applied the Clause to penal laws. *See, e.g.*, Lindsey v. Washington, 301 U.S. 397 (1937); Weaver v. Graham, 450 U.S. 24 (1981); Lynce v. Mathis, 519 U.S. 433 (1997).

the prosecutor and any victim, and the offender's record while incarcerated, as well as an assessment of the likelihood that the offender will recidivate upon release, is a smaller price to pay than allowing offenders to languish in prison for a period of time that society now deems to be excessive.

Conclusion

The work you do, most especially in the area of criminal justice, has a dramatic impact on the lives of real people—both the victims and perpetrators of crime and their families—and helps to shape how people view our criminal justice system in terms of its effectiveness and its fairness. Over the years, I have dealt with many people of goodwill from across the political and ideological spectrum who approach these issues from different perspectives. Some believe the system should be changed because of systemic racism; others believe that we incarcerate too many people—often referring to this as "mass incarceration"—and that the economic and noneconomic costs associated with this are too high relative to any resulting public safety benefits; still others believe that we do not place enough emphasis and focus on rehabilitation and that we underestimate the capacity of those who violate our criminal laws to redeem themselves.

Though I do not agree with all of these perspectives, I acknowledge that the people who espouse these divergent viewpoints believe them passionately and sincerely. In speaking to these thought leaders, I have often been struck by how much agreement there is on many of the measures that *ought* to be taken to improve our criminal justice system, even if there is broad disagreement about *why* those measures are warranted. Sadly, I have also often been struck by the fact that such measures fail to get enacted either because people get caught up in the latter and don't focus on the former or because they insist on an all-or-nothing approach with respect to the specific proposals they support. As you continue your deliberations on these important issues, I would urge you to focus on your areas of agreement and not let the perfect be the enemy of the good.

I thank you for inviting me here to testify today and would be happy to answer any questions you might have.

* * *

Ms. JACKSON LEE. Thank you.

We thank all the witnesses for their testimony. This is a crucial, crucial, crucial crisis in our Nation, and all of you are contributing to our discussion.

We will now proceed under the 5-minute Rule with questions. I will begin by recognizing myself for 5 minutes. Just for a moment, I'll ask if the Ranking Member of the Full Committee desires at this time to have his 5 minutes.

Mr. Jordan?

Mr. BIGGS. Madam Chair, I think Mr. Jordan has left. So, I think he'll waive that for now. If he comes back, I'll let you now.

Ms. JACKSON LEE. We'll extend that courtesy. Thank you so very much.

Mr. BIGGS. Thank you so much.

Ms. JACKSON LEE. Ms. Barkow, for decades Congress passed extremely harsh laws that undermined public safety, created racial disparities and chaos in the Federal courts. Congress' approach to crack cocaine and the entire framework of mandatory minimum sentences is one example of how the failed war on drugs destroyed communities for generations.

Those of us who live in certain communities are always reminded of neighbors, friends, and extended family Members who were just simply standing on a street corner and were caught with conspiracy charges and drugs and got 25 years. They were, like Mr. Underwood, 17, 18, 19, or 20.

What mistakes did Congress make in its approach to punishment? What are the steps to developing laws that are rooted in sound policies?

Ms. Barkow?

Ms. BARKOW. Thank you, Madam Chair.

I would say there were several mistakes that I'd like to highlight, and the first one was that the way to solve issues of drug addiction, or use, or sale is by long sentences, which, as I said in my initial statement, the evidence just doesn't bear that out. When you arrest and incarcerate one person, they are easily replaced by someone else. So, those long sentences really did nothing to address the underlying problems of drug abuse.

In addition, as you mentioned, it ended up that using those really harsh sentences destroyed families, neighborhoods, communities, lives, with no public safety benefit attached to them at all. We really miss out on the valuable contributions of these people locking them away.

When Congress made these decisions, they did so in an environment that was essentially data and evidence free. It was all based on intuition and a kind of gut instinct that, "We'll just lock this problem away."

Unfortunately, Congress did it at a time when it had also established an expert agency, the Sentencing Commission, which was supposed to help

Congress address sentencing policy. Before even giving the Commission a chance, it went and passed sweeping mandatory minimums, the Armed Career Criminal Act, a whole bunch of laws that had no evidentiary basis for them, other than this underlying premise of, "Let's be as harsh as possible."

I think that harsh reality fell disproportionately on young people and on communities of color. What we know about that is those young people would have aged out of their criminal behaviors, but they are serving sentences far beyond what they would have ever needed to do that.

So, I would just urge all of you to look at all the evidence we now have to see that these sentences are really grossly excessive.

Just the last point I will make in that regard. You can have great confidence that you can reduce sentences because we've seen it. We've seen it done at the Federal level. The Sentencing Commission reduced all Federal drug sentences on average by a couple of years.

Those recidivism rates stayed low. They were no different than people who served their full sentences. We've seen State after State dramatically cut sentences. They've reduced their incarceration rates. They've reduced crime at the same time.

So, we have the evidence that reducing sentencing works. I would just urge Congress to take that new path.

Ms. JACKSON LEE. Thank you very much.

Let me, Mr. Underwood, again thank you for your powerful testimony and the work of your daughter, who is also in this work.

You were sentenced to life without parole. Might you tell us how old you were?

What do you think is a more effective approach than extreme penalties like life sentence? What would have been the appropriate sentence for you in light of what you were doing? You're a father. There is a basis of rehabilitation in the prison concept.

Mr. Underwood?

Mr. UNDERWOOD. Yes, Chair. Yes, ma'am.

Ten years would have been an appropriate sentence. I say 10 years because 3,650 days, 24 hours a day, when you're doing time in prison you have an opportunity to commit to either you want to go down that road and stay on that road and go down the road of perdition or you want to go down the road to redemption. You have a choice yourself to make whether you want to play chess, play cards, play basketball, and play all these other things.

In a real sense, that day in and day out, you have to begin to deal with you're doing time, and that doesn't change, and that you destroyed some families, destroyed your family, and destroyed the community bonds. You have to be an individual that wants to commit to bettering themselves and educating themselves.

The system is—I mean, while we do have law libraries or libraries per se with educational tools in them, they are not adequately staffed to prepare an individual for re-entry. I've seen that over and over, especially with young people.

They don't have—we live in a—we have typewriters—what do you call those things? It is a skeleton. Basically, you can email people, but you can't really do—they have the vehicles there, they have the tools there, so put a flash drive in full of educational access for young men and young women, but they don't do that. They use these for GED programs.

It's really a joke. Everybody in, at least on my side, knew that was a joke. You come into a room, there is, like, 50 computers potentially set up to teach young people how to code and to do something, to give them some incentive to want to learn how to do things. They are just in there, just skeletons.

It's a waste of money. They basically impart to people, you come in—if you are on the list to go take your GED, well, if you don't go to the GED class, you get a shot. That's a write-up.

Ms. JACKSON LEE. Thank you.

Mr. UNDERWOOD. If you do go, you get an incentive and they give you $25.

So, what I'm saying is the individual himself has to aspire to really want to change themselves. You come across a lot of young kids that really do, but they don't have the tools themselves, and they rely on elder inmates or people with education in prison basically to help them reach their goals.

Ms. JACKSON LEE. Thank you very much, Mr. Underwood.

My time has expired. I had additional questions. I will yield now to the gentleman from Ohio, Mr. Chabot, for 5 minutes. Thank you very much.

Mr. CHABOT. Thank you, Madam Chair. Thank you very much. I want to start off by thanking all the witnesses for being here, both in person and by video.

A little over a year ago, in the wake of the death of George Floyd, protesters in cities and communities all over the country proclaimed—at least some of them—that because he and others, particularly minorities, have been killed by police officers, that police departments needed to be defunded, even in some cases dismantled.

We then saw a number of cities do just that, cutting billions of dollars from police resources across the country. For example, here in our Nation's

Capital, in Washington, DC, $15 million was cut out of their budget; Baltimore, not far from here, they cut 20 million; L.A., $150 million cut, and the Big Apple, New York City, a billion dollars was cut from the police budget.

Well, as they say, you reap what you sow. Here in Washington, DC, a 43 percent increase in homicides this year compared to this point last year. Baltimore's violent crime went up, so they decided to add back $27 million for the police. L.A. experienced a 12 percent increase in homicides, so its mayor proposed adding back $50 million to the $150 million that they cut. In New York City, they experienced a 97 percent increase in shootings and a 45 percent increase in their homicides.

Last year, in the city that I represent, Cincinnati—most of it is in my district—they experienced the deadliest year on record, with 94 homicides—when compared with some other cities that may not sound like a lot, but that's the most in the city's history—and an increase in violent crimes in the months of civil unrest that followed George Floyd's death.

Ms. Snider and Mr. Malcolm, I'd like to direct this to you folks, if I could.

Could you comment on the impact that the defunding the police and the over-the-top criticism of law enforcement by many in the media and by some of the protesters, again, not all, but many that have criticized the police—and this threat came from Congress—to eliminate qualified immunity, which would have meant that police officers could be sued in their personal capacity?

So, your house, your savings, and your kids' college funds. If you made a mistake or were accused of it, even if you hadn't done anything wrong, you still have tremendous attorney's fees and that sort of thing. To take away qualified immunity.

So, all of this, do you have an opinion as to what impact that has had on the recruitment of police officers across the Nation?

Do you have an opinion as to whether that whole emphasis against the police has had an impact on the homicides and the rates going up in this country? The defunding, is there a relationship there?

I'd ask either one to take that, or both.

Mr. MALCOLM. Ms. Snider has said that I can go first. I think that the defund the police movement is insane.

There is no question that there are problematic relations between police officers and the communities that they serve. Both suffer as a result of that.

While there are certainly issues that need to be worked through, I think one needs to keep in mind that the far bigger problem is the violence happening, primarily in our inner cities that are underpoliced.

With respect to things like qualified immunity, certainly the defund the police movement, the hostility to the police has got to have an impact on recruitment. It probably also leads to an expansion of what's been referred to as the Ferguson effect.

While I am not a big fan of many of the court interpretations involving qualified immunity, I fear that completely doing away with qualified immunity would have a very, very bad impact in terms of recruitment for police officers at a time when they are most needed, particularly among African Americans and Hispanics in terms of recruiting qualified officers from those communities.

Mr. CHABOT. Ms. Snider? You're a former New York police officer yourself if I'm not mistaken. Is that right?

Ms. SNIDER. Yes. Yes, I am.

So, I am going to say I completely agree with Mr. Malcolm's perspective. I do not at all support the rhetoric around defunding the police. I could get on board with maybe changing the verb to "diverting" funding somewhat to programs that will inevitably lead to less reliance on policing.

In terms of morale, the word "defund," it demoralizes police officers. It makes them feel like the public doesn't appreciate what they are there doing every single day. Obviously, their goal is to protect and to serve their community Members.

In terms of qualified immunity, I think what we need to do is ensure that police officers know that as long as they do their work within the scope within the law, and they still are entitled to an indemnification policy, where they would not be subject to liability if they were sued civilly, I think we need to put parameters in effect like that to ensure that we don't lose the recruitment.

As you saw, New York City police officers, I think we lost about 15 percent in the last year or two. A lot of officers who are eligible for retirement are running to the pension section to retire. I think that the defund the police movement is really encouraging people to want to leave the profession.

Mr. CHABOT. Thank you very much.

My time has expired, Madam Chair. I yield back.

Ms. JACKSON LEE. I thank the gentleman.

I now yield to the gentlelady from Georgia, Ms. McBath, for 5 minutes.

Ms. MCBATH. Thank you, Madam Chair.

Thank each and every one you for your testimony today. We really, really appreciate you being here.

Last March so much of our society changed as we tried to reckon with the danger of COVID–19. We reexamined many of our systems as we tried to keep our people safe, and including our criminal justice system, our prisons, and our jails.

State and Federal officials took many different approaches to doing this, and including using home confinement authority, expediting parole, and other methods of reevaluating where and for how long people would actually serve their sentences.

Critically, officials wanted to make changes while maintaining public safety and, avoiding a rise in recidivism. The goal was to release individuals.

That was a decision that we ourselves were trying to make here in Congress, were to move them to home confinement or to protect their health and the health of those who work in prisons, while also not releasing anyone who might be posing a danger or risk to the public.

I'm going to ask each of you if you would chime in briefly, and anyone is free to answer this question.

Can any of you speak to whether these goals were actually achieved, and how we might study the effects of these different kinds of actions that were taken, and what they can teach us about using home confinement for elderly individuals or for those who have health conditions?

Mr. Underwood, you look like you might want to chime in.

Mr. UNDERWOOD. Well, ma'am, the elderly, for the most part, are left defenseless in prison. I actually watched—well, I'm 67. So, I watched men that were in their fifties actually, first, when it hit, we immediately realized when we were locked down, the televisions were off, and we just listened on NPR and whatever else, other news we could garner that this thing is viral. I mean, it was airborne, it's going around the world, because it is moving too fast, and it is just destroying too many lives.

I saw men that were sick from diabetes and whatever other ailments they had and it really attacked them first the most. I could actually see them physically deteriorate. They served no purpose being in there around, I couldn't see anything that they were doing for them.

So, for them, especially when you have older men that are really for the most part—their sentences are almost done. They certainly don't want to come out into the world and commit any more crime.

It's basically a service that you're doing to let them die at home or let them die in the free world as opposed to dying in jail, because you could actually really physically see people dying, deteriorating from—

Ms. MCBATH. Thank you for that. I'm sorry that you had to witness that.

Mr. UNDERWOOD. It was a traumatic thing to see.

Ms. MCBATH. Anyone else?

Mr. MALCOLM. So, Congresswoman, I'm a little unclear about your question. I gather you're asking about for elderly incarcerated individuals whether compassionate release and home confinement makes sense?

Ms. MCBATH. Well, actually, for any individuals that were confined during COVID at that time.

Mr. MALCOLM. Ah.

Ms. MCBATH. The things that we tried to appropriate, the things that we tried to do to make sure that we were alleviating the possibility that some of those confined would actually end up having to stay incarcerated when they could actually have been released.

We wanted to know the efforts that we tried to put forth that were done specifically within the prison system, was any of that helpful?

Mr. MALCOLM. Yeah. I don't know about the adequacy of those. Certainly, the impetus on making those changes for nonviolent offenders was important, not only in terms of protecting people who are being held involuntarily by the State because they've been incarcerated, but there are people who work in those prisons, who if they are exposed to a pandemic—which hopefully we are passing through—then bring that disease back to their loved ones in the community.

I think that people tried hard to make sure that prisons weren't a petri dish. Probably some succeeded better than others.

Ms. MCBATH. Thank you for that.

Ms. Nelson, your testimony notes that we can reduce our prison populations by getting to the root of the causes of crime. So, how can evidence-based violence intervention programs make our communities much safer?

Ms. NELSON. Thanks for asking that. I really appreciated at the time that we're certainly hearing a lot about the crime rates that have been going up in the last year, which not coincidentally corresponds with a worldwide pandemic and occurred independently of police being funded or defunded.

In some places where funding for the police went up, crime still went up. This is happening in every city, rural places, and suburban places. So, it is really independent of all that.

I think this is an opportunity for us to learn from what we did wrong in the 1990s when crime was up as well, and to look at, again, at what actually stops people from shooting each other wherever they are.

There are a number of evidence-based solutions out there, including the Cure Violence intervention, which is a public health intervention for shooting. Focused deterrence, which is a similar intervention, but does include the participation of the police. Hospital-based interventions, in which folks go to victims of shootings who are in the hospital and try to stop retaliation from happening. Then again, funding communities so they have the resources and the bandwidth to be able to withstand this very stressful time that we are in.

We have an opportunity now to jump on this, but we need to do that now before the violence continues to increase.

Ms. JACKSON LEE. Thank you very much for your questioning.

I now recognize the gentlelady from Pennsylvania, Ms. Dean, Representative Dean, for 5 minutes.

Ms. DEAN. Thank you, Madam Chair.

Just an extraordinary day that you are all here, but also the celebration of Juneteenth.

So, congratulations on your hard fought and well-deserved victory on that front for our country.

Ms. JACKSON LEE. Thank you.

Ms. DEAN. I wanted to thank all of you for your compelling testimony about the area of the disproportionate—the crazy disparities, frankly—and the unsuccessful measures that we have put in place around sentencing.

I thank you for speaking truth to the issues of addiction and the connection to the criminal justice system, and the racist sentencing disparities that have cast a shadow over our country for the last 50 years, since the beginning of the so-called war on drugs.

You eloquently, Mr. Underwood, said, if it were a war on drugs it would have been applied equally, and it never was.

You eloquently talk about how it actually has been so unsuccessful. It hasn't made us any safer.

My own family is touched by addiction, which I have spoken about publicly. My middle son, Harry, is 8 years and 7 months, and some days in long-term recovery from opioid addiction.

As he reports to me—he was a young man and a young father when he was falling deeply into addiction, stopped by the police many times. As he says to us in our family, he was treated unfairly fair. Has no record. Never spent time behind bars. Was never separated from his infant daughter. He was treated unfairly fair. It is time we recognize that.

So, may I start with you, Ms. Frederique? My sympathies to you and your family in the loss that you have suffered.

I want to talk about my support for the EQUAL Act, commonsense legislation championed by our Chair and colleague and friend Representative

Jeffries, that addresses the sentencing disparities between crack and cocaine. The bill notably provides for retroactivity.

Would you kindly speak to the importance of retroactivity? I'm thinking of a question that one of the testifiers said today: What will it say about us as a society if we change this and make it retroactive?

What I think it says about us, if we do this, is that we as a society get a second chance to admit a mistake.

What are your thoughts on retroactivity?

Ms. FREDERIQUE. Thank you very much for that question.

So, the EQUAL Act introduced by Representative Jeffries is long overdue. It is actually pretty incredible that we have people that are pushing for this moment.

It is imperative that as we move forward, and as we progress and put forward legislation that fixes the choices that we've made in the past, that those choices apply to the people that are languishing behind.

What it says about our country is that everyone is worth the redemption, everyone is worth the progress, and that we are strong enough to recognize when we've done something wrong, we are strong enough to say this was a mistake and we will atone and acknowledge that that has happened.

I think this is a lesson we teach young people in preschool and in middle school, in high school and college and adults, and we say, you made a mistake, let's talk about it, let's talk through our feelings, and let's move forward. I don't think anything impedes us as a Nation from doing that for other people.

We know the harm we've done with the disparate sentencing around crack cocaine. It doesn't save us anything to not reverse those decisions for people that are inside. It makes us stronger. It makes us stronger, but it also makes us truthful.

Ms. DEAN. Exactly right. Well said. Thank you.

Mr. Underwood, you said in your testimony there's got to be a better way, and I couldn't agree with you more.

I had the chance to hear the Pope speak to prisoners at Curran-Fromhold prison in Philadelphia when he visited a couple of years ago. He said that Jesus comes to save us from the lie that says no one can change, the lie of thinking no one can change. I think you spoke to that.

Could you tell us what we should be doing differently here in Congress to talk about those second chances in redemption?

Mr. UNDERWOOD. There are so many men, Congresswoman Dean, and women, that are geniuses sitting behind bars, that have sat 10, 15, 20, or 30 years. So, just to interact with them and hear their stories, it is incredible.

These are people that could make a difference in their communities. These are people that actually they have atoned a long time ago. They really don't want to be part of a system that—any criminal organization or any kind of crime. They want to do the right thing. They just don't have the opportunity to do the right thing.

Education is important, education is vital. In this new age where you have DSPs that dominate, and we all know digital service providers that dominate the landscape, to have a prison industry that's basically they sit around and teach you how to make furniture and clothes, that's not a productive or adequate use of time for someone that's coming home to a world now that's dominated by technology.

We have so much to offer out here in the society to offer those that are on their way home, that could make a difference in the world, that could do those jobs, that could help provide—pardon me.

Ms. DEAN. Thank you, Madam Chair. I yield back.

Ms. JACKSON LEE. The gentlelady's time has expired.

First, we all are very engaged in this testimony and we are allowing Members to sort of spill over because it is such an important day.

Fifty years in your life, Mr. Underwood, is testimony of how wrong the policy was.

I know that Members know that this is a travel day, so we ask all of us—I have some questions at the end, but we will try to be consistent in our hearing.

These are important times and important stories. So, Members, I do want to have you on the record. I thank you for your participation.

The fact that the two gentlewomen from Georgia and Pennsylvania are so close together we called them back to back. So, we will now call Mr. Owens. Then, Members, we will call another Republican member. Then we'll come to the Democratic side. So, we thank you for understanding equity and fairness.

Mr. Owens, you have 5 minutes at this time. Thank you.

Mr. OWENS. Thank you. Thank you, Chair Jackson Lee and Ranking Member Biggs, for holding this hearing.

Thank you to all the witnesses for your participation.

Mr. Underwood, thank you for your unique perspective. Really appreciate it.

Citizen reform is an issue that's near and dear to my heart. Several years ago, I had the opportunity to mentor a young college football player. He showed great promise and was a close friend to one of my children.

Unfortunately, during his summer break this young man, whose father had abandoned him, and his mother got involved with his uncle's drug trafficking operation, he was caught by authorities. Though it was his first offense, he was sentenced to prison.

He was given a choice by a prosecutor who never lost and a public defender who never won. His plea offer: Ten years if he did not fight the charge or 15 if he did.

He chose 10 years. Like tens of thousands of Black men, he was ripped away from his family. His 1-year-old son, like him, was also destined to be raised without a father.

It will be 26 years, an entire generation, before the 2018 Trump criminal justice reform bill would be passed to begin to address this heartless mandatory sentencing of the 1994 Clinton-Biden crime bill.

I would like to make clear that the criminality, murder, destruction we are seeing in Black communities across our country is not baked into our genes due to slavery 200 years ago.

My upbringing in the segregated 1950s and 1960s proved what can happen to any community where there is a commitment to both mothers and fathers to their children.

It was the proud Black community of my youth that led our country to the growth of the middle class. Men matriculated from college, men committed to marriage and proceeded to become entrepreneurs.

So, I'm pleased to participate in this hearing today, but I do think it has been misnamed. It should be "The Undoing of the Damage of Decades of Terrible Progressive, Anti-Black Policies."

While sentencing reform is a very, very important issue that I support, we can't overstate the damage of decades of policies that have decimated urban Black communities and minority communities.

These policies include high minimum wage, a big benefit to increase the wages of skilled union workers but devastating to poor Black youth attempting to get work experience. Welfare incentives that force young single mothers into government dependency and our young men into self-centered narcissism. Sadly, having babies and abandoning them over the decades has become acceptable—in many cases, unfortunately, even fashionable.

Anti-marriage tax incentives that penalize men and women who commit to marriage. Anti-school choice forcing poor children to remain in failing public schools, never learning to read, write, or think. The racist 1931 Davis-Bacon Act which prioritized White Federal unions over Black entrepreneurs and small business owners.

We are in a country that believes in second chances. Correcting overly harsh sentences for those who have hurt the innocent in our communities should be important to all of us, as important as raising our young boys and girls in an environment that gives them a moral compass to give to their community instead of taking from it.

It is imperative to raise them to understand that life obstacles are destined to come their way, but that they can overcome them as they learn to love God, country, family, respect women, authority, and themselves.

Ms. Snider, according to the National Commission on COVID–19 and Criminal Justice, homicides and aggregated assaults rose significantly beginning in late May and June 2020. After almost 30 years of a crime rate going down, why are we seeing this particular spike?

Ms. SNIDER. Thank you for that question, Congressman.

What we fail to realize and what the media has been telling us is crime rates are surging, violent crime rates are so high, but they are still not as high as they were in the 1980s and in the 1990s.

So, yes, they have gone up. To date, I can't tell you personally why the crime rate has surged in the last year, but I'm going to say COVID–19 has been a very significant contributing factor. People were confined to their homes, people are losing economic resources, people don't have jobs. I'm going to say people probably got a little stir crazy staying at home for 15 months. Those are all factors that could contribute to aggression, behavioral changes, and an increase in crime.

Mr. OWENS. Do you have any other insights that you would like to share in the last few seconds here on the current State of crime and the police force in our Nation?

Ms. SNIDER. I'm sorry.

Mr. OWENS. Do you have anything else you'd like—any other insights you would like to share with us in terms of the current State of the crime that we are experiencing now or the police force in our Nation?

Ms. SNIDER. Not at this time.

Mr. OWENS. Thank you.

I will give back my time. Give back my time.

Ms. DEAN. [Presiding.] The gentleman yields back. At this time, the Chair recognizes Rep. Spartz.

Ms. SPARTZ. Thank you, Madam Chair.

As we know, the criminal justice system is one of the core functions of the government, to protect people's rights to life, liberty, and property.

As a former State legislator, I believe there are a lot of things that States are doing, and sometimes it seems to me that there is a redundancy with Federal crimes. Also, it makes it more complicated.

When the system gets complicated, it is kind of stacked against the people who don't have the money. Maybe that's why it's good to have some CPAs, not just attorneys, in these committees. It is definitely a learning curve for me, and I appreciate your input.

It's important that punishment does fit the crime. As one of my retired judges in my State told me, "Victoria, since we don't put people in jails for life, it is important that we rehabilitate and provide second chances to people. It is also important that we have prevention."

So, I would like to get, Mr. Malcolm, you discussed sentencing and the proposed bills. Do you have any thoughts also on the probation and supervised release mechanism within the Federal system?

As a Federal prosecutor, give me some insight. Are there some things that maybe could be improved there to provide more people opportunities?

Because I think it's extremely important that we have this mechanism that gets people back into really being valuable and productive members of the society.

Mr. MALCOLM. You've raised a number of important points during your remarks just now. You've talked about the overfederalization of crime, where there are duplicative laws among Federal and States laws, which dilutes accountability and takes scarce Federal resources and diverts them into matters that have traditionally been left to the States.

With respect to probation, people who are returning citizens after they have been incarcerated, it is important that the scarce resources for the probation officers are focused on people who are most likely to recidivate.

I think that we have a problem with too many technical violations, returning people to prison too quickly. On the flip side, you'll get people who repeatedly commit violations and who are not dealt with in a timely manner. Before you know it, they have returned fully to a life of crime.

Professor Barkow actually in her opening remarks talked about the problem of collateral consequences that are imposed upon people who are released that make it extremely difficult for them to reintegrate into society and become law-abiding Members of society, productive and being support to their family.

So, part of the probation and parole process is also trying to make it easier by easing up on some of these collateral consequences to make it so that they have an opportunity to become productive members of society.

Ms. SPARTZ. Any comments you have on supervised release?

Mr. MALCOLM. Well, look, supervised release is—there is no problem having supervised release. I wouldn't necessarily say that it is a substitute for incarceration.

For certain nonviolent felons, depending on the circumstances of their offense, depending on the circumstances of their home life and their criminal history—so I know you are considering bills with respect to caretakers—supervised release is certainly an option, as are alternative sentencing mechanisms.

A lot of States have things like drug courts, veterans' courts, and mental health courts. These are all things that are worthy of exploration.

So long as the phrase "evidence-based studies," so long as this is all evidenced based, I think these are all worthy of consideration and possible legislative changes.

Ms. SPARTZ. Thank you. I yield back.

Ms. DEAN. The gentlewoman yields back.

The Chair recognizes the gentlewoman from Pennsylvania, Representative Scanlon, for 5 minutes.

Ms. SCANLON. Thank you, Chair Dean.

The right to trial is established in our Constitution. However, we know that over the past few decades plea bargains have largely replaced trials in our justice system. When defendants choose to go to trial, they often face massive sentences if they lose.

This so-called "trial penalty" punishes individuals for exercising their constitutional right. I'm really concerned about how the pressure to avoid the trial penalty impacts younger defendants and often women.

Ms. Givens, I have several questions for you. Some of these structural things that are driving mass incarceration, including the sentencing guidelines and such. Also, the fact that public defenders are often underfunded, overwhelmed, and cannot adequately protect their clients.

Can you speak to the impact of having less than adequate legal resources for folks who are in our system?

Ms. GIVENS. Obviously, when we don't properly fund and support public defenders, we're not able to really deliver the services under the Constitution that people deserve.

I will say, as a Federal public defender, I think that I have a lot of resources. I want to just shout out that be mindful of the difference between State and Federal public defenders. State public defenders are often saddled with higher caseloads, far fewer resources.

As a Federal public defender, I wouldn't say it's perfect, but I have a little more. I think Federal public defenders across the country deliver some of the best legal services around.

It is that trial penalty, the mandatory minimums, and the discretion in sentencing taken away from judges and given to prosecutors that really informs our outcomes.

Ms. SCANLON. Right. Certainly, the Philadelphia public defender's office is legendarily wonderful. You're absolutely right, that often it's the State system. I believe Representative Deutch on our Committee has a bill, the EQUAL Defense Act, that was also sponsored by our current Vice President last term. So, we know there's work to be done there.

I'd like to direct your attention to something that's kind of mentioned obliquely in your testimony, which is the "girlfriend problem" that we've seen with mandatory minimum sentencing.

Before coming to Congress, I had the opportunity to participate in the Clemency 2014 Project and actually helped coordinate representation for two women who were sentenced to very long sentences as part of these ploys to get people to flip even though they weren't prime offenders.

One of them was Michelle Miles, a first-time nonviolent drug offender. She received a mandatory minimum sense of 30 years for conspiracy to possess and served 19 years before she received clemency. Basically, this was on the basis of her older boyfriend being someone who was running a drug ring.

Similarly, Cindy Shank, whose odyssey became the subject of a Sundance Award-winning HBO documentary, also a young woman who was taken advantage of by an older guy who was running a drug ring, and prosecutors threw the book at both of them.

Can you talk a little bit about how mandatory sentencing is disproportionately impacting women, particularly women of color?

Ms. GIVENS. Yes. Mandatory minimum sentences are disproportionately impacting people of color of all genders. I understand your question about girlfriends taking the fall for their boyfriends involved in various trades, most representative drug trade.

I think part of the problem is in the definition of cooperators, and how we define cooperation, and what type of things that we offer cooperators.

A girlfriend of a boyfriend who is involved in the drug trade can be linked to his primary activities, even if she has a very peripheral role.

That is something that is worth looking into it in how we can really separate the actions of a low-level involved person to the decisions of the primary person.

Ms. SCANLON. Can I just get to one thing—one other thing, because my time is almost out? You did mention also the impact on juvenile defendants or folks who are younger and how the pressure to plead creates issues. Can you speak to that as well?

Ms. GIVENS. Yeah, this a big problem, and I want to say distinctly that when I'm talking about young people, I'm talking about 18 to 26. When we're talking about evidence-based sentencing, we must remember that the data says that people between 18 and 26, they're not traditionally our view of juveniles, but they are in developmental adolescence.

These young people, it takes a whole bunch of different skills to present to them these long sentences and what that means for their life. I think they get pressured and feel pressure to plea because they are overcharged. They don't have a lot of other choices.

Ms. SCANLON. I see my time has expired, but Madam Chair, I would ask unanimous consent to enter into the record a report from the National Association of Criminal Defense Lawyers, entitled, "The Trial Penalty, the Sixth amendment Right to Trial on the Verge of Extinction and How on Save It." With that, I yield back.

Ms. DEAN. [Presiding.] Without objection, it is so ordered.

[The information follows:]

The Trial Penalty: The Sixth Amendment Right to Trial on the Verge of Extinction and How to Save It

Rick Jones
President, NACDL
New York, NY

Barry J. Pollack
Immediate Past President, NACDL
Washington, DC

Norman L. Reimer
Executive Director, NACDL
Washington, DC

Kyle O'Dowd
Associate Executive Director for Policy, NACDL
Washington, DC

Gerald B. Lefcourt
President, FCJ
New York, NY

NACDL Trial Penalty Recommendation Task Force

Andrew Birrell
Co-Chair
Minneapolis, MN

Ramon de la Cabada
Co-Chair
Miami, FL

Martín A. Sabelli
Co-Chair
San Francisco, CA

John Cline
San Francisco, CA

Daniella Gordon
Marlton, NJ

David Patton
New York, NY

Barry J. Pollack
Washington, DC

James Felman
Tampa, FL

JaneAnne Murray
Minneapolis, MN

Marjorie Peerce
New York, NY

Todd Pugh
Chicago, IL

About the National Association of Criminal Defense Lawyers

The National Association of Criminal Defense Lawyers (NACDL) is the preeminent organization in the United States advancing the goal of the criminal defense bar to ensure justice and due process for persons charged with a crime or wrongdoing. *NACDL envisions a society where all individuals receive fair, rational, and humane treatment within the criminal justice system.*

Founded in 1958, NACDL has a rich history of promoting education and reform through steadfast support of America's criminal defense bar, *amicus curiae* advocacy, and myriad projects designed to safeguard due process rights and promote a rational and humane criminal justice system. NACDL's many thousands of direct members — and 90 state, local and international affiliate organizations totalling up to 40,000 members — include private criminal defense lawyers, public defenders, active U.S. military defense counsel, and law professors committed to preserving fairness in America's criminal justice system. Representing thousands of criminal defense attorneys who know firsthand the inadequacies of the current system, NACDL is recognized domestically and internationally for its expertise on criminal justice policies and best practices.

About the Foundation for Criminal Justice

The Foundation for Criminal Justice (FCJ) is a 501(c)(3) charitable non-profit organized to preserve and promote the core values of America's criminal justice system guaranteed by the Constitution — among them access to effective counsel, due process, freedom from unreasonable search and seizure, and fair sentencing. The FCJ supports NACDL's charitable efforts to improve

America's public defense system, and other efforts to preserve core criminal justice values through resources, education, training, and advocacy tools for the public and the nation's criminal defense bar.

Foreword

A grand jury presentation can consist entirely of information that would be inadmissible at trial. A prosecutor may knowingly use illegally-obtained evidence to obtain an indictment, and if she has evidence in her possession that substantially exculpates the target, she may withhold it from the grand jury. The presentation need only establish probable cause to believe the target committed the crime. If 11 of the 23 grand jurors are unconvinced that even that low threshold has been met, an indictment can still be obtained. And of course it's all *ex parte*, so no one is even there to question the prosecutor's presentation.

What accounts for all this? Why do our Supreme Court decisions and federal rules establish a charging process that *guarantees* that imperfect, ill-advised criminal charges can make it through if the prosecutor presses them? The answer is simple: because of trials. Those imperfect, ill-advised charges will come out in the wash when they are subjected to the cleansing effects of a criminal trial in open court. Indeed, when prosecutors know that such charges will go to trial, where they must be proved beyond a reasonable doubt to the satisfaction of a unanimous jury based on admissible evidence that is subject to vigorous challenge by defense counsel to whom exculpatory evidence must be disclosed, they are not likely to bring them in the first place.

This report is a major contribution to the discussion of one of the most important issues in criminal justice today: the vanishing trial. Once the centerpiece of our criminal justice ecosystem, the trial is now spotted so infrequently that if we don't do something to bring it back, we will need to rethink many other features of our system that contribute to fair and just results only when trials occur in meaningful numbers.

The first task in solving a problem is identifying its causes, and this report nails that step. Mandatory minimum sentencing provisions have played an important role in reducing our trial rate from more than 20% thirty years ago to 3% today. Instead of using those blunt instruments for their intended purpose — to impose harsher punishments on a select group of the most culpable defendants — the Department of Justice got in the habit long ago of using them broadly to strong-arm guilty pleas, and to punish those who have the temerity to exercise their right to trial. The Sentencing Guidelines also play an important role, providing excessively harsh sentencing ranges that frame plea discussions when mandatory sentences do not. Finally, the report correctly finds that federal sentencing judges are complicit as well. In too many cases, excessive trial penalties are the result of judges having internalized a cultural norm that when defendants "roll the dice" by "demanding" a trial, they either win big or lose big. The same judges who will go along with a plea bargain that compromises a severe Guidelines range are too reticent to stray very far from the sentencing range after trial.

The report's principles and recommendations will stimulate some much-needed discussion. Today's excessive trial penalties, it concludes, undermine the integrity of our criminal justice system. Putting the government to its proof is a constitutional right, enshrined in the Sixth Amendment; no one should be required to gamble with years and often decades of their liberty to exercise it. The report properly raises the "innocence problem," that is, the fact that prosecutors have become so empowered to enlarge the delta between the sentencing outcome if the defendant pleads guilty and the outcome if he goes to trial and loses that even innocent defendants now plead guilty. But there's an even larger hypocrisy problem. Our Constitution claims to protect the guilty as well, affording them a presumption of innocence and protecting them from punishment unless the government can *prove them guilty* beyond a reasonable doubt. A system characterized by extravagant trial penalties produces guilty pleas in cases where the government cannot satisfy that burden, hollowing out those protections and producing effects no less pernicious than innocents pleading guilty.

The report's recommendations range from the sweeping (ban those mandatory minimums) to the technical (eliminate the motion requirement for the third "acceptance" point), and include suggested modifications to the "relevant conduct" principle at the heart of the Guidelines, pre-plea disclosure requirements, "second looks" at lengthy sentences, and judicial oversight of plea discussions. A particularly attractive recommendation would require judges sentencing a defendant who went to trial to pay greater attention to the sentences imposed on co-defendants who pled guilty; few things place today's excessive trial penalty in sharper relief.

There is no such thing as a perfect criminal justice system. But a healthy one is constantly introspective, never complacent, always searching for injustices within and determined to address them. The sentencing reform movement a generation ago disempowered judges and empowered prosecutors. Federal prosecutors have used that power to make the trial penalty too severe, and the dramatic diminution in the federal trial rate is the result. Our system is too opaque and too severe, and everyone in it – judges, prosecutors, and defense attorneys — is losing the edge that trials once gave them. Most important of all, a system without a critical mass of trials cannot deliver on our constitutional promises. Here's hoping that this report will help us correct this problem before it is too late.

John Gleeson
Partner, Debevoise & Plimpton
Former United States District Judge,
Eastern District of New York

Acknowledgments

This report was truly a joint project, reflecting a remarkable collaboration among numerous entities, all determined to understand and redress the phenomenon of the trial penalty. NACDL's members and many clients contributed to this effort, as did various leaders, and a magnificent team of volunteers from a major law firm. They all deserve the appreciation of the legal profession and the society it serves.

NACDL thanks the Foundation for Criminal Justice and various other donors whose financial support helped make this project possible. NACDL also extends its deep appreciation to the team of attorneys at firm of Skadden Arps Slate Meagher & Flom LLP who worked diligently on the extensive research and drafting involved in this critical project. The Skadden team of attorneys, led by Esther Bloustein, Elisa Klein, and Pro Bono Counsel Donald P. Salzman, also included Justin Barrett, Alison Bloch, Warren Feldman, Mari Guttman, Lauren Haberman, Wallis Hampton, Maximillian Hirsch, Parker Justi, Brittany Libson, Daniel Mayerfeld, Sonya Mitchell, Shayla Parker, Stefania Rosca, Rachel Schiffman, Deepa Vanamali, Caroline Ferris White, and Michael Wiesner.

NACDL also extends its thanks to the members of the NACDL Trial Penalty Recommendation Task Force who dedicated their time and effort to this report and the development of its principles and recommendations: Co-Chairs Andrew Birrell, Ramon de la Cabada, and Martín A. Sabelli; and Members John Cline, James Felman, Daniella Gordon, JaneAnne Murray, David Patton, Marjorie Peerce, NACDL Immediate Past President Barry J. Pollack, and Todd Pugh. In addition, Barry Pollack's long-standing support for this project is deeply appreciated. NACDL also thanks the many lawyers and their clients who contributed their stories and insights to this project, some of whom saw or suffered the impact of the trial penalty first hand.

Thanks also to the following NACDL staff for the careful editing and helpful suggestions: Norman L. Reimer, Executive Director; Kyle O'Dowd, Associate Executive Director for Policy; Quintin Chatman, Editor of *The Champion*®; and Ivan J. Dominguez, Director of Public Affairs & Communications. NACDL would also like to thank Cathy Zlomek, NACDL Art Director and her department for the design of the report.

Executive Summary

The Scope of the Problem

In the words of John Adams, "[r]epresentative government and trial by jury are the heart and lungs of liberty. Without them we have no other fortification against being ridden like horses, fleeced like sheep, worked like cattle, and fed and clothed like swine and hounds."[328] President Adams' colorful language reflected the strength of his view — a view shared by his contemporaries — that the right to trial by jury protects our liberties every bit as much the right to cast votes for our representatives.

> There is ample evidence that federal criminal defendants are being *coerced* to plead guilty because the penalty for exercising their constitutional rights is simply too high to risk.

To the modern ear, this view comes as a surprise. While Americans celebrate the notion of representative government just as much now as they did in the time of the Framers, few still think of trial by jury as a bulwark against the arbitrary and capricious use of government power. Why does this notion seem so surprising to the modern observer? What has become of the sense — so natural for Mr. Adams and his contemporaries — that trial by jury protects freedom?

The answer, is simple: over the last fifty years, trial by jury has declined at an ever-increasing rate to the point that this institution now occurs in less

[328] *See* THE REVOLUTIONARY WRITINGS OF JOHN ADAMS 55 (C. Bradley Thompson ed., 2000).

than 3% of state and federal criminal cases.[329] Trial by jury has been replaced by a "system of [guilty] pleas"[330] which diminishes, to the point of obscurity, the role that the Framers envisioned for jury trials as the primary protection for individual liberties and the principal mechanism for public participation in the criminal justice system.

> The trial penalty cannot be attributed to any single cause. Rather, many shortcomings across the criminal justice system combine to perpetuate this injustice.

Guilty pleas have replaced trials for a very simple reason: individuals who choose to exercise their Sixth Amendment right to trial face exponentially higher sentences if they invoke the right to trial and lose. Faced with this choice, individuals almost uniformly surrender the right to trial rather than insist on proof beyond a reasonable doubt, defense lawyers spend most of their time negotiating guilty pleas rather than ensuring that police and the government respect the boundaries of the law including the proof beyond a reasonable doubt standard, and judges dedicate their time to administering plea allocutions rather than evaluating the constitutional and legal aspects of the government's case and police conduct. Equally important, the public rarely exercises the oversight function envisioned by the Framers and inherent in jury service. Further, the pressure to plead guilty, and plead early, is often accompanied by a requirement that accused persons waive many valuable rights, including the right to challenge unlawfully procured evidence and the

---

329 In 1970, for example, 15 percent of federal cases went to trial. Hindelang Criminal Justice Research Ctr., Univ. at Albany, Sourcebook of Criminal Justice Statistics Online tbl.5.22.2010 (Kathleen Maguire ed.), *available at* http://www.albany.edu/sourcebook/pdf/t5222010.pdf. But this percentage started rapidly declining in the ensuing decades, to a low of 2.9 percent in 2015. U.S. Sentencing Commission, Overview of Federal Criminal Cases Fiscal Year 2015, at 4 (2016), *available at* http://www.ussc.gov/sites/default/files/pdf/research-and-publicalions/research-publicalions/2016/FY15_Overview_Federal_Criminal_Cases.pdf. The state statistics duplicate the federal pattern, and, indeed, indicate that less than two percent of state cases proceed to trial today. Jed S. Rakoff, *Why Prosecutors Rule the Criminal Jus6ice System—and What Can Be Done About It*, 111 NW. U. L. REV. 1429, 1432 (2017). At the same time, and hardly coincidentally, the number of prosecutions rose. In 1970, according the Hindelang Criminal Research Ctr. Sourcebook on Criminal Justice Statistics, federal prosecutors filed charges against 36,356 defendants. By 2011, this number had almost tripled to a peak of 102,617 filings. John Gramlich, *Federal Criminal Prosecu6ions Fall to Lowest Level in Nearly Two Decades*, Pew Research Center, Mar. 28, 2017, *available at* http://www.pewresearch.org/fact-tank/2017/03/28/federal-criminal-proseculions-fall-to-lowest-level- in-nearly-two-decades/. It has since declined to 77,152. *Id.*

330 *LaZler v. Cooper*, 566 U.S. 156, 170 (2012).

right to appeal issues which have an impact not only in their cases but also for society at large.

While scholars still debate the theoretical justifications for and against plea bargaining, neither the government nor the public have exhibited any significant resistance to its rise to dominance. This is not altogether surprising given the ostensible advantages of plea bargaining. Trials are lengthy, expensive processes that can leave victims waiting for years to obtain restitution and closure. Plea bargaining presents a seemingly reasonable alternative that promotes efficiency while providing defendants an opportunity for leniency and putting them on an early road to rehabilitation. Conventional wisdom understandably views this as a win/win solution, particularly because the Constitution affords defendants the right to choose to go to trial if they wish to do so.

> The virtual elimination of the option of taking a case to trial has so thoroughly tipped the scales of justice against the accused that the danger of government overreach is ever-present. And on a human level, for the defense attorney there is no more heart-wrenching task that explaining to client who very likely may be innocent that they must seriously consider pleading guilty or risk the utter devastation of the remainder of their life with incalculable impacts on family.

For most, however, the right to a trial is a choice in name only. Empirical studies and exoneration data have revealed that the pressures defendants face in the plea bargaining process are so strong even innocent people can be convinced to plead guilty to crimes they did not commit.[331] This disturbing figure casts doubt on the assumption that defendants who plead guilty do so voluntarily.

As this Report illustrates, there is ample evidence that federal criminal defendants are being *coerced* to plead guilty because the penalty for exercising their constitutional rights is simply too high to risk. This "trial penalty" results from the discrepancy between the sentence the prosecutor is willing to offer in exchange for a guilty plea and the sentence that would be imposed after a trial. If there were no discrepancy at all, there would be far less incentive for defendants to plead guilty. But the gap between post-trial and post-plea sentences can be so wide, it becomes an overwhelming influence in a defendant's consideration of a plea deal. When a prosecutor offers to reduce a multi-decade prison sentence to a number of years — from 30 years to 5 years,

---

[331] *See, e.g., infra* notes 14, 15, 29 & 30.

for example — any choice the defendant had in the matter is all but eliminated. Although comprehensive data regarding plea offers remains largely unavailable, anecdotal evidence suggests that offers of this nature are common. Prosecutors enjoy enormous discretion to force a defendant's hand. While some may view prosecutors' actions as generous, their willingness to reduce sentences so drastically raises serious doubt that the initial sentences were reasonable in the first place.

Indeed, the ability of prosecutors to threaten exorbitant sentences permeates the federal criminal justice system and has spurred a mounting wave of criticism in recent years. In 2013, Human Rights Watch published a report detailing the ways federal prosecutors use the sentencing laws to coerce federal drug defendants to plead guilty. Building off of that work, NACDL has conducted its own study to examine the structures and mechanisms in the federal system that perpetuate the trial penalty in criminal cases across the board. In particular, NACDL canvassed previous scholarly research, judicial precedent and commentary, the history of and recent amendments to federal sentencing statutes and guidelines, and data and statistical studies published by the U.S. Sentencing Commission. NACDL also conducted a survey, interviewed defense counsel, and examined the case files of dozens of federal criminal defendants to identify real world instances of the trial penalty at play. The following report is the result of those efforts.

As explained in greater detail below, the trial penalty cannot be attributed to any single cause. Rather, many shortcomings across the criminal justice system combine to perpetuate this injustice. Prosecutors — who serve in an adversarial role and are personally incentivized to achieve speedy convictions — enjoy unbridled discretion and informational advantages at the preliminary stages of criminal proceedings that have a significant impact on the sentence that will ultimately be imposed. That influence is exacerbated by the federal Sentencing Guidelines, which call for formulaic calculations that are ripe for manipulation, that often result in sentences far out of proportion with a defendant's actual culpability, and that deliberately reward defendants who agree to plead guilty and do so quickly. Although judges nominally retain discretion to decide a defendant's ultimate sentence, that discretion is frequently hampered by mandatory minimum statutory penalties which are triggered solely by the prosecutor's charging decisions. In addition, many judges are reticent to meaningfully exert their discretion, preferring to cling to the tidy Guidelines calculations, which are virtually immune from reversal on appeal. As a result, when the rare defendant insists on his right to a trial, these forces converge to inflict excruciating penalties. Those penalties then serve as a warning to the next defendant who will know his only hope of obtaining a fair sentence is to forego the right to a trial.

Criminal defense lawyers have long known that trials are vanishing. This is an unacceptable development, and not just because the art of trying a case is atrophying. The virtual elimination of the option of taking a case to trial has so thoroughly tipped the scales of justice against the accused that the danger of government overreach is ever-present. And on a human level, for the defense attorney there is no more heart-wrenching task that explaining to client who very likely may be innocent that they must seriously consider pleading guilty or risk the utter devastation of the remainder of their life with incalculable impacts on family.

This Report documents the corrosive effect of the trial penalty on the system of criminal justice. It examines the relationship between the trial penalty and numerous characteristics of modern criminal justice including virtually unfettered prosecutorial charging discretion,[332] mandatory minimum sentencing statutes,[333] and the federal Sentencing Guidelines. The Report highlights specific cases to demonstrate that individuals are being punished simply for holding the government to its burden of proof and, in some cases, that the trial penalty has coerced innocent individuals, later exonerated, to plead guilty for fear of devastating long post-trial sentences.

In calling out these mechanisms that perpetuate the trial penalty, NACDL does not intend to censure any particular participants or constituencies. Nor is the goal of this report to denounce or abolish plea bargaining. Instead, in identifying the flaws in the plea bargaining and sentencing processes, NACDL seeks to provoke a larger conversation on how those processes can be

[332] The most important driver of pleas is the government's leverage in plea bargaining. *See* JOHN PFAFF, LOCKED IN: HOW OUR FRACTURED CRIMINAL JUSTICE SYSTEM CREATES MASS INCARCERATION (2017) [hereinafter LOCKED IN]; Jed. S. Rakoff, *Why Do Innocent People Plead Guilty*, N. Y. REV. OF BOOKS, Nov. 20, 2014, *available at* http://www.nybooks.com/arlicles/2014/11/20/why-innocent-people- plead-guilty/. Harsh new sentencing statutes and guidelines introduced in the 70s, 80s, and 90s permitted prosecutors to threaten greatly enhanced sentences if the defendant was convicted at trial. These sentences were "largely on the books for bargaining purposes," as the Supreme Court finally acknowledged in 2012. *Missouri v. Frye*, 566 U.S. 134, 144 (2012) (*quo6ing* Barkow). *See also* Gary Fields & John Emschwiller, *Many Failed E9forts to Count Na6ion's Federal Criminal Laws*, WALL ST. J., July 23, 2011, *available at* https://www.wsj.com/arlicles/SB10001424052702304319804576389601079728920.

[333] The government can further up the ante by offering to withdraw, or threatening to file, charges carrying mandatory minimum penalties, or penalties that can be enhanced based on the defendant's prior criminal record. In fact, one judge notes that prosecutors' use of prior felony statements to enhance a defendant's sentence "have played a key role in helping to place the federal criminal trial on the endangered species list." *United States v. Kupa*, 976 F. Supp. 2d 417, 420 (2013) (Gleeson, J.).

reformed to reduce the prevalence of coercion. To that end, NACDL offers a series of recommendations for specific reform in various areas of the criminal justice process in the hope that, by enacting these reforms, criminal defendants can be truly free to choose to exercise their constitutional rights.

> As trials and hearings decline, so too does government accountability. Government mistakes and misconduct are rarely uncovered,[334] or are simply resolved in a more favorable plea bargain.[335] Moreover, the ease of conviction can encourage sloppiness, and a diminution of the government's obligation to fairness.

A system that insulates a prosecution from the searing light of a public trial invites the misuse and abuse of the criminal law. The notion that the exercise of a fundamental constitutional right should be so burdened contravenes a core value that is at the heart of a democracy founded upon the concept that the power of government should be limited. Accused persons should not have to gamble with years of their lives in order to have their day in court. No one should be subjected to geometrically increased punishment merely for putting the government to its proof. And no government should be able to wield the power to prosecute and condemn in a process that is rigged so that it virtually never has to show its hand. A system that has effectively consigned the right to a trial to the dustbin of history should not be tolerated.

Finally, while this report focuses on federal criminal practice, it is well-established that the trial penalty is just as prevalent in state and local criminal prosecutions, and that the virtual extinction of jury trials is just as prevalent in these jurisdictions. NACDL hopes to partner with its many affiliates and other criminal justice reform groups to tackle the roots causes of the trial penalty and restore the balance essential to a fair and just criminal justice system.

The Impact of the Trial Penalty

The trial penalty has profoundly altered a criminal justice system designed as an adversarial battle between the government and defense lawyers, presided over by a judge, with a jury as the final arbiter of guilt.

---

334 *See, e.g.*, Joel Rudin, *Disciplining Errant Prosecutors*, 80 FORDHAM L. REV. 537 (2011); Keith A. Findley & Michael S. Scott, *The Mul6iple Dimensions of Tunnel Vision in Criminal Cases,* 2006 WIS. L. REV. 291, 327-31 (2006).

335 *Id.*

- The trial penalty has made the government the most powerful player in the criminal justice system. Although the defendant is cloaked in the presumption of innocence and the prosecutor theoretically has the burden of proof, as the Report makes clear, the mere decision to charge triggers a domino effect making a guilty plea the only rational choice in most cases. And as trials and hearings decline, so too does government accountability. Government mistakes and misconduct are rarely uncovered,[7] or are simply resolved in a more favorable plea bargain.[8] Moreover, the ease of conviction can encourage sloppiness, and a diminution of the government's obligation to fairness.
- Defense counsel, whose role is to ensure that "all other rights of the accused are protected,"[336] spend most of their time negotiating plea bargains and drafting sentencing memoranda. As a result of the trial penalty, not only are defense counsel trying fewer cases, they are frequently forced to settle cases before meaningful investigation and litigation of the government's case.[337]
- The prevalence of guilty pleas sidelines judges from their traditional supervisory role. Rather than scrutinizing the sufficiency and legality of the government's case, they are reduced to rubber-stamping plea bargains. If a mandatory minimum sentencing statute controls, judges do not even exercise their traditional sentencing role.
- The decline in the number of trials, and the litigation that precedes them, also causes advocacy skills to atrophy on both sides of the adversarial system. The federal courthouse in Manhattan, for example, held only 50 trials in 2015. Many defense lawyers and prosecutors have not tried cases in years, and many of the federal judges have similarly not presided over a trial in years.[338] As one judge summed up the impact of the vanishing trial: "The entire system loses an edge and . . . the quality of justice in our courthouses has suffered as a result."[339]

---

[336] *Penson v. Ohio*, 488 U.S. 75, 84 (1988).

[337] *See* David E. Patton, *Federal Public Defense in an Age of Inquisi6ion*, 122 YALE L.J. 2578 (2013).

[338] Benjamin Weiser, *Trial by Jury, a Hallowed American Right, Is Vanishing*, N.Y. TIMES, Aug. 7, 2016, *available at* https://www.nylimes.com/2016/08/08/nyregion/jury-trials-vanish-and-juslice-is-served-behind-closed- doors.html?_r=0.

[339] *Id.*

> The pressure defendants face to plead guilty can even cause innocent people to plead guilty. Of the 354 individuals exonerated by DNA analysis, 11% had pled guilty to crimes they did not commit,14 and the National Registry of Exonerations has identified 359 exonerees who pled guilty.15 . . . besides a trial, the defendant gives up many protections designed to ensure that no innocent defendant faces punishment.

- The capacity of the government to process large caseloads without hearings or trials has resulted in an exponential increase in incarceration. Wreaking devastation in lives and communities, and selectively concentrated among the poor and people of color, the nation's *mass incarceralion* has rightly been described as "the great unappreciated civil rights issue of our time."[340]
- Exoneration research has revealed one of the most tragic aspects of the criminal justice system: The pressure defendants face to plead guilty can even cause *innocent people* to plead guilty. Of the 354 individuals exonerated by DNA analysis, 11% had pled guilty to crimes they did not commit,[341] and the National Registry of Exonerations has identified 359 exonerees who pled guilty.[342] Additionally, the potential for such wrongful convictions is compounded in bargained-for-justice because, besides a trial, the defendant gives up many protections designed to ensure that no innocent defendant faces punishment.
- Finally, the decline in jury trials deprives society of an important community check on excesses of criminal justice system. **Juries** not only determine whether the prosecutors have met their high burden. They also apply their own sense of fair play — frequently convicting of lesser-included offenses or even acquitting entirely where the prosecution is perceived as over-reaching.[343] They are a reminder that

---

340 Walter Dellinger, *Supreme Court Breakfast Table*, Slate.com, June 25, 2014, *available at* http://www.slate.com/arlicles/news_and_polilics/the_breakfast_table/features/2014/scotus_roundup/supreme_court_roundup_does_today_s_cellphone_decision_mean_the_court_like.html.

341 https://www.innocenceproject.org/dna-exoneralions-in-the-united-states/ (last visited Feb. 8, 2018).

342 http://www.law.umich.edu/special/exoneralion/Pages/detaillist.aspx?View={FAF6EDDB-5A68-4F8F-8A52- 2C61F5BF9EA7}&FilterField1=Group&FilterValue1=P (last visited Feb. 8, 2017).

343 *See United States v. Polizzi*, 549 F. Supp. 2d 308, 404-32 (E.D.N.Y. 2008) (Weinstein, J.) (describing history of jury nullification), vacated sub nom., 564 F.3d 142 (2d Cir. 2009).

the government is not omnipotent, but instead remains subject to the will of the people. As the U.S. criminal justice system churns some 11 million people through its courtroom doors every year,[344] trial by jury actively engage the public in this critical process of democracy.

Principles and Recommendations

Principles

1. The trial penalty — the substantial difference between the sentence offered prior to trial versus the sentence a defendant receives after a trial — undermines the integrity of the criminal justice system.
2. Trials protect the presumption of innocence and encourage the government to charge cases based only on sufficient, legally-obtained evidence to satisfy the reasonable doubt standard.
3. The decline in the frequency of trials impacts the quality of prosecutorial decision-making, defense advocacy, and judicial supervision.
4. The decline in the frequency of trials tends to encourage longer sentences thereby contributing to mass incarceration, including mass incarceration of people of color and the poor.
5. The decline in the frequency of trials erodes the oversight function of the jury thereby muting the voice of lay people in the criminal justice system and also undercuts the role of appellate courts in supervising the work of trial courts.
6. The trial penalty creates a coercive effect which profoundly undermines the integrity of the plea bargaining process.
7. A reduction for accepting responsibility through a guilty plea is appropriate. The same or similar reduction should be available after trial if an individual convicted at trial sincerely accepts responsibility after trial regardless of whether the accused testified at trial or not.
8. No one should be punished for exercising her or his rights, including seeking pre-trial release and discovery, investigating a case, and filing and litigation of pre-trial statutory and constitutional motions.
9. Mandatory minimum sentences undermine the integrity of plea bargaining (by creating a coercive effect) and the integrity of the

---

[344] *See* https://ucr.Lbi.gov/crime-in-the-u.s/2015/crime-in-the-u.s.-2015/tables/table-29 (last visited Feb. 8, 2018).

sentencing process (by imposing categorical minimums rather than case-by-case evaluation). At the very least, safety valve provisions should be enacted to permit a judge to sentence below mandatory minimum sentences if justice dictates.

10. If mandatory minimums are not abolished, the government should not be permitted to use mandatory minimum sentences to retaliate against an accused person's decision to exercise her or his constitutional or statutory rights. That is, the state should not be allowed to file charges carrying mandatory minimum sentences in response to a defendant rejecting a plea offer or invoking her or his rights including the right to trial or to challenge unconstitutional government action.

Recommendations

1. Relevant Conduct: USSG §1B1.3 should be amended to prohibit the use of evidence from acquitted conduct as relevant conduct.
2. Acceptance of Responsibility: USSG §3E1.1(b) should be amended to authorize courts to award a third point for acceptance of responsibility if the interests of justice dictate without a motion from the government and even after trial.
3. Obstruction of Justice: USSG §3C1.1 should be amended to clarify that this adjustment should not be assessed solely for the act of an accused testifying in her or his defense. Application Note 2 should also be clarified in this respect.
4. Mandatory Minimum Sentencing: Mandatory minimum sentencing statutes should be repealed or subject to a judicial "safety valve" in cases where the court determines that individual circumstances justify a sentence below the mandatory minimum.
5. Full Discovery: Defendants should have full access to all relevant evidence, including any exculpatory information, prior to entry of any guilty plea.
6. Remove the Litigation Penalty: The government should not be permitted to condition plea offers on waiver of statutory or constitutional rights necessary for an accused person to make an intelligent and knowing decision to plead guilty. This includes an accused person's decision to seek pre-trial release or discovery, investigate a case, or litigate statutory or constitutional pre-trial motions.
7. Limited Judicial Oversight of Plea-Bargaining: There should be mandatory plea-bargaining conferences in every criminal case

supervised by a judicial officer who is not presiding over the case unless the defendant, fully informed, waives the opportunity. These conferences would require the participation of the parties but could not require either party to make or accept an offer. In some cases, one or more parties might elect not to participate beyond attendance.
8. Judicial "Second Looks": After substantial service of a sentence, courts should review lengthy sentences to ensure that sentences are proportionate over time.
9. Proportionality Between Pre-Trial and Post-Trial Sentencing: Procedures should be adopted to ensure that the accused are not punished with substantially longer sentences for exercising their right to trial, or its related rights. Concretely, post-trial sentences should not increase by more than the following: denial of acceptance of responsibility (if appropriate); obstruction of justice (if proved); and the development of facts unknown before trial.
10. Amendment to 18 U.S.C. § 3553(a)(6): In assessing whether a post-trial sentencing disparity is unwarranted, the sentencing court shall consider the sentence imposed for similarly situated defendants (including, if available, a defendant who pled guilty in the same matter) and the defendant who was convicted after trial. The sentencing court shall consider whether any differential between similarly situated defendants would undermine the Sixth Amendment right to trial.

Introduction

For decades, criminal justice in this country has remained largely hidden from public scrutiny, relegated to backroom "negotiations" between prosecutors and defendants, where the defendant agrees to forego fundamental constitutional rights in exchange for the hope of leniency in sentencing. Year after year, the trend has seen the percentage of federal defendants pleading guilty continuing to rise. In 2016, 97.3% of defendants in the federal criminal justice system opted to concede their guilt. And in 2017, that number held steady at 97.2%. That means that in recent years *fewer than 3%* of federal criminal defendants chose to take advantage of one of the most crucial constitutional rights.[345]

> In 2016, 97.3% of defendants in the federal criminal justice system opted to concede their guilt. And in 2017, that number held steady at 97.2%. That means that in recent years *fewer than 3%* of federal criminal defendants chose to take advantage of one of the most crucial constitutional rights.[18]

Plea bargaining has become so widely accepted that these statistics are unlikely to shock the average reader. But they should be deeply troubling. In a recent article in the *New York Times*, one federal judge highlighted the important role of the jury trial "not only as a truth-seeking mechanism and a means of achieving fairness, but also as a shield against tyranny. As Thomas Jefferson famously said, 'I consider [trial by jury] as the only anchor ever yet imagined by man, by which a government can be held to the principles of its constitution.'"[346]

Indeed, jury trials offer the average citizen an opportunity to directly participate in the criminal justice process to prevent the government from overstepping its authority. The public may still decry overcriminalization and the soaring prison population from afar. But the proliferation of plea bargaining has largely eliminated the public's traditional ability to nullify the government's overreach in individual cases. Despite the clear intentions of the country's founders, American society has willingly handed their authority back to the very institutions that juries were meant to keep in check.

What's more, they have done so not in the name of justice but of efficiency. The current public attitude echoes the same justification the Supreme Court gave when it jettisoned its historical skepticism of plea bargaining: "'If every criminal charge were subjected to a full-scale trial, the States and the Federal Government would need to multiply by many times the

---

345 United States Sentencing Commission, 2016 Sourcebook of Federal Sentencing Statistics, Figure C, *available at* https://www.ussc.gov/sites/default/files/pdf/research-and-publicalions/annual-reports-and- sourcebooks/2016/FigureC.pdf & United States Sentencing Commission, 2017 Sourcebook of Federal Sentencing Statistics, Figure C, *available at* https://www.ussc.gov/sites/default/files/pdf/research-and-publicalions/annual-reports-and- sourcebooks/2017/FigureC.pdf. *See also* Statistical Tables for the Federal Judiciary — June 2016. Table D-4, Criminal Defendants Terminated by Type of Disposition & Offense, *available at* http://www.uscourts.gov/stalislics/table/d-4/stalislical-tables-federal-judiciary/2016/06/30. This figure includes defendants who were acquitted after trial. It does not include those whose charges were dismissed by means other than acquittal.

346 Jed. S. Rakoff, *Why Innocent People Plead Guilty*, N.Y. TIMES, Nov. 20, 2014.

number of judges and court facilities.'"[347] However appealing the efficiency argument may be, it completely eviscerates the myriad protections secured by a jury trial. Defendants who go to trial enjoy the right:

- To be found guilty only by a jury of their peers, selected with the input of defendants' counsel and under restrictions to prevent discrimination that could cause the jury's decision to be unfairly biased;[348]
- To discover exculpatory and impeachment evidence that jurors would likely find material;[349]
- To confront and cross-examine witnesses to ensure live, adversarial testing of the prosecution's case;[350]
- To eliminate any adverse comments by the prosecution regarding the defendants' choice to remain silent;[351]
- To be found guilty only by a unanimous decision from the jury that they found evidence of guilt beyond a reasonable doubt after proper instructions to ensure that they understand the necessary level of proof and the burden on the prosecution to prove its case.[352]
- To raise constitutional and other legal challenges to the manner in which the government acquired evidence to support prosecution; and
- To appeal the conviction and any ancillary rulings underlying the conviction.

None of these protections is available to a defendant who pleads guilty.[353] Popular arguments about greater efficiency thus inevitably lead to an

---

[347] Suja A. Thomas, THE MISSING AMERICAN JURY 50 (2016) (quoting John H. Langbein, *On the Myth of Written Cons6itu6ions: The Disappearance of Criminal Jury Trial*, HARV. J.L. & PUB. POL'Y, 119, 125 (1992)). *See also* Chief Justice Burger's majority opinion in *Santobello v. New York*, 404 U.S. 257, 260 (1970).

[348] *See Batson v. Kentucky*, 476 U.S. 79 (1986); *J.E.B. v. Alabama ex rel. T.B.*, 511 U.S. 127 (1994).

[349] *Brady v. Maryland*, 373 U.S. 83 (1963); *Giglio v. United States*, 405 U.S. 150 (1972).

[350] *Crawford v. Washington*, 541 U.S. 36 (2004).

[351] *Gri9fin v. California*, 380 U.S. 609 (1965).

[352] *Cage v. Louisiana*, 498 U.S. 39 (1990).

[353] *United States v. Ruiz*, 536 U.S. 622, 630 (2002) (holding that defendants who plead guilty do not have a constitutional right to obtain impeachment evidence from prosecution prior to entering plea: "[T]he Constitution, in respect to a defendant's awareness of relevant circumstances, does not require complete knowledge of the relevant circumstances, but permits a court to accept a guilty plea, with its accompanying waiver of various constitutional rights, despite various forms of misapprehension under which a defendant might labor."); *United States v. Moussaoui*, 591 F.3d 263, 285 (4th Cir. 2010) (explaining

uncomfortable conclusion: however important these constitutional rights are, this country *cannot afford* to uphold them save in 3% of criminal cases.

There are undoubted advantages in allowing defendants to plead guilty — for the government, for society, and for defendants themselves. But do those advantages come at the expense of fairness and justice?

There are undoubted advantages in allowing defendants to plead guilty — for the government, for society, and for defendants themselves. But do those advantages come at the expense of fairness and justice? The astounding percentage of defendants who so willingly relinquish important Constitutional protections alone demands closer scrutiny of plea bargaining. Despite the nominal right of individual defendants to insist on a trial, recent studies have revealed that the plea bargaining process can be so coercive it can influence even innocent defendants to plead guilty. As this report details, there is ample evidence that many defendants are compelled to forego their right to a trial because the penalties they would otherwise face are too steep to risk.

This "Trial Penalty" — the discrepancy between the sentence offered during plea negotiations and the sentence a defendant will face after trial — has received much attention in recent years. In 2013, Human Rights Watch published a report detailing how prosecutors use the trial penalty to force federal drug defendants to plead guilty.[354] Joining that effort, NACDL has undertaken its own study to examine the mechanisms that contribute to the trial penalty in federal criminal cases across the board.

The United States Sentencing Commission's data on federal sentencing confirms the existence of a trial penalty. In 2015, in most primary offense categories, the average post-trial sentence was more than triple the average post-plea sentence. In antitrust cases, it was more than eight times as high. (*See* Figure 1, below.) Although these averages do not represent the precise choice faced by any individual defendant, NACDL has also conducted a survey and identified numerous real-world instances of the trial penalty — where defendants who went to trial faced extreme penalties compared to the sentences they were offered during plea negotiations or the sentences of their

---

that right to access exculpatory evidence "is a *trial* right" not available to defendants who plead guilty). Almost invariably, federal prosecutors will require, as a condition of the plea agreement, that the defendant waive the right to file pre-trial motions to suppress and the right to appeal.

[354] *An O9fer You Can't Refuse: How US Federal Prosecutors Force Drug Defendants to Plead Guilty*, Human Rights Watch (2013).

similarly-situated co-defendants. Because plea negotiations are off the record and because most cases plead out, data regarding plea offers is largely unavailable, so there is no way to accurately calculate the full extent of the trial penalty. Nevertheless, a combination of anecdotal evidence and an analysis of prosecutorial practices, sentencing laws, and judicial decisions strongly suggests that coercion plays a major role in the ever-increasing percentage of defendants who forego their right to a trial.

Because plea negotiations are off the record and because most cases plead out, data regarding plea offers is largely unavailable, so there is no way to accurately calculate the full extent of the trial penalty. . . . a combination of anecdotal evidence and an analysis of prosecutorial practices, sentencing laws, and judicial decisions strongly suggests that coercion plays a major role in the ever-increasing percentage of defendants who forego their right to a trial.

Federal prosecutors, who are already personally incentivized to achieve speedy convictions, have virtually unbridled discretion over decisions that will dictate a defendant's ultimate sentence. They possess nearly exclusive authority in selecting what charges to bring, and in most cases, any number of criminal statutes could apply to a defendant's conduct, each carrying a different potential sentence. Prosecutors thus have wide discretion to choose to add or drop charges in an effort to achieve a guilty plea. On the other hand, defendants presented with plea offers are often at an informational disadvantage and are unable to adequately assess the likelihood that they could be acquitted of the charges the prosecutor has selected, even with the benefit of effective assistance of counsel.

The federal sentencing laws in turn provide prosecutors with an arsenal of tools that can be manipulated to convince defendants to plead guilty. The federal Sentencing Guidelines, which are the starting point for sentencing in all federal cases, can result in excruciatingly steep penalties that are frequently disproportionate to a defendant's actual culpability, and important reductions from those penalties are generally only available to defendants who plead guilty. Although judges retain ultimate authority over final sentences, mandatory minimum sentencing statutes — which are only triggered by a prosecutor's decision to charge under the statute — curb judges' discretion in many instances. Even when there is no mandatory penalty in play, many judges are reticent to meaningfully exercise their discretion and instead cling to the familiar Guidelines calculations which are unlikely to be overturned on appeal. In short, the system is stacked against a defendant who insists on his right to a trial because the only way to ensure a fair sentence is to plead guilty.

Fortunately, the mechanisms that contribute to the trial penalty are not cemented in stone. In this report, NACDL has highlighted some of the specific ways defendants are unfairly coerced to forego their right to a trial with the goal of making progress toward reducing the impact of the trial penalty. To that end, NACDL has proposed several specific recommendations for reform. NACDL is hopeful that this effort will spur a broader movement to eliminate the coercive forces at play in plea bargaining and restore true freedom of choice for criminal defendants.

Measuring the Trial Penalty

Based on the data files published by the Sentencing Commission, NACDL has calculated the discrepancy between average sentences post-trial as opposed to those imposed following a guilty plea.[*]* (*See* Figure 1, below) When compared within each primary offense category, the results tend to confirm the existence of a trial penalty. For instance, in 2015, the average sentence for fraud was three times as high for defendants who went to trial versus those who pled guilty. And for burglary/breaking and entering and embezzlement it was nearly eight times as high.[355] Although this analysis does not take into account every factor in each individual case that may have led to a higher sentence, the fact that post-trial sentences tend to be significantly higher in most primary offense categories suggests that defendants are in fact being penalized for going to trial.

---

[*] *For the purposes of the more granular, o9fense-specific data analysis set forth in this report, the U.S. Sentencing Commission data files underlying the 2015 Sourcebook were studied in depth.*

[355] These calculations are based on data from the United States Sentencing Commission's datafiles for individual offenders, *available at* http://www.ussc.gov/research/datafiles/commission-datafiles. The calculations exclude death sentences (which are beyond the datafiles' scope), 144 sentences of life in prison, and 2 cases where an unspecified term of imprisonment was imposed. Those sentences are excluded from this analysis because they do not meaningfully lend themselves to a comparison of sentences on a scale of years. Because a life sentence is far more likely to be imposed post-trial than post-plea, the average discrepancy is in all likelihood greater than what has been calculated.

It may be difficult to calculate how much higher a post-trial sentence would need to be in order to coerce a defendant to plead guilty. But there is strong evidence that these discrepancies can compel even an innocent person to plead guilty.[356]

It may be difficult to calculate how much higher a post-trial sentence would need to be in order to coerce a defendant to plead guilty. But there is strong evidence that these discrepancies can compel even an innocent person to plead guilty.[29] Numerous scholars have examined the innocence problem of plea bargaining and have estimated that anywhere from 1.6% to 27% of defendants who plead guilty may be factually innocent.[357] Even assuming only the lowest of these estimates to be accurate, such outcomes cannot be condoned. The National Registry of Exonerations has identified 359 specific instances where defendants were later determined to be innocent of the crimes they originally pled guilty to.[358] A few cases are particularly worthy of note:

- Marcellus Bradford pled guilty to aggravated kidnapping in a case involving the kidnapping, rape, and murder of a 23-year-old woman in Chicago in 1986. In exchange for his testimony against a co-defendant, the prosecution agreed to drop the murder and rape charges. Bradford agreed, pled guilty, and was sentenced to 12 years in prison. But, after testifying at trial, Bradford recanted his statements, saying police had coerced him into falsely confessing and that he did so only to avoid a life sentence. DNA testing later confirmed that Bradford had not been involved in the crime.[359]
- Michael Marshall, who pled guilty after being charged with aggravated assault, armed robbery, possession of a firearm during a felony, and possession of a firearm by a convicted felon, faced potentially decades in prison. He was sentenced to four years on a charge of theft by taking. Marshall later wrote a letter to the Georgia

---

[356] Lucian E. Dervan, *Bargained Jus6ice: Plea-Bargaining's Innocence Problem and the* Brady *Safety-Valve*, 2012 UTAH L. REV. 51, 95 (2012) ("At some point, the sentencing differential becomes so large that it destroys the defendant's ability to act freely and decide in a rational manner whether to accept or reject the government's offer.").

[357] Dervan, 2012 UTAH L. REV. at 85. *See also* Donald A. Dripps, *Guilt, Innocence, & Due Process of Plea Bargaining*, 57 WM. & MARY L. REV. 1343, 1360-63 (2016).

[358] http://www.law.umich.edu/special/exoneralion/Pages/detaillist.aspx?View={FAF6EDDB-5A68-4F8F-8A52- 2C61F5BF9EA7}&FilterField1=Group&FilterValue1=P (last visited Feb. 8, 2017).

[359] http://www.innocenceproject.org/cases/marcellius-bradford/ (last visited Feb. 8, 2017).

Innocence Project claiming, "I plead guilty out of being scared." Marshall was released after DNA testing showed his DNA did not match the evidence from the crime.[360]

- Viken Keuylian pled guilty to one count of wire fraud based on an alleged failure to repay a bank loan and false statements to the bank. After pleading guilty, his attorney obtained documents in a civil lawsuit with the bank showing that the bank was in fact aware that the money would not be immediately repaid and that the bank was part of an arrangement to support certain business efforts by Keuylian. Keuylian then filed a motion seeking to withdraw his guilty plea, explaining that he always believed the fraud allegation was false but could not prove it until he obtained crucial evidence from the civil lawsuit. He also alleged that he was told that if he did not plead guilty he would be charged with money laundering and would face a significantly larger sentence and that his sister would be charged with fraud as well. The court granted his motion to withdraw his guilty plea and his conviction was vacated. Ultimately, the court granted a motion to dismiss the charge.[361]
- James Ochoa pled guilty to carjacking and armed robbery against his attorney's advice after a judge threatened him with a sentence of 25 years to life if a jury found him guilty. Pre-trial testing eliminated Mr. Ochoa as a possible contributor to the DNA evidence in his case, and news media reported that a deputy district attorney had called the lab to ask a lab analyst to change this report before it was released to Mr. Ochoa's counsel (the analyst refused). Nonetheless, Mr. Ochoa pled guilty and was sentenced to two years in prison. He was later released and his conviction vacated after the DNA was matched to another man arrested in an unrelated crime who later confessed to this crime.[362]

These examples show that the threat of a substantially greater sentence following a conviction at trial is a powerful incentive for even an innocent person to forego his or her Constitutional rights. And, as Mr. Ochoa's case demonstrates, this is true even where the government's case is relatively weak. Although most of these examples involve state court convictions, the same

---

360 http://www.innocenceproject.org/cases/michael-marshall/ (last visited Feb. 8, 2017).

361 http://www.law.umich.edu/special/exoneralion/Pages/casedetail.aspx?caseid=4471 (last visited Feb. 8, 2017).

362 http://www.innocenceproject.org/cases/james-ochoa/ (last visited Feb. 8, 2017).

incentives to plead guilty plague the federal criminal justice system. Moreover, in most federal cases, there is rarely biological evidence to look to for purposes of exoneration. Indeed, one of the key determinants of guilt or innocence in many criminal cases is intent — something that cannot be scientifically determined. Accordingly, these defendants are even less likely to risk a lengthy sentence — even if they know they did not intend to commit fraud.

As the discussion that follows will show, the influences that weigh on a defendant's decision to exercise the right to trial and the advantages that are skewed toward achieving guilty pleas leave little doubt that innocent defendants could be coerced to plead guilty.

A Brief History of Plea Bargaining and the Federal Sentencing Guidelines

Plea Bargaining and the Supreme Court: A Shift from Distrust to Dependency

Even before the time of this country's founding, juries had traditionally served as a check on the various branches of government,[363] allowing citizens to interpret how and when the law should be applied and "'"plac[ing] the real direction of society in the hands of the governed.'"'[364] As one scholar has explained, the criminal jury enjoyed the privilege to "decid[e] not to enforce a law where they believe[d] it would be unjust or misguided to do so, allow[ing] average citizens, through deliberations, to limit the scope of the criminal sanction."[365] Today, the critical role that juries historically played has all but disappeared as plea bargaining has become the overwhelming norm for resolving criminal cases.

---

[363] Thomas, *supra* note 20, at 43-48 (describing how the jury's original power was transferred "to the very parts of government that that jury was intended to check").

[364] Stephan Landsman, *So What? Possible Implica6ions of the Vanishing Trial Phenomenon*, 1 J. EMP. L. STUDIES 973, 974 (2004) ("In its political aspect, the jury is a 'republican' body that 'places the real direction of society in the hands of the governed.' It is drawn from the community at large and speaks with a voice unmediated by either a political appointment process or a requirement of professional training. The jury is the most effective instrument for incorporating the diverse ethnic, economic, religious, and social elements of American society into the justice system.").

[365] CLAY S. CONRAD, JURY NULLIFICATION: THE EVOLUTION OF A DOCTRINE (2014).

The practice of plea bargaining came into greater prominence in the early twentieth century, when crime was on the rise — arguably as a result of overcriminalization — and the criminal justice system was bending under its weight.[366]

Bargained-for justice — trading an admission of guilt for a lesser sentence — is assumed to be acceptable. But not too long ago, guilty pleas secured through promises of leniency or threats of higher sentences were actually deemed to be unconstitutional. The practice of plea bargaining came into greater prominence in the early twentieth century, when crime was on the rise — arguably as a result of overcriminalization — and the criminal justice system was bending under its weight.[39] Yet the practice was generally regarded by courts with deep suspicion, and the Supreme Court outright disapproved of it in a number of opinions.[367] In 1941, the Court ruled that a defendant's guilty plea induced by the prosecutor's threat to seek a higher sentence was unconstitutional. The Court determined that the defendant had been "deceived and coerced into pleading guilty."[368] These sentiments were echoed in several later opinions. Most notably, in *United States v. Jackson*, the Court held that the federal kidnapping statute imposed an "impermissible burden on the exercise of a constitutional right" because it called for the death penalty only for defendants convicted by a jury.[369] According to the Court, "the evil in the federal statute is not that it necessarily *coerces* guilty pleas and jury waivers but simply that it needlessly *encourages* them."[370] The Court readily acknowledged that the statute did not preclude defendants from acting voluntarily. Nevertheless, the *tendency* of the statute *to discourage* defendants from insisting on their innocence was enough to overturn it.[371] By 1968, the

---

[366] *See also* Dervan, *supra* note 29, at 59-61 (describing meteoric rise in plea bargaining as means of settling criminal disputes which was in part in response to "drive to create new criminal laws, a phenomenon that only added to the courts' growing caseloads"). *See also* Lucian E. Dervan, *Overcriminaliza6ion 2.0: The Symbio6ic Rela6ionship Between Plea Bargaining and Overcriminaliza6ion*, 7 J. OF L., ECON. & PLCY. 645, 649 (2011) (noting that number of federal criminal cases concluding in guilty pleas rose sharply from 50% in the early 1900s to 90% in 1925).

[367] *See generally* Dervan, *supra* note 29, at 65-76.

[368] *Walker v. Johnston*, 312 U.S. 275, 279-86 (1941).

[369] *United States v. Jackson*, 390 U.S. 570, 572 (1968).

[370] *Id.* at 583.

[371] *Id.* ("Thus the fact that the [statute] tends to discourage defendants from insisting on their innocence and demanding trial by jury hardly implies that every defendant who enters a guilty plea to a charge under the [statute] does so involuntarily. The power to reject coerced guilty pleas and involuntary jury waivers might alleviate, but it cannot totally eliminate the constitutional infirmity in the capital punishment provision of the [statute].").

Supreme Court had rejected "every guilty plea induced by threats of punishment or promises of leniency that had arrived on its docket."[372]

Despite its prior distrust of plea bargaining, in 1970, the Supreme Court made an astonishing about-face and ruled that it was *not* unconstitutional for prosecutors to offer inducements to obtain a guilty plea — even if such inducements were in the form of threats to seek a higher sentence after trial. In *Brady v. United States*, the Supreme Court held that a guilty plea is not unconstitutionally coerced when "motivated by the defendant's desire to accept the certainty or probability of a lesser penalty rather than face ... a higher penalty authorized by law for the crime charged."[373] The Court came to the same conclusion in *Parker v. North Carolina*, stating that "an otherwise valid plea is not involuntary because induced by the defendant's desire to limit the possible maximum penalty to less than that authorized if there is a jury trial."[374] With these opinions, the Supreme Court reversed decades of skepticism and ushered in a regime of unrestrained plea bargaining.

Indeed, a mere eight years later, the Court was going out of its way to defend the practice; not even the threat of life in prison was enough to convince the Court that the defendant was being unconstitutionally coerced to give up his right to a trial.[375] Although such threats might discourage defendants from going to trial, "'the imposition of these difficult choices [is] an inevitable' — and permissible — 'attribute of any legitimate system which

[372] Dervan, *supra* note 29, at 58-76, 76 (2012) (citing *Machibroda v. United States*, 368 U.S. 487 (1962) (if defendant's allegations were true that prosecutor had threatened to bring additional charges if defendant did not cooperate, then defendant "is entitled to have his sentence vacated"); *Lynum v. Illinois*, 372 U.S. 528 (1963) (striking defendant's confession as a statement made after threats of punishment and promises of leniency)).

[373] *Brady v. United States*, 397 U.S. 742, 751 (1970). This case should not be confused with the better-known case of *Brady v. Maryland*, 373 U.S. 83 (1963), where the Supreme Court held that the prosecution is required to turn over evidence to the defendant that could help prove his or her innocence.

[374] *Parker v. North Carolina*, 397 U.S. 790, 795 (1970).

[375] *See Bordenkircher v. Hayes*, 434 U.S. 357 (1978). In *Bordenkircher*, the defendant was charged with uttering a single forged check in the amount of $88.30, an offense that carried a term of two to ten years in prison. The prosecutor offered to recommend a sentence of five years if the defendant pled guilty. But if the defendant did not plead guilty and "save the court the inconvenience and necessity of a trial," the prosecutor would return to the grand jury to seek an indictment under a Habitual Criminal Act that would subject the defendant to a mandatory sentence of life imprisonment. The defendant rejected the plea and the prosecutor obtained the indictment under the Habitual Criminal Act. After the defendant was found guilty at trial, he was sentenced to life in prison. The Court rejected the defendant's argument that, by making good on his threat to seek a more serious charge carrying a substantially greater sentence, the prosecutor had violated the Constitution's Due Process Clause. 434 U.S. at 365.

tolerates and encourages the negotiation of pleas.'"[376] The Court was no longer asking whether the system *should* encourage the negotiation of pleas; it took this as a given. Many scholars have surmised the reason for this abrupt change of tune — plea bargaining had become critical to maintaining an efficient criminal justice system.[377]

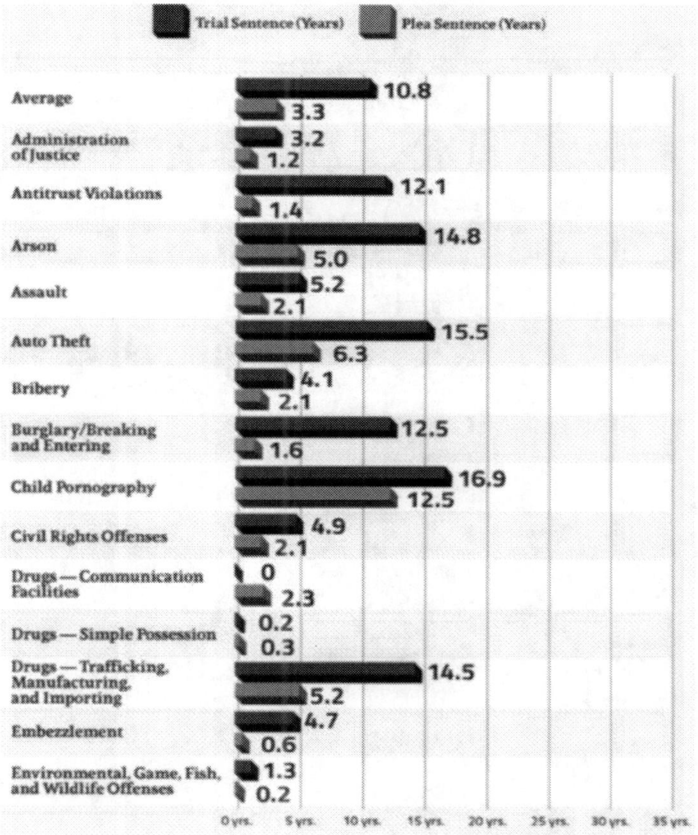

Figure 1. (Continued).

[376] *Bordenkircher v. Hayes*, 434 U.S. at 364 (citing *Cha9fin v. Stynchcombe*, 412 U.S. 17, 31 (1973)).

[377] Dervan, *supra* note 29, at 56, 81-82 (describing *Brady* as a "great compromise" necessitated by strains on the criminal justice system resulting from additional rights afforded to defendants under due process jurisprudence in the 1960s and ever-increasing numbers of criminal cases).

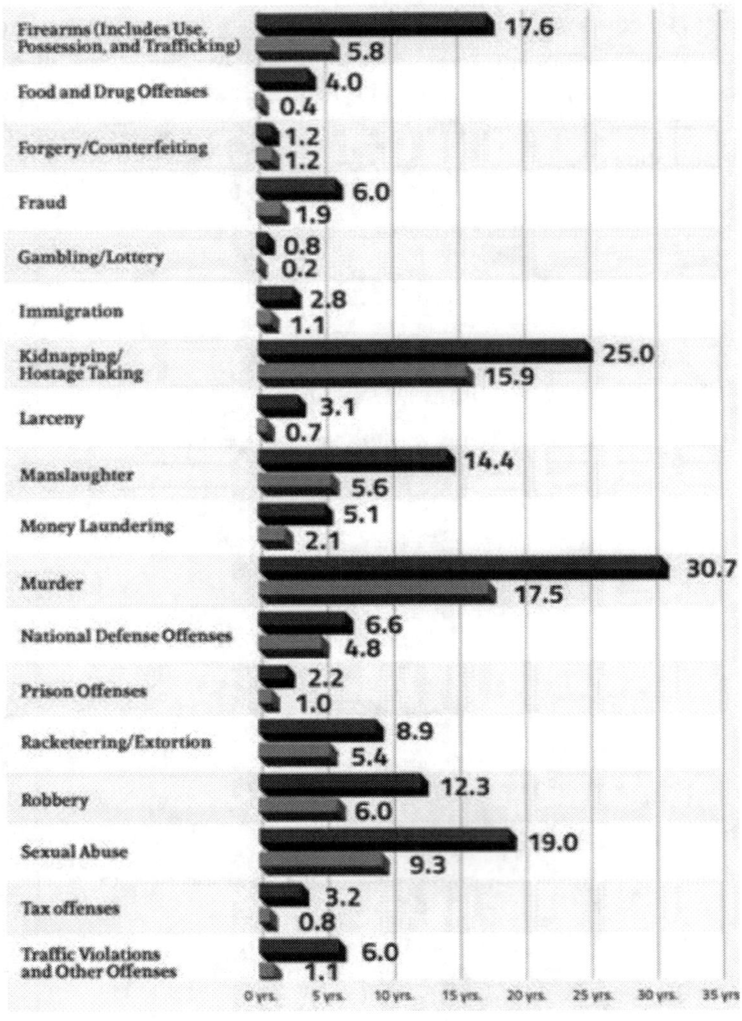

Figure 1. Sentence (Years) x Primary Offense x Plea/Trial.

The Sentencing Reform Act of 1984, United States v. Booker, and Judicial Discretion in Sentencing

Around the same time that the Supreme Court officially endorsed plea bargaining, significant reforms were underway in how criminal defendants were sentenced. Prior to 1984, federal district judges possessed discretion to impose any sentence on a defendant, constrained only by the Constitution and applicable statutory limitations. In response to concerns that this discretion produced wide disparities among similarly-situated defendants — depending largely on geography and the idiosyncrasies of individual judges — Congress passed the Sentencing Reform Act of 1984, instituting a commission to establish "guidelines … for use of a sentencing court in determining the sentence to be imposed in a criminal case …."[378] When the Guidelines were initially adopted, they were considered mandatory. Absent particular circumstances identified in the Guidelines themselves,[379] judges had no discretion to depart from the calculated sentencing range even if they believed the sentences they were imposing were unfair.

Prosecutors have maintained an inordinate amount of discretion over a defendant's ultimate sentence, in part, because the Guidelines are skewed in their favor.

Under these Guidelines, judges select a specific sentence from a range of sentences that is arrived at through a compilation of mathematical calculations. First, the judge calculates the defendant's offense level by: (1) identifying the applicable Guideline based on the statute of conviction; (2) determining the base offense level; evaluating the relevant conduct of the defendant and any others involved in the offense to apply specific offense characteristics;[380] and (4) making any applicable adjustments based on, for example, particular characteristics of the victims, the defendant's role in the

---

[378] 28 U.S.C. § 994(a)(1). The Sentencing Commission is an independent commission of the judicial branch of the federal government, and consists of seven voting members, appointed by the President with the advice and consent of the Senate. 28 U.S.C. § 991(a). At least three of the members must be federal judges, and no more than four may be members of the same political party. *Id.* The Attorney-General or his/her designee serves as an ex officio, non-voting member of the Commission. *Id.* Each Commissioner serves for a term of six years.

[379] These circumstances include, among other things, the provision of "substantial assistance" to the government in the prosecution of other defendants or crimes (§ 5K1.1) and the fact that a defendant was operating under coercion or duress (§5K2.12). *See also generally* 2016 Guidelines Manual, Chapter 5, Part K.

[380] "Relevant conduct" for purposes of calculating the offense level is not limited to conduct that the defendant actually engaged in himself. It can also include the conduct of others involved in the same criminal scheme, as long as the conduct was "reasonably foreseeable" in connection with "jointly undertaken criminal activity." Guidelines Section 1B1.3. This definition of "jointly undertaken criminal activity" was recently amended in 2015. But the Commission explained that it was "not intended as a substantive change in policy." *See* Amendments submitted to Congress April 30, 2015, at 15, *available at* http://www.ussc.gov/guidelines/amendments/reader-friendly-version-amendments-submitted-congress-april- 30-2015-eNfeclive-november-1-2015.

offense, whether the defendant accepted responsibility, and/or whether the defendant obstructed justice. Then, the judge calculates the defendant's criminal history category based on any prior convictions. After determining these two variables — offense level and criminal history category — the judge then plots the point at which they intersect on the Sentencing Table.[381] That intersection yields a sentencing range from which the judge can select a specific sentence.

To aid judges in their selection of an appropriate sentence, a probation officer will conduct an investigation and prepare a Presentencing Report (PSR). In the PSR, the probation officer will include details of the underlying conduct of the offense and the defendant's criminal history, will perform the calculations under the Guidelines, and then make a recommendation to the judge as to an appropriate sentence within the applicable Guidelines range. Both the prosecution and the defense then have an opportunity to review the PSR and raise any objections to the probation officer's calculation. After reaching a conclusion as to the appropriate Guidelines calculation, the judge considers the probation officer's recommendation and the positions of the parties and determines the final sentence.

As discussed more fully in the sections that follow, prosecutors have maintained an inordinate amount of discretion over a defendant's ultimate sentence, in part, because the Guidelines are skewed in their favor. By way of example, the Guidelines offer substantial incentives to defendants to plead guilty quickly, before defense counsel has been able to meaningfully evaluate the merits of the prosecution's case. And the overly-broad definition of "relevant conduct" allows prosecutors to introduce evidence of conduct that was not previously charged or of which the defendant was actually acquitted. "No other common law in the world enables the prosecutor to seek a sentence based on criminal conduct never charged, never subject to adversary process, never vetted by a grand jury or a jury, or worse, charges for which the defendant was acquitted."[382]

In 2005, the Supreme Court finally struck down the provision of the Sentencing Reform Act that made the Guidelines mandatory. *United States v. Booker* is considered a landmark decision because, in theory, it returned sentencing discretion to the judiciary. However, it is widely acknowledged

---

[381] The most recent version of the Sentencing Table is available at http://www.ussc.gov/sites/default/files/pdf/guidelines-manual/2016/Sentencing_Table.pdf.

[382] Nancy Gertner, Bruce Brower & Paul Shechtman, *'Why the Innocent Plead Guilty': An Exchange*, N.Y. TIMES, Jan. 8, 2015.

that the Guidelines continue to have a pervasive impact on sentences. Because the Supreme Court has held that the Guidelines are still the presumptive "starting point and the initial benchmark" for all sentences in the federal system, in every case, judges must still calculate the sentence called for by the Guidelines and consider that recommendation in imposing a sentence.[383] As Justice Sotomayor recently explained, "[i]n most cases, it is the range set by the Guidelines, not the minimum or maximum term of imprisonment set by statute, that specifies the number of years a defendant will spend in prison."[384]

Moreover, despite wishful thinking that *Booker* would encourage federal judges to assume a more active role in determining sentences, data show that over 80% of sentences are still within the Guidelines range.[385] The Supreme Court recently eliminated defendants' ability to challenge the Guidelines on grounds of vagueness, further entrenching their preeminence in a sentencing judge's calculations.[386] Because many sentencing judges have been reluctant to closely scrutinize the application of the Guidelines and because the Supreme Court has encouraged that reluctance, prosecutors may continue to rely on the Guidelines to threaten increasingly harsh sentences, pressuring defendants to plead guilty.

---

[383] *Gall v. United States*, 128 S. Ct. 586, 596 (2007).

[384] *Beckles v. United States*, 580 U.S. (Mar. 6, 2017) (Sotomayor, J., concurring).

[385] *See id.*; United States Sentencing Commission, 2015 Sourcebook of Federal Sentencing Statistics, Figure G, *available at* https://www.ussc.gov/sites/default/files/pdf/research-and-publicalions/annual-reports-and- sourcebooks/2015/FigureG.pdf. The Sentencing Commission reports that nearly 50 percent of sentences are within the Guidelines range, but the "below-range" classification is misleading because more than 40 percent of those sentences are the result of downward departures expressly recognized by the Guidelines. So the percentage of cases where judges choose to exercise their discretion to depart from the Guidelines is actually much lower than 50 percent.

See also Frank O. Bowman, III, *'Loss' Revisited: A Guarded Defense of the Centerpiece of the Federal Economic Crime Sentencing Guideline*, 82 MO. L. REV. 1, 3 (2017) ("Critical to any discussion of the post-*Booker* era is the understanding that the Guidelines, theoretically advisory though they may be, retain a powerful effect on the sentences defendants actually receive. Just under half of all sentences are still imposed within the judicially calculated guideline range, and most sentences imposed outside the applicable range remain fairly close to that range.") (citing Frank O. Bowman, III, *Dead Law Walking: The Surprising Tenacity of the Federal Sentencing Guidelines*, 51 HOUSTON L. REV. 1227, 1244 -50) (2014)). *See also Rita v. United States*, 551 U.S. 338 (2007) (Stevens, J., concurring) ("I am not blind to the fact that, as a practical matter, many federal judges continue to treat the Guidelines as virtually mandatory after our decision in *Booker*.").

[386] *Beckles v. United States*, 580 U.S. (Mar. 6, 2017).

Plea "Bargaining" and Coercive Prosecutorial Discretion

Today, the Federal Rules of Criminal Procedure explicitly recognize and sanction plea bargaining. In exchange for a defendant's agreement to plead guilty, prosecutors may offer to not bring certain charges or to dismiss certain charges.[387] They may agree to recommend, or not to oppose, a particular sentence or sentencing range.[388] In addition, they may agree to argue for or against the application of particular sentencing factors.[389] The flip side of all of these options is that prosecutors may also threaten to add charges or to recommend increased sentences if defendants refuse to plead guilty.

> As one federal judge has acknowledged, "most judges, happy for their own reasons to avoid a time-consuming trial, will barely question the defendant beyond the bare bones of his assertion of guilt, relying instead on the prosecutor's statement (untested by any cross-examination) of what the underlying facts are."[66]
>
> Because plea negotiations take place outside the purview of the court, both the judiciary and the public are cut off from exercising any oversight. The result is that prosecutors possess nearly unchecked discretion in plea negotiations.

In one of its early opinions favoring plea bargaining, the Supreme Court expressed a concern that failing to constitutionally approve the practice would drive it "back into the shadows from which it ha[d] so recently emerged."[390] The problem is, since that time, plea bargaining has largely remained in the shadows. Judicial scrutiny of guilty pleas is extremely limited. Unlike in some states, judges at the federal level are prohibited from participating in the plea bargaining process.[391] Although they are required to determine that a guilty plea is voluntary before accepting it, voluntariness is all but presumed as long as the judge has reminded a defendant of his or her right to a trial and recited

---

387 FED. R. CRIM. P. 11(c)(1)(a).

388 FED. R. CRIM. P. 11(c)(1)(b).

389 FED. R. CRIM. P. 11(c)(1)(c).

390 *Bordenkircher*, 434 U.S. at 365.

391 Multiple states have explicitly condoned participation by judges in the plea bargaining process, while others have allowed it without comment. *See* Risha Raj Batra, *Judicial Par6icipa6ion in Plea Bargaining: A Dispute Resolu6ion Perspec6ive*, 76 OHIO ST. L.J. 566, 577-79 (2015).

rote language listing the protections a trial affords.[392] As one federal judge has acknowledged, "most judges, happy for their own reasons to avoid a time-consuming trial, will barely question the defendant beyond the bare bones of his assertion of guilt, relying instead on the prosecutor's statement (untested by any cross-examination) of what the underlying facts are."[393]

Because plea negotiations take place outside the purview of the court, both the judiciary and the public are cut off from exercising any oversight. The result is that prosecutors possess nearly unchecked discretion in plea negotiations.

An Imbalance of Negotiating Power

In theory, plea bargaining is a negotiation between the government and the defendant. But the two sides do not come to the bargaining table as equal adversaries. The prosecutor is almost always at an informational advantage because he is not required to share information from his investigation with the defendant before offering and requiring the acceptance of a plea deal, leaving the defendant to guess what the prosecutor will be able to prove beyond a reasonable doubt. In addition (as discussed in greater depth in the following sections), many provisions built into the fabric of the sentencing system strengthen the prosecutor's bargaining leverage.[394] In fact, because certain key sentencing benefits are only available to defendants who plead quickly, there is even greater pressure to secure a plea agreement before the defendant or defense counsel have had any opportunity to evaluate the merits of the prosecution's case.

---

[392] *See* Darryl K. Brown, *Judicial Power to Regulate Plea Bargaining*, 57 WM. & MARY L. REV. 1225, 1273 (2016) ("Judges should be concerned with little more than whether a defendant had competent legal assistance and had not '*misunderstood the choices* that were placed before him;' constitutional law has almost nothing to say about whether choices the state creates for defendants are fair or coercive."); Stephanos Bibas, *Designing Plea Bargaining from the Ground up: Accuracy and Fairness without Trials as Backstops*, 57 WM. & MARY L. REV. 1055, 1074 (2016) ("Rules of criminal procedure require judges to provide defendants with a laundry list of procedural rights at plea colloquies, resulting in a near-monologue interrupted only by the defendant's perfunctory 'Yes' to each question. This information comes too late in the process to make a difference; by the time of the plea colloquy, the plea is *a fait accompli*."). *See also id.* at 1059 (noting that judges "may require only bare-bones allocution of factual and legal guilt, and do not have to speculate about the odds of conviction or the collateral consequences.").

[393] Rakoff, *supra* note 19.

[394] *See* notes 93-239, *infra*, and accompanying text.

Specific Bargaining Tactics

Charge Bargaining

Sentences are highly influenced by the specific crimes that are charged — a decision that is entirely within the discretion of the prosecution.[395] Because any number of criminal statutes might apply to a defendant's conduct, there is usually a wide array of charges from which the prosecutor can choose. Thus, prosecutors may threaten to charge under the statute carrying the highest maximum penalty in order to obtain bargaining leverage.[396] They may also intimidate defendants by threatening charges that carry mandatory minimum penalties.[397] There is no legal basis for a defendant to challenge the sufficiency of a grand jury indictment in federal court, and a grand jury may indict on mere hearsay without ever hearing evidence favorable to the accused. So

---

[395] There is no judicial scrutiny of the prosecution's selection of charges. *See Bordenkircher v. Hayes*, 434 U.S. at 364 (1978) ("In our system, so long as the prosecutor has probable cause to believe that the accused committed an offense defined by statute, the decision whether or not to prosecute, and what charge to file or bring before a grand jury, generally rests entirely in his discretion."). As one commentator has noted, "Assuming the prosecutor has a legal right of plenary discretion, it then subordinates the defendant's rights to the tactical exercise of that discretion." Dripps, *supra* note 30, at 1370.

[396] H. Mitchell Caldwell, *Coercive Plea Bargaining*, 61 CATHOLIC U. L. REV. 63, 83 n.147 (2011). Cynthia Alkon, *The U.S. Supreme Court's Failure to Fix Plea Bargaining: The Impact of* Lafler *and* Frye, 41 HASTINGS CONST. L.Q. 561, 587 (Apr. 10, 2014) ("A prosecutor can now routinely decide whether to charge the same act as a misdemeanor or a felony; whether to add an enhancement . . .; whether to add a prior conviction; or whether to allege the offense happened 'in a school zone' or another location that will increase the potential punishment. Adding charges, enhancements, or prior convictions can substantially increase the severity of a sentence."). Although the U.S. Attorneys' Manual instructs prosecutors not to file charges simply to exert leverage to induce a plea, it also instructs them to "seek a plea to the most serious offense that is consistent with the nature and full extent of the defendant's conduct and likely to result in a sustainable conviction." U.S. Attorneys' Manual § 9-27.000, *available at* https://www.juslice.gov/usam/united-states-attorneys-manual. *See also* Mary Patrice Brown and Stevan E. Bunnell, *Nego6ia6ing Jus6ice: Prosecutorial Perspec6ives on Federal Plea Bargaining in the District of Columbia*, 43 AM. CRIM. L. REV. 1063, 1077 (2006) (DOJ policy, reflected in various memoranda issued by attorneys general from Richard Thornburgh to John Ashcroft providing guidance on plea bargaining, [is/has been] to require federal prosecutors to charge and pursue the most serious, readily provable offense(s)).

[397] Yue Ma, *Prosecutorial Discre6ion and Plea Bargaining in the United States, France, Germany, and Italy: A Compara6ive Perspec6ive*, 12 INT'L CRIM. JUSTICE REV. 1, 27 (2002) ("Apart from filing multiple charges, another powerful weapon available to prosecutors is charging defendants under penalty-enhancing statutes."). *See also United States v. Angelos*, 345 F. Supp. 2d 1227 (D. Utah 2004) (drug defendant charged with twenty counts, including five § 924(c) counts, after rejecting a plea offer to plead guilty to a drug distribution count and one § 924(c) count; "the government made clear to Mr. Angelos that if he rejected the offer, the government would obtain a new superseding indictment adding several § 924(c) counts").

prosecutors retain the upper hand to threaten more serious charges, even if they are supported by evidence that would be inadmissible at trial, can be defeated by countervailing evidence, or are wholly unsupported by the law.[398] Because so few defendants are willing to risk going to trial, prosecutors' charging decisions are largely free from judicial scrutiny.

> The consequences for those who insist on their right to trial are even more severe because, many prosecutors believe that, once they have made a threat, they cannot hesitate to follow through — no matter how outrageous the threat is. Otherwise, their threats will not be taken seriously in the future and they will undermine their bargaining leverage.

Charge bargaining strategies enable the prosecutor to exert considerable pressure over defendants to plead guilty.[399] Professor Lucian Dervan recently highlighted a case that starkly illustrates the power prosecutors have over sentences because of their unbridled discretion to select charges. Lea Fastow was the wife of Enron's former chief financial officer, Andrew Fastow. Initially, prosecutors charged her with six felony conspiracy and tax fraud counts, which, under the Sentencing Guidelines, carried a potential sentence of 8 to 10 years in prison.[400] Under a plea agreement, the prosecution agreed to seek a sentence of only five months. When the presiding judge rejected the plea agreement given that probation officers had recommended a sentence of 10-16 months, Ms. Fastow changed her plea to not guilty.[401] To maintain her cooperation and the cooperation of her husband (who was also facing prosecution on separate charges), prosecutors then withdrew the original charges and reached an agreement with Ms. Fastow for her to plead guilty. The revised plea agreement involved a misdemeanor tax charge carrying a

---

[398] Caldwell, *supra* note 69, at 85.

[399] *Id.* at 77; Lindsey Devers, *Plea and Charge Bargaining: Research Summary*, at 2 (Bureau of Justice Assistance, U.S. Dep't of Justice 2011) ("Overall, the majority of evidence illustrates that those who accept a plea are likely to receive a lighter sentence compared with those who opt for a trial. This disparity exists because prosecutors are granted wide discretion when reducing charges."), *available at* https://www.bja.gov/Publicalions/PleaBargainingResearchSummary.pdf.

[400] Indictment, *U.S. v. Fastow*, Cr. No. H-03- (S.D. Tex. Apr. 30, 2003), *available at* http://news.findlaw.com/wsj/docs/enron/usleafstw43003ind.pdf; Lucian E. Dervan & Vanessa A. Edkins, *The Innocent Defendant's Dilemma: An Innova6ive Empirical Study of Plea Bargaining's Innocence Problem*, 103 J. CRIM. L. & CRIMINOLOGY 1, 16 n.91 (2013) ("Given an alleged loss amount of $17 million and more than fifty victims, Fastow, who had no prior criminal record, faced a sentencing range of 97-121 months.").

[401] *Lea Fastow Plea Deal Scrapped*, CNNMoney (Apr. 7, 2004, 6:06 p.m.), *available at* http://money.cnn.com/2004/04/07/news/midcaps/enron_fastow/.

potential sentence of 10-16 months under the Guidelines. Both sides requested a sentence of ten months, and the court imposed a sentence of 12 months. At the second plea hearing, the court commented: "The Department of Justice's behavior might be seen as a blatant manipulation of the federal justice system and is of great concern to this court."[402]

Such manipulation is indeed troubling. But it is all too common. The consequences for those who insist on their right to trial are even more severe because, many prosecutors believe that, once they have made a threat, they cannot hesitate to follow through — no matter how outrageous the threat is. Otherwise, their threats will not be taken seriously in the future and they will undermine their bargaining leverage.

Fact Bargaining

Apart from selecting charges, prosecutors can also influence sentences by bargaining with defendants regarding what facts will be considered when determining their sentences.[403] In considering the facts relevant to sentencing, judges rely on the probation officer's presentence report (PSR).[404] The probation officer is supposed to conduct an independent investigation into the defendants' conduct and criminal background. But in reality, the description of the offense in the PSR is usually derived from information provided by the prosecutor in the indictment.[405]

> With fewer and fewer defendants opting for trial, judicial scrutiny of the terms of plea agreements is increasingly limited, as is judicial scrutiny of police conduct because defendants are coerced into waiving the right to challenge misconduct before the trial court or on appeal.

---

402 *Lea Fastow Pleads — Who's Next?* CNNMoney (May 6, 2004, 5:46 p.m.), *available at* http://money.cnn.com/2004/05/06/news/midcaps/enron_lfastow/.

403 Kate Stith & José A. Cabranes, FEAR OF JUDGING: SENTENCING GUIDELINES IN THE FEDERAL COURTS 136 (1998) ("Plea bargaining that takes the form of 'fact bargaining' under a regime of mandatory sentencing guidelines is, for all intents and purposes, *sentence* bargaining.").

404 FED. R. CRIM. P. 11(c)(3)(A).

405 Probation Officers' Survey, 8 FED'L SENT. REP. 303, 303 (1996) ("[I]n most districts the Probation Officer prepares the Offense Conduct section of the presentence report with information supplied by the government."); Felicia Sarner, '*Fact Bargaining' Under the Sentencing Guidelines: The Role of The Proba6ion Department*, 8 FED. SENT'G REP. 328, 329 (1996) (arguing that the Probation Office has a pervasive law enforcement bias; "The prosecutor's version [of the facts] tends to be adopted in its entirety, almost without exception."); Stith & Cabranes, *supra* note 76, at 138-39 ("The description of the offense in most presentence reports in most districts is prepared largely or exclusively on the basis of information provided by the prosecutor.").

When a defendant pleads guilty, he typically reaches an agreement with the prosecution regarding the relevant facts, and that stipulation is expressly set forth in the plea agreement.[406] Judges may also take such stipulations into account at sentencing. In fact, when the statement of facts included in the plea agreement differs from that included in the PSR, courts tend to defer to the plea agreement.[407] So the factual details that will be used to evaluate the defendant's sentence under the Guidelines is yet another item for the prosecutor to trade, and the incentive for a defendant to reach agreement with the prosecutor becomes even greater.[408]

FedEx, UPS, and the Trial Penalty

In 2013, the federal government accused both FedEx and UPS of illegally conspiring to distribute controlled substances by delivering packages containing pharmaceuticals purchased from Internet pharmacies. Neither company was actually aware of what was in the packages. Despite the novel theory of the government's case, UPS quickly entered a non-prosecution agreement and succumbed to a fine of approximately $40 million and a slew of corporate governance reforms. By contrast, when FedEx opted to take its case to trial, the government sought fines of $1.6 billion — forty times the amount it was willing to accept from UPS in exchange for the non-prosecution agreement. FedEx ultimately prevailed after the presiding judge expressed skepticism of the case and the government dropped its charges. While the trial judge declared that FedEx was factually innocent of the charges, the only reason the judge even got involved was because FedEx insisted on challenging the charges at trial. UPS had engaged in the same conduct and was equally innocent, but incurred a $40 million fine because it gave up its right to a trial in exchange for leniency.

---

406 Brown & Bunnell, *supra* note 69, at 1068-70.

407 Probation Officers' Survey, *supra* note 78, at 304 ("[W]hile courts do weigh both sides and often hold hearings, they almost universally defer to the plea agreement, especially when it is more favorable to the defendant than the presentence report.").

408 Melissa Hamilton, *McSentencing: Mass Federal Sentencing and the Law of Unintended Consequences*, 35 CARDOZO L. REV. 2199, 2235- 2236 (2014) ("With the guidelines, a plethora of facts are specifically relevant to increase and decrease sentencing recommendations. And these fact-based modifications reach much farther than statutory offense enhancements. In essence, fact bargaining here represents more a form of sentence bargaining than plea bargaining because the relevant facts are usually external to the elements of the specific offense(s) of conviction.").

Although the Department of Justice has consistently instructed prosecutors to only stipulate to facts they know to be true and to disclose to the court all facts relevant to Guidelines calculations,[409] fact bargaining persists.[410] When no defendants in a criminal conspiracy exercise their right to a trial — as is almost always the case — there is likely no way to know that fact bargaining has occurred. So by continuing to take advantage of their discretion to force pleas, prosecutors can prevent their own manipulation from being uncovered.

Many prosecutors will not hesitate to use the full extent of their bargaining power to secure guilty pleas.

Draconian Plea Agreements and "Rights Bargaining"

In addition to charge and fact bargaining, prosecutors also have wide discretion to dictate the terms and timing of plea agreements, and they can insist on objectionable terms knowing that those terms will likely never be scrutinized. For instance, in many districts, it is common practice to require defendants to waive the right to appeal their sentence or important legal rulings including, for example, the legality of the criminal statutes or police conduct, including the legality of a stop, search, or seizure, or the acquisition of other

---

[409] *See, e.g.*, U.S. Attorneys' Manual § 9-27.430, *supra* note 69 ("[T]he Department's policy is only to stipulate to facts that accurately reflect the defendant's conduct. If a prosecutor wishes to support a departure from the guidelines, he or she should candidly do so and not stipulate to facts that are untrue."); Memorandum from Attorney General Richard Thornburgh on Plea Policy for Federal Prosecutors: Plea Bargaining Under the Sentencing Reform Act (1989) ("The Department's policy is only to stipulate to facts that accurately represent the defendant's conduct. If a prosecutor wishes to support a departure from the guidelines, he or she should candidly do so and not stipulate to facts that are untrue."), *available at* https://www.fd.org/sites/default/files/criminal_defense_topics/essenlial_topics/sentencing_resources/useful_reports/thornburgh_memos_3.13.89_and_6.16.89.pdf; Memorandum from Attorney General John Ashcroft on Department Policies and Procedures Concerning Sentencing Recommendations and Sentencing Appeals 2 (July 28, 2003) ("If readily provable facts are relevant to calculations under the Sentencing Guidelines, the prosecutor must disclose them to the court, including the Probation Office."), *available at* https://www.justice.gov/sites/default/files/ag/legacy/2009/03/20/ag-072803a.pdf.

[410] Sonja B. Starr and M. Marit Rehavi, *Mandatory Sentencing and Racial Disparity: Assessing the Role of Prosecutors and the E9fects of Booker*, 123 YALE L.J. 2, 12 (2013) ("Plea agreements usually include factual stipulations, and, even though DOJ has long directed prosecutors not to bargain over these facts, many studies have documented the persistence of fact-bargaining."). A 1996 survey of probation officers suggested a widespread perception that fact bargaining occurred regularly and that the stipulated facts in a plea agreement often were not accurate or complete. Probation Officers' Survey, *supra* note 78, at 303.

forms of evidence.[411] And where a defendant has already litigated such an issue, waiver of the right to appeal an adverse determination is frequently a condition of the guilty plea. Increasingly, prosecutors are requiring defendants to waive their right to receive exculpatory evidence in the possession of the government.[412] Very few defendants will refuse to accede to such terms because the only other choice is to take the case to trial and face a much higher sentence. So prosecutors can make plea offers on an all-or-nothing basis, confident that defendants will accept any terms to avoid an excessive sentence and that judges will rubberstamp the deal because they do not want to deny a defendant the benefit of a bargained-for lower sentence. With fewer and fewer defendants opting for trial, judicial scrutiny of the terms of plea agreements is increasingly limited, as is judicial scrutiny of police conduct because defendants are coerced into waiving the right to challenge misconduct before the trial court or on appeal. In the rare case where a defendant goes to trial and challenges the prosecutor's draconian terms, the prosecutor will likely object to the court invading its domain. For example, in one federal case, the defendant was offered a plea agreement that would preclude him from making arguments at sentencing comparing his culpability to one of his co-defendants — a comparison which the law requires of the sentencing judge.[413] The prosecutor was only willing to remove that term from the plea agreement if the defendant first agreed to plead to additional counts that would ultimately result in exposure to a lengthier maximum sentence.[414] When the defendant attempted to raise the unfair plea agreement terms to the court's attention, the prosecutor berated him, arguing that if he "wants to enter into a contract with the government, his choices are perforce constrained by what the government is prepared to agree to."[415]

---

[411] Alexandra W. Reimelt, *An Unjust Bargain: Plea Bargains and Waiver of the Right to Appeal*, 51 B.C. L. REV. 871 (2010).

[412] This waiver implicates defendants' due process rights as set forth in *Brady v. Maryland,* 373 U.S. 83. This practice effectively encourages prosecutors to withhold exculpatory evidence during the plea bargaining process. *See also Alvarez v. City of Brownsville*, 860 F.3d 799 (5th Cir. 2017), rehearing en banc docketed, No. 16-40772 (5th Cir. Nov. 2, 2017) (addressing the question, via a § 1983 action, of whether under the U.S. Constitution a prosecutor may withhold proof of innocence while a defendant pleads guilty).

[413] *See* 18 U.S.C. § 3553.

[414] *See* Memorandum in Support of Motion by Defendant James Fields for a Rule 11 Hearing, Notice of Acceptance of Terms of Plea Offer, and Limited Objection Based on 18 U.S.C. § 3553(a)(6) and the Due Process Clause in *United States v. Latorella and Fields*, No. 10-cv-10388-DPW (D. Mass. Mar. 21, 2012).

[415] *See* Government's Memorandum in Response to Defendant James Fields's Motion for a Rule 11 Hearing in *United States v. Latorella and Fields*, No. 10-cv-10388-DPW (D. Mass. Mar. 21, 2012), at 4.

The Department of Justice frequently pushes Congress and the Sentencing Commission for higher and higher penalties, further evidence of a strong desire to enhance their negotiating leverage.

Perhaps the most extreme example of draconian plea terms was only recently limited by action of former Attorney General Eric Holder. In many districts, prosecutors were seeking a waiver of a prospective claim of ineffectively assistance of counsel as a condition of a guilty plea. In other words, to avoid the trial penalty an accused would have to agree that she would never challenge the fact that the plea itself was the result of ineffective representation of the very counsel who assisted the defendant in understanding the strength of the case and, in the vast majority of cases, recommended the guilty plea. NACDL and various state entities determined that this practice was unethical, and after a challenge to a rule proscribing this kind of waiver was rejected by the Supreme Court of Kentucky, the Department of Justice barred the conduct.[416]

But the capacity of prosecutors to construct ever more onerous conditions for a guilty plea cannot be overstated. Indeed, federal prosecutors now seek even the waiver of rights under the Freedom of Information Act.[417]

David Anthony Taylor and the Trial Penalty

David Anthony Taylor was a member of a gang in Southwest Virginia that was implicated in a string of 10 robberies in 2012. The gang targeted drug dealers because they would typically have drug proceeds in their homes and would be reluctant to report the crimes to the authorities for fear of arrest themselves. George Fitzgerald, the leader of the gang, conducted the

416 National Association of Criminal Defense Lawyers Ethics Advisory Committee Formal Op. No. 12-02 (2012), *available at* https://www.nacdl.org/ethicsopinions/12-02/; *United States v. Kentucky Bar Associa6ion*, 439 S.W.3d 136 (Ky. Aug. 21, 2014); Press Release, Department of Justice, Attorney General Holder Announces New Policy to Enhance Justice Department's Commitment to Support Defendants' Right to Counsel (Oct. 14, 2014), *available at* http://www.jusIice.gov/opa/pr/attorney- general-holder-announces-new-policy-enhance-jusIice-departments-commitment-suppoet.

417 *See Class v. United States,* 2018 WL 987347, *3, S.Ct. (U.S. Feb. 21, 2018) ("…express waivers included…various rights to request or receive information concerning the investigation and prosecution of his criminal case."). *See also* Tim Cushing, *Court Tells Government S6icking FOIA Waivers in Plea Agreements Is Probably a Bad Idea*, techdirt, Aug. 11, 2017, *available at* https://www.techdirt.com/arIicles/20170805/10120837932/court-tells-government-sIicking-foia-waivers-plea- agreements-is-probably-bad-idea.shtml.

surveillance of the victims, decided who would participate in each home invasion, and divided up the proceeds afterwards. He also took a cut of the proceeds from all 10 robberies.

Taylor, on the other hand, was a low-level member who participated in only 3 of the 10 break-ins. He was not involved in planning any of them. Fitzgerald described that Taylor's role was to act as a human shield; as the first member of the gang to enter the house, he was the one most likely to be shot if the victims were armed.

When the gang members were indicted, all of them except Taylor pled guilty. Fitzgerald, the ringleader, was sentenced to 22 years in jail, after receiving a reduction for cooperating with the government against the other gang members. The other low-level members received sentences between 7 and 14 years.

The prosecutor initially offered Taylor a plea deal — it would agree to indict him for only one count of robbery and one count of brandishing a gun. But if Taylor refused the deal, the prosecutor threatened to file additional charges. Taylor chose to exercise his right to a trial, and the prosecutor made good on his threat — he filed a superseding indictment adding two more counts, including an additional gun charge which stacked another mandatory 25 years onto Taylor's potential sentence.

Taylor's first trial resulted in a hung jury, but the second jury convicted him of three of the four counts in the superseding indictment. He was acquitted of one of the gun charges.

Although the prosecutor had moved at trial to exclude evidence regarding Taylor's potential sentence from being presented to the jury (because it might confuse them), after conviction, he sought a 42-year sentence — an upward variance from the Guidelines. In support of that onerous penalty, the prosecutor argued that he could have charged Taylor with participation in another, separate robbery, and that the Guidelines did not appropriately account for Taylor's failure to accept responsibility for his crimes.

Taylor was ultimately sentenced to 28 years in jail, longer than any of his co-defendants, even the ringleader.

Prosecutorial Attitudes and Incentives to Coerce

One criticism of constitutional jurisprudence on plea bargaining is that it fails to acknowledge that prosecutors, as officials of the state, have obligations beyond their own personal interests.[418] In our adversarial system, prosecutors face strong personal, professional, and institutional incentives to secure pleas. Prosecutors, however, are ethically obliged to do justice and not win at any cost. Prosecutors are required to act as an arm of justice and not merely as an adversary to the defendant. Unfortunately, many prosecutors will not hesitate to use the full extent of their bargaining power to secure guilty pleas.[419]

While most prosecutors will not acknowledge that defendants should be punished for going to trial, most adopt the attitude that leniency is only for those defendants who admit their guilt before trial which, of course, amounts to same thing. If a prosecutor finds himself in the difficult position of having to support a much harsher sentence than he was originally willing to accept in exchange for a guilty plea, the most common refrain is that he is merely applying the law. That is a hard argument to swallow, however, because prosecutors actively advocate for amendments to the law to increase their bargaining power. The Department of Justice frequently pushes Congress and the Sentencing Commission for higher and higher penalties, further evidence of a strong desire to enhance their negotiating leverage.

Inadequate Constitutional Protections for Defendants during Plea Bargaining

In 2012, the Supreme Court finally acknowledged that plea bargaining had replaced trials as the nearly universal means of resolving criminal cases: "'It is not some adjunct to the criminal justice system; it is the criminal justice system.'"[420] Because the ultimate fate of defendants is now almost always decided before trial, the Court's landmark decisions in *Missouri v. Frye* and *LaZler v. Cooper* recognized that defendants are entitled to effective assistance of counsel during plea negotiations. But, while this is certainly a welcome concession, it does not remedy the imbalance of power between prosecutors and defendants.[421] Defendants who are represented by effective counsel are still up against the prosecution's unrestrained charging discretion and informational advantages. And, as discussed in more detail below, the exorbitant Sentencing Guidelines and statutes skew the playing field even more in the prosecutor's favor.

---

418 *See* Darryl K. Brown, *supra* note 65, at 1274.

419 Jenn Rolnick Borchetta & Alice Fontier, *When Race Tips the Scales in Plea Bargaining: New Research Finds That Prosecutors Give White Defendants Better Deals Than Black Defendants*, Slate.com, Oct. 23, 2017.

420 *Missouri v. Frye*, 132 S. Ct. 1399, 1407 (2012).

421 *See* Darryl K. Brown, *supra* note 65, at 1275.

Kevin Ring and the Trial Penalty

Kevin Ring was a lobbyist involved in the Jack Abramoff bribery scandal in the mid-2000s. Abramoff and several of his law firm colleagues were accused of providing bribes and gratuities to White House staffers, Congressional aides and other government officials in an attempt to, among other things, influence legislation permitting gambling on Indian reservations. Ring, who worked for Abramoff at the time, was indicted for conspiracy to commit honest services fraud and pay illegal gratuities.

Abramoff and his fellow mastermind in the scheme, Michael Scanlon, were also accused of orchestrating a kickback conspiracy where they actually lobbied against their clients' interests to extort higher fees from them. Ring was largely uninvolved in the kickback conspiracy.

Both Abramoff and Scanlon pled guilty and were sentenced to 4 years and 20 months, respectively. The other lobbyist defendants also pled guilty and the government recommended that they be sentenced either to home confinement or only a few months in prison. The court sentenced one to thirty days in prison and the others to probation.

Ring, however, chose to go trial. After an initial hung jury, the second jury found him guilty. At sentencing, the prosecution calculated Ring's Guidelines range to be between 17 to 21 years, far longer than either Abramoff or Scanlon had received.

In supporting that calculation, the prosecution urged the court to consider the benefits the lobbyists' clients had received in exchange for the bribes — even though it had not argued that those facts were relevant to sentencing any of Ring's co-defendants. The prosecution dismissed any suggestion of fact bargaining, claiming that it had only recently acquired evidence establishing the extent of the benefits.

In a presentencing opinion, the court explained that, although it was not clear that fact bargaining had occurred, courts have little ability to uncover or police such tactics when they are used:

> In criminal cases involving plea agreements, the Court and the probation office are frequently at the mercy of the parties to disclose and explain relevant facts [and] may not always get a full picture of the defendant's offense conduct, nor do [they] have the means to learn the information on [their] own.

The judge ultimately rejected the prosecution's argument and sentenced Ring to 20 months in jail:

> Employing a dramatically different methodology for calculating the Guidelines range of those who plead guilty would … undermine the very purpose of the Guidelines, and give prosecutors even more power over sentencing than is already the case.

Prosecutors Leverage Excessive Sentencing Guidelines to Force Pleas

The enormous discretion that prosecutors wield to pressure defendants to plead guilty through traditional mechanisms like charge and fact bargaining is even greater in light of the Sentencing Guidelines. Although the Guidelines were adopted as a means of addressing unwarranted disparity in sentencing, they have been largely ineffectual in meeting that goal.[422] The Supreme Court has made clear that individual judges are best suited to weigh disparities on a case-by-case basis.[423] But the pipe dream of administering "uniform" justice has held sway, reinforcing the influence of the Guidelines which rely on mathematical calculations at the expense of fairness in individual cases.

As judges, scholars, and even former prosecutors have observed, overemphasis on the amount of loss often leads to sentences that are disproportionate to the seriousness of the offense.[115]

Indeed, although several federal judges are quite outspoken about their disagreement with the Guidelines — referring to them as arbitrary and having been "drawn from nowhere"[424] — many, many more remain reluctant to deviate from them. One federal judge recently admitted that she would not have imposed a 360-month sentence, but she felt compelled to do so because the Guidelines called for that sentence.[425] In fact, because judges are still required to begin their sentencing analysis by calculating the Guidelines range,

---

[422] *See, e.g.*, *United States v. Diaz*, No. 11-CR-00821-2 (JG), 2013 U.S. Dist. LEXIS 11386, at *94 & n.164 (E.D.N.Y. 2013) (citing numerous studies disputing notion that adherence to Guidelines would create greater parity among sentences).

[423] *See Kimbrough v. United States*, 552 U.S. 85, 107-108 (2007).

[424] Jed S. Rakoff, *Why the Federal Sentencing Guidelines Should Be Scrapped*, 26 FED. SENT'G REP. 6, 7 (2013).

[425] *Beckles v. United States*, 580 U.S. (Mar. 6, 2017) (Sotomayor, J., concurring).

there may be a psychological predisposition to sentence within that range.[426] It is also possible that the Guidelines have maintained their pervasive force because they represent the path of least resistance. Within-Guidelines sentences are virtually immune from review on appeal, so judges who do not like to be overturned can ensure a good record by sticking to the Guidelines.[427] Others may cling to the Guidelines because they are used to them. Most of the federal judiciary is made up of judges who began their tenure under a system in which the Guidelines were mandatory, and they may find it difficult to divorce themselves from such a familiar crutch. But whatever their reasons or motivations for doing so, the fact remains that many judges continue to adhere to the Guidelines, preventing any truly meaningful check on federal prosecutors who can use the increasingly harsh Guidelines sentences to coerce defendants to plead guilty.

Economic Crimes As an Example of the Guidelines' Overreach

One of the most flagrant examples of how the Guidelines call for the imposition of excessive sentences is Section 2B1.1, the Guideline that applies to economic crimes. Section 2B1.1 has long been criticized for resulting in sentences that are grossly disproportionate to a defendant's actual culpability. Judges have referred to sentences under this Guideline as "patently absurd on their face,"[428] "a black stain on common sense,"[429] and, "fundamentally flawed."[430] Because defendants' sentences are so inflated under the Guidelines, prosecutors have enormous leverage in economic crime cases to force guilty pleas.[431]

---

[426] Jillian Hewitt, Note, *Fi7ty Shades of Gray: Sentencing Trends in Major White-Collar Cases*, 125 YALE L.J. 1018, 1022 (2016) (noting that there is a "significant body of scholarship" suggesting judges are predisposed to anchor their sentences to the Guidelines range because they are required to begin their analysis with the Guidelines) (citing Mark W. Bennett, *Confron6ing Cogni6ive 'Anchoring E9fect' and 'Blind Spot' Biases in Federal Sentencing: A Modest Solu6ion for Reforming a Fundamental Flaw*, 104 J. CRIM. L. & CRIMINOLOGY 489, 492-93 (2014); Daniel M. Isaacs, Note, *Baseline Framing in Sentencing*, 121 YALE L.J. 426, 439-41 (2011)).

[427] Rakoff, *supra* note 97, at 8. *See also Rita v. United States*, 551 U.S. 338 (2007) (holding that appellate courts may presume that within- Guidelines sentences are reasonable).

[428] *United States v. Adelson*, 441 F. Supp. 2d 506, 515 (S.D.N.Y. 2006) (Rakoff, J.) (rejecting Guidelines sentence of life imprisonment and imposing sentence of three and half years).

[429] *United States v. Parris*, 573 F. Supp. 2d 744, 754 (E.D.N.Y. 2008) (Block, J.) (rejecting Guidelines sentence of 360 months to life and imposing sentence of 5 years).

[430] *United States v. Corsey*, 723 F.3d 366, 377 (2d Cir. 2013) (Underhill, J., concurring in ruling reversing life sentence).

[431] *See* Todd K. Lester, Jeffrey B. Jenson & Matthew P. Diehr, *Federal Sentencing For Economic Crimes — Are We There Yet?*, 1 INVESTIGATIONS Q. 11 (2014) ("white collar criminal

Increased Penalties for Indeterminate Loss Amounts

Although it is commonly referred to as the "fraud guideline," Section 2B1.1 covers a vast array of offenses and offenders, more than any other guideline. It determines the sentences for more than 300 federal criminal statutes and applies to offenses ranging from illegally downloading digital music to massive fraudulent investment schemes.[432] Individuals sentenced under this provision of the Guidelines made up 12.2% of all defendants sentenced in federal courts.[433] Despite the breadth of criminal conduct covered, sentences under Section 2B1.1 are principally driven by a single factor: the amount of loss that actually resulted, or was intended to result, from the offense.[434]

This factor has become increasingly significant in enhancing sentences for economic crimes.[435] The amount of loss is factored into a defendant's total offense level, which is one of the two variables for determining an ultimate sentencing range. When the Guidelines were first adopted, the amount of loss could result in, at most, a 13-level enhancement to a defendant's total offense level. Over the intervening years, the loss table was adjusted to add more categories of loss with higher and higher enhancements.[436] Under the current

---

defendants are particularly incented to enter plea agreements because of the draconian penalties resulting from the overemphasis on loss as a component in sentencing.").

[432] *See* Alan Ellis, John R. Steer, & Mark H. Allenbaugh, *At a 'Loss' for Jus6ice: Federal Sentencing for Economic O9fenses*, 25 CRIM. JUST. 34, 35 (2011) (noting that Section 2B1.1 applies to more than 300 federal criminal statutes, which is far more than any other guideline).

[433] *See* United States Sentencing Commission, 2015 Sourcebook of Federal Sentencing Statistics, Table 17, *available at* http://www.ussc.gov/research/sourcebook-2015. In 2015, only two other guidelines were applied more frequently: Section 2D1.1 (drug crimes) represented 29.1 percent and Section 2L1.2 (immigration) represented 21.7 percent. *Id.* Section 2B1.1 has consistently been one of the most frequently applied guidelines for over 15 years. Note that these figures reflect percentages of all *measured* cases. As the 2015 Sourcebook indicates, 6,381 cases were excluded from Table 17's calculations because there was incomplete information regarding which guidelines were applied in those cases.

[434] *See* § 2B1.1(b)(1).

[435] *See* Testimony of James E. Felman, on behalf of the American Bar Association, before the United States Sentencing Commission for the hearing on Proposed Amendments to the Federal Sentencing Guidelines regarding the Dodd-Frank Act and the Patient Protection and Affordable Care Act, Feb. 16, 2011, at 13 (arguing that reliance on loss to drive sentencing "is simply out of control" because amount of loss in 1987 could increase sentence only five-fold, and now it can increase it 40-fold), *available at* http://www.ussc.gov/sites/default/files/pdf/amendment-process/public-hearings-and-meeIings/20110216/TesIimony_ABA_%20Felman.pdf.

[436] *See* Ellis, Steer & Allenbaugh, *supra* note 105, at 36-37 (explaining that, because of adjustments to loss table, sentence for offense involving loss of over $20 million effectively tripled between 1987 and 2003); Frank O. Bowman, III, *Damp Squib: The Disappoin6ing Denouement of the Sentencing Commission's Economic Crime Project (And What They Should Do Now)*, 27 FED. SENT'G REP. 270, 272 (2015) (describing historical

Guidelines, the amount of loss can result in an enhancement of as much as 30 levels.[437] This means that where a defendant's sentence falls in a range between 0-6 months and 15-20 years will be determined by a single factor.

In cases where losses are particularly difficult to calculate, prosecutors have even greater leverage to force pleas.[123]

This consistent, upward ratcheting of the loss table is out of sync with the Commission's initial purpose for economic crimes. Originally, the Commission sought to provide a short but definite period of confinement in cases that had traditionally resulted in sentences of probation.[438] Over the years, however, the amount of loss enhancements were inflated, not as the result of any empirical analysis suggesting sentences were too low, but rather, in response to directives from Congress who were facing political pressure in the wake of major financial crises.[439] The framers of the Guidelines settled on loss as the driving factor for economic crimes because they believed it to be a reasonable approximation of the seriousness of an offense, and it was common to all covered offenses.[440] But, while the amount of loss may have been an effective means of selecting a sentence somewhere between probation and a

---

adjustments to loss table and noting that "the sentencing effect of an $80 million loss in 1989 was more than doubled by the 2001 guidelines").

[437] Section 2B1.1 begins with a base offense level of 6 or 7 (depending on the maximum sentence in the criminal statute the defendant is charged under) and adds an increasing number of offense levels depending on the amount of loss. There are 16 categories of loss, with the lowest category ($6,500 or less) requiring no increase in a defendant's offense level and with the highest category ($550,000,000 or greater) requiring an increase of 30 levels. For healthcare offenses involving a government healthcare program, the amount of loss could add as many as 34 levels. *See* § 2B1.1(b)(6).

[438] *See* Mark H. Allenbaugh, '*Drawn From Nowhere*': *A Review of The U.S. Sentencing Commission's White-Collar Sentencing Guidelines and Loss Data*, 26 FED. SENT'G REP. 19, 19 (2013) (describing Commission's process for drafting initial set of guidelines for economic crimes).

[439] *See* Ellis, Steer & Allenbaugh, *supra* note 105, at 36 (initial adjustment was in response to savings and loan crisis of the late 1980s); Bowman, III, *supra* note 109, at 272 (explaining that "political furor" following Enron scandal and passage of Sarbanes-Oxley Act were impetus for even further adjustments even though Commission had just raised sentences to historic levels only months earlier, which "no one, outside of Congress, felt to be unduly lenient"); *see also United States v. Corsey*, 723 F.3d 366, 379 (2d Cir. 2013) (Underhill, J., concurring) (noting that "loss guideline ... was not developed by the Sentencing Commission using an empirical approach based on data about past sentencing practices" and arguing that "history of bracket inflation directed by Congress renders the loss guideline fundamentally flawed, especially as loss amounts climb").

[440] *See* Rakoff, *supra* note 97, at 7 (explaining that one of the primary goals of the framers of Section 2B1.1 was to eliminate the disparity in sentencing between white collar crimes and "street" crimes).

few years imprisonment, as the upper range of sentences has risen, it has become far harder to justify basing sentences so heavily on this single factor.[441]

As judges, scholars, and even former prosecutors have observed, overemphasis on the amount of loss often leads to sentences that are disproportionate to the seriousness of the offense.[442] Defendants are plugged into specific slots along the broad spectrum of the loss table without any consideration for other factors that are arguably more significant when measuring a defendant's relative culpability, for instance, the scope and duration of the offense, how much the defendant gained from it, or the defendant's motivation.[443] In addition, individual defendants are frequently held accountable for all losses caused by participants in the same scheme, even if the defendant was not involved in his co-defendants' conduct, did not intend for the losses to occur, and did not personally profit from them.[444] A

---

[441] *See* Ellis, Steer & Allenbaugh, *supra* note 105, at 39-40 (illustrating that tranches in loss table are arbitrary by comparing loss amounts and sentences for various high-profile white collar defendants).

[442] *See United States v. Emmenegger*, 329 F. Supp. 2d 416, 427 (S.D.N.Y. 2014) (Lynch, J.) ("In many cases, including this one, the amount stolen is a relatively weak indicator of the moral seriousness of the offense or the need for deterrence."); Rakoff, *supra* note 97, at 7 ("[I]t should be obvious that in a great many, perhaps most, cases the weight of the drug or the amount of loss does not fairly convey the reality of the crime or the criminal."); Allenbaugh, *supra* note 111, at 25 ("Although the concept of loss has intuitive appeal as a measure of economic offense seriousness, it is far too abstract in its current form to serve as an appropriate sentencing factor for so many diverse types of offenses and offenders."); Letter from former U.S. Attorneys to the Honorable Linda R. Reade, in *United States v. Rubashkin*, 2:08-cr-01324-LRR (N.D. Iowa), dated April 26, 2010 (urging court to depart from guidelines sentence of life in prison).

[443] *See* Ellis, Steer & Allenbaugh, *supra* note 105, at 37 ("While the fraud guideline focuses primarily on aggregating monetary loss and victimization, it fails to measure a host of other factors that may be important, and may be a basis for mitigating punishment…."); Hewitt, *supra* note 99, at 1033-34 (noting that loss enhancements overwhelm other, arguably more relevant factors, and comparing loss table — which contemplates up to a 30-level adjustment — to role in the offense calculations under Section 3B1.1-2 — which can result in, at most, a 4-level adjustment); Douglas A. Berman, *Fiddling with the Fraud Guidelines as* Booker *Burns*, 27 FED. SENT'G REP. 267, 268 (2015) (explaining how emphasis on loss is in tension with Congress's statutory sentencing instructions in 18 U.S.C. § 3553(a) because loss only captures the "nature and circumstances of the offense" but ignores other relevant factors, such as the need "to afford adequate deterrence to criminal conduct" or "to impose similar punishment on similar offenders").

[444] Gain is factored in only where loss cannot reasonably be determined or when it acts as an aggravating factor (on top of the loss enhancement) in cases involving more than $1 million in gross receipts obtained from a financial institution. § 2B1.1 (Application Note 3B); § 2B1.1(b)(16)(A). Because the "court need only make a reasonable estimate of loss," (§2B1.1 (Application Note 3C)) gain is rarely used as an alternative, even though, in cases involving multiple defendants, it is arguably a more accurate gauge for each co-defendant's culpability.

defendant's subjective intent with respect to loss will only be considered under the Guidelines if he or she intended more loss than what actually occurred, meaning intended loss can only increase a defendant's sentence, not lower it.[445]

What's more, in the situation of an unsuccessful fraud — where no loss occurs — intended losses can still increase a defendant's sentence even if the fraudulent scheme is so outlandish that it never could have succeeded in the first place. For instance, one federal district judge imposed a 20-year sentence on defendants who used AOL email accounts to impersonate Buryatian nationals and Yamasee tribesmen seeking a five billion dollar loan to rebuild a pipeline across Siberia.[446] Unsurprisingly, the only person who was "defrauded" by the scheme was a government informant. Even though the defendants had no chance of succeeding in the scheme and no loss could possibly have occurred, the judge imposed a 20-year sentence largely based on an *intended loss* of $3 billion. The Second Circuit reversed, finding that no legitimate investor would have fallen prey to such an outlandish scheme. The concurring judge noted that "[e]ven if it were perfect, the loss guideline would prove valueless in this case, because the conduct underlying these convictions

---

445 *See* Section 2B1.1(b)(2). Coupled with the lower "reasonable foreseeability" standard of the relevant conduct Guideline (Section 1B1.3), this provision means that any defendant involved in a scheme that causes higher losses than he personally intended will be held accountable for the same amount of losses as his co-conspirators, even if they subjectively intended the losses and he did not. *See* Bowman, III, *supra* note 58, at 27-32 (acknowledging one of the downfalls of fraud guideline is how it weighs intended versus actual loss).

The Commission recently amended the definition of intended loss to clarify that intent is a subjective standard — "pecuniary harm the defendant purposely sought to inflict." §2B1.1 (Application Note 3A). But this may have little real-world impact. For one thing, judges are permitted to adopt an evidentiary presumption that a defendant subjectively intended losses if they were reasonably foreseeable. *See* Testimony of Michael Caruso on behalf of Federal Public and Community Defenders to the United States Sentencing Commission regarding the Public Hearing on Economic Crime and Inflation Adjustments, March 12, 2015, at 10-13 (arguing that clarification may not make that much difference because evidentiary standard allows judge to presume the defendant intended losses if they were reasonably foreseeable), *available at* http://www.ussc.gov/sites/default/files/pdf/amendment-process/public-hearings-and-meelings/20150312/Caruso.pdf. Second, many courts, when considering relevant conduct under Section 1B1.3, include all losses that anyone in the fraudulent scheme subjectively intended, as long as they were reasonably foreseeable to the defendant. *See id.* at 10 (citing *United States v. Otuya*, 720 F.3d 183, 191 (4th Cir. 2013) (attributing losses that defendant did not personally intend because co-conspirators intended them)). The result is that the objective "reasonably foreseeable" standard often trumps subjective intent.

446 *See United States v. Corsey*, 723 F.3d 366, 367-71, 377 (2d Cir. 2013).

is more farcical than dangerous."[447] Despite cases like this, the Guidelines permit sentencing judges to rely entirely on intended loss.

Even when actual loss has occurred, loss calculations need not be precise or certain. The sentencing judge is only required to make a "reasonable estimation" of loss.[448] Nor is the prosecution required to prove losses beyond a reasonable doubt; the significantly lower preponderance of the evidence standard applies at sentencing.[449] In other words, a defendant considering whether to exercise his right to trial knows that, even if he decides to put the prosecution to its proof and is acquitted of certain charged conduct, he may still face an enhancement for that conduct at sentencing. In cases where losses are particularly difficult to calculate, prosecutors have even greater leverage to force pleas.[450] They may even use novel theories for calculating losses during plea negotiations to overstate the severity of a defendant's likely sentence.[451] Lower-level members of a fraudulent scheme are more susceptible to these threats because they rarely know the full extent of the loss. Unless contrary information is presented at sentencing, a sentencing judge is permitted to rely solely on the loss amount that the parties stipulate to in a plea agreement.[452] Thus, few defendants will risk going to trial if they can secure the prosecution's agreement to a low loss amount by pleading guilty.

In addition to these tactics, the government may also engage in sentencing entrapment. In such cases, the government uses an undercover agent to investigate criminal conduct but then exacerbates the magnitude of the defendant's conduct to boost the Guidelines calculation and create a sentence that will be high enough to coerce a guilty plea. The government may do this

---

447 *Id.* at 377 (Underhill, J., concurring).

448 Section 2B1.1 (Application Note 3C). *See also* Lawrence J. Zweifach et al., *Loss Causa6ion and the Criminal Prosecu6ion of Securi6ies Law Viola6ions*, *in* SECURITIES LITIGATION AND ENFORCEMENT INSTITUTE 2005, at 327 (PLI Corp. and Prac. Course, Handbook Series No. 6746, 2005).

449 *See, e.g.*, *United States v. Watts*, 519 U.S. 148, 157 (1997) ("[A] jury's verdict of acquittal does not prevent the sentencing court from considering conduct underlying the acquitted charge, so long as that conduct has been proved by a preponderance of the evidence.").

450 *See, e.g.*, Hanni Fakhoury, *How the Sentencing Guidelines Work Against Defendants in CFAA Cases*, Electronic Frontier Foundation, April 9, 2013 (noting particular difficulty of calculating precise loss amount in computer fraud cases and describing case involving stolen articles from website JSTOR where prosecution threatened $2 million in loss that would result in 16-level increase to offense level if defendant refused to plead guilty).

451 *See United States v. Olis*, 429 F.3d 540, 547, n.11 (5th Cir. 2005) (recognizing that prosecutors were "persistently adopt[ing] aggressive, inconsistent, and unsupportable theories of loss" in securities fraud cases).

452 *See United States v. Granik*, 386 F.3d 404, 414 (2d Cir. 2004) (citing commentary to Section 6B1.4). *See also* notes 76-83, *supra*, and accompanying text for a more in-depth discussion of how prosecutors use "fact bargaining" to secure pleas.

by prolonging its investigation even after it has sufficient evidence to obtain an indictment. This practice is entirely permissible in many federal Circuits because judges are unwilling to invade the government's discretion to investigate crimes.[453] In other cases involving crimes like those subject to Section 2B1.1 — where sentences depend so heavily on quantities involved in the crime — the government may also instruct its agents to deliberately increase those quantities to in turn increase the applicable Guidelines ranges that will apply.

Overlapping Enhancements Double-Count the Same Conduct

On top of the enhancement for amount of loss, Section 2B1.1 contains 29 specific offense characteristics ("SOCs") that call for additional enhancements to a defendant's total offense level.[454] At first glance, the SOCs could be viewed as an attempt to more accurately distinguish between the seriousness of different types of economic crimes. But the SOCs almost always aggravate sentences rather than reduce them. So more offense levels are piled on to sentences that are already bloated and out of proportion with culpability because of the onerous loss enhancement. The SOCs are thus serving no distinct purpose other than to give prosecutors more leverage to threaten higher sentences.[455] Additionally, many of the SOCs involve factors that are already taken into account in the loss calculation itself. Frank Bowman — one of the drafters of the modern version of the fraud Guideline (and now an outspoken critic of it)[456] — has explained that the loss calculation was originally intended to serve as a proxy for multiple factors relevant to the seriousness of an offense.[457] Over time, however, the Commission added more

---

453 *See, e.g.*, *United States v. Bala*, 236 F.3d 87, 93 (2d Cir. 2000).

454 The SOCs are listed in Sections 2B1.1(b)(2) through (19). Many have multiple subsections. The Commission recently proposed another SOC for fraud in the context of government benefits for social security and veterans' assistance. *See* United States Sentencing Commission, Proposed Amendments to the Sentencing Guidelines, Dec. 19, 2016, at 65, *available at* http://www.ussc.gov/sites/default/files/pdf/amendment-process/reader-friendly- amendments/20161219_rf_proposed.pdf.

455 Professor Bowman has reasoned that, because the current loss table can increase the offense level so high, there is little room left for the SOC enhancements and role adjustments under Section 3B1.1 to have a meaningful impact in distinguishing relative culpability. *See* Bowman, III, *supra* note 109, at 278-79.

456 Professor Bowman was one of the "principal architects" of the 2001 version of the Guideline that consolidated Section 2B1.1 with Section 2F1.1. He has since acknowledged that numerous errors were made in fashioning the combined Guideline. *See* Bowman, III, *supra* note 58, at 1.

457 Frank O. Bowman, III, *Sentencing High-Loss Corporate Insider Frauds a7ter* Booker, 20 FED. SENT'G REP. 167, 170 (2008) (explaining that, by giving SOC factors independent weight, Commission imposed disproportionate increases in prison time).

and more SOCs to the Guideline but failed simultaneously to decrease the enhancements under the loss table.[458] So factors that were already incorporated into a defendant's sentence through the loss enhancement are now frequently double-counted.[459]

By way of example, the Guidelines stack additional offense levels on top of the loss enhancement when the offense involves a certain number of victims.[460] But higher loss crimes are already much more likely to include a large number of victims because they involve high losses.[461] The same could be said for the "sophisticated means" enhancement, which adds two levels where the defendant "intentionally engaged in or caused [] conduct constituting sophisticated means."[462] As losses are higher, it becomes far more likely that the defendant will have needed to use "sophisticated means" to achieve them.[463] The definition of "sophisticated means" does not provide much guidance on when the enhancement should apply: "especially complex or especially intricate offense conduct pertaining to the execution or concealment of an offense."[464] The application notes provide only two specific examples, one of which is now included in the text of the Guideline itself.[465] This makes it ripe for use by the prosecution as leverage during plea negotiations.[466]

---

458 Like the loss table adjustments, many of the SOCs were added to fulfill directives from Congress in response to financial crises/scandals. *See* Ellis, Steer & Allenbaugh, *supra* note 105, at 36-37 (SOC for conduct that "substantially jeopardized the safety and soundness" of a financial institution was added in response to savings and loan crisis in the 1980s and SOC for director or officer of an organization or more than 250 victims added in connection with passage of Sarbanes-Oxley Act).

459 As Professor Bowman has explained, the drafters of the 2001 consolidated guideline "failed to consider carefully the *combined e9fect* of the very large increases at the mid-to-high end of the new loss table and all the specific offense characteristics that survived the transition from the old separate guidelines to the new consolidated one." Bowman, III, *supra* note 109, at 272.

460 Section 2B1.1(b)(2).

461 Randall D. Eliason, *The Fraud Guideline: The Proposed Amendments, DOJ"s Opposi6ion, and Where We Go from Here*, 27 FED. SENT'G REP. 284, 285 (2015).

462 Section 2B1.1(b)(10).

463 *See* Eliason, *supra* note 134, at 285; Bowman, III, *supra* note 109, at 280 (admitting that, although he advocated for enhancement in 1998, he "no longer think[s] it serves a useful purpose" because "[i]f loss is moderately large, courts virtually always find sophisticated means in any but the very simplest schemes, and often even in those").

464 Section 2B1.1(b)(10) (Application Note 9).

465 Application notes offer interpretation from the Sentencing Commission on how the Guidelines should be applied, and they are generally followed by the parties and the court.

466 *See* Testimony of James E. Felman to United States Sentencing Commission, March 12, 2015, Tr. at 186 (describing how prosecutors use sophisticated means enhancement to penalize defendants who choose to go to trial: "If you go to trial, it was sophisticated, if I'm bargaining, they're willing to say, okay, if you plead, it's not...."), *available at*

The SOCs can also overlap with each other and other Guideline provisions. For example, Section 3B1.3 calls for a 2-level increase to the offense level if the defendant used a special skill.[467] "Special skill" is not defined, so in many cases, both the sophisticated means SOC and the special skill SOC could apply to the very same conduct. The Commission has generally acknowledged this phenomenon of "factor creep," explaining that "as more and more adjustments are added to the sentencing rules, it is increasingly difficult to ensure that the interactions among them, and their cumulative effect, properly track offense seriousness."[468] However, because the Guidelines do not counsel against applying multiple SOCs even when they overlap, prosecutors can rely on them to threaten higher sentences if defendants refuse to plead guilty.[469]

> Because the Guidelines are untethered from determinations of actual culpability, prosecutors have the power to threaten sentences for economic offenders that are generally reserved for the most heinous of violent criminals.

A most egregious instance of double-counting occurs in securities fraud cases involving public companies. A small impact on a large public company can easily result in losses exceeding $20 million, and securities fraud will involve a large number of victims by its very nature.[470] So even before considering any SOCs, defendants in these cases are almost always facing

http://www.ussc.gov/sites/default/files/pdf/amendment-process/public-hearings-and-meelings/20150312/Felman.pdf.

467 Section 3B1.3.

468 *See* "Fifteen Years of Guidelines Sentencing: An Assessment of How Well the Federal Criminal Justice System is Achieving the Goals of Sentencing Reform," United States Sentencing Commission (November 2004) at 137-38, *available at* http://www.ussc.gov/sites/default/files/pdf/research-and-publicalions/research-projects-and-surveys/miscellaneous/15-year-study/15_year_study_full.pdf. *See also* Bowman, III, *supra* note 130, at 170 (explaining that, in his view, Guidelines do a "commendable" job of identifying relevant factors but a poor job of quantifying appropriate sentences when multiple factors interact).

469 *See, e.g.*, Fakhoury, *supra* note 123 (explaining that using certain devices to commit computer fraud can qualify as both "sophisticated means" and "special skill" and citing case where judge applied both, resulting in two separate 2-level increases for the same conduct).

470 *See* Lester, Jenson & Diehr, *supra* note 104, at 13 (explaining that average market capitalization for company listed on NYSE is $8.9 million, meaning that a loss of only 0.5 percent would equate with $44.5 million).

offense levels in the high-20s.[471] But because so many SOCs potentially apply in these cases, sentences can easily reach life imprisonment, even where the loss amount is relatively low.[472] For instance, under the current Guideline, an officer or director of a public company convicted of securities fraud could receive:

Base offense level, §2B1.1(a)(1)	7
More than $3.5 million loss, §2B1.1(b)(1)	+18
Substantial financial hardship to 25 or more victims, §2B1.1(b)(2)	+6
Sophisticated means, §2B1.1(b)(10)	+2
More than $1 million in gross receipts, §2B1.1(b)(16)	+2
Violation of securities laws	
by officer of public company, §2B1.1(b)(19)(A)	+4
Aggravating role in offense, §3B1.1(a)[473]	+4
TOTAL OFFENSE LEVEL:	43 (life)

As the above calculation illustrates, Section 2B1.1 can result in harsher sentences than those typically imposed in cases of murder, kidnapping, and sexual abuse.[474] Even if one were to argue that a multi-decade sentence is truly appropriate in a particular case, the Guidelines are so onerous that the sentencing judge may be required to *depart downward* from the Guidelines range to reach that sentence.[475] Because the Guidelines are untethered from

---

[471] Even considering the Sentencing Commission's 2015 amendments, an offense causing $20 million in loss affecting just 10 victims would result in an offense level of 29. *See* Section 2B1.1(b)(1) & (2).

[472] *See* Bowman, III, *supra* note 130, at 168 & n.20 (explaining that a corporate officer presiding over fraud causing only slightly more than $2.5 million could qualify for life imprisonment based on a base offense level of 7, an 18-level increase for loss greater than $2.5 million, a 2-level increase for deriving more than $1 million in gross receipts, a 6-level increase for more than 250 victims, a 2- level increase for sophisticated means, a 4-level increase for violation of the securities laws by an officer of a publicly traded company, and a 4-level increase for an aggravated role under Section 3B1.1). *See also* Ellis, Steer & Allenbaugh, *supra* note 105, at 37 (noting that a 2-level enhancement for abuse of trust could also apply in many of these cases).

[473] In some jurisdictions, sentencing judges may impose the 4-level increase for an "organizer" or "leader" under Section 3B1.1(a) simply because the defendant is the highest officer of the company, even if he already received a 4-level increase as an officer of a public company under Section 2B1.1(b)(19)(A). *See, e.g.*, *United States v. Duncan*, 42 F.3d 97, 105-06 (2d Cir. 1994). This is double- counting in its truest sense.

[474] The average sentence in 2015 for murder was approximately 24 years, for kidnapping was approximately 20 years, and for sexual abuse was approximately 10 ½ years. *See* United States Sentencing Commission, 2015 Sourcebook of Federal Sentencing Statistics, Table 13, *available at* https://www.ussc.gov/sites/default/files/pdf/research-and-publicalions/annual-reports-and- sourcebooks/2015/Table13.pdf.

[475] *See* Bowman, III, *supra* note 130, at 168 & n.20 (citing 25-year sentence of Bernie Ebbers (WorldCom) and Jeffrey Skilling (Enron) and noting that, had the judge relied on the then-

determinations of actual culpability, prosecutors have the power to threaten sentences for economic offenders that are generally reserved for the most heinous of violent criminals.[476] Although they may be lenient when a defendant agrees to plead guilty, they exhibit no restraint in seeking the highest sentence possible when defendants dare to exercise their right to trial.[477]

The Commission's 2015 Amendments: A Tepid Attempt at Reform

In a series of well-publicized cases following *Booker*, a few federal judges flexed their newly-acquired discretion and spoke out against the absurdly lengthy sentences produced by the fraud Guideline. In 2006, Judge Rakoff of the Southern District of New York rejected a Guidelines sentence of life imprisonment for a first-time non-violent offender accused of securities fraud and instead imposed a sentence of 42 months.[478] In explanation, he noted "the utter travesty of justice that sometimes results from the guidelines' fetish with abstract arithmetic, as well as the harm that guideline calculations can visit on human beings if not cabined by common sense."[479]

In 2012, the Commission announced that it was beginning a multi-year effort to study sentences for economic crimes and that it intended to make

---

current guidelines, he would have been required to depart downward 19 levels to reach those sentences).

[476] *See, e.g.*, *United States v. Adelson*, 441 F. Supp. 2d 506, 508-09 (S.D.N.Y. 2006) (noting that Guideline calculation in securities fraud case for first-time, non-violent offender resulted in an "off-the-chart" offense level of 55, "a level normally only seen in cases involving major international narcotics traffickers, Mafia dons, and the like. How could it possibly apply here?").

[477] Admittedly, this has not been true of all prosecutors. Even though the defendant in *United States v. Parris* took his case to trial, the AUSA readily admitted that the life sentence recommended by the Guidelines put the sentencing judge in a difficult position and acknowledged that "a reasonable sentence 'may well be less, perhaps significantly less, than the guidelines range.'" 573 F. Supp. 2d 744, 751 (E.D.N.Y. 2008).
But the Department of Justice and some U.S. Attorney's Offices continue to oppose any attempts at reform that would decrease guidelines sentences. *See* notes 160-162, *infra*, and accompanying text. In addition, as explained further below, prosecutors are willing to support 70-80 percent departures from the Guidelines in many cases involving economic crimes where the defendants plead guilty and cooperate in the prosecution of other offenders. *See* notes 173-193, *infra*, and accompanying text. This suggests that they do not really view the outrageously high Guidelines sentences as just; they are only pressing for greater leverage to secure pleas. *See also* Bowman, III, *supra* note 130, at 170 (noting magnitude of sentencing discounts for cooperators in WorldCom scandal was an "acknowledgement by both prosecutors and courts that the starting point for departures in these cases should be far lower than the Guidelines nominally require").

[478] *See United States v. Adelson*, 441 F. Supp. 2d 506 (S.D.N.Y. 2006).

[479] *Id.* at 512.

reform to Section 2B1.1 a priority.[480] Those efforts culminated in a series of amendments to Section 2B1.1 that took effect in November 2015. The loss table was tweaked to account for inflation, the victims table was amended to focus less on quantity and more on victim impact, and the definition of intended loss was rewritten to clarify that it is a subjective standard.[481] Although these changes were welcome, most commentators agree that the Commission's reforms did not go far enough, and many predict that the amendments will have little real-world significance.[482] By way of example, the Commission revised the victims table so that higher-level enhancements are applied only if the relevant offense conduct caused "substantial financial hardship."[483] But, as one commentator has pointed out, focusing on victim impact will still favor prosecutors since most of the evidence will likely be in the form of hearsay, and defendants will have no access to that information before sentencing and no meaningful way to challenge it.[484] Another commentator explained that virtually all high-loss defendants will still get at least the 2-level enhancement for 10 or more victims, and many will still get a 4 to 6-level enhancements because it is likely that at least a few of their victims suffered substantial financial hardship.[485] Ultimately, loss continues to overwhelm other sentencing considerations, and the amendments did nothing to address the increasing number of overlapping SOC enhancements.[486]

In rejecting more sweeping change, the Commission maintained that the fraud Guideline was not fundamentally "broken," as some had argued.[487] But

---

480 *Adop6ion of Economic Crime Amendments*, 27 FED'L SENT. RPTR. 322, 322 (2015) (publishing key portions of Commission's press release and Chair Patti B. Sarris's speech regarding the amendments).

481 *See* 2016 Guidelines Manual, Supplement to Appendix C, Amendments 791 & 792.

482 *See* James E. Felman, *ReZlec6ions on the United States Sentencing Commission's 2015 Amendments to the Economic Crimes Guideline*, 27 FED. SENT'G REP. 288, 290 (2015) (lamenting that "new amendments do virtually nothing to allow courts to consider the host of culpability considerations absent from the guideline"); Eliason, *supra* note 134, at 284 (observing that amendments were "merely a cautious first step"); Bowman, III, *supra* note 109, at 280 (calling results of Commission's multi-year study "damp squib").

483 Section 2B1.1(b)(2).

484 Felman, *supra* note 155, at 288.

485 Bowman, III, *supra* note 109, at 277.

486 *See* Berman, *supra* note 116, at 268; Letter from National Association of Criminal Defense Lawyers to the United States Sentencing Commission regarding Comments on Proposed Amendments for 2015 Cycle (Mar. 18, 2015), at 8, *available at* http://www.ussc.gov/sites/default/files/pdf/amendment-process/public-comment/20150318/NACDL.pdf.

487 *Adop6ion of Economic Crime Amendments*, *supra* note 153, at 324. *See also* Transcript of Public Hearing on 2015 Proposed Amendments, March 12, 2015, at 205 (acknowledging that Commission had not found a good way of dealing with high loss crimes in a way that it could "explain to Congress [was] different from just lowering punishments, for the

it reached that conclusion based on sentencing data that was overwhelmingly the result of plea bargaining. In other words, the Commission failed to consider how the Guidelines operate in the abstract, absent the prosecution's willingness to bargain away otherwise applicable enhancements.[488] Because of that, the fraud Guideline remains a daunting tool in the hands of prosecutors.

The Department of Justice and U.S. Attorney's Office, for their part, opposed many of the changes the Commission did make to Section 2B1.1, revealing a deep-seated unwillingness to relinquish the power to coerce pleas.[489] While they admitted that the fraud Guideline was imprecise, they simultaneously maintained their position that sentences for economic crimes were not harsh enough. For instance, in 2011, then U.S. Attorney for the Southern District of New York Preet Bharara acknowledged that the Guidelines do not offer "meaningful guidance for differentiating among financial criminals and accurately gauging their relative culpability," but as a solution he proposed two new aggravating SOCs for insider trading offenses and a floor for mortgage fraud cases that would set a default loss amount even in cases where the victim banks did not actually suffer any loss.[490] In recent years, the Department of Justice has pushed for more and more SOC enhancements with the specific purpose of further increasing sentences for economic offenders.[491]

---

fraudsters who cause the most harm"), *available at* http://www.ussc.gov/sites/default/files/transcript_3.pdf.

488 Bowman, III, *supra* note 109, at 274.

489 *See* Letter from Jonathan J. Wroblewski, Department of Justice Director of the Office of Policy and Legislation, to United States Sentencing Commission, March 9, 2015, at 13 (opposing long-anticipated changes to Section 2B1.1 because "[l]essening penalties for economic crimes would be contrary to the overwhelming societal consensus that exists around these offenses"), *available at* http://www.ussc.gov/sites/default/files/pdf/amendment-process/public-hearings-and- meelings/20150312/DOJ.pdf.

490 Statement of Preet Bharara, United States Attorney for the Southern District of New York, to U.S Sentencing Commission, Feb. 16, 2011, *available at* http://www.ussc.gov/sites/default/files/pdf/amendment-process/public-hearings-and-meelings/20110216/Teslimony_DOJ_%20Bharara.pdf.

491 *See* Letter from Jonathan J. Wroblewski, Department of Justice Director of the Office of Policy and Legislation to United States Sentencing Commission, June 28, 2010, at 5 (referring to Bradley Stinn's 12-year sentence as "unacceptable," arguing that "the recent economic crisis" called for the imposition of "significant imprisonment terms"), *available at* http://sentencing.typepad.com/files/annual_letter_2010_final_062810.pdf; *id.* at 5, n.2 (suggesting Commission add enhancement to Section 2C1.1 that would increase penalties for cases involving military procurement fraud that occurs overseas).

Bradley Stinn, Friedman's Jewelers, and the Trial Penalty

As CEO of Friedman's Jewelers, Bradley Stinn had led his company from a failing regional business with $40 million in debt to a thriving, national chain with over 700 stores throughout the country. Stinn was one of Friedman's largest shareholders and was unswervingly devoted to its success during his eleven years with the company.

Unbeknownst to Stinn, Friedman's CFO, Vic Suglia, and its controller, John Mauro, had been aiding one of Friedman's vendors in a fraudulent loan scheme. When the SEC and DOJ began investigating Friedman's involvement in the scheme, they also uncovered questionable accounting practices that had allowed Friedman's to overstate its earnings. The government brought criminal charges against Suglia and Mauro related to the loan fraud and five accounting violations. Both admitted the charges and pled guilty.

Although the government agreed that Stinn knew nothing of the loan fraud, it indicted him for securities fraud because Suglia and Mauro's accounting manipulations had allegedly resulted in misleading statements in Friedman's public filings. The government offered Stinn a 5-year maximum sentence if he pled guilty, but Stinn did not take the deal because he'd had no personal involvement in preparing the financial statements and said he would not be able to truthfully admit that he knew they were false. Suglia and Mauro both testified against him at trial, and Stinn was convicted.

Members of the jury explained after the trial that they had convicted Stinn because they believed he knew about one of the alleged accounting violations and should have disclosed it. But they explained that they understood Stinn's role in the offense to be minimal. The presentence report ignored this evidence and based its analysis on the facts alleged in the indictment, even though members of the jury had admitted to having rejected most of those allegations. The presentence report calculated $100 million in losses and applied a host of specific offense characteristics to reach an offense level of 48. The recommended sentence was 70 years.

As a first-time offender who had already suffered significant losses from his own large investment in Friedman's — and who faced a restitution penalty on top of that — Stinn argued for leniency. Former colleagues, one of the jurors, and even a long-time Friedman's investor who had lost money in the fraud wrote in support of Stinn's request. But the prosecution vehemently defended the Guidelines calculation and urged the court to impose a lengthy sentence. The judge ultimately sentenced Stinn to 12 years in prison.

Suglia and Mauro — who had actually manipulated Friedman's accounting records and participated in the separate fraudulent loan scheme — were sentenced after Stinn. In stark contrast, the prosecution recommended no jail time, and they were sentenced to probation.

The result of efforts to amend Section 2B1.1 reveals a flaw in the Commission's procedures for internal reform. Although the Commission collects a vast amount of data each year on the application of the Guidelines and conducts an annual process to amend them, those efforts rarely, if ever, look at how the Guidelines can be manipulated by prosecutors to force guilty pleas. The full impact of the Guidelines — absent negotiated reductions — can only truly be tested if defendants go to trial. Thus, fewer trials masks the need for reform, keeping onerous Guidelines in place, which perpetuates prosecutors' leverage to force pleas, in turn decreasing the number of trials, and the cycle endlessly repeats.

The full impact of the Guidelines — absent negotiated reductions — can only truly be tested if defendants go to trial. Thus, fewer trials masks the need for reform, keeping onerous Guidelines in place, which perpetuates prosecutors' leverage to force pleas, in turn decreasing the number of trials, and the cycle endlessly repeats.

Departure Provisions in the Sentencing Guidelines Put Even More Power in the Hands of Prosecutors

Because many judges are reticent to deviate from the Guidelines, qualifying for a reduction or departure that is expressly sanctioned by the Guidelines can be critical for defendants to obtain a fair sentence. Yet, two of the most important provisions of the Guidelines allowing for reductions/downward departures — acceptance of responsibility (§ 3E1.1) and substantial assistance (§ 5K1.1) — can be obtained only if a defendant pleads guilty. In many cases, the only way to secure leniency from the onerous penalties imposed under the Guidelines or statutory mandatory enhancements is to give up the constitutional right to a trial.

Acceptance of Responsibility

Section 3E1.1 of the Guidelines allows for a two-level reduction in a defendant's offense level if the defendant "clearly demonstrates acceptance of responsibility for his offense." Despite the title of this provision, in practice it has nothing to do with the level of remorse a defendant feels or expresses at sentencing. Instead, it is almost uniformly treated as a discount awarded to defendants who plead guilty.

> In many cases, the only way to secure leniency from the onerous penalties imposed under the Guidelines or statutory mandatory enhancements is to give up the constitutional right to a trial.

When first formulating the Guidelines in 1987, the Commission considered a proposal for an automatic discount in guilty plea cases but rejected it because a fixed reduction "would not be in keeping with the public's perception of justice."[492] Under the earliest version of Section 3E1.1, a defendant was not automatically entitled to the two-level reduction merely because he pleaded guilty, nor was he necessarily disqualified from the reduction merely because he chose to go to trial.[493] Two years later, however, the Commission added an application note making clear that, except in rare circumstances, the "adjustment is not intended to apply to a defendant who puts the government to its burden of proof at trial," even if the judge later determines that the defendant has exhibited genuine remorse. That has remained the rule ever since. So, for all intents and purposes, "acceptance of responsibility" has become synonymous with pleading guilty.

Section 3E1.1 also allows for an additional one-level reduction when a defendant "timely" notifies authorities of his intention to plead guilty and assists the government in the investigation and prosecution of his own misconduct.[494] Colloquially referred to as "super acceptance of

---

[492] *See* William W. Wilkins, Jr., *Plea Nego6ia6ions, Acceptance of Responsibility, Role of the O9fender, and Departures: Policy Decisions in the Promulga6ion of Federal Sentencing Guidelines*, 23 WAKE FOREST L. REV. 181, 191 (1988).

[493] *1987 Federal Sentencing Guidelines Manual* § 3E1.1 ("(b) A defendant may be given consideration under this section without regard to whether his conviction is based upon a guilty plea or a finding of guilt by the court or jury or the practical certainty of conviction at trial. (c) A defendant who enters a guilty plea is not entitled to a sentencing reduction under this section as a matter of right."), *available at* http://www.ussc.gov/sites/default/files/pdf/guidelines-manual/1987/manual- pdf/Chapter_3.pdf.

[494] Section 3E1.1(b) only applies if a defendant's offense level is at least 16 before applying the two-level reduction of subsection (a).

responsibility," this additional reduction exists for the express purpose of "permitting the government to avoid preparing for trial" and allowing the government and the court to "allocate their resources efficiently."[495] Although the reduction has been available to defendants since 1992, it was significantly restricted in 2003, with the passage of the Feeney Amendment. Now Section 3E1.1(b) requires a motion by the government stating that the defendant's plea was timely and that it helped to conserve the costs of preparing for trial. Since then, most Circuits have interpreted the language "upon motion of the government" to vest prosecutors with the exclusive authority to decide who should receive the additional benefit under Section 3E1.1(b).[496] They will only overturn a prosecutor's decision to withhold a supporting motion if there is evidence of unconstitutional motive.[497] Thus, most defendants remain at the mercy of the prosecution and know they must plead quickly to benefit from the additional reduction. This, in turn, discourages transparency and tends to insulate the government from the consequences of failing to identify and disclose exculpatory evidence.

Both versions of the acceptance of responsibility reduction unfairly penalize defendants who go to trial. Even where defendants feel no genuine remorse, they can expect to receive the reduction as long as they are willing to save the government the time and expense of a trial. On the other hand, prosecutors may rely on the acceptance of responsibility provision to argue for disparately higher sentences for defendants who choose to exercise their right to a trial.

While a two- or three-level reduction may not seem significant enough to coerce someone to plead guilty, it can have a substantial impact on a defendant's ultimate sentence. For instance, a defendant with an offense level of 33 ordinarily would face a sentence between 11 and 14 years. But if he timely notifies authorities of his intention to plead guilty and secures a government motion in support of the full three-level reduction, he can reduce

---

[495] Section 3E1.1(b).

[496] *See* Alexa Chu Clinton, *Taming the Hydra: Prosecutorial Discre6ion under the Acceptance of Responsibility Provision of the US Sentencing Guidelines*, 79 UNIV. OF CHI. L. REV. 1467, 1468-69 (2012).

[497] The First, Fifth, Seventh, Eighth, Ninth, and Tenth Circuits permit prosecutors to withhold a supporting motion under Section 3E1.1(b) as long as their refusal is "rationally related to a legitimate government end" and is not "animated by an unconstitutional motive." *See United States v. Moreno-Trevino*, 432 F.3d 1181, 1186 (10th Cir. 2005); *see also United States v. Beatty*, 538 F.3d 8, 15 (1st Cir. 2008); *United States v. Newson*, 515 F.3d 374, 378 (5th Cir. 2008); *United States v. Debery*, 576 F.3d 708, 711 (7th Cir. 2009); *United States v. Smith*, 422 F.3d 715, 726 (8th Cir. 2005); *United States v. Johnson*, 581 F.3d 994, 1001 (9th Cir. 2009).

his sentence by almost 4 years. Even at the low end of the sentencing table, where only the two-level reduction is available, there is still a significant inducement to plead guilty because it may mean the difference between having to serve jail time or being permitted to serve the sentence in home detention or on probation.[498]

> Particularly in cases where the question of guilt turns on a subjective assessment of a defendant's knowledge or intent, it is fundamentally unfair to punish a person for asserting the right to have a jury make that determination.

Although it may not be inherently objectionable to incentivize defendants to plead guilty by offering them a modest benefit, the reduction for acceptance of responsibility does not operate in the abstract. In most cases, some form of prosecutorial bargaining has already resulted in a reduced sentence because of dismissed charges or stipulated facts. Because prosecutors possess immense discretion to influence sentencing outcomes before the Guidelines are even applied, the reduction for guilty pleas that is built into the Guidelines only serves to compound their formidable power to extract guilty pleas.[499]

James Fields and the Trial Penalty

In 2010, James Fields and Jon Latorella, the chief financial officer and chief executive officer of LocatePlus Holdings Corporation, were both

[498] If a defendant's sentence falls within Zone B of the Sentencing Table, a judge is permitted to impose a sentence of community confinement or home detention *as an alterna6ive* to imprisonment, meaning the defendant need not serve any jail time. *See* Section 5C1.1. If the sentence falls within Zone A, the entire term of the sentence may be served as probation. *See* Section 5B1.1. A two-level reduction can easily bump a sentence from Zone C to Zone B or from Zone B to Zone A.

See also Shana Knizhnik, *Failed Snitches and Sentencing S6itches: Substan6ial Assistance and the Cooperator's Dilemma*, 90 N.Y.U. L. REV. 1722, 1730 (2015) (noting that a two-level reduction "can reduce the floor of the range by anywhere from three months (constituting a 75 percent sentence reduction from an original floor of four months) to 68 months (constituting an 18.9 percent reduction from an original floor of 360 months)").

[499] *See* Albert W. Alschuler, *Departures and Plea Agreement Under the Federal Sentencing Guidelines*, 117 F.R.D. 459, 473 (1988) (warning that, without limits on prosecutorial plea bargaining, acceptance of responsibility reduction "could become simply an 'add on' — an extra benefit that a defendant receives after striking a bargain with an Assistant United States Attorney: 'Come to our showroom; make your best deal with one of our friendly sales personnel; and then use the enclosed certificate — Guidelines Section 3E1.1 — to receive an additional 20 percent discount from the price of your new car.'").

charged with securities fraud, money laundering, and aggravated identity theft. The government offered the defendants the same deal — in exchange for their guilty pleas, it would recommend a sentence of 5 years. The defendants would be prohibited from arguing for a lower sentence. However, if they both pled guilty, the government would allow them to recommend a sentence of not less than 4 years.

Latorella took the deal. But Fields rejected it because he believed that the terms of the plea agreement violated his right to due process. Fields went to trial and was ultimately found guilty.

At sentencing, the prosecutor admitted that "[a]s to core culpability, there is nothing to distinguish Fields from Latorella." Despite that admission, he advocated for a nine-year sentence for Fields — nearly twice what Latorella got in his plea bargain.

In support of the lengthier sentence, the prosecutor protested Fields' vigorous defense of his case, arguing that the 390 docket entries and "scorched-earth litigation" tactics evidenced that Fields had not accepted responsibility for his crimes.

The sentencing judge disagreed, expressing discomfort with the prosecution's arguments because they suggested that the reason Fields should receive a higher sentence was not because he lacked remorse but because he chose to go to trial:

> [I]n my turn, do I say he went to trial, he consumed vast quantities of Canadian forest with his paper in this context, consequently he gets a higher sentence? … [A]m I engaging in a pretext when I said it is not because he went to trial[,] it is because he lacked remorse…?

The judge ultimately sentenced Fields to the same 5 years as Latorella, rejecting the prosecutor's invitation to equate the choice to go to trial with a failure to accept responsibility:

> There is, of course, embedded in the Sentencing Guidelines a concept of acceptance of responsibility. It is, as I indicated from my perspective, a Faustian bargain made by the Sentencing Commission in recognition of practices that have developed, but frankly I am indifferent to it in making my own judgment about what the proper sentence should be.

The other, perhaps unintended, consequence of providing an express sentencing discount for pleading guilty in the Guidelines themselves is that it predisposes prosecutors and judges to overlook instances where defendants are being unfairly punished for exercising their right to a trial. Indeed, the prosecutors in the Kevin Ring case were unashamed in their position that he deserved harsher punishment because "he is the only lobbyist who went to trial and chose not to plead guilty…."[500] Particularly in cases where the question of guilt turns on a subjective assessment of a defendant's knowledge or intent, it is fundamentally unfair to punish a person for asserting the right to have a jury make that determination. There is no reason why a person who genuinely believes he did not knowingly commit a crime cannot sincerely accept responsibility after a jury of his peers renders judgment. But the Guidelines expressly discourage judges from individually assessing a defendant's level of remorse and instead impose an automatic penalty for not pleading guilty, condoning the notion that the assertion of the constitutional right to a trial imposes an unfair burden on the government.

Indeed, those judges who cling to the Guidelines have a ready-made defense when faced with the argument that a trial penalty is being imposed: a harsher sentence is fair because the defendant failed to "accept responsibility." Because the Guidelines sanction this way of thinking, judges can rely on this rote defense and may turn a blind eye to the unfairness of the sentences they are imposing.

Those judges who cling to the Guidelines have a ready-made defense when faced with the argument that a trial penalty is being imposed: a harsher sentence is fair because the defendant failed to "accept responsibility." Because the Guidelines sanction this way of thinking, judges can rely on this rote defense and may turn a blind eye to the unfairness of the sentences they are imposing.

Substantial Assistance

Another Guideline provision that has a significant impact on inducing guilty pleas is Section 5K1.1, which permits a downward departure from the applicable Guidelines range where a defendant has provided substantial assistance to the government in the investigation or prosecution of another

[500] *See* Sept. 20, 2011 Memorandum Opinion in 1:08-cr-00274-ESH (D.D.C.) at 7-8 (quoting prosecution's oral argument in support of its initial sentencing recommendation).

offender.[501] To qualify for this departure, defendants must first admit their own guilt and then provide the prosecution with information about the criminal conduct of their co-conspirators or about other crimes.[502] At least one federal Circuit Court of Appeals has recognized that "obtaining a substantial assistance motion from the government represents a particularly critical point in [the criminal] process" because of the profound effect it can have on a defendant's sentence.[503]

§5K1.1 Substantial assistance departure cases: degree of decrease for offenders in each primary offense category[504]

PRIMARY OFFENSE	N	Median Sentence in Months	Median Decrease G in Months From guideline Minimum	Median Percent G Decrease From m guideline Minimu
TOTAL	8,084	31	30	50.4
Murder	10	92	194	60.6
Manslaughter	1	—	—	—
Kidnapping/Hostage Taking	3	120	47	40
Sexual Abuse	45	72	60	47.5
Assault	5	48	18	35.3
Robbery	74	42	20	30.7
Arson	21	38	36	53.9
Drugs — Trafficking	4,705	42	41	48.4
Drugs — Communication Facility	36	7	24	85.8
Drugs — Simple Possession	1	—	—	—
Firearms	723	48	36	44.4
Burglary/B&E	2	—	—	—
Auto Theft	11	2	29	80
Larceny	54	8	22	69
Fraud	1,288	12	21	73.5

501 *See* 2016 Guidelines Manual, § 5K1.1.

502 *See* Section 5K1.1, Application Note 2 (distinguishing substantial assistance from acceptance of responsibility because it "is directed to the investigation and prosecution of criminal activities by persons other than the defendant").

503 *United States v. Leon6i*, 326 F.3d 1111, 1114, 1117 (9th Cir. 2003). *See also* Richard L. Lippke, *Rewarding Coopera6ion: The Moral Complexi6ies of Procuring Accomplice Tes6imony*, 13 NEW CRIM. L. REV. 90, 91 (2010) ("Criminal defendants who face formidable sentences and have few prospects for leniency otherwise are eager, perhaps desperate, to offer authorities 'substantial assistance' and thereby reduce the time they will end up serving behind bars").

504 United States Sentencing Commission, 2015 Sourcebook of Federal Sentencing Statistics, Table 6, *available at* https://www.ussc.gov/sites/default/files/pdf/research-and-publicalions/annual-reports-and- sourcebooks/2015/Table06.pdf.

PRIMARY OFFENSE	N	Median Sentence in Months	Median Decrease G in Months From guideline Minimum	Median Percent G Decrease From m guideline Minimu
Embezzlement	16	7	14	67.5
Forgery/Counterfeiting	46	10	11	57.8
Bribery	66	5	21	83.1
Tax	79	0	16	100
Money Laundering	155	12	24	72.2
Racketeering/Extortion	196	24	25	52.6
Gambling/Lottery	13	0	6	100
Civil Rights	6	11	56	86.5
Immigration	241	12	12	45.5
Child Pornography	59	120	72	40
Prison Offenses	9	8	8	33.7
Administration of Justice Offenses	68	0	12	100
Environmental/Wildlife	23	0	18	100
National Defense	24	23	33	58.9
Antitrust	6	15	16	52.3
Food & Drug	9	0	18	100
Other Miscellaneous Offenses	89	0	18	100

Unlike acceptance of responsibility — which has a fixed benefit — Section 5K1.1 places no limit on how far a defendant's sentence can be reduced in exchange for providing substantial assistance. In 2015, the median departure in 5K1.1 cases was 50.4%. For cases involving certain specific types of crimes, it was much higher. For example, the median departure in fraud and money laundering cases was over 70%. In bribery and civil rights cases it was over 80%.

Prosecutors are incentivized to be extremely lenient with cooperators because the information cooperators provide allows the government to secure more convictions with fewer resources.[505] And, although prosecutors merely make recommendations at sentencing, judges are generally inclined to accept their recommendations because they believe the prosecutors are in the best position to quantify the significance of the cooperators' assistance.[506] Where

[505] *See* Knizhnik, *supra* note 171, at 1748 (noting that there is an especially strong incentive on the prosecution's part to sign up cooperators in antitrust and fraud cases because those types of crimes are almost impossible to prove without some inside information).

[506] *See* Section 5K1.1(a)(1) (one of the factors courts should consider in evaluating "the significance and usefulness of the defendant's assistance" is "the government's evaluation of the assistance rendered"). *See also id.*, Application Note 3 (advising judges that

prosecutors are authorized to cut defendants' sentences by half — or more — there is a powerful inducement for defendants to plead guilty. Prosecutors take full advantage of this incentive; in 2015, 12.4%, or one out of every eight, federal defendants received a departure for substantial assistance.[507]

Not every defendant has the chance to take advantage of the departure, however. Originally, Rule 35 of the Federal Rules of Criminal Procedure allowed defendants to appeal directly to the sentencing judge for leniency and the judge could give them credit for attempting to cooperate, even if the government chose not to acknowledge their efforts.[508] But, with the advent of the Guidelines, there was a shift in authority. Section 5K1.1 now requires the government to file a motion supporting the departure.[509] A prosecutor's decision to withhold a supporting motion is reviewable only if the defendant can demonstrate that the prosecutor had an unconstitutional motive for doing so.[510] Moreover, prosecutors are usually only willing to file supporting motions in exchange for information that can help them secure additional convictions.[511] Thus, a defendant who wants to receive a substantial assistance

---

"[s]ubstantial weight should be given to the government's evaluation of the extent of the defendant's assistance").

507 This figure has been relatively consistent for the past 10 years: 14.4 percent in 2006, 14.4 percent in 2007, 13.5 percent in 2008, 12.4 percent in 2009, 11.5 percent in 2010, 11.2 percent in 2011, 11.7 percent in 2012, 12.1 percent in 2013, 12.8 percent in 2014, 12.4 percent in 2015, 11.1 percent in 2016. *See* Table N in United States Sentencing Commission Sourcebook Archives, *available at* https://www.ussc.gov/research/sourcebook/archive. The rate of substantial assistance departures significantly varies from one jurisdiction to another. In the Tenth Circuit, only 5.9% of cases involved substantial assistance departures in 2015. But in the D.C. Circuit, 29.8% of defendants received the departure. These figures also do not capture those defendants who pled guilty in the hope of receiving a substantial assistance motion but did not get one.

508 *See The Use of Federal Rule of Criminal Procedure 35(b)*, United States Sentencing Commission, at 3 (2016) (explaining that "[b]efore the enactment of the Sentencing Reform Act of 1984, Rule 35(b) contained a strict time limitation but included no substantive restrictions on the bases by which a court could reduce or modify a sentence"), *available at* http://www.ussc.gov/sites/default/files/pdf/research-and-publicalions/research-publicalions/2016/Rule35b.pdf.

509 *See* § 5K1.1. Rule 35(b) was also amended to account for this shift in authority by adopting the "government motion" requirement from the Guidelines. Courts have since interpreted this amendment as a change in the purpose of Rule 35(b). Instead of providing an opportunity for defendants to seek leniency, it now "confer[s] an 'entitlement on the government' that allow[s] it to obtain 'valuable assistance' and then ask a sentencing court to reduce the defendant's sentence as 'compensation' for that assistance." *The Use of Federal Rule of Criminal Procedure 35(b)*, *supra* note 181, at 3 (quoting *United States v. Shelby*, 584 F.3d 743, 745 (7th Cir. 2009)).

510 *See Wade v. United States*, 504 U.S. 181, 185-86 (1992).

511 George C. Harris, *Tes6imony for Sale: The Law and Ethics of Snitches and Experts*, 28 PEPP. L. REV. 1, 17 (2000) ("The *sine qua non* of [cooperation] agreements is proffered testimony that will support the conviction of an accomplice or another suspect."); *see id.* at

departure ordinarily must offer to disclose information that the government does not already have.[512]

Annette Trujillo and the Trial Penalty

Annette Trujillo was a legal assistant at a law firm in Florida during the housing boom in the mid-2000s. Shortly after hiring her, Trujillo's employer delegated to her the task of conducting real estate closings. She soon became caught up in a mortgage fraud scheme perpetrated by a group of mortgage brokers, realtors and several straw buyers who used fraudulent loan applications to extract more money from banks than they would have otherwise been prepared to lend. To cover up the scheme, the co-conspirators included false information on the settlement documents regarding how the proceeds of the loans would be disbursed. As the closing agent, Trujillo signed off on the settlement documents.

When the scheme was eventually uncovered, Trujillo was indicted on charges of bank fraud and wire fraud in connection with the two properties for which she had acted as the closing agent. The government also indicted her on a charge of conspiracy, alleging that she had conspired with the other defendants to commit the fraud. Trujillo maintained that she had not intended to defraud anyone and she had not received any financial gain from the fraud. Because she believed she was innocent of conspiracy, she took her case to trial. The jury ultimately returned a guilty verdict on the bank and wire fraud counts but acquitted her of the conspiracy charge.

Trujillo's co-defendants — the masterminds who concocted the scheme, the mortgage brokers who provided false information on the loan applications, and the straw buyers who had allowed their names to be used on the applications — all pled guilty and all received reductions for acceptance of responsibility.

Trujillo was sentenced to 5 years, 5 months, more than double the sentences of the mortgage brokers and straw buyers, who had actually benefitted from the fraud.

---

50 (noting that prosecutorial authority is never exercised if the defendant proffers evidence exculpating others).

[512] *See* Michael A. Simon, *Retribu6ion for Rats: Coopera6ion, Punishment, and Atonement*, 56 VAND. L. REV. 1, 16 (2003) (noting that prosecution will look to "whether the defendant's information is cumulative of other evidence that [it] already has or can obtain").

Although she had been convicted in connection with only two properties, the prosecution sought to apply a loss amount arising out of five properties, based on evidence of a separate mortgage fraud scheme it had only recently discovered. Trujillo protested the injustice of being held responsible for conduct she had not even been charged with and which she had had no opportunity to contest at trial. But the judge remained unsympathetic. In supporting her ultimate sentence, the judge expressed the view that Trujillo deserved harsher punishment than her co-defendants because she had not accepted responsibility for her crimes.

A defendant who wants to receive a substantial assistance departure ordinarily must offer to disclose information that the government does not already have.[513]

This creates additional pressure for defendants to plead quickly, before they have had much time to consider their options. If defendants wait too long to offer to cooperate, they run the risk that someone else will cooperate before them and the information they have to trade will no longer be of any value to the government.[514]

This creates additional pressure for defendants to plead quickly, before they have had much time to consider their options. If defendants wait too long to offer to cooperate, they run the risk that someone else will cooperate before them and the information they have to trade will no longerbe of any value to the government.[186] It also entices defendants to embellish the facts, or even

---

[513] *See* Ellen Yaroshefsky, *Coopera6ion with Federal Prosecutors: Experiences of Truth Telling and Embellishment*, 68 FORDHAM L. REV. 917, 929 (1999) (describing the "race to the station house" among co-conspirators because "[t]he longer a defendant waits to cooperate, the less likely he is to have information that is still useful to the government"). In her interviews with defense attorneys, Professor Yaroshefsky heard complaints that, because speed is crucial, the attorneys were often forced to discuss cooperation with their clients before having any opportunity to fully review the case or even develop an attorney-client relationship with them. *Id.* at 929-30. *See also* Harris, *supra* note 184, at 53 ("Decision regarding offers of leniency may depend as much on the skill and promptness of defense counsel in soliciting a deal as on a carefully considered assessment of relative culpability.").

[514] John Wesley Hall, Jr., *5K1.1 to be Obtained by Perjury — What to Do, What to Do?*, 7 OHIO STATE J. OF CRIM. L. 667 (2010) (criminal defense lawyer admitting that 5K1.1 puts "hydraulic pressure" on defendants to cooperate, and that many "will offer to say anything to cut their exposure"); Richard L. Lippke, *Rewarding Coopera6ion: The Moral Complexi6ies of Procuring Accomplice Tes6imony*, 13 NEW CRIM. L. REV. 90, 111-17 (2010) (describing "powerful incentive" defendants have "to please prosecutors at some predictable cost to their truthfulness in revealing what they and their accomplices have done.").

lie, in the hopes of providing new information that will earn them a substantial assistance motion.[187] There is an extensive body of scholarly work discussing the unreliability of cooperator testimony.[515] A study conducted in 1999 concluded that prosecutors are quick to believe cooperators when they offer testimony that will secure additional convictions, but they frequently lack sufficient evidence to corroborate that testimony.[516] Despite widespread concerns about reliability, there may be little opportunity to challenge cooperator testimony in individual cases. Even defendants who take their cases to trial are limited in their ability to impeach cooperating witnesses because they do not always have discovery into discussions between the prosecution and a cooperating witness.[517] For instance, prosecutors are not required to take notes of their meetings with cooperating witnesses, so there may be little available to defense attorneys in the way of written discovery. Moreover, the jury may not be able to assess the witness's motives because they will likely not know the extent of the sentencing reduction the witness is receiving since prosecutors often delay sentencing for cooperating witnesses until after they have testified.[518] Those defendants who are unwilling to risk the harsh consequences of losing at trial may be forced to plead guilty because of false cooperator testimony.[519]

Gil Lopez and the Trial Penalty

Gil Lopez was the Chief Accounting Officer of Stanford Financial Group, a company that provided legal and accounting services to a group of entities owned and managed by Allen Stanford. For decades, Allen

---

[515] *See, e.g.,* Lippke, *supra* note 187, at 111-117; Yaroshefsky, *supra* note 186.

[516] *See* Yaroshefsky, *supra* note 186, at 943 (citing interview with former AUSA: "The incentives to please you are great and you might not even recognize them because you have come to develop what you believe to be a trusting relationship with your cooperator."); *id.* at 936 (citing another interview: "[A] cooperator can tell you about a telephone conversation he had with a defendant. When you ask for the date, the telephone records establish that they did, indeed, have a conversation on that date. So that's the corroboration for the substance of the conversation. You have no independent way to know the substance of the conversation.").

[517] *See* Harris, *supra* note 184, at 49 (arguing that procedural safeguards during trial are not adequate to uncover false cooperator testimony in part because defense counsel is at an informational disadvantage, having had no opportunity to meet with the cooperator or take pretrial discovery).

[518] *See* Knizhnik, *supra* note 171, at 1740.

[519] *See* Lippke, *supra* note 187, at 117 (noting "likelihood that many individuals implicated by their former associates will find it in their best interest to reach their own plea agreements with prosecutors").

Stanford had been appropriating credit deposit investments in Stanford International Bank (SIB) for his own personal benefit, using the funds to support the rest of his companies and to bankroll his lavish lifestyle. While Stanford was the overall mastermind of the scheme, it was undisputed that his Chief Financial Officer, James Davis, was the next in line. Davis admitted that he orchestrated the cover-up efforts by falsifying revenue disclosures in SIB's annual reports and bribing government regulators and the company's external auditor.

As the government later conceded, Lopez was completely unaware that Davis had paid bribes to cover up Stanford's scheme. But, in his role as Chief Accounting Officer, he did review drafts of SIB's annual reports before they were made public. So when the fraud was eventually uncovered, Lopez was indicted along with Stanford and Davis.

Davis quickly pled guilty and agreed to testify against Stanford and Lopez in exchange for a 5K1.1 motion from the government. The only person who Lopez could have testified against was Davis himself. Lopez met with the Assistant U.S. Attorney to discuss a plea, but because Davis had gotten there first, he had no information to trade, and no formal plea offer was ever made. He decided instead to take his case to trial, and the jury convicted him, largely based on Davis's testimony.

Davis received a downward departure for his cooperation and was sentenced to five years. Lopez — who was indisputably less culpable than Davis and who gained nothing from the fraud other than his regular salary — was sentenced to 20 years in prison.

When he raised this gross disparity on appeal, the Fifth Circuit brushed it off. Although the panel readily admitted that plea bargaining "often does lead to more lenient sentences for more culpable defendants who choose to cooperate," it expressed no sympathy for defendants like Lopez, who are unwittingly punished in the process. According to the Court, "[t]his is simply the way that cases against multiple co-defendants are often prosecuted."

Lopez was 70 years old when he was sentenced and will likely die in prison.

Probably the most perverse aspect of the substantial assistance departure, however, is that it disproportionately favors the most culpable defendants. Those at the highest levels of a criminal conspiracy are usually the ones who know the most about it and are most valuable to prosecutors.

Probably the most perverse aspect of the substantial assistance departure, however, is that it disproportionately favors the most culpable defendants. Those at the highest levels of a criminal conspiracy are usually the ones who know the most about it and are most valuable to prosecutors. On the other hand, defendants who have had only minimal involvement are unlikely to have much information of value to trade.[520] The Guidelines allow prosecutors complete discretion to decide who qualifies for the departure, and many judges are unwilling to challenge that discretion at sentencing. So it is frequently the least culpable defendants who face the harshest penalties.[521]

Statutory Mandatory Minimum Sentencing Enhancements Exacerbate Already Out-of-Control Guidelines Sentences

Beyond the overreaching Sentencing Guidelines, there are other mechanisms in the federal criminal justice system that create significant barriers for exercising the right to a trial. In certain cases, federal statutes require mandatory enhancements to sentences that judges are required to tack on. But these apply only if the prosecution has first charged the defendant with conduct triggering the enhancement. Thus, prosecutors have yet another tool in many cases to persuade defendants to plead guilty.

---

520 *See* Charles Doyle, *Federal Mandatory Minimum Sentencing Statutes*, Congressional Research Service, at 9 (2013) (describing "inverted sentencing" that often results from substantial assistance departure: "a situation in which 'the more serious the defendant's crimes, the lower the sentence — because the greater his wrongs, the more information and assistance he had to offer to a prosecutor,' while in contrast the exception is of no avail to the peripheral offender who can provide no substantial assistance."), *available at* https://fas.org/sgp/crs/misc/RL32040.pdf.

521 Knizhnik, *supra* note 171, at 1726 (noting that low-level defendants can be held liable for conspiracy based on cooperator testimony even when they themselves have no information about the conspiracy and thus have no opportunity to benefit from a substantial assistance departure).

This disparity can quickly balloon out of control when combined with other factors. For instance, before the departure for substantial assistance is even considered, nearly every cooperating defendant will first get a reduction in their guidelines range because they accepted responsibility. Again, that reduction will apply regardless of whether they genuinely feel remorse. It is just as likely, if not more likely, that cooperating defendants plead guilty to take advantage of the benefit of Section 5K1.1 and not because they have truly accepted responsibility for their crimes. *See* Lippke, *supra* note 187, at 107 (arguing that it is implausible to assume genuine remorse "corresponds in any reliable way with the group of defendants who are first apprehended or first able to reach plea agreements with prosecutors").

§ 924(c) — Stacked Penalties for Carrying a Gun

Prosecutors can use the threat of 18 U.S.C. § 924(c) to prompt defendants to plead guilty. Under this statute, any person who "uses or carries a firearm" or possesses a firearm "in furtherance of" a drug trafficking crime or a crime of violence faces a mandatory additional term of 5 years in prison.[522] This additional term must be served on top of the sentence that applies under the Guidelines for the underlying offense. Judges do not have discretion to make the terms concurrent.[523] Where 924(c) applies, defendants are automatically disqualified from receiving probation.[524]

In addition, for every "second or subsequent" firearms offense, defendants face a 25-year enhancement.[525] Sentences for multiple 924(c) violations are "stacked," meaning that a defendant charged with two 924(c) violations in the same indictment will face 5 additional years for the first violation and then 25 more years on top of that for the second violation.

It is entirely up to prosecutors whether or not to charge an eligible defendant with a violation under 924(c).[526] What's more, if they opt to file the charge and the defendant is convicted, the additional penalty is obligatory and the judge must impose it.

---

[522] 18 U.S.C. § 924(c)(1)(A)(i). This term is even longer if the gun is brandished (7 years) or discharged (10 years). 18 U.S.C. § 924(c)(1)(A)(ii) & (iii). It is also increased for particular types of firearms. Short-barreled and semi-automatic guns carry a 10-year minimum increase in sentence, and machine guns or guns equipped with silencers carry a 30-year minimum increase. 18 U.S.C. § 924(c)(1)(B).
Like many provisions of the Sentencing Guidelines, penalties under 924(c) have become significantly harsher over the years since it was first adopted. *See* Firearms Policy Team Report to United States Sentencing Commission on Sentencing for the Possession or Use of Firearms During a Crime, Jan. 6, 2000, at 3 (detailing a history of the increases to penalties under 924(c) since it was adopted in 1968), *available at* http://www.ussc.gov/sites/default/files/pdf/research/working-group-reports/firearms/20000106-use-firearms-during-crime/firearms.pdf.

[523] 18 U.S.C. § 924(c)(1)(D)(ii) ("[N]o term of imprisonment imposed on a person under this subsection shall run concurrently with any other term of imprisonment imposed on the person, including any term of imprisonment imposed for the crime of violence or drug trafficking crime during which the firearm was used, carried, or possessed.").

[524] *See* 18 U.S.C. § 924(c)(1)(D)(i).

[525] *See* 18 U.S.C. § 924(c)(1(C)(i). If the second or subsequent offense involves a machine gun or a gun with a silencer, the defendant faces a mandatory life sentence. 18 U.S.C. § 924(c)(1)(C)(ii).

[526] Firearms Policy Team Report to United States Sentencing Commission on Sentencing for the Possession or Use of Firearms During a Crime, Jan. 6, 2000, at 16 ("Obviously, the length of an offender's prison term can be dramatically affected by" charging decisions of prosecutors.), *available at* http://www.ussc.gov/sites/default/files/pdf/research/working-group- reports/firearms/20000106-use-firearms-during-crime/firearms.pdf.

There has been a barrage of criticism for applying the gun enhancement to drug trafficking crimes because it severely ratchets up sentences even for non-violent drug offenders.[527] But even in the context of crimes of violence, 924(c) poses a significant and unwarranted impairment on the free exercise of the right to a trial. The enhancement has the potential to apply in a wide variety of circumstances. "Crimes of violence" under 924(c) extend well beyond the traditional notion of violent crime, which includes offenses like murder, rape, and assault.[528] For a crime to be "violent" for purposes of imposing the gun enhancement, it is not necessary that any individual actually have been injured or even that the defendant threatened to injure someone.[529] There simply needs to be a *risk* that physical force will be used against the person *or property* of another. Under the broad definition of this so-called "residual clause," burglary of an unoccupied home and obstruction of justice may be deemed crimes of violence.[530] The Supreme Court recently overturned a similar definition of "violent felony" in the Armed Career Offender Act (18 U.S.C. § 924(e)) because it was unconstitutionally vague, but lower federal courts have continued to apply the residual clause in 924(c).[531]

---

[527] *An O9fer You Can't Refuse*, *supra* note 27.

[528] *See* Alice Ristroph, *Criminal Law in the Shadow of Violence*, 62 ALA. L. REV. 571, 604 (2011) (noting that DOJ's consideration of "crimes of violence" involves a much narrower definition).

[529] 18 U.S.C. § 924(c)(3)(B). In construing the term "crime of violence," courts have adopted a categorical approach, meaning that they examine the statutory elements of the crime, rather than the particular details of the defendant's conduct. *See* Ristroph, *supra* note 201, at 604.

[530] *See* Ristroph, *supra* note 201, at 603 (noting that shift in sentencing law from conception of a threat of violence to a mere risk of violence caused the number of crimes that qualify as "violent" to explode and "is helping to fuel the vast expansion of the U.S. prison population").

[531] The Supreme Court recently held that the definition of "violent felony" in § 924(e) is unconstitutionally vague. *See United States v. Johnson*, ___U.S. ___, 135 S. Ct. 2551 (2015). The circuit courts are split on whether the reasoning in *Johnson* should extend "crimes of violence" under § 924(c). *See, e.g.*, *United States v. Prickett*, 839 F.3d 697, 700 (8th Cir. 2016) (joining the Second and Sixth Circuits in upholding Section 924(c)(3)(B) against a vagueness challenge); *United States v. Brown*, 868 F.3d 297, 302 (4th Cir. 2017) (denying to extend the application of *Johnson* outside the ACCA context; finding that *Johnson* only recognized that ACCA's residual clause was unconstitutionally vague and did not touch upon the residual clause at issue in this case). *But see United States v. Cardena*, 842 F.3d 959, 996 (7th Cir. 2016) (holding that "the residual clause in 18 U.S.C. § 924(c)(3)(B) is ... unconstitutionally vague"); *In re Smith*, 829 F.3d 1276, 1280 (11th Cir. 2016) ("extrapolate[ing] from the *Johnson* holding that § 924(c)'s residual clause is ... unconstitutional").

The Sentencing Commission, for its part, recognized that the Guidelines definition of "crime of violence" implicated many of the same concerns as in *Johnson*, and it revised its definition to remove the "risk of physical force" residual clause. *See* United States Sentencing Commission, *Report to the Congress: Career O9fender Sentencing Enhancements*, at 52,

Because of their vast discretion in charging, prosecutors can threaten 924(c) enhancements if defendants refuse to plead guilty. Defendants will know that they have no hope of leniency at sentencing because the enhancements are mandatory. Thus, exercising one's right to trial becomes a treacherous route, and the severity of the consequences can easily sway defendants to plead guilty.

The 924(c) enhancement is both vague and overbroad. It goes well beyond addressing the aim of reducing gun violence.[532] For 924(c) to apply, a defendant only has to carry or possess the gun; he need not ever fire or even brandish it. That means that the defendant will face a firearms enhancement even when the gun is unconnected to the violent nature of the crime. In fact, one commentator conducted a study in 2000 revealing that only a minority of cases involving 924(c) convictions were cases where the firearm was actually used.[533]

Despite the overbreadth of 924(c), there is little judges can do to regulate its use by prosecutors. Because of their vast discretion in charging, prosecutors can threaten 924(c) enhancements if defendants refuse to plead guilty. Defendants will know that they have no hope of leniency at sentencing because the enhancements are mandatory. Thus, exercising one's right to trial becomes a treacherous route, and the severity of the consequences can easily sway defendants to plead guilty.

The three strikes rule thus severely punishes defendants for their past conduct without any means to appeal to the sentencing judge for leniency.[209]

Usually, the only way to obtain relief from prosecutorial overreach is to go to trial in the hope that the weaknesses in the government's charges will eventually be revealed. But because the vast majority of defendants never take

---

available at https://www.ussc.gov/sites/default/files/pdf/news/congressional-tesIimony-and-reports/criminal- history/201607_RtC-Career-ONfenders.pdf. The Commission has called on Congress to similarly amend the various statutory definitions of "crimes of violence," like in §924(c), to focus only "on those offenders with the most serious violent criminal backgrounds." *Id.* at 48.

[532] Paul J. Hoffer, *Federal Sentencing for Violent and Drug Tra9ficking Crimes Involving Firearms: Recent Changes and Prospects for Improvement*, 37 AM. CRIM. L. REV. 41, 74 (2000) (As a whole, firearm sentence enhancement laws "show little or no impact," though enhancement laws have been "associated with a decrease in some types of crimes in a few states.").

[533] *See id.*

their cases to trial, there is no telling how many defendants have succumbed to the threats of prosecutors based on improper 924(c) charges.

§ 3559 — Three Strikes and You're Out

Another weapon prosecutors have to coerce guilty pleas is 18 U.S.C. § 3559(c), the "three strikes" rule, which mandates a sentence of life imprisonment *without parole* for any defendant convicted of a violent felony who has previously been convicted of two or more violent felonies or one violent felony and one serious drug offense. Similar to 924(c), a defendant's sentence under the three strikes rule is entirely dependent on the prosecutor, who must file an information notifying the court and the defendant of the prior offenses supporting the enhancement. The government is perfectly free in any case to choose not to seek the enhancement. On the other hand, if they do seek it, the life sentence is mandatory.[534] Judges have no avenue for mitigating the sentence even if they believe the circumstances do not call for such a harsh penalty.[535] The three strikes rule thus severely punishes defendants for their past conduct without any means to appeal to the sentencing judge for leniency.[536]

Francisco Feliciano and the Trial Penalty

In April 2011, an armed, masked man attempted to rob a bank in Florida, but he abandoned his plan shortly after entering the bank and was driven away from the scene by an accomplice. Ten days later, a similar robbery took place at a nearby bank, involving two-masked men and a third accomplice as the getaway driver. They managed to steal over $10,000 in cash. Although there was evidence that a gun had been used during the

---

534 18 U.S.C. 3559(c) ("a person who is convicted in a court of the United States of a serious violent felony *shall* be sentenced to life imprisonment…") (emphasis added). The only exception to imposing a life sentence is a case where the death penalty applies instead. 18 U.S.C. § 3559(c)(5).

535 *See* American Civil Liberties Union, *10 Reasons to Oppose '3 Strikes, You're Out'* (arguing that three strikes rule "ties the hands of judges who have traditionally been responsible for weighing both mitigating and aggravating circumstances before imposing sentence. Judicial discretion in sentencing, which is admired all over the world for treating people as individuals, is one of the hallmarks of our justice system. But the rigid formula imposed by '3 strikes' renders the role of sentencing judges almost superfluous."), *available at* https://www.aclu.org/other/10-reasons-oppose-3-strikes-youre-out.

536 Federal courts have uniformly rejected the argument that the three strikes rule violates the prohibition against double jeopardy, reasoning that it is not a re-punishment for past conduct but simply increased punishment for the current offense. *See, e.g.*, *United States v. Kaluna*, 192 F.3d 1188, 1198-99 (9th Cir. 1999).

first attempted robbery, neither the bank's surveillance footage nor any eyewitnesses identified a gun at the second robbery.

Following an investigation, three men were indicted as the perpetrators of the two robberies: Steven Trubey and Francisco Feliciano were implicated in both robberies, and Christopher Quinn was identified as their accomplice in the second robbery. Quinn eventually pled guilty. Although he admitted he never saw a gun at the second robbery, he claimed that Feliciano had told him he had gun. Based on that scant evidence, the prosecution threatened Feliciano with stacked gun charges for both robberies and a 25-year enhancement under 924(c) unless he agreed to plead guilty. But Feliciano chose to go to trial, believing that medical evidence would exonerate him. As was well-documented (and as Trubey corroborated), Feliciano had been receiving medical treatment for herniated discs and would not have been able to easily vault the counters (twice) like the masked perpetrator at the second robbery had done.

At trial, the prosecution presented no fingerprints, DNA, or other physical evidence linking Feliciano to the crimes. Quinn was the government's key witness and testified that Feliciano told him he had a gun at the second robbery. Trubey, on the other hand, testified that he had helped Feliciano pawn his gun a week earlier, so they used a shoebox with blinking lights disguised as a bomb at the second robbery instead because they had no gun. Despite this evidence contradicting Quinn's testimony, the jury found Feliciano guilty on all charges, including both gun charges, and he was sentenced to 41 years in jail.

Trubey, who admitted to participating in the second robbery, should have faced a similar penalty. But he pled guilty, was indicted for only the first robbery, and was sentenced to 8 ½ years. Quinn was sentenced to 14 years.

When Feliciano appealed the 25-year enhancement, the government initially defended it, arguing that Quinn's testimony was sufficient to support the second gun charge. But a month later (and conspicuously right after the U.S. Attorney for that district retired) the government changed its tune and filed an amended brief conceding that it was obvious Quinn was lying about the gun and admitting there was not sufficient evidence to support the second gun charge.

In reversing Feliciano's sentence, the Eleventh Circuit expressed concerns that the prosecution had decided to file the second gun charge in the first place: "The government clearly knew there were problems with this charge before trial. … While it is good that the government eventually reached an understanding of the inherent weakness in Count Four, they knew from interviews with Messrs. Trubey and Quinn long before trial that no one saw a gun .... We expect more from United States prosecutors."

The federal three strikes rule was adopted in 1994 as part of the Violent Crime Control and Law Enforcement Act. It followed similar laws in Washington and California that were spurred by public outrage over several high-profile murders committed by convicted felons shortly after they had been released from prison.[537] Proponents of three-strikes laws claim they serve to protect the public from the most dangerous violent criminals by removing them permanently from society.[538] But, like 924(c), the three strikes rule broadly defines "violent felony"; it is not limited to crimes involving serious injury or death. Defendants can face a mandatory life sentence as long as each of their three strikes involves a mere *risk* that physical force will be used.[539] A group of current and former prosecutors who publicly opposed Washington's version of the three-strikes rule provided this hypothetical scenario to illustrate that law's overreach:

An 18-year old high school senior pushes a classmate down to steal his Michael Jordan $150 sneakers — Strike One; he gets out of jail and shoplifts a jacket from the Bon Marche, pushing aside the clerk as he runs out of the store — Strike Two; he gets out of jail, straightens out, and nine years later gets in a fight in a bar and intentionally hits someone, breaking his nose —

---

[537] *See* Meredith McClain, '*Three Strikes and You're Out*': *The Solu6ion to the Repeat O9fender Problem?*, 20 SETON HALL UNIV. LEGIS. J. 97, 97- 100 (1996); David Schultz, *No Joy in Mudville Tonight: The Impact of 'Three Strike' Laws on State and Federal Correc6ions Policy, Resources, and Crime Control*, 9 CORNELL J.L. & PUB. POL'Y 557, 568 (2000) (three strikes laws were passed in "a frenzied emotional setting" when "fears of crime and victimization were running high," "[p]oliticians were appealing to this mood, and the media was increasing its coverage of violent crime").

[538] *See 10 Reasons to Oppose '3 Strikes, You're Out,' supra* note 208.

[539] The definition of "violent felony" emulates crimes of violence under § 924(c). It includes any offense "that has as an element the use, attempted use, or threatened use of physical force against the person of another or *that, by its nature, involves a substanmial risk that physical force against the person of another may be used in the course of commitming the odfense*." 18 U.S.C. § 3559(c)(2)(F)(ii) (emphasis added). Under this definition, the offense must first carry a statutory maximum sentence of at least 10 years. There are also specifically enumerated crimes that automatically qualify as violent felonies, including: murder, manslaughter, assault with the intent to commit murder, assault with the intent to commit rape, aggravated sexual abuse, sexual abuse, abusive sexual conduct, kidnapping, aircraft piracy, robbery, carjacking, extortion, arson, firearms use, and firearms possession under § 924(c). 18 U.S.C. § 3559(c)(2)(F)(i).

criminal behavior, to be sure, but hardly the crime of the century, yet it is Strike Three. He is sent to prison for the rest of his life.[540]

Although harsher penalties may be justified for certain habitual offenders, in most cases imprisonment for life with no opportunity for parole is extreme. The Sentencing Guidelines already contemplate higher sentences for those defendants with a history of criminal conduct.[541] Indeed, the Guidelines consider the defendant's criminal history before calculating the appropriate sentencing range in every case,[542] and they specifically provide for increased sentences for "career offenders" — including those defendants convicted of three or more violent crimes.[543] But at least the Guidelines attempt to tailor sentences for career offenders to their individual conduct and circumstances. The Sentencing Commission recently reported that defendants accused of three or more crimes of violence under the "career offender" Guideline received, on average, a sentence of about 15 years, which, for most defendants, is nowhere near a life sentence.[544] Moreover, the Sentencing Commission has now revised its definition of "crime of violence" to remove the residual clause for crimes that involve a mere risk of physical force.[545] But that vague and overbroad language remains applicable under the three strikes rule.[546] Also, under the career offender Guideline, the judge always retains the authority to

---

540 *See 10 Reasons to Oppose '3 Strikes, You're Out,' supra* note 208.

541 When the Commission was first promulgating the Guidelines, Congress directed it to set sentences for habitual offenders "at or near the maximum term authorized." Sentencing Reform Act of 1984, 18 U.S.C. § 944(h).

542 *See* § 4A1.1(a)-(c).

543 *See* Section 4B1.1.

544 *See Report to the Congress: Career O9fender Sentencing Enhancements*, *supra* note 204, at 34. Because the career offender guideline also applies to repeat drug offenders, the Commission divided its study into three groups: those convicted of only drug trafficking offenses, those convicted of only violent offenses, and those convicted of a mix of both. *Id.* at 27. According to the Commission's study, 47.4 percent of "violent only" career offenders received a sentence below the Guidelines range. *Id.* at 35 (Figure 15). *See also* Nkechi Taifa, *'Three-Strikes-and-You're-Out' — Mandatory Life Imprisonment for Third Time Felons*, 20 UNIV. OF DAYTON L. REV. 717, 721 (1995) (noting that a defendant convicted of assault with two prior offenses will receive, on average, a sentence of 68 months).

545 United States Sentencing Commission, *Amendments to the Sentencing Guidelines*, at 4-5, *available at* https://www.ussc.gov/sites/default/files/pdf/amendment-process/oNficial-text- amendments/20160121_Amendments_0.pdf.

546 In a recent report, the Sentencing Commission urged Congress to amend the definitions "crime of violence" under § 924(c) and "violent felony" under § 924(e) to remove the residual "risk of physical force" clause. The Commission pointed out "that the guideline's criminal history rules already take into account an individual's increased culpability and likelihood of recidivism." *Report to the Congress: Career O9fender Sentencing Enhancements*, *supra* note 204, at 55. The Commission did not extend its recommendation to "violent felonies" under 3559(c), although it is unclear why. The same reasoning should apply.

depart upward or downward if the circumstances warrant a harsher or more lenient sentence. In contrast, the three strikes rule automatically imposes an arbitrary life sentence that cannot be adjusted under any circumstances.

Even when prosecutors do not believe a life sentence is truly warranted, there is nothing preventing them from threatening to apply the three strikes rule if the defendant insists on going to trial.

Because repeat offenders already face substantial penalties under the Guidelines and other statutory enhancements — likely keeping them in prison well into middle-age — there seems little added benefit to perpetual incarceration. Most violent crime is committed by young men, and recidivism rates in general drop steadily and significantly after age 25.[547] On the other hand, the expense of incarceration rises precipitously as prisoners age.[548] The three strikes rule thus imposes significant costs on the government by keeping habitual offenders in prison long after they have ceased to be a threat to society.

Recent data published by the Sentencing Commission suggests that, in many cases, even prosecutors do not support the imposition of a life sentence.[549] Nonetheless, the three strikes rule can be a powerful tool for securing guilty pleas. Even when prosecutors do not believe a life sentence is truly warranted, there is nothing preventing them from threatening to apply the three strikes rule if the defendant insists on going to trial. For instance, in the case of Demetrius Derden, the prosecutor included a concession in the plea agreement stating that she would not seek a life sentence under 3559(c) if he

---

547 *See also* United States Sentencing Commission, *Recidivism Among Federal O9fenders: A Comprehensive Overview*, at 23 (noting that only 16 percent of individuals over 60 who were released from prison in 2005 recidivated, compared to 67.6 percent of those below age 21), *available at* http://www.ussc.gov/sites/default/files/pdf/research-and-publicaIions/research- publicaIions/2016/recidivism_overview.pdf.

548 *See* Center for Justice at Columbia University, *Aging in Prison: Reducing Elder Incarcera6ion and Promo6ing Public Safety*, at 24-26, *available at* http://centerforjusIice.columbia.edu/files/2015/10/AgingInPrison_FINAL_web.pdf.

549 Although data is not available to show the rate at which the government chooses to forgo applying the three strikes enhancement, the Sentencing Commission has examined sentences where the career offender guideline would apply for "violent only" offenses. And those cases necessarily qualify for the three strikes enhancement. According to the Commission's study, the government supported a below-guidelines sentence for 24.6 percent "violent only" career offenders in 2014. That means that, in at least a quarter of the cases where the three strikes rule would otherwise apply, the prosecution has not chosen to seek it. *Report to the Congress: Career O9fender Sentencing Enhancements*, *supra* note 204, at 35.

pled guilty.[550] At Derden's plea colloquy, both the prosecutor and the presiding judge emphasized that concession. "MS. ALLYN: *You might not have qualified for that anyway*, but regardless the government is saying we're not even to look at that [sic], we're not going to seek that. … THE COURT: You can't get a life sentence unless the government seeks it. … So if the government is not seeking a life sentence, you are not going to get a life sentence."[551] The judge later admitted that "[t]hroughout these proceedings, it has never appeared likely that Derden would qualify for a life sentence under § 3559(c)(1)."[552] In fact, one of Derden's prior offenses *by defini6ion* could not qualify as a violent felony under the statute because it was not one of the enumerated offenses and was not punishable by at least 10 years in prison.[553] But nothing prevented the prosecutor from emphasizing that the three strikes rule might apply in order to obtain Derden's guilty plea.

> Thus, defendants facing three-strikes charges are at a severe disadvantage in negotiating plea deals and have little hope of contesting the charges if they choose to go to trial.

Even in cases where the three strikes rule might arguably apply, the prosecution still retains the upper hand in plea negotiations. All the prosecutor need do is establish that the elements of the previous offenses meet the definition of "violent felony"; the government has no obligation to evaluate the defendant's actual conduct. But if the defendant wants to rebut that argument, *he* must prove with *clear and convincing evidence* that there was no serious threat of harm to any person.[554] Indeed, establishing the absence of a physical injury is often an insurmountable burden because the official records of prior offenses may not contain any evidence regarding injury and the prior offenses may be so old that defendants cannot gather evidence

550 *United States v. Derden*, No. 12-cr-0012 (PJS/SER), 2016 WL 5858638, at *1 (D. Minn. Oct. 5, 2016).
551 *Id.* at *3.
552 *Id.* at *2.
553 *Id.* at *2, n.2.
554 *See* 18 U.S.C. § 3559(c)(3). Robbery and unenumerated offenses that otherwise meet the definition of "violent felony" will not count as one of the defendant's three strikes if the defendant proves that no firearm or dangerous weapon was used or threatened to be used and that the offense did not result in death or serious bodily injury. § 3559(c)(3)(A). Arson will not count as a strike if the defendant proves that the offense posed no risk to human life and that the defendant reasonably believed it posed no threat to human life. § 3559(c)(3)(B).

anew.[555] Federal courts have held that placing the burden of proof on defendants in these instances does not violate due process, but at least one Court of Appeals judge disagreed, noting that, in a case involving a 25-year old robbery conviction, "[witnesses to such an ancient event are often gone; physical evidence has almost certainly disappeared."[556] Thus, defendants facing three-strikes charges are at a severe disadvantage in negotiating plea deals and have little hope of contesting the charges if they choose to go to trial.

Denandias Watson and the Trial Penalty

Denandias Watson grew up in an "environment of great deprivation and neglect." His father was killed by a police officer under the influence of alcohol; he subsequently watched his mother endure years of physical and verbal abuse at the hands of his step-father. As his defense counsel explained, he "hasn't been shown any human kindness by anybody" in his entire life. Dealing with depression, he dropped out of school, turned to alcohol and drugs, and embraced the streets.

On two separate occasions in 1997 and 1998, Watson was arrested for possession with the intent to distribute cocaine. He allegedly assaulted the arresting officers during the first offense. And he was accused of carrying a firearm during both offenses. In each instance, he pled guilty.

Several years later, he was arrested again in connection with an armed robbery at a restaurant. In their pursuit of the robbers, a few of the arresting officers sustained minor injuries.

During plea negotiations for the robbery, the prosecution offered to recommend a sentence of 15 years and a downward departure if Watson cooperated in the investigation of his co-defendants. But they threatened to seek the 3559(c) enhancement if he insisted on going to trial. Watson's two co-conspirators — who also had criminal records — pled guilty and were each sentenced to twenty-two years in prison.

When Watson ultimately chose to exercise his right to a trial, the prosecution followed through on their threat and filed an information seeking to impose a life sentence. Although Watson objected that one of his prior convictions had been obtained through an invalid guilty plea, the

[555] *See* Daniel R. O'Connor, *Defining the Strike Zone — An Analysis of the Classifica6ion of Prior Convic6ions under the Federal Three Strikes and You're Out Scheme*, 36 B.C. L. REV. 847, 878 (1994-1995).

[556] *See United States v. Kaluna*, 192 F.3d 1188, 1201 (9th Cir. 1999) (Thomas, J., dissenting).

sentencing judge did not believe he had the authority to reconsider that conviction even for purposes of sentencing Watson's most recent offense.

Because the judge was bound by the prosecution's decision to seek the three-strikes enhancement, he had no choice but to sentence Watson to life in prison. The only way Watson could have avoided that sentence was to give up his constitutional right to a trial.

Judicial Reticence to Mitigate Unwarranted Disparities

Except where mandatory minimums apply, federal judges do retain a significant amount of discretion over sentencing in individual cases. Indeed, after *Booker* was decided, federal judges were afforded an important tool to aid in the exercise of their newly-granted discretion. Chapter 18, Section 3553(a) of the U.S. Code instructs judges to impose sentences that are "sufficient, but not greater than necessary," to achieve the recognized goals of sentencing. It then lists several factors the sentencing judge should consider, including:

- the nature and circumstances of the offense and the history and characteristics of the defendant;
- the kinds of sentences available;
- the Sentencing Guidelines;
- policy statements of the Sentencing Commission;
- the need to avoid unwarranted sentence disparities among similarly situated defendants; and
- the need to provide restitution to any victims of the offense.[557]

These requirements existed even when the Guidelines were mandatory, but the factors in 3553(a) had little independent significance because judges were compelled to sentence within the Guidelines range. Now that the Guidelines are advisory, one would expect the other 3553(a) factors to have a larger influence over sentences. That has not proved to be the case, however.

---

[557] *See* 18 U.S.C. § 3553(a). *See also Judicial Responsibility for Jusbice in Criminal Courts*, NACDL, FCJ, and the Monroe Freedman Institute for the Study of Legal Ethics at Hofstra University's Maurice A. Deane School of Law (2017), *available at* https://www.nacdl.org/judicialresponsibilityforjuslicereport/.

In two cases, *Gall* and *Nelson*, the Supreme Court made clear that sentencing judges must consider the 3553(a) factors independent of the Guidelines themselves; they cannot presume that a within-Guidelines sentence is reasonable.[558] But that mandate has little practical significance because appellate courts *are* permitted to affirm within-Guidelines sentences based on the presumption that they are reasonable.[559] As Justice Souter recognized in a dissenting opinion:

> Without a powerful reason to risk reversal on the sentence, a district judge faced with evidence supporting a high subrange Guidelines sentence will … sentence within the high subrange. This prediction is weakened not a whit by the Court's description of within-Guidelines reasonableness as an "appellate" presumption …. What works on appeal determines what works at trial.[560]

Sentencing judges thus know that within-Guidelines sentences are unlikely to be overturned, and their consideration of the 3553(a) factors is usually a rote recitation without any meaningful explanation of how the factors have been applied.[561] In addition, the Sentencing Commission's "Statement of Reasons" reporting form encourages judges to ignore their obligations under 3553(a) because, in the vast majority of cases, the form does not require judges to provide any written explanation of sentencing decisions that are within the Guidelines range.[562]

---

[558] *See Nelson v. United States*, 555 U.S. 350, 352 (2009) ("Our cases do not allow a sentencing court to presume that a sentence within the applicable Guidelines range is reasonable."); *Gall v. United States*, 552 U.S. 38, 49-50 (2007) ("The Guidelines are not the only consideration …. [A]fter giving both parties an opportunity to argue for whatever sentence they deem appropriate, the district judge should then consider all of the § 3553(a) factors to determine whether they support the sentence requested by a party. In so doing, he may not presume that the Guidelines range is reasonable.").

[559] *See Rita v. United States*, 551 U.S. 338 (2007) (endorsing presumption of reasonableness for federal appellate courts).

[560] *See id.* at 391 (Souter, J., dissenting).

[561] One panel of the Second Circuit has complained that the Commission's "Statement of Reasons" form encourages judges to ignore their obligations under 3553(a). *United States v. Pruitt*, 813 F.3d 90 (2d Cir. 2016). Judges are required to complete a form identifying their reasons for the selected sentence in each case. However, the form does not require them to provide any written explanation for a sentence within the Guidelines range, as long as the high end of the range is no more than 24 months.

[562] The Statement of Reasons form only requires a written explanation of a within-Guidelines sentence if the Guidelines range is wider than 24 months. As one panel of the Second Circuit has noted, 82.3 percent of all Guidelines ranges in 2014 were no wider than 24 months, so the form "conveys to sentencing judges that as long as they stay within a range that is not wider than 24 months, no reasons for the sentence are necessary. That message

Except where mandatory minimums apply, federal judges do retain a significant amount of discretion over sentencing in individual cases … Now that the Guidelines are advisory, one would expect the other 3553(a) factors to have a larger influence over sentences. That has not proved to be the case, however.

Circuit court decisions since *Gall* and *Nelson* have also watered down judges' discretion under 3553(a). This is particularly true for 3553(a)(6) — which addresses the need to avoid unwarranted disparities among similarly-situated defendants. Some Circuits have effectively written this paragraph out of the statute, reasoning that the Guidelines calculations already address this concern and that asking individual judges to make determinations about unwarranted disparities is impractical and imprecise.[563] Other Circuits have limited the scope of unwarranted disparity challenges by holding that 3553(a)(6) is only concerned with national disparities; judges need not compare the sentences of defendants involved in the same criminal scheme when considering unwarranted disparities.[564]

Courts have allowed outrageous sentencing disparities among co-defendants, even in cases where the nature and circumstances of their offenses is practically identical and the only significant difference is that one defendant insisted on a trial.

---

conflicts with the mandate in § 3553…." *United States v. Pruitt*, 813 F.3d 90, 94 (2d Cir. 2016).

563 *See, e.g.*, *United States v. Mason*, 410 F. App'x 881, 886 (6th Cir. 2010) ("As this court has previously stated, it is pointless for defendants who receive within-Guidelines sentences to raise unwarranted-disparity claims.") (internal quotation marks omitted); *United States v. Vaughn*, 431 F. App'x 507, 509-10 (7th Cir. 2011) ("because the guidelines are designed to avoid unwarranted disparities, a sentence such as Vaughn's that is within the guidelines range necessarily complies with § 3553(a)(6)"). *See also United States v. Treadwell*, 593 F.3d 990, 1011 (9th Cir. 2010) ("A district court need not, and, as a practical matter, cannot compare a proposed sentence to the sentence of every criminal defendant who has ever been sentenced before."); *United States v. Willingham*, 497 F.3d 541, 544-55 (5th Cir. 2007) ("National averages of sentences that provide no details underlying the sentences are unreliable to determine unwarranted disparity because they do not reflect the enhancements or adjustments for the aggravating or mitigating factors that distinguish individual cases.").

564 Most circuits allow co-defendant comparisons but have held that judges are not required to consider them. Matthew Benjamin, *Beyond Anecdote: Informing the Sentencing Court's 3553(a)(6) Duty*, 26 FED. SENT'G REP. 35, 38 n.34 (2013). *See, e.g.*, *United States v. Dowdy*, 216 F. App'x 178, 181 (3d Cir. 2007) (district courts are not required to consider sentencing disparities among co-defendants, and defendants cannot challenge their sentences on appeal based on disparity among co-defendants).

Even judges who are generally willing to consider disparity among co-defendants may decide it is irrelevant if one co-defendant goes to trial. According to some judges, the concern about unwarranted disparities does not even apply in this circumstance because a defendant who chooses to go to trial is necessarily differently-situated from his co-defendants who pled guilty.[565] Admittedly, if judges were *required* to impose identical sentences on co-defendants, that would virtually eliminate the incentive to plead guilty in every case. But even a judge who feels compelled to honor the bargained-for sentence in a plea agreement is not prevented from imposing an appropriately proportional sentence on a similarly-situated co-defendant who has gone to trial. A flat-out refusal to consider 3553(a)(6) at all if a defendant goes to trial effectively condones *any* disparity in sentencing among co-defendants, regardless of how extensive the disparity is. Courts have allowed outrageous sentencing disparities among co-defendants, even in cases where the nature

[565] *United States v. Rodriguez-Milian*, 820 F.3d 26, 35 (1st Cir. 2016), *cert. denied*, 137 S. Ct. 138 (2016) (finding that it is settled law in the circuit "that a co-conspirator who has elected to plead guilty is not similarly situated to a co-conspirator who has elected to stand trial.") (citing *United States v. Dávila–González,* 595 F.3d 42, 50 (1st Cir. 2010)); *United States v. Ebbers*, 458 F.3d 110, 129 (2d Cir. 2006) (mentioning that § 3553 is aimed at eliminating national sentencing disparity [and not disparity between similarly situated defendants.]); *United States v. Spence*, No. 15-2593, 2017 WL 2983003, at *4 (3d Cir. July 13, 2017) (finding that identically situated conspirators can receive different sentences because some of them pled guilty, as "[a] court may extend[ ] leniency in exchange for a plea of guilty and ... not extend[ ] leniency to those who have not demonstrated those attributes on which leniency is based.") (citing *Corbitt v. New Jersey*, 439 U.S. 212, 224 (1978)) (internal quotations omitted); *United States v. Brainard*, 745 F.2d 320, 324 (4th Cir. 1984) (holding that disparity in sentences between a defendant who stands trial and a co-defendant who pleads guilty does not require appellate reversal); *United States v. Cannon*, 552 F. App'x 512, 517, 522 (6th Cir. 2014) (finding that a district court did not abuse its discretion by allowing a disparity between two co-conspirators, when one pled guilty and one went to trial, and that this leniency was the whole point of plea bargaining); *United States v. Pisman*, 443 F.3d 912, 916 (7th Cir. 2006) (noting corresponding reduction to sentence of defendant who pled guilty, when compared to a defendant who went to trial, was not an unwarranted disparity) (citation omitted); *United States v. Herra-Herra*, 860 F.3d 1128, 1133 (8th Cir. 2017) (noting that district court did not abuse its discretion in finding a disparity between a co-conspirator who went to trial and others who pled guilty); *United States v. Carter*, 560 F.3d 1107, 1121 (9th Cir. 2009) (noting that, so long as there is no indication of retaliation against a defendant for choosing to go to trial, taking into account that one defendant chose to go to trial while a similarly situated defendant pled guilty when sentencing is not unreasonable); *United States v. Lunnin*, 608 F. App'x 649, 665 (10th Cir. 2015) (acknowledging that choosing to plead guilty vs. go to trial is grounds for permitting disparity between otherwise similarly situated defendants); *United States v. Langston*, 590 F.3d 1226, 1237 (11th Cir. 2009) (finding no unwarranted disparity where a defendant who pled guilty received a lesser sentence than a defendant who chose to go to trial); *United States v. Mejia*, 597 F.3d 1329, 1344 (D.C. Cir. 2010) (noting that accepting responsibility by pleading guilty creates a disparity that merits a reduction in sentence compared to similarly situated defendants).

and circumstances of their offenses is practically identical and the only significant difference is that one defendant insisted on a trial.

Allmendinger's case is a telling example of the pervasive and pernicious impact of the Guidelines. Although the judge applied a variance of *80 years*, that did Allmendinger little good. He was still going to end up spending nearly the rest of his life in prison because the sentence under the Guidelines was astronomical. If, instead of using the Guidelines as a baseline, the judge had started with Oncale's sentence — which everyone agreed was sufficient — and moved upward, Allmendinger likely would have received a fairer sentence. In isolation of the Guidelines, it would have been hard for the judge to determine that 40 additional years in prison was "sufficient, but not greater than necessary" to account for the distinctions between Oncale and Allmendinger. But where the presumptive starting point for a sentence is in excess of the entire lifespan of most people, locating a sentence "sufficient, but not greater than necessary" can easily turn into an arbitrary task.[566] In many cases, the excessive pull of the Guidelines prevents judges from meaningfully exercising their discretion under 3553(a).

Allmendinger's case amounts to an endorsement of a 35-year penalty for exercising the right to a trial. But neither the sentencing judge nor the appellate court bothered to concern themselves with the effect that disparity could have on later defendants who are faced with the decision to relinquish their constitutional rights. With outcomes like this, it is little wonder that only 3 out of 100 defendants are willing to risk going to trial.

Christian Allmendinger and the Trial Penalty

In 2004, Christian Allmendinger and Brent Oncale founded a company called A&O to sell bonded life settlement investments — interests in life insurance policies protected by a reinsurance bond. Investors were guaranteed a pay-out based on the life insurance policies, which would remain in force as long as the premiums on the life insurance policies were current.

[566] It is possible that judges find the 3553(a) factors complicated or even contradictory and so they opt to rely on the Guidelines range that has been calculated according to a defined and familiar formula. *See* "It's Time To Rethink Or Junk Entirely 18 U.S.C. § 3553(a)," HERCULES AND THE UMPIRE, Blog by Judge Richard George Kopf, District of Nebraska (entry posted July 27, 2014) (expressing frustration that the 3553(a) factors "provide no meaningful guidance to the sentencing judge"), *available at* https://herculesandtheumpire.com/2014/07/.

In marketing their products to investors, the partners made false statements about the size and staff of A&O and their record of earning returns. They also mispresented the use of invested funds. Instead of being segregated in a separate account and used solely to pay premiums, the funds were comingled with A&O's general operating account. The partners used that account to pay millions of dollars to themselves.

Following a series of regulatory inquiries, the partners agreed to sell A&O to another company "Blue Dymond." Unbeknownst to Allmendinger, Blue Dymond was actually a shell company created by Oncale, who intended to continue running the business after it was sold. In late 2007 — long after Allmendinger left the business — Oncale and another associate appropriated $11 million of investor funds from the company and ceased making premium payments, causing the life insurance policies to lapse and forcing the company into bankruptcy. A&O's investors lost over $100 million.

Allmendinger and Oncale were both indicted. Oncale pled guilty as part of a cooperation agreement and was sentenced to 10 years in prison (later reduced to 5 years after testifying against Allmendinger). Allmendinger chose to go to trial, was convicted, and faced a sentence of 125 years in prison under the Guidelines — a shocking disparity given the similarity between the two partners.

There were only two material differences between them. While Oncale stayed on and eventually participated in the decision to cease making premium payments, ultimately causing investors' losses, Allmendinger left the business at a time when premium payments were current on a sufficient number of policies to pay off A&O's investors. On the other hand, while Oncale immediately offered to cooperate with investigators, Allmendinger initially hid some of the proceeds of the fraud after he was indicted and initially contemplated flight but eventually appeared for trial. In all other respects, the two original partners were identically culpable.

The judge agreed to grant Allmendinger a variance of 80 years, that still left him with 45 years — 9 times higher than Oncale's sentence. In supporting that sentence, the judge referred to Allmendinger's crimes as "heinous." He did not explain why Allmendinger deserved such a harsh sentence compared to his partner.

On appeal, the Fourth Circuit rejected Allmendinger's argument of unwarranted disparity, finding that the sentencing judge's explanation was adequate to meet the requirements of 3553(a). Allmendinger was 39 when he was sentenced. His 45-year sentence will keep in him in prison for nearly the rest of his life.

Principles and Recommendations

Principles

1. The trial penalty — the substantial difference between the sentence offered prior to trial versus the sentence a defendant receives after a trial — undermines the integrity of the criminal justice system.
2. Trials protect the presumption of innocence and encourage the government to charge cases based only on sufficient, legally-obtained evidence to satisfy the reasonable doubt standard.
3. The decline in the frequency of trials impacts the quality of prosecutorial decision-making, defense advocacy, and judicial supervision.
4. The decline in the frequency of trials tends to encourage longer sentences thereby contributing to mass incarceration, including mass incarceration of people of color and the poor.
5. The decline in the frequency of trials erodes the oversight function of the jury thereby muting the voice of lay people in the criminal justice system and also undercuts the role of appellate courts in supervising the work of trial courts.
6. The trial penalty creates a coercive effect which profoundly undermines the integrity of the plea bargaining process.
7. A reduction for accepting responsibility through a guilty plea is appropriate. The same or similar reduction should be available after trial if an individual convicted at trial sincerely accepts responsibility after trial regardless of whether the accused testified at trial or not.
8. No one should be punished for exercising her or his rights, including seeking pre-trial release and discovery, investigating a case, and filing and litigation of pre-trial statutory and constitutional motions.
9. Mandatory minimum sentences undermine the integrity of plea bargaining (by creating a coercive effect) and the integrity of the sentencing process (by imposing categorical minimums rather than case-by-case evaluation). At the very least, safety valve provisions should be enacted to permit a judge to sentence below mandatory minimum sentences if justice dictates.

10. If mandatory minimums are not abolished, the government should not be permitted to use mandatory minimum sentences to retaliate against an accused person's decision to exercise her or his constitutional or statutory rights. That is, the state should not be allowed to file charges carrying mandatory minimum sentences in response to a defendant rejecting a plea offer or invoking her or his rights including the right to trial or to challenge unconstitutional government action.

Recommendations

1. Relevant Conduct: USSG §1B1.3 should be amended to prohibit the use of evidence from acquitted conduct as relevant conduct.
2. Acceptance of Responsibility: USSG §3E1.1(b) should be amended to authorize courts to award a third point for acceptance of responsibility if the interests of justice dictate without a motion from the government and even after trial.
3. Obstruction of Justice: USSG §3C1.1 should be amended to clarify that this adjustment should not be assessed solely for the act of an accused testifying in her or his defense. Application Note 2 should also be clarified in this respect.
4. Mandatory Minimum Sentencing: Mandatory minimum sentencing statutes should be repealed or subject to a judicial "safety valve" in cases where the court determines that individual circumstances justify a sentence below the mandatory minimum.
5. Full Discovery: Defendants should have full access to all relevant evidence, including any exculpatory information, prior to entry of any guilty plea.
6. Remove the Litigation Penalty: The government should not be permitted to condition plea offers on waiver of statutory or constitutional rights necessary for an accused person to make an intelligent and knowing decision to plead guilty. This includes an accused person's decision to seek pre-trial release or discovery, investigate a case, or litigate statutory or constitutional pre-trial motions.
7. Limited Judicial Oversight of Plea-Bargaining: There should be mandatory plea-bargaining conferences in every criminal case supervised by a judicial officer who is not presiding over the case unless the defendant, fully informed, waives the opportunity. These conferences would require the participation of the parties but could

not require either party to make or accept an offer. In some cases, one or more parties might elect not to participate beyond attendance.

8. Judicial "Second Looks": After substantial service of a sentence, courts should review lengthy sentences to ensure that sentences are proportionate over time.
9. Proportionality Between Pre-Trial and Post-Trial Sentencing: Procedures should be adopted to ensure that the accused are not punished with substantially longer sentences for exercising their right to trial, or its related rights. Concretely, post-trial sentences should not increase by more than the following: denial of acceptance of responsibility (if appropriate); obstruction of justice (if proved); and the development of facts unknown before trial.
10. Amendment to 18 U.S.C. § 3553(a)(6): In assessing whether a post-trial sentencing disparity is unwarranted, the sentencing court shall consider the sentence imposed for similarly situated defendants (including, if available, a defendant who pled guilty in the same matter) and the defendant who was convicted after trial. The sentencing court shall consider whether any differential between similarly situated defendants would undermine the Sixth Amendment right to trial.

Conclusion

In closing, it is important to reiterate what is at stake if the trial penalty continues to hold sway over defendants' free exercise of their Constitutional rights. A system that coerces even one innocent person to plead guilty should not be condoned. Nor should the rights of the accused to hold the government to its burden of proof be impeded by fear of severe retribution. Unless the freedom of choice to exercise the right to a jury trial is fully restored, a great hypocrisy will endure — one that espouses lofty principles of criminal justice but insists that the system for administering criminal justice cannot afford to honor those principles except in an insignificant percentage of cases.

NACDL readily acknowledges the difficulty of fashioning a sentencing system that allows for individualized sentences tempered by concerns for national parity, and then administering that system in a just and efficient way. This study should not be viewed as a disparagement of the federal prosecutorial bar, the federal judiciary, or the Sentencing Commission as a whole. However, as an organization dedicated to promoting civil rights and liberties that are fundamental to democracy, NACDL is gravely concerned that the current system unfairly infringes on one of the most precious Constitutional rights.

As the years go on, fewer and fewer defendants are choosing to take advantage of the right to a trial. When the risks of exercising this crucial human right are too great for all but 3% of federal criminal defendants, the system is in need of repair.

* * *

Ms. DEAN. Next, the Chair recognizes the gentleman from California, Mr. Lieu.

Mr. LIEU. Thank you, Madam Chair, and thank you to all the witnesses who are here today, as well as for your expertise. I just want to first say that mandatory minimum sentences are stupid, and they're stupid because we stupidly force every fact pattern, every life case, into these rigid little boxes that don't reflect reality. The whole reason we have judges and juries and prosecutors and defense attorneys, instead of robots and computers, is to provide individualized justice for each unique case. Mandatory minimums strip that away. It's had devastating consequences for society and overly harsh punishments.

I'm a former prosecutor in the United States Military. We didn't have mandatory minimum sentences for drug offenses. We're talking about folks that fly fighter jets with weapons on them, drive tanks, sit in missile silos. We didn't have individualized—or mandatory minimum sentences, because we believe in individualized justice, so should the Federal civilian side. I look forward to working with the Committee to eliminate mandatory minimum sentences for drug offenses.

What I'd like to focus on today is pretrial detention, and Professor Barkow, you had mentioned in your witness statement, a section on pretrial detention, and you stated that individuals detained pretrial are more likely to plead guilty than defendants who are not detained, and that pretrial detention also leads to longer sentences regardless of a defendant's risk, crime, or criminal history. Can you elaborate on why that is?

Ms. BARKOW. Yes. Thank you, Representative Lieu, for the question. I think that what we see when people are detained pretrial is they would like to leave, and, so, it's an even more coercive plea-bargaining environment than for someone who is not detained.

If you're thinking about fighting your case but you're under detention, and you're offered any kind of time-served sort of thing, people are more likely to take it. So, they take worse deals, they get longer sentences as a result.

Then the other thing we know about pretrial detention is that it is really disruptive on people's lives, right? If you take somebody who was working, their employer is unlikely to keep them. Even if they're just detained a short period of time, it's not something that they're particularly forgiving about, Hey, I've got to serve out a little bit of time in jail, can I still keep my job? The answer is typically no, so they lose their jobs.

They often get evicted from their housing. These are people that are living at the margins. They lose custody of their children. So, it's an enormous disruptive event in somebody's life.

So, separate and apart from whatever they're accused of doing, when you detain them pretrial and you take them away from all of those things, their job, their housing, and their children, you can see why when they are ultimately released from that, it's harder to get on a path to stay law-abiding.

So, they're actually at an increased risk of committing crimes than if we just kept them out in the first place and didn't detain them. We have lots of evidence from the States now, places that are reforming their pretrial defense practices where they're really lowering their detention numbers and crime rates are going down, they're saving money. Again, it's one of those win-win areas.

Mr. LIEU. Thank you, Professor Barkow. I gather from your answer that you believe that pretrial detention reform, also known in some places as bail reform, would be a critical part of sentencing reform, right?

Ms. BARKOW. I think it is urgent, absolutely, 100 percent.

Mr. LIEU. Thank you. I also note that pretrial detention has sky-rocketed in the Federal system, from 19 percent in 1985 to 75 percent in 2019.

In addition, Federal pretrial detention rates are much higher than States, who are at about 75 percent, compared to 38 percent for States with large urban counties.

That's one reason I introduced the pretrial reform bills. I have two of them, and I look forward to working with this Subcommittee to get those bills marked up.

I'd like to ask a question of Ms. Givens. First, thank you for your service as a Federal public defender. Can you explain a little bit what the effect of pretrial detention has on some of your clients who, let's say, are unable to leave pretrial detention?

Ms. GIVENS. Pretrial detention, in the Federal system, has a devastating effect. I agree with Rachel Barkow wholeheartedly. It affects families, their lives, employment, but most importantly, I think we need to look at the data, which is, if you release people pretrial, they don't abscond, and they're not a community safety risk, which are the only two questions that you're supposed to be answering at a pretrial detention hearing.

The evidence just doesn't suggest that these people represent those two risks. We could save a lot of money and divert people into drug treatment and mental health treatment before detaining them.

Mr. LIEU. Thank you so much. I yield back.

Ms. DEAN. The gentleman yields back. The Chair recognizes the representative from Wisconsin, Representative Tiffany, for 5 minutes.

Mr. TIFFANY. Thank you, Madam Chair.

Ms. Barkow, we're hearing a lot about that mental health is needed here. Mental health treatment is a consistent message here in regard to drug problems, that type of stuff.

So, we had this great deinstitutionalization that happened, what was that, back in the 1970s, and did we make a mistake in not getting people mental health? Because, perhaps, changes should have been made in the '70s, but did we, by deinstitutionalizing—because I hear people, in regards to the homeless problem, they speak frequently about those people have significant mental health problems, but they're not getting them, whereas perhaps they did get them earlier. Did we miss the mark 50 years ago?

Ms. BARKOW. Well, I think the deinstitutionalization movement, it was the right idea, because these big mental hospitals were really abusive and awful places. They actually had a lot in common in what we see in prisons today.

The idea behind it was they were supposed to be deinstitutionalized to community mental health facilities. So, there were supposed to be community-based places for them to go, and that's where it went awry, there was no replacement for what had been offered. So, I don't think the answer would be a return to institutionalizing people, but I do think the idea of providing community-based care is critical, and that was the piece that was missing from that movement previously.

I think you're entirely right to draw the connection, though, between people with mental health needs and a hearing on sentencing, because for many of the people that we see cycling in and out of prisons and jails, they have an underlying mental health issue, so you're not really doing anything by incarcerating them.

Mr. TIFFANY. Sure. So, we didn't have a replacement for what happens which is classic.

Ms. Givens, what I heard from you is, you were saying the Federal Government has a problem in regards to this issue, that you would more effectively deal with this—or it would be more effectively dealt with if the Federal Government didn't do certain things. Is that correct?

Ms. GIVENS. The Federal Government—I heard your question, as the Federal Government is a problem, and they need to do certain other things. I'm not sure what you're asking me.

Mr. TIFFANY. So, when I heard your testimony, you talked about harsh mandatory minimums, some of the requirements that the Federal Government has in place, that they end up being counterproductive. Is that accurate?

Ms. GIVENS. I would agree.

Mr. TIFFANY. Is that accurate?

Ms. GIVENS. Yes.

Mr. TIFFANY. Yeah. Okay. So, I sure hope this committee, that we look at this in a way that is introspective and making sure that we're not creating problems for the States. Maybe this is something that we should defer to the States. I'm hearing about some success stories from States, that they think they're handling it better.

This is classic, where we have the laboratory of the States, the 50 States, where they, maybe, more effectively deal with something like this, rather than trying to get this one-size-fits-all approach that comes from the Federal Government.

Number three, Ms. is it Frederick? I wasn't here for your testimony.

Ms. FREDERIQUE. Frederique.

Mr. TIFFANY. Frederique. Thank you. Can you assure—if we make these changes that you're calling for, can you assure us there will not be a spike in violent crime?

Ms. FREDERIQUE. I think what you're seeing is that the things that we have currently have not assured that either, so what I can say is that the things that we are pushing for is an investment in communities and providing people support, and that those things are important as we move forward.

Mr. TIFFANY. I respect the goals that you have laid out here for what we should try to do in laying out, perhaps, a roadmap to make this happen, but I can tell you, if we continue to see the unprecedented increase in violent crime that's happening in our cities right now—so my district, I'm in Wisconsin, but I'm right next to Minneapolis and St. Paul. That's in Wisconsin, it's 15 minutes away.

They are seeing an unprecedented increase in violent crime in Minneapolis right now, and it largely affects minority communities of color. That's who is being hit the worst with this. I look at the feed on my phone each day, and I had two today, that regularly get these crime updates from Minneapolis, and it's unbelievable the number of people that are being harmed, whether it's carjackings, murders, and stuff like that.

We have to make sure that we do a smart job here about this, because if crime continues to increase the way it is in our major cities across America, people are not going to stand for this, because this is what happened after the '60s and '70s, people said, That's enough. We want our communities to be safe. We could be right back here with the public saying, we want tougher—we want you to be much tougher on crime if we don't do this properly.

Anyhow, my time is up, and I yield.

Ms. JACKSON LEE. [Presiding.] The gentleman yields back. I thank him for his testimony. We now acknowledge the Vice Chair of the Subcommittee, Ms. Bush from Missouri, for 5 minutes. You're recognized.

Ms. BUSH. I thank you, Chair, for convening this important hearing. Let me just say, being tough on crime—let me start with, being tough on crime is the reason why we're here today. It is not because social safety nets were being taken care of. It was the tough-on-crime work of people that even are in this Chamber.

So, 50 years, that's how long our government has waged a war, not on drugs, but on people. Our people, they are not statistics. A lot of my colleagues even here today in Congress aren't where I'm from. They haven't seen what I've seen, the people and communities harmed by this racist, White supremacist war on drugs.

Those folks are my neighbors, they're my friends, they're my classmates, they're my loved ones. I will never forget how in a 2-year window, as a young person, I lost 40–50 friends. Imagine losing friends or community members so frequently that loss and trauma become your norm.

In fact, I lost more friends to the war on drugs than not. I had a very, very close loved one of mine who was killed, shot straight in the head because of this nightmare. For those of us that lived through this war, we lived through daily and tragic deaths. What the war on drugs ignited was an actual warfare on our streets.

Our grandparents were forced to put their homes up for bond, and when the government threw us in jail and left us without any social safety nets, it was that this was what was needed. No, many grandparents were forced to become guardians because the war on drugs devastated an entire generation of parents.

Children were forced to be caretakers for their parents who fell victim to the cycle of abuse. I watched young boys fall into the trap of selling drugs as a means of survival. Survival. Youth are joining gangs as a way to secure their homes and their streets from police violence.

I know because I was a part of that. It's not something that I read or that I heard, like some folks on here.

I saw young women and girls unwillingly fall victim to trafficking, abuse, and exploitation to survive this war on drugs.

As a young child and a young adult, I didn't think I had a voice to do anything about what I was seeing, but now as a Congress-woman and as a nurse, I can speak for all my friends whose lives were cut too short. I can speak for those friends who are still behind bars even to this day, and I can say, unequivocally, that the war on drugs was a failure of policy. It was a failure many leaders in this very Chamber are responsible for.

Ms. Frederique, thank you for your thorough testimony and providing solutions. The war on drugs has not meaningfully reduced drug use. In what ways has it worsened drug use and overdose deaths?

Ms. FREDERIQUE. Thank you so much, Congresswoman, for your question. Unequivocally, our choices around policy, our Draconian investments, our focus on incarceration and criminalization, have not only not deterred people from using drugs, but they have also made drug use more risky and more dangerous.

Prohibition itself has made our drug supply risky and dangerous. Our choice—that was a choice—to create prohibition, and to really push and focus on criminalization, has made our drug supply poisoned.

What we are seeing with the overdose rates is that people:

1. Don't have the education that they need to understand drug use and to make sure that they don't die, which is basic.
2. Our drug supply is poisoned because people are adulterating it because of the incentivization of prohibition.
3. Our communities don't have the resources necessary to navigate addiction because we are bloating our criminal justice system as opposed to the public health infrastructure that people need to navigate addiction.

As a social worker, it is very clear to me that we need community supports and resources to navigate people's choices around risky drug use. Our focus on criminalization, not only makes it difficult for people to ask for help or to get them, and it also makes it really difficult for us to control the kinds of substances that people are using.

Ms. BUSH. Thank you. Thank you, Ms. Frederique.

Ms. Barkow, you have written extensively on the role of the President and the role he can play in reversing the harms of the war on drugs for those who are serving time. Can you talk about these proposals?

Ms. BARKOW. Yeah. Whatever you do in Congress—and I urge you to do as much as you can—the President can use the clemency power to reduce sentences. So, anyone, for example, who is serving a sentence under any of these mandatory minimums that's too harsh, the people who are on home confinement that someone asked about earlier, keeping them out, the President can do all that through clemency. There's no reason to send any of those folks back. A blanket clemency order would keep them home. He can use the clemency power to reduce these Draconian drug sentences that people are serving, and I certainly hope that he uses that power.

Ms. BUSH. Thank you very much, and I'll close here. For years and years our communities were duped, our communities were told that these criminal policies were necessary to keep our streets safe, but we know that that was a lie.

We know that these policies made substance use, health issues even worse, and I implore my colleagues to join us in legislating to promote health and not perpetuate harm. Thank you, and I yield back.

Ms. JACKSON LEE. I thank the gentlelady for important questions, and I thank her for yielding back. Now, recognize the Ranking Member, Mr. Biggs, for 5 minutes of questioning.

Mr. BIGGS. I thank the Chair, and this has been a very interesting hearing, and I really thank you for holding this hearing. This is an important hearing.

As a person who practiced law in the criminal field for a number of years and tried many cases, I will tell you that I think that it's interesting to me that we have—so much of what I've heard I find fascinating. I think there are things that we can have points of agreement on, and if I could, at some point, I would encourage us to be able to sit down, put aside our partisan differences, and see if there was some way to find concord at least in certain areas that we could move forward. That's very difficult to do.

I would just want—and I have to respond to something that was just said in the last speaker, that these were institutionally racist policies. I just point out in 1971, New York had a huge heroin epidemic. It was just a terrible problem in the early '70s. Then Congressman Rangel from Harlem urged then-President Nixon to ramp up drug-fighting efforts more aggressively and said, quote, "We could bring a halt to this condition which is killing off American youth," close quote. That's what he told President Nixon. I don't think this was done intentionally, on a racist basis—

You know, could I have a point of order? That's—Madam Chair?

Mr. COHEN. Sorry. I apologize. Will you yield?

Mr. BIGGS. That is absurd. That is absurd.

Mr. COHEN. It is not absurd. Will you yield?

Ms. JACKSON LEE. It's Mr. Biggs time.

Mr. BIGGS. I would ask for my time to be restored to where I was before I was interrupted.

Ms. JACKSON LEE. Your time is being restored, and I'll—do you wish to yield to the gentleman for his question?

Mr. BIGGS. No, I don't. I don't, Madam Chair. I will not yield to him.

Ms. JACKSON LEE. We'll provide you with that time.

Mr. BIGGS. Thank you.

The reality is, that's what I'm talking about. That kind of interruption prevents us from being able to set aside partisan bickering and get to where there's concord to move things forward.

I'll tell you about a case where a client I represented one time with regard to drug abuse. This individual was charged and he was probably the most respectful defendant I'd ever had an opportunity to work with. Very respectful, very kind, very gracious.

His charge was first-degree murder. While under the influence of drugs, he had gone into a home of a man that he had met and killed him. He strangled him. There was very little defense to that. I mean, that's what he did. He was under the influence of drugs.

We had to wait to do the trial because while under the influence of drugs, he had gone into a restaurant with two friends and semiautomatic weapons and robbed the entire restaurant. We had to wait for that trial to be completed before we could go forward, and we had to move the motions that were necessary regarding that.

I tell you that because I asked him what he thought the root of his problem was. He said it was drugs. He said it was clearly—he said, when I was under the influence of drugs, it just messed everything up, and we had an extensive talk and conversation about that. It ended up ruining his life and many others.

I tell you that because I do think drug use and trafficking can have very serious consequences tangential to personal use.

I was taken by something that Mr. Underwood said about training individuals who are going to be coming out, so they don't recidivate. There's a Department of Corrections—and this is one thing I think Mr. Tiffany was correct on. I think the States have gotten way ahead of the Feds on a lot of sentencing reform. They use private sector groups.

I'll give you an example. They use the Home Builders Association. That Home Builders Association provides training in the trades, whether it's framing, plumbing, *et cetera*, to build homes and commercial facilities. Why is that important? Because Arizonans can never find enough—there's always employment available in those trades. So, we want individuals to be able to get out, be able to find employment, and go forward.

We have unique problems. Every State does. I think in the comments that Mr. Malcolm indicated, my note at the beginning of his comments after listening to him, was that, and I think a lot of you have shared that, is, an individual charged with a crime, those are particularized situations and circumstances for that individual, and sometimes the larger view, the generic view, doesn't take those into account.

I'll have more to say on this later, Madam Chair, and I'll yield back.

Ms. JACKSON LEE. The gentleman yields back. We thank him for taking a moment of personal privilege, indicating that we may have some common ground, and we do thank you for acknowledging that. I think it is now appropriate to yield to Mr. Cohen for 5 minutes.

Mr. COHEN. Thank you, Madam Chair, and I should not have laughed, except I had to, because I was reading a quote from John Ehrlichman, a top Nixon adviser and former Watergate co-conspirator, who later revealed the true reason for the war on drugs in a 1994 interview with Harper's Magazine.

Mr. Ehrlichman didn't bring up Charlie Rangel. Mr. Ehrlichman said, "You want to know what this is really about." The Nixon campaign in 1968 and the Nixon White House after that had two enemies: The anti-war left and Black people. You understand what I'm saying? We know we couldn't make it illegal to be either, against the war or Black, but by getting the public to associate the hippies with marijuana and Blacks with heroin, and then criminalizing both heavily, we could disrupt those communities. We could arrest their leaders, raid their homes, break up their meetings, and vilify them night after night on the evening news. Did you know we were lying about the drugs? Of course, we did.

So, that's a pretty laughable thing to follow-up with Charlie Rangel influenced President Nixon to start the war on drugs. That was absurd.

If you go back into history with Harry Anslinger, which is back in the '30s, it was all about African Americans and Mexicans. It was racist, racist, racist, and always has been and still is. The war on drugs is a big failure. "Just say no" is a joke, a simplistic answer to a difficult situation.

I've worked—I think Ms.—is it Barlow? She brought up—somebody brought up about commutations and sentencing. I've got pardon legislation to mend our pardon power, to take away the ability to pardon your cronies, your family Members, your associates who work with you and your campaign, your people in your Administration, which is what basically what the previous President did.

He'd had a few cases where he took care of a few people who knew a lady that was originally from Memphis, moved to Arizona, and somebody she brought up. He didn't go through and try to take care of a bunch of people sentenced for long drug sentences. He didn't do that. He took care of Manafort, and he took care of Flynn, and he took care of Roger Stone, and all those criminals.

We need to change our pardon power and make it to where it is mercy and justice and not taking care of cronies and covering up crimes, which is what we just experienced.

I was not totally over-enamored with what President Obama did, but at least he got 1,800 people out of the criminal justice system, people he didn't know. They weren't favors. He set up a system that was rather rigid and lengthy, but a system.

He didn't get to probably another 8,000 people who at least deserved justice and should have had their sentences commuted because it was such a difficult process. At least 1,800 people got out, and it was something pretty amazing in American history, that somebody—a President pardoned people who he didn't know, who never made a campaign contribution and never covered up a crime for them, but he pardoned them because they did meet some criteria that showed they were in prison unnecessarily and too long a period of time, and they were drug sentences.

We need to use the pardon power early on to help filter out people who shouldn't be in the criminal justice system. We need to use compassionate release and get rid of older people and sick people and whatever and do whatever we can.

Mr. Malcolm, in your testimony, you said you don't like to call the drug problem a victimless crime or whatever, because of the fact that in the chain of distribution, there's a likelihood of there being violence and guns and all that stuff. That's true.

Do you still think that because that the people who are possessing should be penalized harshly like we do it?

Mr. MALCOLM. No. So, what I said in my written testimony is that I'm always uncomfortable with the phrase "nonviolent drug offense," because there is, inherent in any drug deal, the risk of overdose, in addition to the fact that a lot of it is gang-related, and there is a lot of violence that comes from that, but—

Mr. COHEN. Let's take marijuana. Let's take marijuana. Would a person possessing marijuana, he's not going to overdose?

Mr. MALCOLM. I'm going to separate out—so, all I'm saying is that people who just routinely use the phrase "nonviolent drug offense" doesn't sit well with me. That is a different issue from how long we should incarcerate people and how long we should punish them.

As I said, I was in favor of the First Step Act, which cut back on mandatory minimum sentences for repeat drug offenders, and I am open to reforming sentencing laws. That's what I have said in my testimony.

Mr. COHEN. Okay. Let me ask you this. Mr. Chabot mentioned in his questioning—and Mr. Chabot's my friend, but he brought up the idea of, does defund the police hurt the police's attitude, and he stressed all the defund the police, which Republicans do, and that's one of our problems here. Most Democrats—I'd say that less than two hands can you count people who are for defunding the police.

Do you think that Republicans who voted against the Congressional Gold Medal for police and other policemen—and there were 20—I think there were 21 of them voted again—more than 21— voted against giving them a Congressional Gold Medal. Do you think that hurts the feeling of the police about their support and their attitudes?

Mr. MALCOLM. Congressman, that's a political question that I've given no thought to. I certainly applaud the heroic efforts of the people who kept you safe on January 6th.

Mr. COHEN. What about somebody—and one of our Members said that the officer who shot Ms. Babbitt when she tried to break through the glass window that had been broken and come into the Speaker's lobby, he called that Capitol Policeman an assassin. Do you think that hurts the people in the Capitol Police Department's mood and feeling?

Mr. MALCOLM. I've heard that view expressed. I do not agree with that. The officer who killed Ms. Babbitt was clearly protecting you. You were about to have a group of people breaking through a window—

Ms. JACKSON LEE. The gentleman's time is expired.

Mr. MALCOLM. Okay.

Mr. COHEN. Thank you, sir.

Mr. MALCOLM. Sure.

Mr. COHEN. Thank you.

Ms. JACKSON LEE. The gentleman's time is expired. Thank you so very much.

Let me take a moment, Members, to first acknowledge Members who desire to be here. Again, Members of this committee, I want to thank you for being here, the Representatives Bass, Demings, McBath, Dean, Scanlon, Bush, Cicilline, Lieu, Correa, Escobar, and Cohen. These are all faithful Members, and in some ways, Members were called away when I acknowledged them: Representative Biggs, of course, our Ranking Member Chabot, Representatives Gohmert, Steube, Tiffany, Massie, Spartz, Fitzgerald, and Owens.

My Subcommittee is a very faithful committee. I want to acknowledge that Members had a number of obligations, but we thank them for their presence.

Mr. Biggs, did you want to take some follow-up questions?

Mr. BIGGS. I unfortunately have to go, but I want to submit that—Madam Chair, I unfortunately have to go. I'd like to submit this article for the record, if that's possible.

Ms. JACKSON LEE. Without objection, so ordered.

[The information follows:]

Profile: Charles Rangel and the Drug Wars

Aug 17, 2013
by Brian Mann

In March 1971, New York City faced a growing heroin epidemic. That year, Charles Rangel — then just 41 years old — was part of a delegation of newly-elected black congressman who won a closed-door meeting at the White House with President Richard Nixon.

It was a historic moment. Nixon had already begun the process of criminalizing drugs in new ways, ramping up the federal effort to crack down on dealers and addicts. Over the decades that followed, those policies would send millions of young black men to prison. Some African American leaders were already voicing doubts and concerns.

But during the meeting, Rangel didn't urge Nixon to rethink his drug war strategy. Instead, the Harlem Democrat urged Nixon to ramp up drugfighting efforts more aggressively, more rapidly.

"We could bring a halt to this condition which is killin off American youth," Rangel told Nixon.

In their encounter, secretly taped by Nixon's White House recording system and broadcast here for the first time, Rangel called on Nixon to use America's military and diplomatic power to stop the importation of drugs.

He urged the the president to view the spread of heroin and cocaine as a "national crisis" and warned that if Nixon didn't act fast, more Americans would demand that narcotics be legalized.

"It seems to me that more white America is saying, let's legalize drugs because we can't deal with the problem," Rangel cautioned.

Just three months later, Nixon formally launched his national war on drugs, echoing much of the language Rangel used that day at the White House. "Public enemy number one in the United States is drug abuse. In order to fight and defeat this enemy, it is necessary to wage a new, all-out offensive," he said.

Rangel would later write warmly of his partnership with Nixon on drug war issues. "Nixon was tough on drugs," he recalled in his 2007 memoir. "[We] worked closely together on what was the beginning of our international war on drugs."

In the decade that that followed, Rangel himself emerged as one of the black community's toughest and most persistent voices on drug issues, pushing for more money and manpower for the police, and for more military drug interdiction overseas.

He lobbied for the creation of a special House subcommittee on narcotics and then served as its chairman, using the post to support creation of the Drug Enforcement Agency and a national Drug Czar.

Under his leadership, many members of the Congressional Black Caucus voted in favor of some of the most punitive drug-war era legislation, expanding mandatory minimum sentences, funding more prisons and boosting penalties for crack cocaine.

In a profile in *Ebony* magazine in 1989, Rangel bragged about pressuring Nixon and President Ronald Reagan to get even tougher on drugs, blasting them for what he called a "lackadaisical attitude."

Even as questions and doubts about the drug war grew, Rangel wrote editorials mocking the idea of drug decriminalization and describing narcotics as a "genocidal" poison.

In the early '90s, Rangel appeared in a televised debate with William F. Buckley Jr. Buckley, a prominent white conservative, had concluded that the drug war was a costly, violent and racially divisive mistake.

But again and again, Rangel pushed back. "In order to fight the drug war, we need all of these factors working together," he insisted, praising police effort, as well as overseas drug interdiction. "We should not allow people to be able to distribute this poison without fear that they might be arrested and put in jail," he said.

"Would you describe what kind of fear you have in mind that isn't already there by, for instance, Nelson Rockefeller's suggestion of life in prison?" Buckley asked.

During the debate, Rangel called for the appointment of a more effective Federal drug czar, suggesting that Army General Colin Powell take over leadership of the drug war.

Rangel's views of the drug war did slowly evolve. In the 2000s, he began sponsoring legislation to ease sentencing disparities between crack and powder cocaine. Rangel published editorials acknowledging that tough crime laws — which he called "well intentioned" — were hurting many African American families.

But with nearly a million African Americans behind bars and one out of every 10 young black men tangled up in the criminal justice system, Rangel sometimes seemed out of touch. "I don't remember the last time anyone was arrested in the city of New York for marijuana," Rangel said during a 2009 congressional hearing in Washington. "I mean smoking marijuana on the streets of Manhattan, the copy may say 'Don't do it on my beat,' but nobody's getting arrested," he said.

In fact, tens of thousands of people, many of them black and Hispanic, are arrested every year for marijuana possession in New York City.

In 2011, however, Rangel did co-sponsor federal legislation that would decriminalize marijuana. That bill failed to pass.

In recent years, many black leaders and organizations, including the NAACP and the Congressional Black Caucus, have called for an end to the drug war that Rangel helped wage. Eric Holder, the nation's first black

Attorney General, has said that those policies "decimated" some black and Hispanic communities.

But speaking with WNYC, Rangel, now 83 years old, stuck by his long support for the drug fight. He said it's important to remember that the heroin and cocaine epidemics were a horror for families in his Harlem district.

"People were absolutely in panic that the drug dealers had taken over the street," Rangel recalled. "Break-ins and burglaries were prevalent and there was an all-time high in fear of how far this would go."

In his memoir published in 2007, Rangel maintained that America's 40-year drug war did help clean up many black neighborhoods, arguing that "a lot of the drug-related bleeding was staunched."

* * *

Mr. BIGGS. Thank you.

Ms. JACKSON LEE. Thank you. You have a very effective substitute, so thank you.

I am going to take a moment to submit some statements into the record that I think are appropriate. First, without objection, I will be submitting a statement from the Leadership Conference into the record, submitting a statement from the ACLU into the record without objection.

Then an article, "They Let People Die, U.S. Prison Bureaus Denied Tens of Thousands Compassionate Release During COVID." Mr. Underwood indicated that he was released for his own record but also under that process.

The data shows officials approved fewer applications during the pandemic and the year before despite risks from the virus. I ask unanimous consent to submit that, without objection.

Also, "Drug reform advocates call Supreme Court ruling on crack sentences 'a shocking loss,' "which just recently came out on Friday, and then an article in The Hill from Mr. Loewenstein, "Why the War on Drugs Must End." There's a dangerous myth that it is over. In reality, the drug war has never been more ferocious, targeting minorities and the most vulnerable in the U.S. and abroad.

I ask unanimous consent to have those submitted into the record.

[The information follows:]

Statement of Jesselyn Mccurdy, Managing Director of Government Affairs and Sakira Cook, Senior Director, Justice Program, the Leadership Conference on Civil and Human Rights, United States House of Representatives, Committee on the Judiciary, Subcommittee on Crime, Terrorism, and Homeland Security, "Undoing the Damage of the War on Drugs: A Renewed Call for Sentencing Reform," June 17, 2021

Chairwoman Jackson Lee, Ranking Member Biggs, and members of the Subcommittee, thank you for the opportunity to submit a statement for the record for this critical hearing. On behalf of The Leadership Conference on Civil and Human Rights, a coalition charged by its diverse membership of more than 220 national organizations to promote and protect civil and human rights in the United States, I write to underscore the critical need for sentencing reform and urge the Subcommittee and all of Congress to heed President Biden's call for the end of mandatory minimums and other overly-punitive policies that undermine the very foundation of justice in our country.

Over the past five decades, U.S. criminal-legal policies have driven an increase in incarceration rates that is unprecedented in this country's history and unmatched globally: the United States incarcerates more people than any other country in the world, with more than 2 million people currently incarcerated in U.S. prisons and jails.[567] Over-criminalization and over-incarceration have devastating impacts on those ensnared in the criminal-legal system and on their families, do not produce any proportional increase in public safety, and disproportionately harm low-income communities and communities of color. In particular, mandatory minimum penalties are a key driver of the burgeoning prison population, and eliminating them is crucial to any sentencing reform legislation. The Leadership Conference is categorically opposed to mandatory minimums sentences, and urges Congress to take steps toward repairing the damage wrought by these penalties by ending blanket policies that do not allow for judicial discretion and promoting alternatives to arrest and incarceration.

---

[567] "Trends in U.S. Corrections." *The Sentencing Project*. Last Updated May 2021. Pg. 2. https://www.sentencingproject.org/wp-content/uploads/2021/06/Trends-in-US-Corrections.pdf.

Mandatory Minimums and the War on Drugs Have Fueled Explosive Prison Population Growth

Since the mid-20th century, Congress has expanded its use of mandatory minimum penalties by broadening it to include different offenses and lengthening the mandatory minimum sentences.[568] The proliferation of the use of mandatory minimum sentences has fueled skyrocketing prison populations.[569] The federal prison population has increased from approximately 25,000 in FY1980 to nearly 152,894 today.[570] For each year between 1980 and 2013, federal prisons added almost 6,000 more inmates than the previous year.[571] As of 2016, 55% of the federal prison population was comprised of those who had been sentenced under a mandatory minimum provision.[572] While drops in prosecutions and in the severity of sentences for drug-related crime, as well as releases due to the COVID-19 pandemic, have led to a decline in the federal prison population in recent years, by and large these piecemeal changes are insufficient to reverse nearly forty years of explosive growth.[573] The Bureau of Prisons' (BOP) budget has grown in tandem: the President's FY22 budget request for BOP is $8 billion, which

---

568 "Mandatory Minimum Penalties in the Federal Criminal Justice System." *The U.S. Sentencing Commission*. Oct. 2011. Ch. 2, Pg. 22. https://www.ussc.gov/sites/default/files/pdf/news/congressional-testimony-and-reports/mandatory-minimum-penalties/20111031-rtc-pdf/Chapter_02.pdf.

569 *See, e.g.*, Samuels, Julie, & La Vigne, Nancy, & Thomson, Chelsea. "Next Steps in Federal Corrections Reform: Implementing and Building on the First Step Act." *Urban Institute*. May 2019. https://www.urban.org/sites/default/files/publication/100230/next_steps_in_federal_corrections_reform_1.pdf; Travis, Jeremy, & Western, Bruce, & Redburn, Steve. "The Growth of Incarceration in the United States: Exploring Causes and Consequences." *Nat'l Research Council*. 2014. Pg. 336. http://blogs.law.columbia.edu/praxis1313/files/2019/04/Chapter-13-NAS.pdf.

570 "Statistics: Total Federal Inmates." *Federal Bureau of Prisons*. Last updated June 10, 2021. https://www.bop.gov/about/statistics/population_statistics.jsp.

571 James, Nathan. "The Federal Prison Population Buildup: Options for Congress." *Congressional Research Service*. May 20, 2016. Pg. 1. https://crsreports.congress.gov/product/pdf/R/R42937.

572 "An Overview of Mandatory Minimum Penalties in the Federal Criminal Justice System." *United States Sentencing Commission*. Jul. 2017. Pg. 49. https://www.ussc.gov/sites/default/files/pdf/research-and-publications/research-publications/2017/20170711_Mand-Min.pdf.

573 Ghandnoosh, Nazgol. "U.S. Prison Decline: Insufficient to Undo Mass Incarceration." *The Sentencing Project*. May 19, 2020. https://www.sentencingproject.org/publications/u-s-prison-decline-insufficient-undo-mass- incarceration/; "Policy Shifts Reduce Federal Prison Population." *United States Courts*. April 25, 2017. https://www.uscourts.gov/news/2017/04/25/policy-shifts-reduce-federal-prison-population.

accounts for nearly a quarter of the Department of Justice's (DOJ) entire budget.[574]

Draconian drug laws and their resulting enforcement are the source of much of this growth. Under the banner of the War on Drugs, the Reagan administration imposed particularly harsh mandatory minimum penalties for drug offenses under the Anti-Drug Abuse Act of 1986 and dedicated more than a billion dollars ($2.3 billion in today's dollars) to law enforcement efforts to increase drug arrests. The Violent Crime Control and Law Enforcement Act of 1994 (known colloquially as the 1994 Crime Bill) instituted a "three strikes" penalty that mandated a life sentence for anyone convicted of certain prior drug or violent felonies and incentivized states to adopt similar 'tough-on-crime' policies.[575] The "arrest-first" policies of the 1980s and '90s led to a surge in drug arrests, with a particularly large impact on cannabis arrests,[576] and an attendant use of long mandatory minimum sentences that caused the federal prison population to explode. The Urban Institute has found that increases in expected time served for drug offenses was the largest contributor to growth in the federal prison population between 1998 and 2010.[577] The Charles Colson Task Force on Federal Corrections, a Congressionally-mandated, bipartisan organization, attributes the growth both to the number of people admitted to prison for drug crimes as well as to the increased length of their sentences.[578] Currently, people convicted of drug offenses make up 46.3 percent of the BOP population.[579]

---

574 "Federal Prison System (BOP) FY22 Budget Request." *Department of Justice*. https://www.justice.gov/jmd/page/file/1398986/download.

575 "Violent Crime Control and Law Enforcement Act of 1994: U.S. Dep't of Justice Fact Sheet." *U.S. Dep't of Justice*. Oct. 24, 1994. https://www.ncjrs.gov/txtfiles/billfs.txt. The First Step Act of 2018 reduced this sentence to 25 years. Pub. L. No. 115-391 (2018).

576 "Crime in the United States 1996. Section V. Drugs in America: 1980-1995." *FBI Uniform Crime Reporting*. 1996. Pg. 280. https://ucr.fbi.gov/crime-in-the-u.s/1996/96sec5.pdf.

577 Mallik-Kane, Kamala & Parthasarathy, Barbara & Adams, William. "Examining Growth in the Federal Prison Population, 1998 to 2010." *Urban Institute*. 2012. Pg. 3. https://www.urban.org/sites/default/files/publication/26311/412720-Examining-Growth-in-the-Federal-Prison- Population--to--.PDF.

578 "Drivers of Growth in the Federal Prison Population." *Charles Colson Task Force on Federal Corrections*. March 2015. https://www.urban.org/sites/default/files/publication/43681/2000141-Drivers-of-Growth-in-the-Federal- Prison-Population.pdf.

579 "Statistics: Inmate Offenses." *Federal Bureau of Prisons*. Updated June 5, 2021. https://www.bop.gov/about/statistics/statistics_inmate_offenses.jsp.

Overly Punitive Sentencing Does Not Deter Crime and Exacerbates Racial Disparities

Yet, despite the dramatic uptick in incarceration, there is no indication that these sentences deter crime, protect public safety, or decrease drug use or trafficking. Increasing the severity of punishment has little impact on crime deterrence, and studies of federal drug laws show no significant relationship between drug imprisonment rates and drug use or recidivism.[580] The punishment-based approach to the War on Drugs, with its dramatic increase in the use of mandatory minimums — and corresponding increase in incarceration — has produced lasting harm in communities across the country while having little effect on actual drug use or crime. Unfortunately, the myth that punishment and harsh mandatory minimums will reduce drug use and crime persists in real and consequential ways: just this past April, Congress extended the temporary "class wide" emergency scheduling of fentanyl-related substances, which will exacerbate untenable federal sentencing trends and give rise to harsh mandatory minimum penalties for offenses involving fentanyl analogues.[581] Statistics about the growth in mass incarceration due to mandatory minimums, combined with data showing they have no positive effect on public safety, illustrate the harmful impact of these sentences on prison growth and the need to turn away from such antiquated "tough on crime" policies.

Mandatory minimums also eliminate judicial discretion, preventing judges from tailoring punishment to a particular defendant by taking into account an individual's background and the circumstances of his or her offenses when determining his or her sentence. Mandatory minimums instead place more power in the hands of prosecutors and their charging decisions, which is particularly concerning given that prosecutors are more likely to charge Black people with a crime that carries a mandatory minimum than a

---

[580] *See, e.g.*, Luna, Erik. "Mandatory Minimums." *The Academy for Justice*. 2017. Pgs. 127-130. https://law.asu.edu/sites/default/files/pdf/academy_for_justice/7_Criminal_Justice_Reform_Vol_4_Mandatory- Minimums.pdf; Nat'l Inst. of Justice. "Five Things about Deterrence." May 2016. https://www.ojp.gov/pdffiles1/nij/247350.pdf; "Federal Drug Sentencing Laws Bring High Cost, Low Return." *Pew Charitable Trusts*. Aug. 27, 2015. https://www.pewtrusts.org/en/research-and-analysis/issue-briefs/2015/08/federal- drug-sentencing-laws-bring-high-cost-low-return.

[581] H.R. 2630, the Extending Temporary Emergency Scheduling of Fentanyl Analogues Act (P.L. 117-12).

White person.[582] Mass incarceration as a whole has had a markedly disproportionate impact on communities of color. Today, BOP reports that 38 percent of its current prison population is Black and 30.2 percent is Hispanic, an enormous disparity given that both groups represent only about one third of the nation's population combined.[583] These disparities are also reflected in mandatory minimum penalties. In a 2017 review of mandatory minimum sentencing policies, the U.S. Sentencing Commission found that Black people in BOP custody were more likely to have been convicted of an offense carrying a mandatory minimum penalty than any other group.[584] Hispanic and Black people accounted for a majority of those convicted with an offense carrying a drug mandatory minimum,[585] despite the fact that White and Black people use illicit substances at roughly the same rate, and Hispanic people use such substances at a lower rate.[586] The study also showed that Black people were the least likely to receive relief from mandatory minimum sentences compared to White and Hispanic people.[587] Finally, the review found racial disparities in convictions of a federal offense subject to a mandatory minimum penalty: 73.2 percent of Black people convicted of a federal offense received a mandatory minimum sentence, compared to 70 percent of White people and 46.9 percent of Hispanic people.[588] It is clear that mandatory minimums create stark racial disparities in federal sentencing.

---

[582] Starr, Sonja B., and M. Marit Rehavi. "Racial Disparity in Federal Criminal Sentences." *University of Michigan Law School Scholarship Repository*. 2014. Pg. 1323. https://repository.law.umich.edu/cgi/viewcontent.cgi?article=2413&context=articles.

[583] "Inmate Statistics." *Federal Bureau of Prisons*. Updated June 5, 2021. https://www.bop.gov/about/statistics/statistics_inmate_race.jsp. Hispanics make up 18.5% of the U.S. population, while Black people make up 13.4%. "United States QuickFacts." *U.S. Census Bureau*. Last updated July 1, 2019. https://www.census.gov/quickfacts/fact/table/US/PST045219.

[584] "An Overview of Mandatory Minimum Penalties in the Federal Criminal Justice System." *United States Sentencing Commission*. Jul. 2017. Pg. 53. https://www.ussc.gov/sites/default/files/pdf/research-and-publications/research-publications/2017/20170711_Mand-Min.pdf.

[585] "Mandatory Minimum Penalties for Drug Offenses in the Federal Criminal Justice System." *United States Sentencing Commission*. Oct. 2017. Pg. 57. https://www.ussc.gov/sites/default/files/pdf/research-and-publications/research-publications/2017/20170711_Mand-Min.pdf.

[586] "Results from the 2018 Nat'l Survey on Drug Use and Health: Detailed Tables." *Substance Abuse and Mental Health Service Administration*. 2018. Table 1.23B. https://www.samhsa.gov/data/sites/default/files/cbhsq-reports/NSDUHDetailedTabs2018R2/NSDUHDetailedTabs2018.pdf.

[587] *Ibid.* at 7.

[588] *Ibid.* at 40.

Congress Can Turn Back the Clock on the War on Drugs

Congress has made some progress toward addressing the harms of mandatory minimums. In 2010, Congress passed the Fair Sentencing Act (FSA), which reduced the disparities between the mandatory penalties for crack and powder cocaine from 100:1 to 18:1. Building on this legislation, the First Step Act of 2018 made necessary, though modest, improvements to the federal sentencing scheme by making the FSA retroactive and through expanding the federal safety valve, which permits a sentencing court to disregard minimum sentences for low-level, nonviolent defendants. Under this provision, judges have discretion to make a person eligible for the safety valve in cases where the seriousness of his or her record is over-represented, or it is unlikely he or she would commit other crimes. The law also reformed and reduced the unfair three-strike mandatory minimum sentence from life to 25 years. The First Step Act further eliminated 924(c) stacking, which had permitted consecutive sentences for gun charges stemming from a single incident committed during a drug crime or a crime of violence. Unfortunately, the law does not make most of its sentencing reforms retroactive, leaving thousands of people in prison. The First Step Implementation Act of 2021, which will soon go to the Senate floor for a vote, makes these key reforms retroactive and further expands the safety valve. Additionally, the House last year voted to address the collateral consequences of federal marijuana criminalization by passing the Marijuana Opportunity Reinvestment and Expungement (MORE) Act, which would, among provisions, provide for the expungement and resentencing of marijuana offenses. We urge you to support this year's version of the MORE Act, H.R. 3617, in order to right the wrongs of decades of this criminalization.

Yet, these small, measured steps cannot adequately redress years of cruel and lengthy sentencing policies. To address fully the immense harms perpetrated by mandatory minimums and other sentencing practices, Congress must go beyond these incremental reforms and pass meaningful and expansive legislation that transforms the federal sentencing scheme. Such reform would reduce unnecessarily lengthy stays, enabling people to rebuild their lives, reducing the exorbitant costs of the prison system, and give redress to those serving unreasonably long sentences.

Conclusion

Mandatory minimum penalties have incurred devastating economic, societal, and human costs, destroying families and irreparably damaging communities of color. The penalties are lengthy, with almost no room for discretion or mercy. As one federal judge has declared, these are sentences that "no one – not even the prosecutors themselves – thinks are appropriate."[589] President Biden has also recognized this destructive impact and has called for an end to federal mandatory minimum sentences and other harmful practices.[590] These sentences, and particularly those for drug offenses, have led to an explosion in the federal prison population with no attendant positive impact on crime deterrence or public safety. As we mark the 50th anniversary of the War on Drugs in 2021, we strongly urge Congress to take bold steps to address the damage wrought by mandatory minimum sentencing and transform our criminal-legal system into one that delivers true justice and equality.

House Committee on the Judiciary, United States House of Representatives, Statement for the Record, American Civil Liberties Union, "Undoing the Damage of the War on Drugs: A Renewed Call for Sentencing Reform," June 17, 2021

We thank the United States House of Representatives' Committee on the Judiciary for holding this hearing to recognize the 50th anniversary of the war on drugs and the need for sentencing reform.

For 100 years, the ACLU has been our nation's guardian of liberty, working in courts, legislatures, and communities to defend and preserve the individual rights and liberties that the Constitution and the laws of the United States guarantee to everyone in this country. Through advocacy and litigation, the ACLU has been seeking an end to the failed war on drugs and our costly addiction to incarceration for decades.

The war on drugs has sent millions of people to prison and seriously eroded our civil liberties and civil rights while costing taxpayers billions of dollars every year. Fifty years later we have nothing to show for these

---

[589] U.S. v. Kupa, 11 CR-345 (E.D.N.Y.). Oct. 9, 2013. Pg. 4. https://img.nyed.uscourts.gov/files/opinions/11cr345SOR.pdf.

[590] "The Biden Plan for Strengthening America's Commitment to Justice." https://joebiden.com/justice/.

sacrifices except our status as the world's largest incarcerator. As you know, those we incarcerate, including in federal prisons, are disproportionately Black and brown. The drug war has deepened racial injustice, shattered neighborhoods, and separated families, all without evidence that it has improved public safety. This anniversary is a shameful one and it is long past time for Congress to recognize the failure of this approach and begin down a radically different path.

From the beginning, the war on drugs was intended to decimate the Black community. John Ehrlichman, the Watergate co-conspirator and President Nixon's domestic affairs aide, told a reporter decades after Nixon declared the war on drugs: "We knew we couldn't make it illegal to be either against the war or black, but by getting the public to associate the hippies with marijuana and blacks with heroin and then criminalizing both heavily, we could disrupt those communities." Ehrlichman continued: "We could arrest their leaders, raid their homes, break up their meetings, and vilify them night after night on the evening news. Did we know we were lying about the drugs? Of course we did."

The drug war has achieved only the harmful purposes President Nixon intended— disrupting, vilifying, and oppressing communities of color.

On this 50th anniversary of the drug war, Congress must take immediate actions to repair the harms the drug war has inflicted on people and communities—especially people and communities of color. Congress must also begin building a new comprehensive drug policy system that prioritizes health and harm reduction over criminalization and incarceration.

Here are 10 things Congress can and must do now to stop the drug war and begin to heal the damage it has wrought:

1. *End mandatory minimum sentencing laws.* Perhaps the single most impactful action Congress can take to reduce mass incarceration is to repeal all existing mandatory minimum sentencing laws and cease passing new ones. Between 1980 and 2013, the federal prison population grew by 750 percent, and that growth is due to lengthy drug sentences. Indeed, nearly half of the people in federal prison are there for drug offenses. Congress must end all mandatory minimum sentencing, beginning with the drug mandatory minimums, by passing measures like the Mandatory Minimum Reform Act, which repeals the drug mandatory minimums. It must also pass legislation to end all mandatory minimum sentencing laws, including the Justice

Safety Valve Act, which allows courts to sentence below the mandatory minimum for any offense.

2. *Ensure retroactive relief for people previously sentenced under the mandatory minimum regime of the drug war.* Congress enacted meaningful sentencing reforms in the FIRST STEP Act of 2018, but people who were sentenced before the law was passed did not benefit. No person should continue serving a sentence Congress has since deemed excessive and unjust. Congress should pass legislation to fix sentencing disparities and not create new ones. Congress must pass the First Step Implementation Act (H.R. 3510/S. 1014), which will make the FIRST STEP sentencing reforms retroactive. Any additional sentencing reforms Congress passes should include retroactive application of the new law. The EQUAL Act (H.R. 1693/S. 79), for example, eliminates the crack/powder disparity and ensures its sentencing reform is made retroactive.
3. *Remove marijuana from the Controlled Substances Act.* Both public opinion and sage public policy have called for an end to marijuana prohibition. In fact, 17 states have legalized adult use of marijuana and 36 states and the District of Columbia have legalized the use of medical marijuana. Yet, at the federal level, marijuana remains a Schedule I substance, subjecting people involved in marijuana activities to harsh penalties and preventing a range of scientific research that could upend decades of propagandized misinformation driven by racism and fear. The consequences of criminalization are felt most harshly by people of color. Though marijuana use is roughly equal among Blacks and whites, Blacks are 3.73 times as likely to be arrested for marijuana possession. The enforcement of these laws burdens individuals with conviction records that harm their ability to work, find housing, and provide for their families and their future. Congress must pass the Marijuana Opportunity, Reinvestment, and Expungement (MORE) Act (H.R. 3617), which will decriminalize marijuana at the federal level while enabling states to set their own regulatory policies without threat of federal interference. Significantly, the bill also addresses the collateral consequences of federal marijuana criminalization and takes steps to ensure the legal marketplace is diverse and inclusive of individuals most adversely affected by prohibition.

4. *End penalties for simple drug possession.* Simply possessing drugs for personal use must be decriminalized by repealing the federal simple possession statute, 21 U.S.C. § 844. In addition, simple possession of a controlled substance and positive drug tests must not be permissible grounds for incarceration when a person is under federal supervision, including pretrial supervision and supervised release. Accordingly, Congress must pass the Drug Policy Reform Act of 2021 to end criminal penalties for personal use drug possession, and pass legislation to end penalties for personal use while under court supervision.
5. *End the presumptions against pretrial release, including the presumption in alleged drug felony cases.* Current federal law turns the presumption of innocence on its head for people awaiting trial on felony drug charges, among other offenses. Under the Bail Reform Act of 1984, courts must adhere to the presumption that people are not safe for release if they are charged with most any felony drug offense. As a result, the federal pretrial detention rate is an appalling 75 percent. In fact, over one-third of people sitting in federal lock-up were denied bond based on the presumption in drug cases. Congress must pass the Smarter Pretrial Detention for Drug Charges Act (S. 309) to end this presumption in drug cases and pass similar legislation to end pretrial detention presumptions in all cases.
6. *Lift the ban on second chances.* After Congress abolished federal parole in the Sentencing Reform Act of 1984, people serving a federal sentence lost any possibility of a second chance, regardless of how strong the evidence is that they are prepared to return to the community. That, coupled with a policy of imposing longer prison sentences, resulted in a 280 percent increase, between 1999 to 2016, in the number of people 55 or older in state and federal prisons. Research shows incarcerating the elderly does not make us safer, since people age out of crime and long sentences do little to deter crime. Congress must pass measures to review lengthy sentences, including the Second Look Act, which gives people who have served 10 or more years of their sentence the opportunity to file a motion in court and present their case for a lower sentence.

7. *End collateral consequences and support successful reentry.* People with criminal records face numerous barriers when they return to the community, particularly when seeking employment, housing, and public benefits. To address these barriers, Congress should pass the Workforce Justice Act (H.R. 1598) to encourage states to adopt "ban the box" policies for private employers; the Medicaid Reentry Act (H.R. 955/S. 285) to allow an individual leaving prison to resume Medicaid and prepare reentry services in the last 30 days of incarceration; and the Fair Chance at Housing Act to lower barriers to housing for people with a criminal record. Congress should also aid reentry efforts by passing measures contained in the NEXT STEP Act that will reinstate the right to vote in federal elections for formerly incarcerated individuals; allow a path to seal records of nonviolent drug offenses and automatically seal or expunge juvenile records; remove the lifetime ban on federal TANF and SNAP benefits for people with nonviolent drug offenses; remove barriers that prevent people with criminal convictions from receiving occupational licenses for jobs such as hairdressers and taxi drivers; and ensure that anyone released from federal prison receives a photo identification, birth certificate, and Social Security card.
8. *End civil asset forfeiture.* Civil asset forfeiture, which allows law enforcement to take property from someone who has not been convicted of a crime, has long been used to carry out the war on drugs and has the same disproportionate impact on people of color. The practice is driven by the billions of dollars it generates annually for law enforcement at all levels because law enforcement is permitted to keep the assets it forfeits. Civil asset forfeiture also contributes to militarized policing because law enforcement departments use profits from forfeitures to purchase military weapons and equipment with little oversight or accountability. For example, between 2008 and 2014, police departments spent $2.5 billion from federal civil forfeiture seizures, with over $177 million of that spent on weapons. In 2018, the DOJ Asset Forfeiture fund amassed a net balance of about $1.5 billion. Moreover, property owners who challenge a seizure bear the burden and the costs of demonstrating a property's "innocence" and are not entitled to a lawyer. Congress must act by passing the Fifth Amendment Integrity Restoration (FAIR) Act (H.R. 2857), to end federal and state/local partnerships known as "equitable sharing" that have been used to circumvent state civil forfeiture

reforms; increase the burden of proof in civil forfeiture proceedings from a "preponderance of evidence" to "clear and convincing evidence" before the government can take someone's property; and provide property owners the right to counsel in all civil forfeiture proceedings.

9. *End penalties for exercising the Sixth Amendment right to trial.* The trial penalty—the enhanced sentence used to penalize people who exercise their right to have a trial instead of pleading guilty—undermines the Constitutional right to a jury trial that is the core of our judicial process. As a result of the trial penalty, only about 2 percent of federal cases go to trial. And those who do, face a higher sentence. Congress should pass legislation that amends the United States Sentencing Guidelines to remove penalties imposed on individuals who exercise their right to trial and right to testify in their own defense. Congress should also ensure that accused people receive all exculpatory evidence prior to entering a guilty plea. Congress should also pass the Prohibiting Punishment of Acquitted Conduct Act (S. 601) so courts will no longer be able to sentence a person based on acquitted conduct.
10. *Ensure the United States Sentencing Commission is a balanced body that considers the interests of people charged with drug crimes.* The United States Sentencing Commission is an independent commission in the judicial branch that establishes sentencing policies for the federal criminal justice system. The Commission is responsible for promulgating the U.S. Sentencing Guidelines which, though not binding on judges, exert enormous influence in determining how long someone will be incarcerated when convicted of a federal crime. In addition to its seven voting members, the Attorney General or the Attorney General's designee serves as a nonvoting member of the Commission. This nonvoting membership gives the prosecution an important opportunity to influence the Commission's work. Current law, however, does not give any comparable influence to the individuals who are the very subject of the Commission's sentencing policies. There is no justification for this one-sidedness. Congress must fix this imbalance by passing measures like the Federal Defender Ex Officio Act, which adds a nonvoting member from the Federal Public Defenders to the Commission so that this important body can consider the interests and perspective of the people who must bear the consequences of its policies.

This Committee's hearing comes at a historic moment: we have spent half a century fighting and losing the war on drugs. This approach was corrupt and racist from the outset and it has not made us safer or reduced the harms drugs can cause. We must stop waging this war on our own communities. Congress should seize on this moment to take bold action that will end this failed experiment. We urge the Committee to exercise its powers accordingly, and appreciate the leadership the Committee has shown in convening this hearing.

'They Let People Die': US Prisons Bureau Denied Tens of Thousands Compassionate Release during Covid

This article is more than 2 years old

The last time Sean McQuiddy called home from federal prison, it was just before Christmas in 2020, and he had just tested positive for Covid-19.

"If I don't make it out of here," his brother recalled him saying, "just know that I love you."

McQuiddy was from Nashville, Tennessee, and was 23 years into a life sentence for selling crack. The two dozen other defendants in his case had already gotten out, including his younger brother Darrell, who had scored a reduced sentence a few years back.

The downturn in approvals came even as the number of people seeking compassionate release rocketed from 1,735 in 2019 to nearly 31,000 after the virus hit. Photograph: Bing Guan/Reuters New data shows officials approved fewer applications during the pandemic than the year before, despite risks from virus.
Keri Blakinger and Joseph Neff for The Marshall Project.
Last modified on Fri 11 Jun 2021 09.31 EDT.

But due to a technicality, 54-year-old Sean wasn't so lucky. And when the pandemic hit, he was worried: he was overweight, with high blood pressure, asthma and other breathing problems. In August, he had begged prison officials for compassionate release, citing the heightened threat of the virus. But court records show the warden ignored his request.

Tens of thousands of federal prisoners like McQuiddy applied for compassionate release after the virus began sweeping through lockups. But new Bureau of Prisons data shows officials approved fewer of those applications during the pandemic than they did the year before.

Philly DA: inside the fight to end mass incarceration in America.

While the BOP director gave the green light to 55 such requests in 2019, a new director who took over in early 2020 approved only 36 requests in the 13 months since the pandemic took hold in March 2020. The downturn in approvals came even as the number of people seeking compassionate release rocketed from 1,735 in 2019 to nearly 31,000 after the virus hit, according to the new figures.

Because the data was compiled for members of Congress, BOP spokesman Scott Taylor said the agency would not answer any questions about the data, "out of respect and deference" to lawmakers.

But Shon Hopwood, a Georgetown law professor, called the bureau's decrease in compassionate releases during the pandemic "mind-boggling."

"They let people die in prison that shouldn't have had to die," he said.

Federal judges stepped in to release thousands of people in the face of bureau inaction. And the bureau continues to face intense scrutiny and several lawsuits over its handling of Covid-19. Since the first reported case last spring, more than 49,000 federal prisoners have fallen ill and 256 have died, according to corrections data tracked by the Marshall Project.

Thirty-five of those who died were waiting for a decision on their release requests – including McQuiddy.

* * *

People in federal prisons seeking early release during the pandemic have two main routes. One is home confinement, which allows low-risk prisoners to finish their sentences at home or in a halfway house. They're still considered in custody, and the decision is entirely up to the Bureau of Prisons. As Covid shutdowns began last March, Congress expanded the eligibility criteria and then the attorney general, Bill Barr, ordered prison officials to let more people go. Since then, more than 23,700 people have been sent to home confinement – though several thousand of them may have to return to prison once the pandemic ends.

Advertisement

The other is through compassionate release. If a warden endorses a prisoner's request, the case goes to BOP's central office, which usually rejects it. If a warden denies a request or 30 days pass with no response, then the incarcerated person can ask a judge to reduce the sentence to time served. The new data showed 3,221 people had been let out on compassionate release since the start of the pandemic – but 99% of those releases were granted by judges over the bureau's objections.

Last fall, the Marshall Project published data showing that the Bureau of Prisons rejected or ignored more than 98% of compassionate release requests during the first three months of the pandemic. Citing that reporting, federal lawmakers in December wrote to the agency to demand more data on both compassionate release and home confinement.

The updated figures outlined in the agency's response to Congress in April showed that BOP wardens actually endorsed slightly fewer compassionate release requests as the pandemic progressed. In the first three months, wardens approved 1.4% of release applications. The central office rejected most of those, with the director, Michael Carvajal, ultimately approving just 0.1%. By the end of April – more than a year into the pandemic, and after more than 200 prisoner deaths – wardens had approved 1.2% of applications, and Carvajal again accepted just 0.1%.

By comparison, federal judges approved 21% of compassionate release requests they considered in 2020, according to a recent report from the US Sentencing Commission.

* * *

The McQuiddy brothers grew up in the projects of Nashville, riding go-karts together and playing football. They both dropped out of high school, and by the late 1980s began selling drugs – running a crack house seemed like a way out of the poverty around them, Darrell McQuiddy said.

In 1997, both brothers got arrested. While Darrell ended up with a little under 25 years in prison, Sean got a mandatory life sentence because he'd paid a 17-year-old to work in the crack house, court records show.

After Congress passed drug sentencing reforms starting in 2010, the brothers grew hopeful they would not die in prison. But only one of them qualified for a shorter sentence under the new laws: Darrell got nearly four years off his time because his pre-sentence report only mentioned powdered cocaine in the description of his crime. But Sean's pre-sentence report also listed crack, so he wasn't eligible for a sentence reduction.

Sean McQuiddy. 'It was so unfair, what happened to him.' Photograph: Courtesy of Darrell McQuiddy.

"It was so unfair what happened to him," Sean's lawyer, Michael Holley, said. "It's the kind of crack case that wouldn't get a life sentence today."

* * *

The bureau has offered little insight into its reasons for denying compassionate release. According to the information BOP sent to Congress, wardens denied nearly 23,000 requests because the person "does not meet criteria." Roughly 3,200 people were denied because their cases were "not extraordinary and compelling," while a little over 1,200 were rejected for not providing enough information or documentation. Four people met the criteria but were denied due to "correctional concerns," the agency said.

Of the 374 prisoners that wardens recommended for compassionate release during the pandemic, the agency's central office rejected or did not respond to just over 90%, apparently without making any note as to why. "The BOP does not track the specific reasons for approval or denial of a compassionate release request at the central office level, as there can be several reasons for a particular decision," wrote the general counsel, Ken Hyle. Some of those reasons, he added, could be opposition from federal prosecutors, a lack of release plan or fear that letting someone out would "minimize the severity of the inmate's offense."

Prisoners who brought their requests to court usually encountered opposition from federal prosecutors. Alison Guernsey, a clinical associate professor at the University of Iowa College of Law, reviewed the cases of all prisoners who have died of the virus, including those who were seeking compassionate release. She said the Department of Justice often said prisoners requesting release couldn't prove they'd asked the warden first. Sometimes, prosecutors argued that the Bureau of Prisons was doing its best to handle the pandemic responsibly, or that the incarcerated person begging for release wasn't really at high risk from the virus.

"In court, prosecutors were fighting release and saying that this person doesn't have a condition that makes them vulnerable – and then they would die, and the BOP would issue a press release saying that the person had underlying conditions," Guernsey said. "The two-faced position of the Department of Justice, which includes the BOP, is really quite shocking."

Often, judges agreed with the prosecutors' reasoning. But in some cases, the judges never made a decision – or the prisoners died first.

Advertisement

By the time the pandemic hit, McQuiddy was not in good health and had already spent several months in a medical prison. Still, several times a day he talked to his brother – who'd been released in 2015 and started a dump truck company, where he hoped Sean would one day work.

When the warden ignored McQuiddy's request for compassionate release, he went to court. Prosecutors opposed him, saying he hadn't made any plan to address his riskiest underlying condition – obesity – and that he'd be safer in prison because no one at the Arkansas facility where he was locked up had died from the virus yet. "Covid-19 is not fatal in most cases," they wrote in a court filing.

But Covid-19 swept through the prison a few weeks later, and McQuiddy fell ill. Christmas came, and he didn't call home. Finally, the prison called in late December and told his family he'd been moved to an outside hospital and put on a ventilator. His brother and daughters went to see him, and his lawyer again asked the judge to consider McQuiddy's plea for release. Once again, prosecutors opposed it, this time saying that it wasn't safe to let him out now that he'd already fallen sick.

The judge didn't rule for more than a month. Finally, in late January, he weighed in.

"All pending motions are DENIED as moot," District Judge William Campbell wrote on 22 January, directing the clerk to close the file.

McQuiddy had died 11 days earlier.

Supreme Court Ruling on Crack Sentences 'a Shocking Loss,' Drug Reform Advocates Say

The ruling on the First Step Act is "contrary to what Congress intended and contrary to common sense," said a lawyer who represents incarcerated people.

June 15, 2021, 9:57 AM EDT
By Jon Schuppe

The Supreme Court's decision restricting the use of a landmark 2018 drug reform law landed like an anvil Monday morning at the Decarceration Collective, a Chicago law firm that seeks to free people serving life sentences for federal drug crimes.

The unanimous ruling said the law — which has been used to cut the sentences of thousands of federal drug offenders, including many accused of handling large amounts of crack cocaine — couldn't be used to reduce the sentences of people convicted of possessing small amounts of crack. The court's ruling came over the objections of the law's authors, who said they intended to help those low-level offenders, and the Biden administration, whose Justice Department declined to argue for the narrow interpretation of the law in court.

"It's a shocking loss," said MiAngel Cody, lead counsel and justice policy analyst at the Decarceration Collective.

Cody said she has represented a "kingpin" convicted of possessing thousands of kilos of crack who was released under the 2018 law, known as the First Step Act, which aimed to ease harsh drug sentencing statutes that has disproportionately punished Black people. But the court's ruling means people convicted of selling less than 28 grams of crack —about the weight of a AA battery — "can't go back into court" to seek a reduction, Cody said.

"They just had the door shut in their face, and that's completely unfair," she said. "That makes no sense from a public safety perspective."

The case was brought by Tarahrick Terry, a Black Florida man who was sentenced to more than 15 years in prison for possessing 3.9 grams of crack cocaine — about the weight of four paper clips. Terry argued that he should be eligible for a reduced sentence under the First Step Act.

President Donald Trump signed the First Step Act at the White House on Dec. 21, 2018.Jim Watson / AFP via Getty Images file.

The 2018 law was Congress' latest attempt to undo 1980s federal drug laws that allowed for much harsher penalties for possession of crack cocaine than for possession of powder cocaine. The first round of changes, passed in 2010, narrowed the disparity, but it didn't apply to people who had already been sentenced or to those sentenced for possession of small amounts of crack. The First Step Act, which was passed in a rush of activity during the final weeks of a lame-duck Congress, made the earlier changes retroactive — but still only explicitly for people sentenced for possession of larger amounts of crack.

Many of the people affected by the Supreme Court's ruling, like Terry, were hit with harsh penalties for possessing small amounts of crack because they had previously been convicted of other drug offenses.

Lower courts ruled against Terry, 33; the Justice Department under then-President Donald Trump argued that the First Step Act didn't apply to him. The agency switched course under Biden — but that didn't convince the Supreme Court.

The court, in a 9-0 decision written by Justice Clarence Thomas, said the First Step Act was limited by a technical omission: It left out the lowest rung of offenders.

Justice Sonia Sotomayor pointed out the discrepancy in a concurring opinion, noting that the law's sponsors urged the court to rule that it be applied to low-level offenders. But the law itself said something different, she wrote, an "injustice" that can be corrected only by Congress.

The ruling frustrated many people who lobbied for the law across the political spectrum.

"I think it's a nonsensical interpretation," said Holly Harris, who pushed for passage of the First Step Act as president and executive director of the Justice Action Network, which recruits lawmakers from the left and the right to support changes in the criminal justice system. "For those of us who were at the table litigating this bill, the one thing we said over and over is we want relief for low-level nonviolent offenders."

Mark Holden, chairman of the board of Americans for Prosperity, a conservative policy group, who pushed for the First Step Act, agreed, saying Congress should pass a law making the relief for low-level offenders unambiguous.

"This should be something done quickly," Holden said.

Sen. Dick Durbin, D-Ill., chairman of the Judiciary Committee, said Monday that the Senate would work to fix the law and that he hoped there would be bipartisan support.

Harris said that while the ruling was disappointing, it is an opportunity to gather support in Congress for more criminal justice reform bills, including one that would clarify the First Step Act's intent for low-level offenders. She is also advocating for the Equal Act, which would eliminate the crack-to-powder cocaine sentencing disparity completely.

In addition, her organization is urging the Biden administration to abandon a Trump Justice Department memo saying 24,000 nonviolent inmates released to home confinement to curb the spread of Covid-19 in prisons must be sent back to prison if their sentences haven't ended.

Jacki Phelps, appellate litigation counsel at the Decarceration Collective, said she believed that the authors of the First Step Act hadn't made a mistake but that the Supreme Court had.

The impact is hard to calculate, because there is no simple way to measure how many prisoners had their paths to potential early release cut off, Phelps said.

Cody and Phelps pointed to one example, in addition to Terry: Jahmal Green, 45, who is serving a life sentence for a 2006 conviction for distributing less than a gram of crack in Iowa after earlier drug convictions.

Jahmal Green, left, in prison last fall with a friend who later died of Covid-19.Courtesy of Delyla Green.

Green, who is Black, had withdrawn all of his pending court motions because he was hoping for a more favorable law to help him, said Cody, who has been following his case. Lawyers representing many prisoners in similar situations also put their appeals on hold to wait for the ruling in Terry's case, Phelps said. They expected it to be in their favor.

"We really don't know how many people are sitting in federal prison for these low-level paper clip-sized amounts whose claims were foreclosed by this Terry decision," Phelps said.

"If these defendants had sold more crack, then they would be eligible for sentencing relief. That's contrary to what Congress intended and contrary to common sense."

Delyla Green, 29, a niece of Jahmal Green's, said in an interview that he is in a prison in Arizona, far from family in Chicago and Minneapolis. He has diabetes and applied for compassionate release but was denied, she said.

"Its just been so tough," she said. "My dad, his brother, just passed, and he wasn't able to be there for that. He missed the birth of my son. He didn't get a chance at life, really."

She said that despite the Supreme Court setback, her family would continue searching for ways to reduce his sentence.

"We're not going to give up until he's free," she said. "Whatever it takes."

Why the War on Drugs Must End

by Antony Loewenstein | Jan. 09, 2020

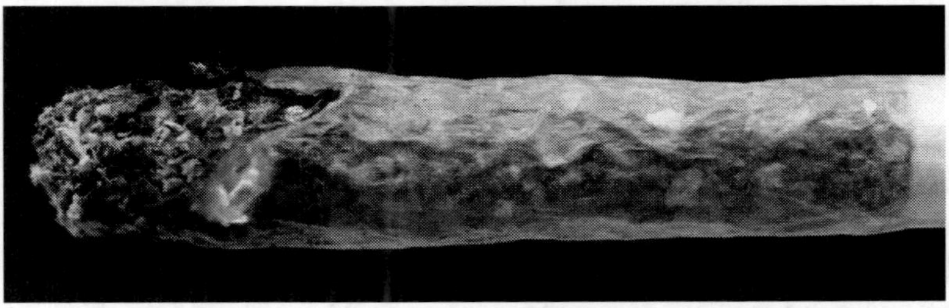

iStock.

There's a dangerous myth in sections of the public that the war on drugs is coming to an end. It's an idea that as cannabis legalization sweeps across the U.S. and many other nations around the world, legal prohibitions against drug use and abuse will soon be reduced or removed entirely.

In reality, the drug war has never been more ferocious, targeting minorities and the most vulnerable in the U.S. and abroad. In the U.S. in 2018, there were more arrests for marijuana than in 2017, despite 11 states now allowing legal cannabis for citizens over 21 years of age. The FBI released figures that detailed 663,367 marijuana arrests in the country in 2018. The majority of Americans, according to a number of polls in the last years, now support marijuana legalization.

"Americans should be outraged that police departments across the country continue to waste tax dollars and limited law enforcement resources on arresting otherwise law-abiding citizens for simple marijuana possession," National Organization for the Reform of Marijuana Laws Executive Director Erik Altieri said.

Cannabis is just the tip of the drug war iceberg. Although President Donald Trump has spoken regularly about escalating the war on drugs, blaming Mexico and drug cartels on the huge amounts of illicit substances entering the U.S., including heroin, cocaine, opioids and fentanyl, he ignores the elephant in the room: Millions of Americans want and need illegal drugs and illegality won't stop them. According to a recent report from the RAND corporation, in 2016 alone U.S. citizens spent $150 billion on cannabis, cocaine, heroin and methamphetamines.

The opioid epidemic is the worst drug crisis in the country's history, killing hundreds of thousands of people and costing trillions of dollars. It was partly caused by pharmaceutical companies that saw an opportunity to make a fortune. Some of the biggest players, such as the Sackler family, are set to walk away from multibillion dollar settlements with billions of dollars still in their bank accounts.

I've spent the last five years investigating the drug war around the world, and what I've seen shocked me. Think of Honduras, a nation wracked by extreme violence and gang warfare. Much of the cocaine flowing into the U.S. from South America transits through Honduras, and the effect is a narco-state fully backed by the Trump administration (and the Obama White House before them). I witnessed what hundreds of millions of dollars of U.S. military support has created in the Central American state, a population that's fleeing its borders in huge numbers. Honduras is a failed state, partly destroyed by the immense power of drug cartels and criminal gangs to control the huge cocaine trade. The President Donald Trump era is seeing many vulnerable Honduran refugees being sent back to Honduras where they face threats and death.

Guinea-Bissau in West Africa is a key cocaine transit hub between South America and Europe. Labelled a "narco-state" by the UN, last year saw the country's biggest ever drug bust, nearly two tonnes of cocaine. Although the nation doesn't suffer the same debilitating violence experienced by Honduras, ongoing political instability ensures that drug cartels view Guinea-Bissau as ripe for abuse.

In the Philippines under President Rodrigo Duterte, at least 30,000 mostly poor civilians have been murdered in the last three and a half years. Duterte remains a popular leader, able to convince a fearful population that his deadly approach on methamphetamine users will bring societal renewal. The Philippines is what happens when a war on drugs becomes quasi-genocidal.

In the UK, conservative governments have continued to punish the most vulnerable people with drug dependence. While drug use and abuse is soaring in the UK, the so-called "Uberisation" of the drug trade in Britain has made it the cocaine capital of Europe, vast parts of the country are being lost to devastating austerity policies. These harsh economic cuts are directly tied to unhealthy use and abuse of cocaine, heroin and other illicit substances. The newly elected Boris Johnson government is deaf to the need for radical changes around drug prohibition.

A Range of Solutions

Despite the ugliness that exists around the drug war, there are encouraging signs of hope. Most of the Democratic candidates for President in 2020 have drug policies that were unimaginable just four years ago. Tulsi Gabbard wants to decriminalize drugs like cocaine and heroin. Bernie Sanders advocates federal cannabis legalisation by executive order, ending the war on drugs, eliminating private prisons and reparations for communities disproportionately affected by the drug war (largely minorities and people of color).

Joe Biden's position on cannabis appears to be that he doesn't support full legalization (making him an outlier in the Democratic field). Elizabeth Warren has been vocal in her opposition to the war on drugs, backs legalised cannabis and safe injecting centres (a practice that already exists successfully in Europe and Australia).

One of the more exciting aspects of future U.S. drug policy revolves around the medical use of psychedelic drugs such as LSD, ecstasy and psilocybin (magic mushrooms). Last year, Oakland became the second U.S. city (after Denver) to decriminalise magic mushrooms. The potential use of these drugs to treat mental health issues, PTSD, addictions and end-of-life trauma are profound, and scientific studies concur. Ecstasy could be legally available through a registered doctor by the beginning of next decade.

Of course, drug legalization is only one aspect of changing societal attitudes towards drugs. The stigmas and stereotypes around drug use and abuse, pushed by many in the media for decades, must change. How we think, write and talk about drugs has contributed to politicians believing that they could prosecute a racialized drug war for over 100 years. For example, racial bias is endemic within the management of the opioid crisis in the U.S.; white sufferers are benefitting from doctors prescribing drugs to treat their problems while black sufferers are either ignored or denied appropriate medication.

Ending the drug war is more imaginable now than at any time in the last half century. It won't happen overnight, nor with President Donald Trump in the White House, but the appeal of harsh prohibition is dwindling. While the Drug Enforcement Administration (DEA) continues to receive obscenely huge amounts of government largesse, so many Americans now use and abuse drugs that it's the height of futility to try and stop it. Punishing individuals who make the personal choice to consume an illicit substance has no place in the 21st century.

Antony Loewenstein is a Jerusalem-based Australian journalist who has written for The New York Times, The Guardian, the BBC, The Washington Post, The Nation, Huffington Post, Haaretz, and many others. His latest book is Pills, Powder and Smoke: Inside the Bloody War on Drugs. He's the author of Disaster Capitalism: Making a Killing Out of Catastrophe; the writer/co-producer of the associated documentary, Disaster Capitalism; and the co-director of an Al-Jazeera English film on the opioid drug tramadol. His other books include My Israel Question, The Blogging Revolution, and Profits of Doom, and he is the co-editor of the books Left Turn and After Zionism, and is a contributor to For God's Sake.

Correction: The amount the U.S. spent in 2016 on cannabis, cocaine, heroin, and methamphetamines has been corrected.

* * *

Ms. JACKSON LEE. Members, I have one or two questions, and I will then conclude. So, let me just quickly ask Ms. Nelson that we know the '70s marked the formal beginning of mass incarceration. We have seen the results of mass incarceration, of what transpired with mass incarceration. So, the question that we have is, why is it important to remember and consider that history, which is evidence of mass incarceration, when undertaking sentencing reform?

Ms. NELSON. Thank you for that question. I think it's important to—and many of the questions on the colloquy today has touched on the history of when we started going down this path in the '70s through the '90s.

It was a period, and as I said in my testimony, right after the civil rights—the achievements of the civil rights era. There was a rise in crime, but it immediately became politicized and racialized in terms of sort of conflating growing crime with criminality of non-White people. That allowed us to come down on people in a very harsh way.

I think now—and certainly we've been hearing about it throughout this testimony—what are the lessons that we've learned from that period, how can we not make those same mistakes, both as we undo the war on drugs, and think again about what we're trying to do when we sentence people.

The framework that we put forward is that when we're sentencing people, we have to have a reason for doing it. We have to actually—need to create actual safety, we have to repair harm, and we have to promote racial justice. An overly harsh mechanism for sentencing does none of that.

There's been lots of testimony from several witnesses about how harsh sentences do not deter crime, and there has been testimony about where we are now in terms of rising crime.

I cannot say strongly enough that as we are in this period, we can learn from what we did wrong in the '70s through the '90s, and take an evidence-based approach to both how we deal with being proactive about crime, and then once crime has occurred, what is the appropriate sentence. It should be a sentence that repairs the harm, not a sentence that holds people in for too long, and to no effect.

Ms. JACKSON LEE. Thank you very much. I think it's clear the challenges we have.

Very quickly to Ms. Givens, you had an important statement in your testimony that what we're doing is really erasing an entire phase of life for an entire generation. We know that brains do not mature until the age of 25.

Explain what this process of mass incarceration and mandatory minimums does to your defendants, particularly in the age 18 to 26, and again how destructive that is.

Ms. GIVENS. Quickly, I guess in a nutshell, I would say that what it does, is, it doesn't give young people the opportunity to do some of the things that Ms. Nelson was just speaking about. It doesn't give them the opportunity to repair and recover.

The brain development piece is so hopeful and so important because what we know from data is, young people's brains develop and they respond in a shorter time, so they don't need these long sentences to make a U-turn in their life.

It takes away their education, takes them away from their family. It actually increases trauma. The Act of incarcerating a young person increases trauma. You really take away connection, mental health, and superimpose on them hypervigilance, anxiety, they don't continue to develop self-esteem.

All of these things will follow them for the rest of their life, but most importantly, it takes young people away from the ability to become good income earners, because we are wasting 5, 10, 20 years of their life where they could get a skill and contribute to society.

Ms. JACKSON LEE. As a Federal defender, you see this all the time?

Ms. GIVENS. All the time. It's why I feel like this about it. I see it all the time.

Ms. JACKSON LEE. Ms. Frederique, I think you might remember a recent news story regarding teens in Ocean City, simply trying to enjoy themselves. They were vaping and came across—or law enforcement came across them. Sizeable amount of violence following the antivaping law obviously. I guess one might say that it was considered a drug.

How does these kinds of laws then wind up with probably violent encounters and young people losing their freedom, and also being unfortunately violently confronted?

Ms. FREDERIQUE. Thank you for that. So, what I would say is what we saw in Ocean City is something that we see all across this country, where people use substances as an excuse, as a pretext, or justification, for law enforcement and violence against young people and people of color.

It's one of the biggest reasons why we need to move away from the current war on drugs, because it creates the space for these encounters. So, it gives excuse for law enforcement to disrupt the fun that young people are having.

I think it's really important to recognize that there are only certain young people that are able to take up public space and to have fun and to be joyful and to be loud and rambunctious.

Then there are other young people that take that time and take up that space and that are met with the State actors, like law enforcement, engaging them in ways that can often escalate and turn into violence.

Drugs, be it things that are legal or illegal, drugs in general— so, tobacco, alcohol, substances—are often used as a pretext for the engagement, or justification for the escalation.

So, one of the things that is super important for us is to figure out, how do we remove those tools so that we can give young people more time to experience life, freedom, liberty, and autonomy, without the constant over-surveillance that we see that the State uses.

Ms. JACKSON LEE. Thank you very much.

Mr. Underwood, because you're so powerful, let me give you the last word. Mr. Underwood, can you turn your mike on? I'm giving you the last word.

You had a sentence of life. Is that correct?

Mr. UNDERWOOD. Yes, ma'am.

Ms. JACKSON LEE. Was that life without parole?

Mr. UNDERWOOD. Yes, ma'am.

Ms. JACKSON LEE. If you don't mind, in the course of your being contrary to the legal system, did you have any Act where someone lost their life?

Mr. UNDERWOOD. In my case?

Ms. JACKSON LEE. Yes.

Mr. UNDERWOOD. Well, I was accused of being the head of a drug ring that—

Ms. JACKSON LEE. But your actual actions did not—

Mr. UNDERWOOD. No, no, not—no, no.

Ms. JACKSON LEE. You got life without parole?

Mr. UNDERWOOD. Yes, ma'am.

Ms. JACKSON LEE. So, if there was not a court intervention and a number of other things and your basic rehabilitation and goodness, you would still be there?

Mr. UNDERWOOD. Absolutely.

Ms. JACKSON LEE. A gentleman with a suit on and tie would still be there?

Mr. UNDERWOOD. Yes, ma'am.

Ms. JACKSON LEE. So, just my final question to you—my final question to you is, the war on drugs, mandatory minimums, how much life is being lost, how much people, value here to this Nation, is being lost by those under the mandatory minimums in our prisons today, particularly our Federal prisons?

Mr. UNDERWOOD. Well, mandatory minimums, Chair, are a travesty, because they don't allow for judges to consider the individual themselves.

I can speak for myself. I made a Sixth amendment challenge to the application of the Federal sentencing guidelines to my case. What that means is, when I went to trial, I understood that the Sixth amendment was initiated in 1791. I went to trial in 1989, but I didn't have Sixth amendment rights because of mandatory minimums.

I was one of the first persons that they used with this case, *McMillan* v. *Pennsylvania*, and—long story. This is the condensed version. After McMillan in 2002, Harris—McMillan was—came out of the '86. I was one of the first persons that they experimented with, McMillan, sentencing factors. Judge can do this. No, the jury has doesn't have to find anything. They don't have to find you guilty of the most heinous act.

If they say you committed murder, then the jury—it should have been a jury question. No, the jury don't have to find that. They say you sold drugs and you're facing a 10-year sentence, and now, because of mandatory minimums, you got life with no parole. Well, that should be a jury question. No, juries don't have to find that. This is drug—I, as the judge, these are sentencing factors, live with it. That's what they did. That's fine.

Time went on, 25 years passed, and this is the irony of doing a lot of time, because you have to understand that your children, grandchildren, friends, and people that love you, that want to help you, that don't know how to help you, the reality is, for them, life, it's like this, because you over there, and life is over here.

If you have families grow, like the Congresswoman said, friends and families you lose along the way. In my case, 25 years went by in Alleyne. We say Alleyne, but it was Alleyne. It's pronounced Alleyne. That came out in 2013, 570 U.S. 99, 2013, it came out. It said, you know what, you were right. Mandatory minimums, to get to the ceiling for maximum, you have to stand on the floor.

So, you have to be found guilty of every element of the offense to get the mandatory minimum. I didn't get that option under the Sixth Amendment, which, I have six cases in the law books, six actual published opinions. Three of them I put there myself.

So, once this happened with the law, and I figured, well, okay, I was going to go home at some point, the reality of this is that they never made any of this retroactive. So from—let me—I digress. Let me go back a little bit; in 1999, *Richardson* v. *United States*, 526 U.S. 813.

Ms. JACKSON LEE. If you can summarize.

Mr. UNDERWOOD. Yes, ma'am, I'll summarize it like this. Richardson was the subsection 848 CCE case that triggered a life sentence if you were found guilty of all elements of that offense. Not only did I have racketeering, and I had drug conspiracy, but I had continued criminal enterprise. I was never given the opportunity to have the jury find me individually guilty of any of those offense. I was found guilty in a general jury verdict, and the judge decided what I was guilty of. I made a Sixth amendment objection at the trial at sentencing.

I just had a general jury verdict, and the judge said, whatever they say, that's, yeah, you're guilty of that. I made these objections at trial, at sentencing—

Ms. JACKSON LEE. You lost a part of your life?

Mr. UNDERWOOD. Yeah, a significant part.

Ms. JACKSON LEE. Well, you have made your repentance to society, and I assume to yourself and four children that you have.

Mr. UNDERWOOD. Yes. My children.

Ms. JACKSON LEE. Your children are in good stead. Your children are—you are proud of your children?

Mr. UNDERWOOD. Absolutely. Yes, ma'am. Absolutely, Chair, absolutely.

Ms. JACKSON LEE. Well, let us learn from where you are today, and what might have happened to those who are not lucky enough, or, how should I say, astute enough to have been in this chair where you are today—that are now languishing.

Mr. UNDERWOOD. Yes, ma'am.

Ms. JACKSON LEE. I hope that this committee, in a bipartisan manner, with Mr. Biggs, the Ranking Member, has made some very important points. Our colleagues have made some very important points and that we can come to some consideration of what is the best approach for this scourge of drugs that was utilized to be a scourge on people and families and humanity.

Forgive me for my extended comment. The Ranking Member is very kind in his indulgence and so are Members, but I want Members to know that we are going to move ahead, because this is the moment that we must deal with this question.

I think there are a lot of minds here that can contribute to the solution, and I hope the minds will be both Republicans and Democrats.

With that in mind, no further comments from my Members, this hearing on the "Undoing the Damage of the War on Drugs: A Renewal Call for Sentencing Reform," is now herefore adjourned. Let me thank all the witnesses for their outstanding testimony. Thank you.

[Whereupon, at 1:16 p.m., the Subcommittee was adjourned.]

Statement for Congressional Record

William R. Underwood

Constitutional Argument: Where is the Rule of Law under the Bill of Rights?

From the moment of my trial and throughout my thirty-three years of incarceration, I continuously made the following constitutional arguments. These arguments were based on the objections I made under the 6th Amendment right to have a jury decide all elements of the offense, but I never received the opportunity to exercise the constitutional objections that I preserved that is now Alleyne vs. United States, 570 U.S. 99 (2013). Nonetheless, I continued to maintain hope, despite the hopelessness of my life without parole sentence and transformed my life while in prison. I devoted my time and energy to studying the law in the law library, being a present and focused father to my children and grandchildren and mentored the young men I encountered throughout my years in federal prison. My devotion to transformation resonated with my children and my eldest daughter, Ebony Underwood, became an advocate for criminal justice reform. In 2017, she founded, WE GOT US NOW, a national nonprofit advocacy organization built by, led by and about children and young adults impacted by parental incarceration. On January 15, 2021, I received a compassionate release from federal prison and less than six months into my freedom I now have the opportunity to present to the United States Congress the story of my constitutional challenge and the profound impact that my daughter's organization has championed throughout these United States.

In 1989-90, during trial, I made a Sixth Amendment challenge to the application of the Federal Sentencing Guidelines to my case. I stated that it was for the jury to determine whether my conduct continued past the effective date of the Sentencing Guidelines. "The issue was squarely raised in the district court at a hearing in February 1990." "[T]he judge explicitly addressed the question and determined ...." The Court of Appeals upholding Cederabaum's ruling stated: "That finding is not clearly erroneous, and we therefore accept it. See 18 U.S.C. S 3742(e)." U.S. v. Underwood, 932 F.2d 1049, 1053-1055 (2nd Cir. 1991).

We now know, under the requirements of the Sixth Amendment, the Second Circuit's ruling in U.S. v. Underwood, 932 F.2d at 1053, that: "McMillan v. Pennsylvania, 477 U.S. 79 (1986), is dispositive of Underwood's claim." Underwood I. And, that the Second Circuit's ruling in Underwood v. U.S., 15 F.3d 16, 19 (2nd Cir. 1993), that: "As we held in Underwood I, the Supreme Court's decision in McMillan v. Pennsylvania, 477 U.S. 79 (1986), is dispositive here." Underwood II. Those decisions which determined the mandatory minimum of life with no parole for Underwood, were wrongly decided. McMillan v. Pennsylvania, 477 U.S. 79 (1986), was overruled in Alleyne v. United States, 570 U.S. 99 (2013). As "inconsistent...with the original meaning of the Sixth Amendment." 570 U.S. at 103.

The definition of **dispositive:** "Being a deciding factor; (of a fact or factor) bringing about a final determination." **Black's Law Dictionary, Bryan A. Garner, Tenth Edition, p. 572 (2014).**

We now know, under the requirements of the Sixth Amendment, Underwood should have been given the opportunity to have a jury determine beyond a reasonable doubt, whether his offense conduct continued past November 1, 1987, the effective date of the mandatory sentencing Guidelines, in order to sentence him to a mandatory minimum life sentence.

We now know, "Justice Sotomayor, with whom Justice Ginsburg and Justice Kagan join, concurring, [stated]. 'I join the opinion of the Court, which persuasively explains why Harris v. United States, 536 U.S. 545 (2002), and McMillan v. Pennsylvania, 477 U.S. 79 (1986), were wrongly decided. Under the reasoning of our decision in Apprendi, ..., and the original meaning of the Sixth Amendment, facts that increase the statutory minimum sentence (no less than facts that increase the statutory maximum sentence) are elements of the offense that must be found by a jury and proved beyond a reasonable doubt.' " Alleyne v. United States, 570 U.S. 99, 118 (2013) (Sotomayor, J.) (Concurring at 1).

Ergo, under the requirement of the Sixth Amendment, when Judge Cedarbaum, stated that she was sentencing Underwood under the old law version of S 848(a), the 10-year minimum up to life sentence maximum. But, she then sentenced Underwood to a mandatory minimum life sentence under the Guidelines. She committed a fundamental sentencing error.

The Supreme Court over the ages, has continually held: "A constitutional right 'may be forfeited in criminal as well as civil cases by the failure to make timely assertion of the right'." Yakus v. United States, 321 U.S. 414, 444 (1944).

The error in Underwood's case can be seen as an error in sentencing—i.e., as the District Court imposing a sentence that it had no actual authority to impose. It can also be seen as an error in the conviction—i.e., as the conviction of a defendant for a crime different then the crime charged in the indictment and for which an element that the defendant was demonstrably prepared to contest was decided by the judge by a preponderance-of-the-evidence standard rather than by a jury beyond a reasonable doubt.

The irony of Underwood's case is that he made a constitutional challenge to every law that was used to incarcerate him and throw away the key, and his objections fell on deaf ears. When the Supreme Court overruled those challenges as unconstitutional, his preserved challenges fell on blind eyes.

The Supreme Court has now stated,

"Together with the right to vote, those who wrote our Constitution considered the right to trial by jury, ' the heart and lungs, the mainspring and the center wheel' of our liberties, without which 'the body must die; the watch must run down; the government must become arbitrary.' .... Just as the right to vote sought to preserve the people's authority over their government's executive and legislative functions, the right to a jury trial sought to preserve the people's authority over its judicial functions....

Together, these pillars of the Bill of Rights ensure that the government must prove to a jury every criminal charge beyond a reasonable doubt, an ancient rule that has 'extend[ed] down centuries'. Apprendi vs. New Jersey, 530 U.S. 466, 477 (2000)....

Before Apprendi, however, this Court had held that facts elevating the minimum punishment not need be proven to a jury beyond a reasonable doubt. McMillian vs. Pennsylvania, 477 U.S. 79 (1986); see also Harris vs. United States, 536 U.S. 545 (2002) (adhering to McMillian).

Eventually, the Court confronted this anomaly in Alleyne. .... This Court reversed. Finding no basis in the original understanding of the 5th and 6th Amendments for McMillian and Harris, the Court expressly overruled those decisions and held that 'the principle applied in Apprendi applies with equal force to facts increasing the mandatory minimum' as it does to facts increasing the statutory maximum penalty. Alleyne, 570 U.S., at 112."

Which begs the question, "Where is the rule of law in the United States Constitution as guaranteed by the Bill of Rights that is supposed to protect its citizenry? When the guarantee under the rule of law does not exist and all of its citizens do not receive equal protection under the law?"

Chapter 2

H. R. 3617: In the Senate of the United States*

April 4 (legislative day, March 31), 2022
Received; read twice and referred to the Committee on Finance

An Act

To decriminalize and deschedule cannabis, to provide for reinvestment in certain persons adversely impacted by the War on Drugs, to provide for expungement of certain cannabis offenses, and for other purposes.

Be it enacted by the Senate and House of Representatives of the United States of America in Congress assembled,

Section 1. Short Title

This Act may be cited as the "Marijuana Opportunity Reinvestment and Expungement Act" or the "MORE Act."

Sec. 2. Findings

The Congress finds as follows:

---

* This is an edited, reformatted and augmented version of "Marijuana Opportunity Reinvestment and Expungement Act," Publication No. HR 3617 RFS, dated April 4 (legislative day, March 31), 2022.

In: Policies to Reverse the Damage Caused by the War on Drugs
Editors: Katie A. Hilbert
ISBN: 979-8-89113-829-2

1) The communities that have been most harmed by cannabis prohibition are benefiting the least from the legal marijuana marketplace.
2) A legacy of racial and ethnic injustices, compounded by the disproportionate collateral consequences of 80 years of cannabis prohibition enforcement, now limits participation in the industry.
3) 37 States, the District of Columbia, Puerto Rico, Guam, and the U.S. Virgin Islands have adopted laws allowing legal access to cannabis, and 15 States, the District of Columbia, the Common wealth of the Northern Mariana Islands, and Guam have adopted laws legalizing cannabis for adult recreational use.
4) A total of 47 States have reformed their laws pertaining to cannabis despite the Schedule I status of marijuana and its Federal criminalization.
5) Legal cannabis sales totaled $20,000,000,000 in 2020 and are projected to reach $40,500,000,000 by 2025.
6) According to the American Civil Liberties Union (ACLU), enforcing cannabis prohibition laws costs taxpayers approximately $3.6 billion a year.
7) The continued enforcement of cannabis prohibition laws results in over 600,000 arrests annually, disproportionately impacting people of color who are almost 4 times more likely to be arrested for cannabis possession than their White counterparts, despite equal rates of use across populations.
8) People of color have been historically targeted by discriminatory sentencing practices resulting in Black men receiving drug sentences that are 13.1 percent longer than sentences imposed for White men and Latinos being nearly 6.5 times more likely to receive a Federal sentence for cannabis possession than non-Hispanic Whites.
9) In 2013, simple cannabis possession was the fourth most common cause of deportation for any offense and the most common cause of deportation for drug law violations.
10) Fewer than one-fifth of cannabis business owners identify as minorities and only approximately 4 percent are black.

11) Applicants for cannabis licenses are limited by numerous laws, regulations, and exorbitant permit applications, licensing fees, and costs in these States, which can require more than $700,000.
12) Historically disproportionate arrest and conviction rates make it particularly difficult for people of color to enter the legal cannabis marketplace, as most States bar these individuals from participating.
13) Federal law severely limits access to loans and capital for cannabis businesses, disproportionately impacting minority small business owners.
14) Some States and municipalities have taken proactive steps to mitigate inequalities in the legal cannabis marketplace and ensure equal participation in the industry.

Sec. 3. Decriminalization of Cannabis

(a) CANNABIS REMOVED FROM SCHEDULE OF CONTROLLED SUBSTANCES.—

(1) REMOVAL IN STATUTE.—Subsection (c) of schedule I of section 202(c) of the Controlled Substances Act (21 U.S.C. 812) is amended—

(A) by striking "(10) Marihuana." and

(B) by striking "(17) Tetrahydrocannabinols, except for tetrahydrocannabinols in hemp (as defined under section 297A of the Agricultural Marketing Act of 1946)."

(2) REMOVAL FROM SCHEDULE.—Not later than 180 days after the date of the enactment of this Act, the Attorney General shall finalize a rulemaking under section 201(a)(2) removing marihuana and tetrahydrocannabinols from the schedules of controlled substances. For the purposes of the Controlled Substances Act, marihuana and etrahydrocannabinols shall each be deemed to be a drug or other substance that does not meet the requirements for inclusion in any schedule. A rulemaking under this paragraph shall be considered to have taken effect as of the date of enactment of this Act for purposes of any offense committed, case pending, conviction entered, and, in the case of a juvenile, any offense committed, case pending, and adjudication of juvenile delinquency entered before, on, or after the date of enactment of this Act.

(b) CONFORMING AMENDMENTS TO CONTROLLED SUBSTANCES ACT.—The Controlled Substances Act (21 U.S.C. 801 et seq.) is amended—

(1) in section 102(44) (21 U.S.C. 802(44)), by striking "marihuana,"

(2) in section 401(b) (21 U.S.C. 841(b))—(A) in paragraph (1)—

(i) in subparagraph (A)—

(I) in clause (vi), by inserting "or" after the semicolon;

(II) by striking clause (vii); and

(III)by redesignating clause (viii) as clause (vii);

(ii) in subparagraph (B)—

(I) in clause (vi), by inserting ''or'' after the semicolon;

(II) by striking clause (vii); and

(III)by redesignating clause

(viii) as clause (vii);

(iii) in subparagraph (C), in the first sentence, by striking ''subparagraphs (A),

(B), and (D)'' and inserting ''subparagraphs (A) and (B)'';

(iv) by striking subparagraph (D);

(v) by redesignating subparagraph (E) as subparagraph (D); and

(vi) in subparagraph (D)(i), as so redesignated, by striking ''subparagraphs (C) and (D)'' and inserting ''subparagraph(C)'';

(B) by striking paragraph (4); and (C) by redesignating paragraphs (5), (6), and (7) as paragraphs (4), (5), and (6), respectively;

(3) in section 402(c)(2)(B) (21U.S.C. 842(c)(2)(B)), by striking, "marihuana,"

(4) in section 403(d)(1) (21 U.S.C. 843(d)(1)), 7by striking "marihuana;"|

(5) in section 418(a) (21 U.S.C. 859(a)), by striking the last sentence;

(6) in section 419(a) (21 U.S.C. 860(a)), by 11 striking the last sentence;

(7) in section 422(d) (21 U.S.C. 863(d))—(A) in the matter preceding paragraph (1), by striking ''marijuana,''; and (B) in paragraph (5), by striking "such as a marihuana cigarette,''; and

(8) in section 516(d) (21 U.S.C. 886(d)), by striking ''section 401(b)(6)'' each place the term appears and inserting ''section 401(b)(5).''

(c) OTHER CONFORMING AMENDMENTS.—

(1) National forest system drug control ACT OF 1986.—The National Forest System Drug Control Act of 1986 (16 U.S.C. 559b et seq.) is amended—

1 (A) in section 15002(a) (16U.S.C. 2559b(a)) by striking ''marijuana and other'';

(B) in section 15003(2) (16 U.S.C. 559c(2)) by striking ‘‘marijuana andother’’;

(C) in section 15004(2) (16U.S.C.559d(2)) by striking ‘‘marijuana and other’’.

(2) INTERCEPTION OF COMMUNICATIONS.—Section 2516 of title 18, United States Code, is amended—

(A) in subsection (1)(e), by striking ‘‘marihuana,’’; and

(B) in subsection (2) by striking ‘‘marihuana’’.

(3) FMCSA PROVISIONS.—

(A) CONFORMING AMENDMENT.—Section 31301(5) of title 49, United States Code, is amended by striking ‘‘section 31306,’’ and inserting ‘‘sections 31306, 31306a, and subsections (b) and (c) of section 31310,’’.

(B) DEFINITION.—Section 31306(a) of title 49, United States Code, is amended—

(i) by striking ‘‘means any substance’’

and inserting the following: ‘‘means—

‘‘(A) any substance’’; and

(ii) by striking the period at the end and inserting ‘‘; and ‘‘(B) any substance not covered under subparagraph (A) that was a substance under such section as of December 1, 2018, and specified by the Secretary of Transportation.’’.

(C) DISQUALIFICATIONS.—Section 31310(b) of title 49, United States Code, is amended by adding at the end the following:

‘‘(3) In this subsection and subsection (c), the term ‘controlled substance’ has the meaning given such term in section 31306(a).’’.

(4) FAA PROVISIONS.—Section 45101 of title 49, United States Code, is amended—

(A) by striking ‘‘means any substance’’ and inserting the following: ‘‘means—

‘‘(A) any substance’’; and

(B) by striking the period at the end and inserting ‘‘; and ‘‘(B) any substance not covered under subparagraph (A) that was a substance under such section as of December 1, 2018, and specified by the Secretary of Transportation.’’

(5) FRA PROVISIONS.—Section 20140(a) of title 49, United States Code, is amended—(A) by striking ‘‘means any substance’’

and inserting the following: ‘‘means—

‘‘(A) any substance’’; and (B) by striking the period at the end and inserting ‘‘; and

''(B) any substance not covered under subparagraph (A) that was a substance under such section as of December 1, 2018, and specified by the Secretary of Transportation.''.

(6) FTA PROVISIONS.—Section 5331(a)(1) of title 49, United States Code, is amended—

(A) by striking ''means any substance'' and inserting the following: ''means—

''(A) any substance''; and (B) by striking the period at the end and inserting ''; and ''(B) any substance not covered under subparagraph (A) that was a substance under such section as of December 1, 2018, and whose use the Secretary of Transportation decides has a risk to transportation safety.''

(d) RETROACTIVITY.—The amendments made by this section to the Controlled Substances Act (21 U.S.C. 801et seq.) are retroactive and shall apply to any offense committed, case pending, conviction entered, and, in the case of a juvenile, any offense committed, case pending, or adjudication of juvenile delinquency entered before, on, or after the date of enactment of this Act.

(e) EFFECT ON OTHER LAW.—Nothing in this subtitle shall affect or modify—

(1) the Federal Food, Drug, and Cosmetic Act (21 U.S.C. 301 et seq.);

(2) section 351 of the Public Health Service Act (42 U.S.C. 262); or

(3) the authority of the Commissioner of Food and Drugs and the Secretary of Health and Human Services—

(A) under—

(i) the Federal Food, Drug, and Cosmetic Act (21 U.S. 301 et seq.); or (ii) section 351 of the Public Health Service Act (42 U.S.C. 262); or (B) to promulgate Federal regulations and guidelines that relate to products containing cannabis or cannabis-derived compounds under the Act described in subparagraph (A)(i) or the section described in subparagraph (A)(ii).

(f) PUBLIC MEETINGS.—Not later than one year after the date of enactment of this Act, the Secretary of Health and Human Services, acting through the Commissioner of Food and Drugs, shall hold not less than one

public meeting to address the regulation, safety, manufacturing, product quality, marketing, labeling, and sale of products containing cannabis or cannabis-derived compounds.

(g) SPECIAL RULE FOR FEDERAL EMPLOYEE TESTING.—Section 503 of the Supplemental Appropriations Act, 1987 (5 U.S.C. 7301 note) is amended by adding at the end the following:

''(h) MARIJUANA.—

"(1) CONTINUED TESTING.—Notwithstanding the Marijuana Opportunity Reinvestment and Expungement Act and the amendments made thereby, the Secretary of Health and Human Services may continue to include marijuana for purposes of drug testing of Federal employees subject to this section, Executive Order 12564, or other applicable Federal laws and orders.

"(2) DEFINITION.—The term 'marijuana' has the meaning given to the term 'marihuana' in section 102 of the Controlled Substances Act (21 6U.S.C. 802) on the day before the date of enactment of the Marijuana Opportunity Reinvestment and Expungement Act.".

(h) SPECIAL RULE FOR CERTAIN REGULATIONS.—(1) IN GENERAL.—The amendments made by this section may not be construed to abridge the authority of the Secretary of Transportation, or the Secretary of the department in which the Coast Guard is operating, to regulate and screen for the use of a controlled substance.

(2) CONTROLLED SUBSTANCE DEFINED.—In this subsection, the term "controlled substance" means—

(A) any substance covered under section 102 of the Controlled Substances Act (21U.S.C. 802) on the day before the date of enactment of this Act; and

(B) any substance not covered under subparagraph (A) that was a substance covered under section 102 of the Controlled Substances Act (21 U.S.C. 802) on December 1, 2018, and specified by the Secretary of Transportation.

Sec. 4. Demographic Data of Cannabis Business Owners and Employees

(a) IN GENERAL.—The Bureau of Labor Statistics shall regularly compile, maintain, and make public data on the demographics of—

(1) individuals who are business owners in the cannabis industry; and (2) individuals who are employed in the cannabis industry.

(b) DEMOGRAPHIC DATA.—The data collected under subsection (a) shall include data regarding—

(1) age;

(2) certifications and licenses;

(3) disability status;

(4) educational attainment;

(5) family and marital status;

(6) nativity;

(7) race and Hispanic ethnicity;

(8) school enrollment;

(9) veteran status; and

(10) sex.

(c) CONFIDENTIALITY.—The name, address, and other identifying information of individuals employed in the cannabis industry shall be kept confidential by the Bureau and not be made available to the public.

(d) DEFINITIONS.—In this section:

(1) CANNABIS.—The term ‘‘cannabis’’ means either marijuana or cannabis as defined under the State law authorizing the sale or use of cannabis in which the individual or entity is located.

(2) CANNABIS INDUSTRY.—The term ‘‘cannabis industry’’ means an individual or entity that is licensed or permitted under a State or local law to engage in commercial cannabis-related activity.

(3) OWNER.—The term ‘‘owner’’ means an individual or entity that is defined as an owner under the State or local law where the individual or business is licensed or permitted.

Sec. 5. Creation of Opportunity Trust Fund and Imposition of Taxes with Respect to Cannabis Products

(a) ESTABLISHMENT OF OPPORTUNITY TRUST FUND.—Subchapter A of chapter 98 of the Internal Revenue Code of 1986 is amended by adding at the end the following new section:

‘‘Sec. 9512. Establishment of Opportunity Trust Fund

‘‘(a) CREATION OF TRUST FUND.—There is established in the Treasury of the United States a trust fund to be known as the ‘Opportunity Trust Fund’ (referred to in this section as the ‘Trust Fund’), consisting of such amounts as may be appropriated or credited to such fund as provided in this section or section 9602(b).

‘‘(b) TRANSFERS TO TRUST FUND.—There are hereby appropriated to the Trust Fund amounts equivalent to the net revenues received in the Treasury from the taxes imposed under chapter 56.

"(c) EXPENDITURES.—Amounts in the Trust Fund shall be available, without further appropriation, only as follows:

"(1) 50 percent to the Attorney General to carry out section 3052(a) of part OO of the Omnibus Crime Control and Safe Streets Act of 1968.

"(2) 10 percent to the Attorney General to carry out section 3052(b) of part OO of the Omnibus Crime Control and Safe Streets Act of 1968.

"(3) 20 percent to the Administrator of the Small Business Administration to carry out section 6(b)(1) of the Marijuana Opportunity Reinvestment and Expungement Act.

"(4) 20 percent to the Administrator of the Small Business Administration to carry out section 6(b)(2) of the Marijuana Opportunity Reinvestment and Expungement Act."

(b) CANNABIS REVENUE AND REGULATION ACT.—
Subtitle E of the Internal Revenue Code of 1986 is
amended by adding at the end the following new chapter:

"Chapter 56—Cannabis Products

"Subchapter A—Tax on Cannabis Products

"Sec. 5901. Imposition of Tax

"(a) IMPOSITION OF TAX.—There is hereby imposed on any cannabis product produced in or imported into the United States a tax equal to—

"(1) for any such product removed during the first 5 calendar years ending after the date on which this chapter becomes effective, the applicable percentage of such product's removal price, and "(2) for any product removed during any calendar year after the calendar years described in paragraph (1), the applicable equivalent amount.

"(b) APPLICABLE PERCENTAGE.—For purposes of subsection (a)(1), the applicable percentage shall be determined as follows:

"(1) For any cannabis product removed during the first 2 calendar years ending after the date on which this chapter becomes effective, 5 percent.

"(2) For any cannabis product removed during the calendar year after the last calendar year to which paragraph (1) applies, 6 percent.

"(3) For any cannabis product removed during the calendar year after the calendar year to which paragraph (2) applies, 7 percent.

"(4) For any cannabis product removed during the calendar year after the calendar year to which paragraph (3) applies, 8 percent.

"(c) APPLICABLE EQUIVALENT AMOUNT.—

"(1) IN GENERAL.—For purposes of subsection(a)(2), the term 'applicable equivalent amount' means, with respect to any cannabis product removed during any calendar year, an amount equal to—

"(A) in the case of any cannabis product not described in subparagraph (B), the product of the applicable rate per ounce multiplied by the number of ounces of such product (and a proportionate tax at the like rate on all fractional parts of an ounce of such product), and "(B) in the case of any THC-measurable cannabis product, the product of the applicable rate per gram multiplied by the number of grams of tetrahydrocannabinol in such product (and a proportionate tax at the like rate on all fractional parts of a gram of tetrahydrocannabinol in such product). "(2) Applicable rates.—

"(A) IN GENERAL.—For purposes of paragraph (1)(A), the term 'applicable rate per ounce' means, with respect to any cannabis product removed during any calendar year, 8 percent of the prevailing sales price of cannabis flowers sold in the United States during the 12-month period ending one calendar quarter before such calendar year, expressed on a per ounce basis, as determined by the Secretary.

"(B) THC-measurable cannabis products.—For purposes of paragraph (1)(B), the term 'applicable rate per gram' means, with respect to any cannabis product removed during any calendar year, 8 percent of the prevailing sales price of tetrahydrocannabinol sold in the United States during the 12-month period ending one calendar quarter before such calendar year, expressed on a per gram basis, as determined by the Secretary.

"(d) TIME OF ATTACHMENT ON CANNABIS PRODUCTS.—The tax under this section shall attach to any cannabis product as soon as such product is in existence as such, whether it be subsequently separated or transferred into any other substance, either in the process of original production or by any subsequent process.

"Sec. 5902. Definitions

"(a) DEFINITIONS RELATED TO CANNABIS PRODUCTS.—For purposes of this chapter—

"(1) Cannabis product.—

"(A) IN GENERAL.—Except as provided in subparagraph (B), the term 'cannabis product' means any article which contains (or consists of) cannabis.

"(B) EXCEPTIONS.—The term 'cannabis product' shall not include an FDA-approved article or industrial hemp.

"(C) FDA-APPROVED ARTICLE.—The term 'FDA-approved article' means any article if the producer or importer thereof demonstrates to the satisfaction of the Secretary of Health and Human Services that such article is—

"(i) a drug—

"(I) that is approved under sec-
tion 505 of the Federal Food, Drug,
and Cosmetic Act or licensed under
section 351 of the Public Health Service Act, or

"(II) for which an investigational use exemption has been authorized under section 505(i) of the Federal Food, Drug, and Cosmetic Act or under section 351(a) of the Public Health Service Act, or "(ii) a combination product (as described in section 503(g) of the Federal Food, Drug, and Cosmetic Act), the constituent parts of which were approved or cleared under section 505, 510(k), or 515 of such Act.

"(D) INDUSTRIAL HEMP.—The term 'industrial hemp' means the plant Cannabis sativa L. and any part of such plant, whether growing or not, with a delta-9 tetrahydrocannabinol con centration of not more than 0.3 percent on a dry weight basis.

"(2) THC-measurable cannabis product.—

The term 'THC-measurable cannabis product' means any cannabis product—

"(A) with respect to which the Secretary has made a determination that the amount of tetrahydrocannabinol in such product can be measured with a high degree of accuracy, or "(B) which is not cannabis flower and the concentration of tetrahydrocannabinol in which is significantly higher than the average such concentration in cannabis flower.

‘‘(3) CANNABIS.—The term ‘cannabis’ has the meaning given such term under section 102(16) of the Controlled Substances Act (21 U.S.C. 802(16)).

‘‘(b) DEFINITIONS RELATED TO CANNABIS ENTER-PRISES.—For purposes of this chapter—

‘‘(1) CANNABIS ENTERPRISE.—The term ‘cannabis enterprise’ means a producer, importer, or export warehouse proprietor.

‘‘(2) PRODUCER.—

‘‘(A) IN GENERAL.—The term ‘producer’ means any person who plants, cultivates, harvests, grows,manufactures, produces, compounds, converts, processes, prepares, or packages any cannabis product.

‘‘(B) PERSONAL USE EXCEPTION.—Subject to regulation prescribed by the Secretary, the term ‘producer’ shall not include any individual otherwise described in subparagraph (A) if the only cannabis product described in such subparagraph with respect to such individual is for personal or family use and not for sale. ‘‘(3) IMPORTER.—The term ‘importer’ means any person who—

‘‘(A) is in the United States and to whom non-tax-paid cannabis products, produced in a foreign country or a possession of the United States, are shipped or consigned, ‘‘(B) removes cannabis products for sale or consumption in the United States from a customs bonded warehouse, or ‘‘

(C) smuggles or otherwise unlawfully rings any cannabis product into the United States.

‘‘(4) Export warehouse proprietor.—

‘‘(A) IN GENERAL.—The term ‘export warehouse proprietor’ means any person who operates an export warehouse.

‘‘(B) EXPORT WAREHOUSE.—The term ‘export warehouse’ means a bonded internal revenue warehouse for the storage of cannabis products, upon which the internal revenue tax has not been paid—

‘‘(i) for subsequent shipment to a foreign country or a possession of the United States, or ‘‘(ii) for consumption beyond the jurisdiction of the internal revenue laws of the United States.

‘‘(5) CANNABIS PRODUCTION FACILITY.—The term ‘cannabis production facility’ means an establishment which is qualified under subchapter C to perform any operation for which such qualification is required under such subchapter.

‘‘(c) OTHER DEFINITIONS.—For purposes of this chapter—

"(1) PRODUCE.—The term 'produce' includes any activity described in subsection (b)(2)(A).

"(2) REMOVAL; REMOVE.—The terms 'removal' or 'remove' means—

"(A) the transfer of cannabis products from the premises of a producer (or the transfer of such products from the bonded premises of a producer to a non-bonded premises of such producer),

"(B) release of such products from customs custody, or "(C) smuggling or other unlawful importation of such products into the United States.

"(3) REMOVAL PRICE.—The term 'removal price' means—"(A) except as otherwise provided in this paragraph, the price for which the cannabis product is sold in the sale which occurs in connection with the removal of such product,

"(B) in the case of any such sale which is described in section 5903(c), the price deterined under such section, and "(C) if there is no sale which occurs in connection with such removal, the price which would be determined under section 5903(c) if such product were sold at a price which cannot be determined.

"Sec. 5903. Liability and Method of Payment

"(a) LIABILITY FOR TAX.—

"(1) ORIGINAL LIABILITY.—The producer or importer of any cannabis product shall be liable for the taxes imposed thereon by section 5901.

"(2) Transfer of liability.—

"(A) IN GENERAL.—When cannabis products are transferred, without payment of tax, pursuant to subsection (b) or (c) of section 5904—

"(i) except as provided in clause (ii), the transferee shall become liable for the tax upon receipt by the transferee of such articles, and the transferor shall thereupon be relieved of their liability for such tax, and "(ii) in the case of cannabis products which are released in bond from customs custody for transfer to the bonded premises of a producer, the transferee shall become liable for the tax on such articles upon release from customs custody, and the importer shall thereupon be relieved of their liability for such tax.

"(B) RETURNED TO BOND.—All provisions of this chapter applicable to cannabis products in bond shall be applicable to such articles returned to bond upon withdrawal from the market or returned to bond after previous removal for a tax-exempt purpose.

“(b) METHOD OF PAYMENT OF TAX.—

“(1) In general.—

“(A) Taxes paid on basis of return.—

The taxes imposed by section 5901 shall be paid on the basis of return. The Secretary shall, by regulations, prescribe the period or the event to be covered by such return and the information to be furnished on such return.

“(B) APPLICATION TO TRANSFEREES.—In the case of any transfer to which subsection (a)(2)(A) applies, the tax under section 5901 on the transferee shall (if not otherwise relieved by reason of a subsequent transfer to which such subsection applies) be imposed with respect to the removal of the cannabis product from the bonded premises of the transferee.

“(C) POSTPONEMENT.—Any postponement under this subsection of the payment of taxes determined at the time of removal shall be conditioned upon the filing of such additional bonds, and upon compliance with such requirements, as the Secretary may prescribe for the protection of the revenue. The Secretary may, by regulations, require payment of tax on the basis of a return prior to removal of the cannabis products where a person defaults in the postponed payment of tax on the basis of a return under this subsection or regulations prescribed thereunder.

“(D) Administration and penalties.—

All administrative and penalty provisions of this title, insofar as applicable, shall apply to any tax imposed by section 5901. “(2) Time for payment of taxes.—

“(A) IN GENERAL.—Except as otherwise provided in this paragraph, in the case of taxes on cannabis products removed during any semi-monthly period under bond for deferred payment of tax, the last day for payment of such taxes shall be the 14th day after the last day of such semimonthly period.

“(B) IMPORTED ARTICLES.—In the case of cannabis products which are imported into the United States, the following provisions shall apply:

“(i) IN GENERAL.—The last day for payment of tax shall be the 14th day after the last day of the semimonthly period during which the article is entered into the customs territory of the United States.

“(ii) SPECIAL RULE FOR ENTRY OF WAREHOUSING.—Except as provided inclause (iv), in the case of an entry for warehousing, the last day for payment of tax shall not be later than the 14th day after the last day of the semimonthly period during which the article is removed from the first such warehouse.

‘‘(iii) FOREIGN TRADE ZONES.—Except as provided in clause (iv) and in regulations prescribed by the Secretary, articles brought into a foreign trade zone shall, notwithstanding any other provision of law, be treated for purposes of this subsection as if such zone were a single customs warehouse.

‘‘(iv) EXCEPTION FOR ARTICLES DESTINED FOR EXPORT.—Clauses (ii) and (iii) shall not apply to any article which is shown to the satisfaction of the Secretary to be destined for export.

‘‘(C) Cannabis products brought into THE UNITED STATES FROM PUERTO RICO.—In the case of cannabis products which are brought into the United States from Puerto Rico and subject to tax under section 7652, the last day for payment of tax shall be the 14th day after the last day of the semimonthly period during which the article is brought into the United States.

‘‘(D) Special rule where due date FALLS ON SATURDAY, SUNDAY, OR HOLIDAY.—

Notwithstanding section 7503, if, but for this subparagraph, the due date under this paragraph would fall on a Saturday, Sunday, or a legal holiday (as defined in section 7503), such due date shall be the immediately preceding day which is not a Saturday, Sunday, or such a holiday.

‘‘(E) Special rule for unlawfully PRODUCED CANNABIS PRODUCTS.—In the case of any cannabis products produced in the United States at any place other than the premises of a producer that has filed the bond and obtained the permit required under this chapter, tax shall be due and payable immediately upon production.

‘‘(3) Payment by electronic fund transfer.—Any person who in any 12-month period, ending December 31, was liable for a gross amount equal to or exceeding $5,000,000 in taxes imposed on cannabis products by section 5901 (or section 7652) shall pay such taxes during the succeeding calendar year by electronic fund transfer (as defined in section 5061(e)(2)) to a Federal Reserve Bank. Rules similar to the rules of section 5061(e)(3) shall apply to the $5,000,000 amount specified in the preceding sentence.

‘‘(c) DETERMINATION OF PRICE.—

‘‘(1) Constructive sale price.—

‘‘(A) IN GENERAL.—If an article is sold directly to consumers, sold on consignment, or sold (otherwise than through an arm’s length transaction) at less than the fair market price, or if the price for which the article sold cannot be determined, the tax under section 5901(a) shall be computed on the price for which such articles are sold, in the ordinary course of trade, by producers thereof, as determined by the Secretary.

‘‘(B) Arm’s length.—

"(i) IN GENERAL.—For purposes of this section, a sale is considered to be made under circumstances otherwise than at arm's length if—

"(I) the parties are members of the same controlled group, whether or not such control is actually exercised to influence the sale price, "

(II) the parties are members of a family, as defined in section 267(c)(4), or

"(III) the sale is made pursuant to special arrangements between a producer and a purchaser.

"(ii) CONTROLLED GROUPS.—

"(I)IN GENERAL.—The term 'controlled group'has the meaning given to such term by subsection (a) of section 1563, except that 'more than 50 percent' shall be substituted for 'at least 80 percent' each place it appears in such subsection.

"(II) Controlled groups WHICH INCLUDE NONINCORPORATED PERSONS.—Under regulations prescribed by the Secretary, principles similar to the principles of subclause (I) shall apply to a group of persons under common control where one or more of such persons is not a corporation.

"(2) Containers, packing and transportation charges.—In determining, for the purposes of this chapter, the price for which an article is sold, there shall be included any charge for coverings and containers of whatever nature, and any charge incident to placing the article in condition packed ready for shipment, but there shall be excluded the amount of tax imposed by this chapter, whether or not stated as a separate charge. A transportation, delivery, insurance, installation, or other charge (not required by the preceding sentence to be included) shall be excluded from the price only if the amount thereof is established to the satisfaction of the Secretary in accordance with regulations.

"(3) Determination of applicable equivalent amounts.—Paragraphs (1) and (2) shall apply for purposes of section 5901(c) only to the extent that the Secretary determines appropriate.

"(d) PARTIAL PAYMENTS AND INSTALLMENT ACCOUNTS.—

"(1) PARTIAL PAYMENTS.—In the case of—

"(A) a contract for the sale of an article wherein it is provided that the price shall be paid by installments and title to the article sold does not pass until a future date notwithstanding partial payment by installments,

"(B) a conditional sale, or "(C) a chattel mortgage arrangement wherein it is provided that the sales price shall be paid in installments, there shall be paid upon each payment with respect to the article a percentage of such payment equal to the rate of tax in effect on the date such payment is due.

"(2) SALES OF INSTALLMENT ACCOUNTS.—If installment accounts, with respect to payments on which tax is being computed as provided in paragraph (1), are sold or otherwise disposed of, then paragraph (1) shall not apply with respect to any subsequent payments on such accounts (other than subsequent payments on returned accounts with respect to which credit or refund is allowable by reason of section 6416(b)(5)), but instead—

"(A) there shall be paid an amount equal to the difference between—

"(i) the tax previously paid on the payments on such installment accounts, and "(ii) the total tax which would be payable if such installment accounts had not been sold or otherwise disposed of (computed as provided in paragraph (1)), except that

"(B) if any such sale is pursuant to the order of, or subject to the approval of, a court of competent jurisdiction in a bankruptcy or insolvency proceeding, the amount computed under subparagraph (A) shall not exceed the sum of the amounts computed by multiplying—

"(i) the proportionate share of the amount for which such accounts are sold which is allocable to each unpaid installment payment, by

"(ii) the rate of tax under this chapter in effect on the date such unpaid installment payment is or was due.

The sum of the amounts payable under this subsection in respect of the sale of any article shall not exceed the total tax.

"Sec. 5904. Exemption from Tax; Transfers in Bond

"(a) EXEMPTION FROM TAX.—Cannabis products on which the internal revenue tax has not been paid or determined may, subject to such regulations as the Secretary shall prescribe, be withdrawn from the bonded premises of any producer in approved containers free of tax and not for resale for use—

"(1) exclusively in scientific research by a laboratory,

"(2) by a proprietor of a cannabis production facility in research, development, or testing (other than consumer testing or other market analysis) of processes, systems, materials, or equipment, relating to cannabis or cannabis operations, under such limitations and conditions as to quantities, use, and accountability as the Secretary may by regulations require for the protection of the revenue, or "(3) by the United States or any governmental agency thereof, any State, any political subdivision of a State, or the District of Columbia, for non-consumption purposes.

"(b) CANNABIS PRODUCTS TRANSFERRED OR REMOVED in Bond From Domestic Factories and Export Warehouses.—

"(1) IN GENERAL.—Subject to such regulations and under such bonds as the Secretary shall prescribe, a producer or export warehouse proprietor may transfer cannabis products, without payment of tax, to the bonded premises of another producer or export warehouse proprietor, or remove such articles, without payment of tax, for shipment to a foreign country or a possession of the United States, or for consumption beyond the jurisdiction of the internal revenue laws of the United States.

"(2) LABELING.—Cannabis products may not be transferred or removed under this subsection unless such products bear such marks, labels, or notices as the Secretary shall by regulations prescribe.

"(c) CANNABIS PRODUCTS RELEASED IN BOND FROM CUSTOMS CUSTODY.—Cannabis products imported or brought into the United States may be released from customs custody, without payment of tax, for delivery to a producer or export warehouse proprietor if such articles are not put up in packages, in accordance with such regulations and under such bond as the Secretary shall prescribe.

"(d) CANNABIS PRODUCTS EXPORTED AND RETURNED.—Cannabis products classifiable under item 9801.00.10 of the Harmonized Tariff Schedule of the United States (relating to duty on certain articles previously exported and returned), as in effect on the date of the enactment of the Marijuana Opportunity Reinvestment and Expungement Act, may be released from customs custody, without payment of that part of the duty attributable to the internal revenue tax for delivery to the original producer of such cannabis products or to the export warehouse proprietor authorized by such producer to receive such products, in accordance with such regulations and under such bond as the Secretary shall prescribe.

Upon such release such products shall be subject to this chapter as if they had not been exported or otherwise removed from internal revenue bond.

"Sec. 5905. Credit, Refund, or Drawback of Tax

"(a) CREDIT OR REFUND.—

"(1) IN GENERAL.—Credit or refund of any tax imposed by this chapter or section 7652 shall be allowed or made (without interest) to the cannabis enterprise on proof satisfactory to the Secretary that the claimant cannabis enterprise has paid the tax on—

"(A) cannabis products withdrawn from the market by the claimant, or

"(B) such products lost (otherwise than by theft) or destroyed, by fire, casualty, or act of God, while in the possession or ownership of the claimant.

"(2) CANNABIS PRODUCTS LOST OR DESTROYED IN BOND.—

"(A) EXTENT OF LOSS ALLOWANCE.—No tax shall be collected in respect of cannabis products lost or destroyed while in bond, except that such tax shall be collected—

"(i) in the case of loss by theft, unless the Secretary finds that the theft occurred withoutconnivance, collusion, fraud, or negligence on the part of the proprietor of the cannabis production facility, owner, consignor, consignee, bailee, or carrier, or their employees or agents,

"(ii) in the case of voluntary destruction, unless such destruction is carried out as provided in paragraph (3), and "(iii) in the case of an unexplained shortage of cannabis products.

"(B) PROOF OF LOSS.—In any case in which cannabis products are lost or destroyed, whether by theft or otherwise, the Secretary 13 may require the proprietor of a cannabis production facility or other person liable for the tax to file a claim for relief from the tax and submit proof as to the cause of such loss. In every case where it appears that the loss was by theft, the burden shall be upon the proprietor of the cannabis production facility or other person responsible for the tax under section 5901 to establish to the satisfaction of the Secretary that such loss did not occur as the result of connivance, collusion, fraud, or negligence on the part of the proprietor of the cannabis production facility, owner, consignor, consignee, bailee, or carrier, or their employees or agents.

"(C) REFUND OF TAX.—In any case where the tax would not be collectible by virtue of subparagraph (A), but such tax has been paid, the Secretary shall refund such tax.

"(D) LIMITATIONS.—Except as provided in subparagraph (E), no tax shall be abated, remitted, credited, or refunded under this paragraph where the loss occurred after the tax was determined. The abatement, remission, credit, or refund of taxes provided for by subparagraphs (A) and (C) in the case of loss of cannabis products by theft shall only be allowed to the extent that the claimant is not indemnified against or recompensed in respect of the tax for such loss.

"(E) APPLICABILITY.—The provisions of this paragraph shall extend to and apply in respect of cannabis products lost after the tax was determined and before completion of the physical removal of the cannabis products from the bonded premises.

“(3) VOLUNTARY DESTRUCTION.—The proprietor of a cannabis production facility or other persons liable for the tax imposed by this chapter or by section 7652 with respect to any cannabis product in bond may voluntarily destroy such products, but only if such destruction is under such supervision and under such regulations as the Secretary may prescribe.

“(4) LIMITATION.—Any claim for credit or refund of tax under this subsection shall be filed within 6 months after the date of the withdrawal from the market, loss, or destruction of the products to which the claim relates, and shall be in such form and contain such information as the Secretary shall by regulations prescribe.

“(b) DRAWBACK OF TAX.—There shall be an allowance of drawback of tax paid on cannabis products, when shipped from the United States, in accordance with such regulations and upon the filing of such bond as the Secretary shall prescribe.

“Subchapter B—Occupational Tax

“Sec. 5911. Imposition and Rate of Tax

“(a) IN GENERAL.—Any person engaged in business as a producer or an export warehouse proprietor shall pay a tax of $1,000 per year (referred to in this subchapter as an ‘occupational tax’) in respect of each premises at which such business is carried on.

“(b) PENALTY FOR FAILURE TO REGISTER.—Any person engaged in business as a producer or an export warehouse proprietor who willfully fails to pay the occupation tax shall be fined not more than $5,000, or imprisoned not more than 2 years, or both, for each such offense.

"Sec. 5912. Payment of Tax

"(a) CONDITION PRECEDENT TO CARRYING ON BUSINESS.—No person shall be engaged in or carry on any trade or business subject to the occupational tax until such person has paid such tax.

"(b) COMPUTATION.—

"(1) IN GENERAL.—The occupational tax shall be imposed—

"(A) as of on the first day of July in each year, or

"(B) on commencing any trade or business on which such tax is imposed.

"(2) PERIOD.—In the case of a tax imposed under subparagraph (A) of paragraph (1), the occupational tax shall be reckoned for 1 year, and in the case of subparagraph (B) of such paragraph, it shall be reckoned proportionately, from the first day of the month in which the liability to such tax commenced, to and including the 30th day of June following.

"(c) METHOD OF PAYMENT.—

"(1) PAYMENT BY RETURN.—The occupational tax shall be paid on the basis of a return under such regulations as the Secretary shall prescribe.

"(2) Stamp denoting payment of tax.—

After receiving a properly executed return and remittance of any occupational tax, the Secretary shall issue to the taxpayer an appropriate stamp as a receipt denoting payment of the tax. This paragraph shall not apply in the case of a return covering liability for a past period.

"Sec. 5913. Provisions Relating to Liability for Occupational Taxes

"(a) PARTNERS.—Any number of persons doing business in partnership at any one place shall be required to pay a single occupational tax.

"(b) DIFFERENT BUSINESSES OF SAME OWNERSHIP AND LOCATION.—Whenever more than one of the pursuits or occupations described in this subchapter are carried on in the same place by the same person at the same time, except as otherwise provided in this subchapter, the occupational tax shall be paid for each according to the rates severally prescribed.

"(c) BUSINESSES IN MORE THAN ONE LOCATION.—

"(1) LIABILITY FOR TAX.—The payment of the occupational tax shall not exempt from an additional occupational tax the person carrying on a trade or business in any other place than that stated in the records of the Internal Revenue Service.

"(2) STORAGE.—Nothing contained in paragraph (1) shall require imposition of an occupational tax for the storage of cannabis products at a location other than the place where such products are sold or offered for sale.

"(3) PLACE.—

"(A) IN GENERAL.—For purposes of this section, the term 'place' means the entire office, plant or area of the business in any one location under the same proprietorship.

"(B) DIVISIONS.—For purposes of this paragraph, any passageways, streets, highways, rail crossings, waterways, or partitions dividing the premises shall not be deemed sufficient separation to require an additional occupational tax, if the various divisions are otherwise contiguous.

"(d) DEATH OR CHANGE OF LOCATION.—

"(1) IN GENERAL.—In addition to the person who has paid the occupational tax for the carrying on of any business at any place, any person described in paragraph (2) may secure the right to carry on, without incurring any additional occupational tax, the same business at the same place for the remainder of the taxable period for which the occupational tax was paid.

"(2) ELIGIBLE PERSONS.—The persons described in this paragraph are the following:

"(A) The surviving spouse or child, or executor or administrator or other legal representative, of a deceased taxpayer.

"(B) A husband or wife succeeding to the business of his or her living spouse.

"(C) A receiver or trustee in bankruptcy, or an assignee for benefit of creditors.

"(D) The partner or partners remaining after death or withdrawal of a member of a partnership.

"(3) CHANGE OF LOCATION.—When any person moves to any place other than the place for which occupational tax was paid for the carrying on of any business, such person may secure the right to carry on, without incurring additional occupational tax, the same business at the new location for the remainder of the taxable period for which the occupational tax was paid. To secure the right to carry on the business without incurring additional occupational tax, the successor, or the person relocating their business, must register the succession or relocation with the Secretary in accordance with regulations prescribed by the Secretary.

"(e) FEDERAL AGENCIES OR INSTRUMENTALITIES.—Any tax imposed by this subchapter shall apply to any agency or instrumentality of the United States unless such agency or instrumentality is granted by statute a specific exemption from such tax.

"Sec. 5914. Application to State Laws

"The payment of any tax imposed by this subchapter for carrying on any trade or business shall not be held to—

"(1) exempt any person from any penalty or punishment provided by the laws of any State for carrying on such trade or business within such State, or in any manner to authorize the commencement or continuance of such trade or business contrary to the laws of such State or in places prohibited by municipal law, or "(2) prohibit any State from placing a duty or tax on the same trade or business, for State or other purposes.

"Subchapter C—Bond and Permits

"Sec.	5921.	Establishment and bond.
"Sec.	5922.	Application for permit.
"Sec.	5923.	Permit.

"Sec. 5921. Establishment and Bond

"(a) PROHIBITION ON PRODUCTION OUTSIDE OF Bonded Cannabis Production Facility.—

"(1) IN GENERAL.—Except as authorized by the Secretary or on the bonded premises of a cannabis production facility duly authorized to produce cannabis products according to law, no cannabis product may planted, cultivated, harvested, grown, manufactured, produced, compounded, converted, processed, prepared, or packaged in any building or on any premises.

"(2) AUTHORIZED PRODUCERS ONLY.—No person other than a producer which has filed the bond required under subsection (b) and received a permit described in section 5923 may produce any cannabis product.

"(3) PERSONAL USE EXCEPTION.—This subsection shall not apply with respect the activities of an individual who is not treated as a producer by reason of section 5902(b)(2)(B).

"(b) BOND.—

"(1) WHEN REQUIRED.—Every person, before commencing business as a producer or an export warehouse proprietor, shall file such bond, conditioned upon compliance with this chapter and regulations issued thereunder, in such form, amount, and manner as the Secretary shall by regulation prescribe. A new or additional bond may be required whenever the Secretary considers such action necessary for the protection of the revenue.

"(2) APPROVAL OR DISAPPROVAL.—No person shall engage in such business until he receives notice of approval of such bond. A bond may be disapproved, upon notice to the principal on the bond, if the Secretary determines that the bond is not adequate to protect the revenue.

"(3) CANCELLATION.—Any bond filed hereunder may be canceled, upon notice to the principal on the bond, whenever the Secretary determines that the bond no longer adequately protects the revenue.

"Sec. 5922. Application for Permit

"(a) IN GENERAL.—Every person, before commencing business as a cannabis enterprise, and at such other time as the Secretary shall by regulation prescribe, shall make application for the permit provided for in section 5923. The application shall be in such form as the Secretary shall prescribe and shall set forth, truthfully and accurately, the information called for on the form. Such application may be rejected and the permit denied if the Secretary, after notice and opportunity for hearing, finds that—

"(1) the premises on which it is proposed to conduct the cannabis enterprise will not be adequate to protect the revenue after commencing operations, or

"(2) such person (including, in the case of a corporation, any officer, director, or principal stock-holder and, in the case of a partnership, any partner) has failed to disclose any material information required or made any materially false statement in the application therefor.

“Sec. 5923. Permit

“(a) ISSUANCE.—A person shall not engage in business as a cannabis enterprise without a permit to engage in such business. Such permit, conditioned upon compliance with this chapter and regulations issued thereunder, shall be issued in such form and in such manner as the Secretary shall by regulation prescribe. A new permit may be required at such other time as the Secretary shall by regulation prescribe.

“(b) SUSPENSION OR REVOCATION.—

“(1) SHOW CAUSE HEARING.—If the Secretary has reason to believe that any person holding a permit—

“(A) has not in good faith complied with this chapter, or with any other provision of this title involving intent to defraud, “(B) has violated the conditions of such permit,

“(C) has failed to disclose any material information required or made any material false statement in the application for such permit, or “(D) has failed to maintain their premises in such manner as to protect the revenue, the Secretary shall issue an order, stating the facts charged, citing such person to show cause why their permit should not be suspended or revoked.

“(2) ACTION FOLLOWING HEARING.—If, after hearing, the Secretary finds that such person has not shown cause why their permit should not be suspended or revoked, such permit shall be suspended for such period as the Secretary deems proper or shall be revoked.

“(c) INFORMATION REPORTING.—The Secretary may require— “(1) information reporting by any person issued a permit under this section, and

“(2) information reporting by such other persons as the Secretary deems necessary to carry out this chapter.

“(d) INSPECTION OR DISCLOSURE OF INFORMATION.—For rules relating to inspection and disclosure of returns and return information, see section 6103(o).

“Subchapter D—Operations

"Sec. 5934. Restrictions relating to marks, labels, notices, and packages.
"Sec. 5935. Restriction on importation of previously exported cannabis products.

"Sec. 5931. Inventories, Reports, and Records

"Every cannabis enterprise shall—

"(1) make a true and accurate inventory at the time of commencing business, at the time of concluding business, and at such other times, in such manner and form, and to include such items, as the Secretary shall by regulation prescribe, with such inventories to be subject to verification by any internal revenue officer,

"(2) make reports containing such information, in such form, at such times, and for such periods as the Secretary shall by regulation prescribe, and

"(3) keep such records in such manner as the Secretary shall by regulation prescribe, with such records to be available for inspection by any internal revenue officer during business hours.

"Sec. 5932. Packaging and Labeling

"(a) PACKAGES.—All cannabis products shall, before removal, be put up in such packages as the Secretary shall by regulation prescribe.

"(b) MARKS, LABELS, AND NOTICES.—Every package of cannabis products shall, before removal, bear the marks, labels, and notices if any, that the Secretary by regulation prescribes.

"(c) LOTTERY FEATURES.—No certificate, coupon, or other device purporting to be or to represent a ticket, chance, share, or an interest in, or dependent on, the event of a lottery shall be contained in, attached to, or stamped, marked, written, or printed on any package of cannabis products.

"(d) INDECENT OR IMMORAL MATERIAL PROHIBITED.—No indecent or immoral picture, print, or representation shall be contained in, attached to, or stamped, marked, written, or printed on any package of cannabis products.

"(e) EXCEPTIONS.—Subject to regulations prescribed by the Secretary, cannabis products may be exempted from subsections (a) and (b) if such products are—

"(1) for experimental purposes, or

''(2) transferred to the bonded premises of another producer or export warehouse proprietor or released in bond from customs custody for delivery to a producer.

''Sec. 5933. Purchase, Receipt, Possession, or Sale of Cannabis Products After Removal

''(a) RESTRICTION.—No person shall—

''(1) with intent to defraud the United States, purchase, receive, possess, offer for sale, or sell or otherwise dispose of, after removal, any cannabis products—

''(A) upon which the tax has not been paid or determined in the manner and at the time prescribed by this chapter or regulations thereunder, or

''(B) which, after removal without payment of tax pursuant to section 5904(a), have been diverted from the applicable purpose or use specified in that section, ''(2) with intent to defraud the United States, purchase, receive, possess, offer for sale, or sell or otherwise dispose of, after removal, any cannabis products which are not put up in packages as required under section 5932 or which are put up in packages not bearing the marks, labels, and notices, as required under such section, or ''(3) otherwise than with intent to defraud the United States, purchase, receive, possess, offer for sale, or sell or otherwise dispose of, after removal, any cannabis products which are not put up in packages as required under section 5932 or which are put up in packages not bearing the marks, labels, and notices, as required under such section.

''(b) EXCEPTION.—Paragraph (3) of subsection (a) shall not prevent the sale or delivery of cannabis products directly to consumers from proper packages, nor apply to such articles when so sold or delivered.

''(c) LIABILITY TO TAX.—Any person who possesses cannabis products in violation of paragraph (1) or (2) of subsection (a) shall be liable for a tax equal to the tax on such articles.

''Sec. 5934. Restrictions Relating to Marks, Labels, Notices, and Packages

''No person shall, with intent to defraud the United States, destroy, obliterate, or detach any mark, label, or notice prescribed or authorized, by this chapter or regulations thereunder, to appear on, or be affixed to, any package of cannabis products before such package is emptied.

‘‘Sec. 5935. Restriction on Importation of Previously Exported Cannabis Products

‘‘(a) EXPORT LABELED CANNABIS PRODUCTS.—

‘‘(1) IN GENERAL.—Cannabis products produced in the United States and labeled for exportation under this chapter—

‘‘(A) may be transferred to or removed from the premises of a producer or an export warehouse proprietor only if such articles are being transferred or removed without tax in accordance with section 5904,

‘‘(B) may be imported or brought into the United States, after their exportation, only if such articles either are eligible to be released from customs custody with the partial duty exemption provided in section 5904(d) or are returned to the original producer of such article as provided in section 5904(c), and

‘‘(C) may not be sold or held for sale for domestic consumption in the United States unless such articles are removed from their export packaging and repackaged by the original producer into new packaging that does not contain an export label.

‘‘(2) Alterations by persons other than ORIGINAL PRODUCER.—This section shall apply to articles labeled for export even if the packaging or the appearance of such packaging to the consumer of such articles has been modified or altered by a person other than the original producer so as to remove or conceal or attempt to remove or conceal (including by the placement of a sticker over) any export label.

‘‘(3) Exports include shipments to PUERTO RICO.—For purposes of this section, section 5904(d), section 5941, and such other provisions as the Secretary may specify by regulations, references to exportation shall be treated as including a reference to shipment to the Commonwealth of Puerto Rico.

‘‘(b) EXPORT LABEL.—For purposes of this section, an article is labeled for export or contains an export label if it bears the mark, label, or notice required under section 5904(b).

"Subchapter E—Penalties

"Sec. 5941. Civil Penalties

"(a) OMITTING THINGS REQUIRED OR DOING THINGS FORBIDDEN.—Whoever willfully omits, neglects, or refuses to comply with any duty imposed upon them by this chapter, or to do, or cause to be done, any of the things required by this chapter, or does anything prohibited by this chapter, shall in addition to any other penalty provided in this title, be liable to a penalty of $10,000, to be recovered, with costs of suit, in a civil action, except where a penalty under subsection (b) or (c) or under section 6651 or 6653 or part II of subchapter A of chapter 68 may be collected from such person by assessment.

"(b) FAILURE TO PAY TAX.—Whoever fails to pay any tax imposed by this chapter at the time prescribed by law or regulations, shall, in addition to any other penalty provided in this title, be liable to a penalty of 10 percent of the tax due but unpaid.

"(c) SALE OF CANNABIS OR CANNABIS PRODUCTS for Export.—

"(1) Every person who sells, relands, or receives within the jurisdiction of the United States any cannabis products which have been labeled or shipped for exportation under this chapter,

"(2) every person who sells or receives such relanded cannabis products, and

"(3) every person who aids or abets in such selling, relanding, or receiving, shall, in addition to the tax and any other penalty provided in this title, be liable for a penalty equal to the greater of $10,000 or 10 times the amount of the tax imposed by this chapter. All cannabis products relanded within the jurisdiction of the United States shall be forfeited to the United States and destroyed. All vessels, vehicles, and aircraft used in such relanding or in removing such cannabis products from the place where relanded, shall be forfeited to the United States.

"(d) APPLICABILITY OF SECTION 6665.—The penalties imposed by subsections (b) and (c) shall be assessed, collected, and paid in the same manner as taxes, as provided in section 6665(a).

"(e) CROSS REFERENCES.—For penalty for failure to make deposits or for overstatement of deposits, see section 6656.

"Sec. 5942. Criminal Penalties

"(a) FRAUDULENT OFFENSES.—Whoever, with intent to defraud the United States—

"(1) engages in business as a cannabis enterprise without filing the application and obtaining the permit where required by this chapter or regulations thereunder,

"(2) fails to keep or make any record, return, report, or inventory, or keeps or makes any false or fraudulent record, return, report, or inventory, required by this chapter or regulations thereunder,

"(3) refuses to pay any tax imposed by this chapter, or attempts in any manner to evade or defeat the tax or the payment thereof,

"(4) sells or otherwise transfers, contrary to this chapter or regulations thereunder, any cannabis products subject to tax under this chapter, or

"(5) purchases, receives, or possesses, with intent to redistribute or resell, any cannabis product—

"(A) upon which the tax has not been paid or determined in the manner and at the time prescribed by this chapter or regulations thereunder, or

"(B) which, without payment of tax pursuant to section 5904, have been diverted from the applicable purpose or use specified in that section, shall, for each such offense, be fined not more than $10,000, or imprisoned not more than 5 years, or both.

"(b) LIABILITY TO TAX.—Any person who possesses cannabis products in violation of subsection (a) shall be liable for a tax equal to the tax on such articles."

(c) STUDY.—Not later than 2 years after the date of the enactment of this Act, and every 5 years thereafter, the Secretary of the Treasury, or the Secretary's delegate, shall—

(1) conduct a study concerning the characteristics of the cannabis industry, including the number of persons operating cannabis enterprises at each level of such industry, the volume of sales, the amount of tax collected each year, and the areas of evasion, and (2) submit to Congress recommendations to improve the regulation of the industry and the administration of the related tax.

(d) ANNUAL REPORTS REGARDING DETERMINATION OF APPLICABLE RATES.—Not later than 6 months before the beginning of each calendar year to which section 5901(a)(2) of the Internal Revenue Code of 1986 (as added by this section) applies, the Secretary of the Treasury, or the Secretary's delegate, shall make publicly available a detailed description of the methodology which the Secretary anticipates using to determine the applicable rate per ounce and the applicable rate per gram which will apply for such calendar year under section 5901(c)(2) of such Code.

(e) CONFORMING AMENDMENTS.—(1) Section 6103(o)(1)(A) of the Internal Revenue Code of 1986 is amended by striking "and firearms" and inserting "firearms, and cannabis products."

(2) The table of chapters for subtitle E of such Code is amended by adding at the end the following new item: "Chapter 56. Cannabis Products".

(3) The table of sections for subchapter A of chapter 98 of such Code is amended by adding at the end the following new item: "Sec. 9512. Establishment of Opportunity Trust Fund."

(f) EFFECTIVE DATE.—

(1) IN GENERAL.—Except as otherwise provided in this subsection, the amendments made by this section shall apply to removals, and applications for permits under section 5922 of the Internal Revenue Code of 1986 (as added by subsection (b)), after 180 days after the date of the enactment of this Act.

(2) ESTABLISHMENT OF OPPORTUNITY TRUST FUND.—The amendment made by subsection (a) shall take effect on the date of the enactment of this Act.

Sec. 6. Opportunity Trust Fund Programs

(a) CANNABIS JUSTICE OFFICE; COMMUNITY REINVESTMENT GRANT PROGRAM.—

(1) CANNABIS JUSTICE OFFICE.—Part A oftitle I of the Omnibus Crime Control and Safe Streets Act of 1968 (34 U.S.C. 10101 et seq.) is amended by inserting after section 109 the following:

"SEC. 110. CANNABIS JUSTICE OFFICE.

"(a) ESTABLISHMENT.—There is established withinthe Office of Justice Programs a Cannabis Justice Office.

"(b) DIRECTOR.—The Cannabis Justice Office shall be headed by a Director who shall be appointed by the Assistant Attorney General for the Office of Justice Programs. The Director shall report to the Assistant Attorney

General for the Office of Justice Programs. The Director shall award grants and may enter into compacts, cooperative agreements, and contracts on behalf of the Cannabis Justice Office. The Director may not engage in any employment other than that of serving as the Director, nor 21 may the Director hold any office in, or act in any capacity for, any organization, agency, or institution with which the Office makes any contract or other arrangement.

''(c) EMPLOYEES.—

''(1) IN GENERAL.—The Director shall employ as many full-time employees as are needed to carry out the duties and functions of the Cannabis Justice Office under subsection (d). Such employees shall be exclusively assigned to the Cannabis Justice Office.

''(2) INITIAL HIRES.—Not later than 6 months after the date of enactment of this section, the Director shall—

''(A) hire no less than one-third of the total number of employees of the Cannabis Justice Office; and

''(B) no more than one-half of the employees assigned to the Cannabis Justice Office by term appointment that may after 2 years be converted to career appointment.

''(3) LEGAL COUNSEL.—At least one employee hired for the Cannabis Justice Office shall serve as legal counsel to the Director and shall provide counsel to the Cannabis Justice Office.

''(d) DUTIES AND FUNCTIONS.—The Cannabis Justice Office is authorized to—

''(1) administer the Community Reinvestment Grant Program; and ''(2) perform such other functions as the Assistant Attorney General for the Office of Justice Programs may delegate, that are consistent with the statutory obligations of this section.''

2) Community reinvestment grant proGRAM.—Title I of the Omnibus Crime Control and Safe Streets Act of 1968 (34 U.S.C. et seq.) is amended by adding at the end the following:

''Part PP—Community Reinvestment Grant Program

''SEC. 3056. AUTHORIZATION.

''(a) IN GENERAL.—The Director of the Cannabis Justice Office shall establish and carry out a grant program, known as the 'Community Reinvestment Grant Program', to provide eligible entities with funds to administer services for individuals adversely impacted by the War on Drugs, including—

"(1) job training;

"(2) reentry services;

"(3) legal aid for civil and criminal cases, including expungement of cannabis convictions;

"(4) literacy programs;

"(5) youth recreation or mentoring programs;

and

"(6) health education programs.

"(b) SUBSTANCE USE DISORDER SERVICES.—The Director, in consultation with the Secretary of Health and Human Services, shall provide eligible entities with funds to administer substance use disorder services for individuals adversely impacted by the War on Drugs or connect patients with substance use disorder services. Also eligible for such services are individuals who have been arrested for or convicted of the sale, possession, use, manufacture, or cultivation of a controlled substance other than cannabis (except for a conviction involving distribution to a minor).

"Sec. 3057. Funding from Opportunity Trust Fund

"The Director shall carry out the program under this part using funds made available under section 9512(c)(1) and (2) of the Internal Revenue Code.

"SEC. 3058. DEFINITIONS.

"In this part:

"(1) The term 'cannabis conviction' means a conviction, or adjudication of juvenile delinquency, for a cannabis offense (as such term is defined in section 13 of the Marijuana Opportunity Reinvestment and Expungement Act).

"(2) The term 'eligible entity' means a non-profit organization, as defined in section 501(c)(3) of the Internal Revenue Code, that is representative of a community or a significant segment of a community with experience in providing relevant services to individuals adversely impacted by the War on Drugs in that community.

''(3) The term 'individuals adversely impacted by the War on Drugs' has the meaning given that term in section 6 of the Marijuana Opportunity Reinvestment and Expungement Act.''.

(b) CANNABIS RESTORATIVE OPPORTUNITY PROGRAM; Equitable Licensing Grant Program.—

(1) Cannabis restorative opportunity PROGRAM.—The Administrator of the Small Business Administration shall establish and carry out a program, to be known as the ''Cannabis Restorative Opportunity Program'', to provide loans and technical assistance under section 7(m) of the Small Business Act (15 U.S.C. 636(m)) to assist small business concerns owned and controlled by socially and economically disadvantaged individuals that operate in eligible States or localities.

(2) Equitable licensing grant program.—The Administrator of the Small Business Administration shall establish and carry out a grant program, to be known as the ''Equitable Licensing Grant Program'', to provide any eligible State or locality funds to develop and implement equitable cannabis licensing programs that minimize barriers to cannabis licensing and employment for individuals adversely impacted by the War on Drugs, provided that each grantee includes in its cannabis licensing program at least four of the following elements:

(A) A waiver of cannabis license application fees for individuals who report an income below 250 percent of the Federal Poverty Level for at least 5 of the past 10 years and who are first-time applicants for a cannabis license.

(B) A prohibition on the denial of a cannabis license based on a conviction for a cannabis offense that took place prior to State legalization of cannabis or the date of enactment of this Act, as appropriate.

(C) A prohibition on restrictions for licensing relating to criminal convictions except with respect to a criminal conviction related to owning and operating a business.

(D) A prohibition on cannabis license holders engaging in suspicionless cannabis drug testing of their prospective or current employees, except with respect to drug testing for safety-sensitive positions required under part 40 of title 49, Code of Federal Regulations.

(E) The establishment of a cannabis licensing board that is reflective of the racial, ethnic, economic, and gender composition of the eligible State or locality, to serve as an oversight body of the equitable licensing program.

(3) DEFINITIONS.—In this subsection:

(A) ELIGIBLE STATE OR LOCALITY.—The term ''eligible State or locality'' means a State or locality that has taken steps to—

(i) create an automatic process, at nocost to the individual, for the expungement, destruction, or sealing of criminal records for cannabis offenses; and

(ii) eliminate violations or other penalties for persons under parole, probation, pre-trial, or other State or local criminal supervision for a cannabis offense.

(B) Individual adversely impacted by THE WAR ON DRUGS.—The term ''individual adversely impacted by the War on Drugs'' means an individual—

(i) who reports an income below 250 percent of the Federal Poverty Level for at least 5 of the past 10 years; and (ii) who has been arrested for or convicted of the sale, possession, use, manufacture, or cultivation of cannabis (except for a conviction involving distribution to a minor), or whose parent, sibling, spouse, or child has been arrested for or convicted of such an offense.

(C) Small business concern owned AND CONTROLLED BY SOCIALLY AND ECONOMICALLY DISADVANTAGED INDIVIDUALS.—The term ''small business concern owned and controlled by socially and economically disadvantaged individuals'' has the meaning given in section 8(d)(3)(C) of the Small Business Act (15 U.S.C. 637(d)(3)(C)).

(D) STATE.—The term ''State'' means each of the several States, the District of Columbia, Puerto Rico, any territory or possession of the United States, and any Indian Tribe (as defined in section 201 of Public Law 90–294 (25 U.S.C. 1301) (commonly known as the ''Indian Civil Rights Act of 1968'')).

(c) STUDY ON PROGRAMS.—

(1) GAO STUDY.—The Comptroller General of the United States, in consultation with the Administrator of the Small Business Administration, shall conduct an annual study on the individuals and entities receiving assistance under the Cannabis Restorative Opportunity and Equitable Licensing Programs. This study shall include the types of assistance by state, and a description of the efforts by the Small Business Administration to increase access to capital for cannabis-related small business concerns owned and controlled by socially and economically disadvantaged individuals, individuals adversely impacted by the War on Drugs, as well as the racial, ethnic, economic and gender composition of the eligible State or locality.

(2) REPORT.—Not later than 1 year after the date of enactment of this Act, the Comptroller General of the United States shall submit a report on the results of the study conducted under paragraph

(1) to—

(A) the Committee on Small Business of the House of Representatives;

(B) the Committee on Small Business and Entrepreneurship of the Senate;

(C) the Committee on the Judiciary of the House of Representatives; and

(D) the Committee on the Judiciary of the Senate.

Sec. 7. Availability of Small Business Administration Programs and Services to Cannabis-Relatedlegitimatebusinesses and Service Providers

(a) Definitions Relating to Cannabis-Related Legitimate Businesses and Service Providers.—

Section 3 of the Small Business Act (15 U.S.C. 632) is amended by adding at the end the following new subsection:

‘‘(gg) CANNABIS-RELATED LEGITIMATE BUSINESSES AND SERVICE PROVIDERS.—In this Act:

‘‘(1) CANNABIS.—The term ‘cannabis’—

‘‘(A) means—

‘‘(i) all parts of the plant Cannabis sativa L., whether growing or not;

‘‘(ii) the seeds thereof;

‘‘(iii) the resin extracted from any part of such plant; and ‘‘(iv) every compound, manufacture, salt, derivative, mixture, or preparation of such plant, its seeds or resin; and

‘‘(B) does not include—

‘‘(i) hemp, as defined in section 297A of the Agricultural Marketing Act of 1946;

‘‘(ii) the mature stalks of such plant, fiber produced from such stalks, oil or cake made from the seeds of such plant, any other compound, manufacture, salt, derivative, mixture, or preparation of such mature stalks (excep the resin extracted therefrom), fiber, oil, or cake, or the sterilized seed of such plant which is incapable of germination; or

‘‘(iii) any drug product approved under section 505 of the Federal Food, Drug, and Cosmetic Act, or biological product licensed under section 351 of the Public Health Service Act.

‘‘(2) Cannabis-related legitimate business.—The term ‘cannabis-related legitimate business’ means a manufacturer, producer, or any person or company that is a small business concern and that—

"(A) engages in any activity described in subparagraph (B) pursuant to a law established by a State or a political subdivision of a State, as determined by such State or political subdivision; and

"(B) participates in any business or organized activity that involves handling cannabis or cannabis products, including cultivating, producing, manufacturing, selling, transporting, displaying, dispensing, distributing, or purchasing cannabis or cannabis products.

"(3) SERVICE PROVIDER.—The term 'service provider'—

"(A) means a business, organization, or other person that—

"(i) sells goods or services to a cannabis-related legitimate business; or

"(ii) provides any business services, including the sale or lease of real or any other property, legal or other licensed services, or any other ancillary service, relating to cannabis; and

"(B) does not include a business, organization, or other person that participates in any business or organized activity that involves handling cannabis or cannabis products, including cultivating, producing, manufacturing, selling, transporting, displaying, dispensing, distributing, or purchasing cannabis or cannabis products.".

(b) SMALL BUSINESS DEVELOPMENT CENTERS.—

Section 21(c) of the Small Business Act (15 U.S.C.648(c)) is amended by adding at the end the following new paragraph:

"(9) Services for cannabis-related LEGITIMATE BUSINESSES AND SERVICE PROVIDERS.—

A small business development center may not decline to provide services to an otherwise eligible small business concern under this section solely becausesuch concern is a cannabis-related legitimate business or service provider.".

(c) WOMEN'S BUSINESS CENTERS.—Section 29 of the Small Business Act (15 U.S.C. 656) is amended by adding at the end the following new subsection:

"(p) SERVICES FOR CANNABIS-RELATED LEGITIMATE BUSINESSES AND SERVICE PROVIDERS.—A women's business center may not decline to provide services to an otherwise eligible small business concern under this section solely because such concern is a cannabis-related legitimate business or service provider.".

(d) SCORE.—Section 8(b)(1)(B) of the Small Business Act (15 U.S.C. 637(b)(1)(B)) is amended by adding at the end the following new sentence: "The head of the SCORE program established under this subparagraph 23 may not decline to provide services to an otherwise eligible small business concern solely because such concern is a cannabis-related legitimate business or service provider.''.

(e) VETERAN BUSINESS OUTREACH CENTERS.—Section 32 of the Small Business Act (15 U.S.C. 657b) is amended by adding at the end the following new subsection:

''(h) SERVICES FOR CANNABIS-RELATED LEGITI-

MATE BUSINESSES AND SERVICE PROVIDERS.—A Veteran Business Outreach Center may not decline to provide services to an otherwise eligible small business concern under this section solely because such concern is a cannabis-related legitimate business or service provider.''.

(f) SECTION 7(a) LOANS.—Section 7(a) of the Small Business Act (15 U.S.C. 636(a)) is amended by adding at the end the following new paragraph:

''(38) Loans to cannabis-related LEGITIMATE BUSINESSES AND SERVICE PROVIDERS.—TheAdministrator may not decline to provide a guarantee for a loan under this subsection, and a lender 18 may not decline to make a loan under this subsection, to an otherwise eligible small business concern solely because such concern is a cannabis-related legitimate business or service provider.''.

(g) DISASTER LOANS.—Section 7(b) of the Small Business Act (15 U.S.C. 636(b)) is amended by inserting after paragraph (15) the following new paragraph:

''(16) Assistance to cannabis-related LEGITIMATE BUSINESSES AND SERVICE PROVIDERS.—

The Administrator may not decline to provide assistance under this subsection to an otherwise eligible small business concern solely because such concern is a cannabis-related legitimate business or service provider.''.

(h) MICROLOANS.—Section 7(m) of the Small Business Act (15 U.S.C. 636(m)) is amended by adding at the end the following new paragraph:

''(14) Assistance to cannabis-related LEGITIMATE BUSINESSES AND SERVICE PROVIDERS.—

The Administrator may not decline to make a loan or a grant under this subsection, and an eligible intermediary may not decline to provide assistance under this subsection to an otherwise eligible borrower, eligible intermediary, or eligible nonprofit entity (as applicable) solely because such borrower, intermediary, or nonprofit entity is a cannabis-related legitimate business or service provider.''.

(i) SMALL BUSINESS INVESTMENT COMPANY DEBENTURES to Finance Cannabis-Related LEGITIMATE BUSINESSES AND SERVICE PROVIDERS.—Part A of title III of the Small Business Investment Act of

1958 (15 U.S.C. 681 et seq.) is amended by adding at the end the following new section:

"Sec. 321. Debentures to Finance Cannabis-Related Legitimate Businesses And Service Providers

"(a) GUARANTEES.—The Administrator may not decline to purchase or guarantee a debenture made under this title to an otherwise eligible small business investment company solely because such small business investment company provides financing to an entity that is a cannabis-related legitimate business or service provider (as defined in section 7(a)(38) of the Small Business Act).

"(b) OTHER ASSISTANCE.—A small business investment company may not decline to provide assistance under this title to an otherwise eligible small business concern solely because such small business concern is a cannabis-related legitimate business or service provider (as defined in section 7(a)(38) of the Small Business Act).".

(j) STATE OR LOCAL DEVELOPMENT COMPANY LOANS.—Title V of the Small Business Investment Act of 1958 (15 U.S.C. 695 et seq.) is amended by adding at the end the following new section:

"Sec. 511. Loans to Finance Cannabis-Related Legitimate Businesses and Service Providers

"(a) LOANS AND LOAN GUARANTEES.—The Administrator may not decline to make or provide a guarantee for a loan under this title to an otherwise eligible qualified State or local development company solely because such qualified State or local development company provides financing to an entity that is a cannabis-related legitimate business or service provider (as defined in section 7(a)(38) of the Small Business Act).

"(b) OTHER ASSISTANCE.—A qualified State or local development company may not decline to provide assistance under this title to an otherwise eligible small business concern solely because such small business concern is a cannabis-related legitimate business or service provider (as defined in section 7(a)(38) of the Small Business Act).".

Sec. 8. No Discrimination in the Provision of a Federal Public Benefit on the Basis of Cannabis

(a) IN GENERAL.—No person may be denied any Federal public benefit (as such term is defined in section 401(c) of the Personal Responsibility and Work Opportunity Reconciliation Act of 1996 (8 U.S.C. 1611(c))) on the basis of any use or possession of cannabis, or on the basis of a conviction or adjudication of juvenile delinquency for a cannabis offense, by that person.

(b) SECURITY CLEARANCES.—Federal agencies may not use past or present cannabis or marijuana use as criteria for granting, denying, or rescinding a security clearance.

Sec. 9. No Adverse Effect for Purposes of the Immigration Laws

(a) IN GENERAL.—For purposes of the immigration laws (a s such term is defined in section 101 of the Immigration and Nationality Act), cannabis may not be considered a controlled substance, and an alien may not be denied any benefit or protection under the immigration laws based on any event, including conduct, a finding, an admission, addiction or abuse, an arrest, a juvenile adjudication, or a conviction, relating to the possession or use of cannabis that is no longer prohibited pursuant to this Act or an amendment made by this Act, regardless of whether the event occurred before, on, or after the effective date of this Act.

(b) CANNABIS DEFINED.—The term ''cannabis''—

(1) means all parts of the plant Cannabis sativa L., whether growing or not; the seeds thereof; the resin extracted from any part of such plant; and every compound, manufacture, salt, derivative, mixture, or preparation of such plant, its seeds or resin; and

(2) does not include—

(A) hemp, as defined in section 297A of the Agricultural Marketing Act of 1946;

(B) the mature stalks of such plant, fiber produced from such stalks, oil or cake made from the seeds of such plant, any other compound, manufacture, salt, derivative, mixture, or preparation of such mature stalks (except the resin extracted therefrom), fiber, oil, or cake, or the sterilized seed of such plant which is incapable of germination; or

(C) any drug product approved under section 505 of the Federal Food, Drug, and Cosmetic Act, or biological product licensed under section 351 of the Public Health Service Act.

(c) CONFORMING AMENDMENTS TO IMMIGRATION AND NATIONALITY ACT.—The Immigration and Nationality Act (8 U.S.C. 1101 et seq.) is amended—

(1) in section 212(h), by striking ''and subparagraph (A)(i)(II) of such subsection insofar as it relates to a single offense of simple possession of 30 grams or less of marijuana'';

(2) in section 237(a)(2)(B)(i), by striking ''other than a single offense involving possession for one's own use of 30 grams or less of marijuana'';

(3) in section 101(f)(3), by striking ''(except as such paragraph relates to a single offense of simple possession of 30 grams or less of marihuana)'';

(4) in section 244(c)(2)(A)(iii)(II) by striking ''except for so much of such paragraph as relates to a single offense of simple possession of 30 grams or less of marijuana'';

(5) in section 245(h)(2)(B) by striking ''(except for so much of such paragraph as related to a single offense of simple possession of 30 grams or less of marijuana)'';

(6) in section 210(c)(2)(B)(ii)(III) by striking '', except for so much of such paragraph as relates to a single offense of simple possession of 30 grams or less of marihuana''; and (7) in section 245A(d)(2)(B)(ii)(II) by striking '', except for so much of such paragraph as relates to a single offense of simple possession of 30 grams or less of marihuana''.

Sec. 10. Resentencing and Expungement

(a) EXPUNGEMENT OF NON-VIOLENT FEDERAL

Cannabis Offense Convictions for Individuals Not Under a Criminal Justice Sentence.—

(1) IN GENERAL.—Not later than 1 year after the date of the enactment of this Act, each Federal district shall conduct a comprehensive review and issue an order expunging each conviction or adjudication of juvenile delinquency for a non-violent Federal cannabis offense entered by each Federal court in the district before the date of enactment of this Act and on or after May 1, 1971. Each Federal court shall also issue an order expunging any arrests associated with each expunged conviction or adjudication of juvenile delinquency.

(2) NOTIFICATION.—To the extent practicable, each Federal district shall notify each individual whose arrest, conviction, or adjudication of delinquency has been expunged pursuant to this subsection that their arrest, conviction, or adjudication of juvenile delinquency has been expunged, and the effect of such expungement.

(3) Right to petition court for EXPUNGEMENT.—At any point after the date of enactment of this Act, any individual with a prior conviction or adjudication of juvenile delinquency for a non-violent Federal cannabis offense, who is not under a criminal justice sentence, may file a motion for expungement. If the expungement of such a conviction or adjudication of juvenile delinquency is required pursuant to this Act, the court shall expunge the conviction or adjudication, and any associated arrests. If the individual is indigent, counsel shall be appointed to represent the individual in any proceedings under this subsection.

(4) SEALED RECORD.—The court shall seal all records related to a conviction or adjudication of juvenile delinquency that has been expunged under this subsection. Such records may only be made available by further order of the court.

(b) SENTENCING REVIEW FOR INDIVIDUALS UNDER

A Criminal Justice Sentence.—

(1) IN GENERAL.—For any individual who is under a criminal justice sentence for a non-violent Federal cannabis offense, the court that imposed the sentence shall, on motion of the individual, the Director of the Bureau of Prisons, the attorney for the Government, or the court, conduct a sentencing review hearing. If the individual is indigent, counsel shall be appointed to represent the individual in any sentencing review proceedings under this subsection.

(2) Potential reduced resentencing.—

After a sentencing hearing under paragraph (1), a court shall—

(A) expunge each conviction or adjudication of juvenile delinquency for a non-violent Federal cannabis offense entered by the court before the date of enactment of this Act, and any associated arrest;

(B) vacate the existing sentence or disposition of juvenile delinquency and, if applicable, impose any remaining sentence or disposition of juvenile delinquency on the individual as if this Act, and the amendments made by this Act, were in effect at the time the offense was committed; and

(C) order that all records related to a conviction or adjudication of juvenile delinquency that has been expunged or a sentence or disposition of juvenile delinquency that has been vacated under this Act be sealed and only be made available by further order of the court.

(c) EFFECT OF EXPUNGEMENT.—An individual who has had an arrest, a conviction, or juvenile delinquency adjudication expunged under this section—

(1) may treat the arrest, conviction, or adjudication as if it never occurred; and

(2) shall be immune from any civil or criminal penalties related to perjury, false swearing, or false statements, for a failure to disclose such arrest, conviction, or adjudication.

(d) EXCEPTION.—An individual who at sentencing received an aggravating role adjustment pursuant to United States Sentencing Guideline 3B1.1(a) in relation to a Federal cannabis offense conviction shall not be eligible for expungement of that Federal cannabis offense conviction under this section.

(e) DEFINITIONS.—In this section:

(1) The term ''Federal cannabis offense'' means an offense that is no longer punishable pursuant to this Act or the amendments made under this Act.

(2) The term ''expunge'' means, with respect to an arrest, a conviction, or a juvenile delinquency adjudication, the removal of the record of such arrest, conviction, or adjudication from each official index or public record.

(3) The term ''under a criminal justice sentence'' means, with respect to an individual, that the individual is serving a term of probation, parole, supervised release, imprisonment, official detention, pre-release custody, or work release, pursuant to a sentence or disposition of juvenile delinquency imposed on or after the effective date of the Controlled Substances Act (May 1, 1971).

(f) STUDY.—The Comptroller General of the United States, in consultation with the Secretary of Health and Human Services, shall conduct a demographic study of individuals convicted of a Federal cannabis offense. Such study shall include information about the age, race, ethnicity, sex, and gender identity of those individuals, the type of community such users dwell in, and such other demographic information as the Comptroller General determines should be included.

(g) REPORT.—Not later than 2 years after the date of the enactment of this Act, the Comptroller General of the United States shall report to Congress the results of the study conducted under subsection (f).

Sec. 11. References in Existing Law to Marijuana or Marihuana

Wherever, in the statutes of the United States or in the rulings, regulations, or interpretations of various administrative bureaus and agencies of the United States—

(1) there appears or may appear the term "marihuana" or "marijuana", that term shall be struck and the term "cannabis" shall be inserted; and

(2) there appears or may appear the term "Marihuana" or "Marijuana", that term shall be struck and the term "Cannabis" shall be inserted.

Sec. 12. Severability

If any provision of this Act or an amendment made by this Act, or any application of such provision to any person or circumstance, is held to be unconstitutional, the remainder of this Act, the amendments made by this Act, and the application of this Act and the amendments made by this Act to any other person or circumstance shall not be affected.

Sec. 13. Cannabis Offense Defined

For purposes of this Act, the term "cannabis offense" means a criminal offense related to cannabis—

(1) that, under Federal law, is no longer punishable pursuant to this Act or the amendments made under this Act; or

(2) that, under State law, is no longer an offense or that was designated a lesser offense or for which the penalty was reduced under State law pursuant to or following the adoption of a State law authorizing the sale or use of cannabis.

Sec. 14. Rulemaking

Unless otherwise provided in this Act, not later than 1 year after the date of enactment of this Act, the Department of the Treasury, the Department of Justice, and the Small Business Administration shall issue or amend any rules, standard operating procedures, and other legal or policy guidance necessary to carry out implementation of this Act. After the 1-year period, any publicly issued subregulatory guidance, including any compliance guides, manuals, advisories and notices, may not be issued without 60-day notice to appropriate congressional committees. Notice shall include a description and justification for additional guidance.

Sec. 15. Societal Impact of Marijuana Legalization Study

The Comptroller General of the United States shall, not later than 2 years after the date of enactment of this Act, provide to Congress a study that addresses the societal impact of the legalization of recreational cannabis by States, including—

(1) sick days reported to employers;

(2) workers compensations claims;

(3) tax revenue remitted to States resulting from legal marijuana sales;

(4) changes in government spending related to enforcement actions and court proceedings;

(5) Federal welfare assistance applications;

(6) rate of arrests related to methamphetamine possession;

(7) hospitalization rates related to methamphetamine and narcotics use;

(8) uses of marijuana and its byproducts for medical purposes;

(9) uses of marijuana and its byproducts for purposes relating to the health, including the mental health, of veterans;

(10) arrest rates of individuals driving under the influence or driving while intoxicated by marijuana;

(11) traffic-related deaths and injuries where the driver is impaired by marijuana;

(12)arrest of minors for marijuana-related charges;

(13) violent crime rates;

(14) school suspensions, expulsions, and law enforcement referrals that are marijuana-related;

(15) high school dropout rates;

(16) changes in district-wide and State-wide standardized test scores;

(17) marijuana-related hospital admissions and poison control calls;

(18)marijuana-related juvenile admittances into substance rehabilitation facilities and mental health clinics;

(19) diversion of marijuana into neighboring States and drug seizures in neighboring States;

(20) marijuana plants grown on public lands in contravention to Federal and State laws; and

(21) court filings under a State's organized crime statutes.

Sec. 16. Study on Marijuana Impairment

(a) IN GENERAL.—Not later than 1 year after the date of enactment of this Act, the Secretary of Transportation shall conduct a study on technologies and methods that law enforcement may use to determine whether a driver is impaired by marijuana.

(b) REQUIREMENTS.—The study conducted under subsection (a) shall be carried out by the National Highway Traffic Safety Administration, in consultation with any other agency the Secretary determines appropriate.

(c) AUTHORIZATION OF APPROPRIATIONS.—There is authorized to be appropriated $10,000,000 to carry out this section.

Sec. 17. Workplace Impact of Marijuana Legalization Study

Not later than one year after the date of enactment of this Act, the National Institute for Occupational Safety and Health shall—

(1) conduct a study and submit to Congress a report on the impact of the legalization of recreational cannabis by States on the workplace; and (2) develop best practices for use by employers that are transitioning their policies related to the use of recreational cannabis, prioritizing the development of best practices for employers engaged in Federal infrastructure projects, transportation, public safety, and national security.

Sec. 18. School Impact of Marijuana Legalization

STUDY.

Not later than one year after the date of enactment of this Act, the Secretary of Education shall—

(1) conduct a study and submit to Congress a report on the impact of the legalization of recreational cannabis by States on schools and school-aged children; and

(2) develop best practices for use by educators and administrators to protect school-aged children from any negative impacts of such legalization.

Passed the House of Representatives April 1, 2022.

Attest: CHERYL L. JOHNSON,

Clerk.

Index

F

G

H

I

L

M

N

O

P

R

S

T

W